PRAISE FOR JOBY WARRICK'S

BLACK FLAGS

"Mr. Warrick . . . has a gift for constructing narratives with a novelistic energy and detail, and in this volume, he creates the most revealing portrait yet laid out in a book of Abu Musab al-Zarqawi, the founding father of the organization that would become the Islamic State. . . . [Warrick] uses his own copious sources within the United States and Jordanian intelligence to flesh out Mr. Zarqawi's story and the crucial role that American missteps and misjudgments would play in fueling his rise and the advance of the Islamic State. . . . Zarqawi comes across as a kind of Bond villain, who repeatedly foils attempts to neutralize him." —*The New York Times*

"This account of the emergence of ISIS examines in painful detail the consequences of the Bush Administration's misadventures in Iraq. . . . Warrick charts Zarqawi's rise from booze-swilling Jordanian street tough to one of the most brutal jihadists in the world. He demonstrates how much the militants of the Islamic State owe to Zarqawi, who was killed in 2006—not only their ideology but even the color of the jumpsuits that prisoners wear in execution videos. The militants of ISIS, one of Warrick's sources explains, are the 'children of Zarqawi.'" —*The New Yorker*

"Warrick's book might be the most thorough and nuanced account of the birth and growth of ISIS published so far. *Black Flags* is full of personalities, but it keeps its gaze carefully focused on the wider arc of history." —*The Boston Globe*

"Joby Warrick [has] a great eye for memorable characters. In *Black Flags* he puts faces on the amorphous organizations we hear about all the time, namely ISIS and the CIA. Learning about the origins of ISIS is key to understanding the organization today—and key to understanding why we failed to halt ISIS's growth." —GQ.com

"A detailed, step-by-step narrative demonstrating how repeated mis-calculations by the United States, Arab leaders and al-Qaeda wound up empowering the Islamic State. . . . *Black Flags* provides answers in this still-unfolding history of what happens when religious radicals try to outdo one another for the mantle of God's favorite."
—*The Dallas Morning News*

"Joby Warrick has written a penetrating and fascinating look at the birth and evolution of the world's most violent terrorist network, ISIS, or ISIL. This is an eye-opening book. . . . The author tells his story through rich details and revealing anecdotes that bring you into the violent world of Islamic extremism. At times, you feel as if you're sitting in a tent in a remote region of Iraq, watching and listening to al-Zarqawi as he claws his way to the top of the terrorist chain. . . . The writing is crisp, the reporting incredible, a combination of extensive digging and terrific use of sources."
—*The Buffalo News*

"Joby Warrick moves easily through the intelligence warrens of Washington and the shattered landscape of the Middle East to tell this insightful narrative of the rise of the Islamic State. *Black Flags* is an invaluable guide to an unfolding tragedy that must be understood before it can be ended."
—Lawrence Wright, author of
Thirteen Days in September and
The Looming Tower

"Joby Warrick is an exceptional storyteller, and *Black Flags* is both illuminating and spellbinding. No book better explains the miscalculations, wrong turns, and bad luck that led to the rise of ISIS."
—Rick Atkinson, author of
The Guns at Last Light: The War in Western Europe, 1944–1945

JOBY WARRICK

BLACK FLAGS

Joby Warrick has been a reporter for *The Washington Post* since 1996. He is a winner of the Pulitzer Prize for journalism, and the author of *The Triple Agent*. *Black Flags* won the Pulitzer Prize for general nonfiction in 2016.

Also by Joby Warrick

The Triple Agent:
The al-Qaeda Mole Who Infiltrated the CIA

BLACK FLAGS

── THE RISE OF ISIS ──

JOBY WARRICK

ANCHOR BOOKS

A DIVISION OF PENGUIN RANDOM HOUSE LLC

NEW YORK

FIRST ANCHOR BOOKS EDITION, SEPTEMBER 2016

Copyright © 2015, 2016 by Joby Warrick

All rights reserved. Published in the United States by Anchor Books,
a division of Penguin Random House LLC, New York, and
distributed in Canada by Random House of Canada, a division
of Penguin Random House Canada Limited, Toronto. Originally
published in hardcover in the United States by Doubleday, a
division of Penguin Random House LLC, New York, in 2015.

Anchor Books and colophon are registered trademarks of
Penguin Random House LLC.

The Library of Congress has cataloged the Doubleday edition
as follows:
Warrick, Joby.
Black flags: the rise of ISIS / Joby Warrick.—First edition.
pages cm
1. IS (Organization)   2. Terrorism—Iraq.   3. Terrorism—Middle East.
4. Terrorism—Religious aspects—Islam.   5. Islamic fundamentalism.
6. Middle East—Politics and government—21st century.   I. Title.
HV6433.I722I8593 2015   956.9104'2—dc23   2015020949

Anchor Books Trade Paperback ISBN: 978-0-8041-6893-9
eBook ISBN: 978-0-385-53822-0

Author photograph © Marvin Joseph / The Washington Post
Book design by Michael Collica

www.anchorbooks.com

Printed in the United States of America
10 9 8 7 6 5 4 3 2 1

To Maryanne
With love and gratitude

I bring the men who desire death as ardently as you desire life.

—Khalid ibn al-Walid (seventh-century Islamic
warrior, companion of Muhammad)

CONTENTS

AUTHOR'S NOTE

The names of several current and former Jordanian intelligence officers interviewed for this book have been altered by mutual agreement due to concerns about threats to their safety. They are referred to in these pages by their informal Arab *kunya* titles, rather than by traditional family names.

LIST OF PRINCIPAL CHARACTERS

Zarqawi and His Generation

Abu Muhmmad al-Maqdisi (given name Aasim Muhammad Tahir al-Barqawi), Jordanian-Palestinian cleric and author, former cellmate and mentor to Zarqawi

Abu Musab al-Zarqawi (given name Ahmad Fadil al-Khalayleh), Jordanian terrorist, founder of al-Qaeda in Iraq

Abu al-Ghadiya, Syrian dentist, senior Zarqawi associate, and supply master

Ayman al-Zawahiri, leader of al-Qaeda's "core" branch, former deputy to Osama bin Laden

Osama bin Laden, founder of al-Qaeda

The Islamic State of Iraq and Its Successors

Abu Omar al-Baghdadi (given name Hamid Dawud Mohamed Khalil al-Zawi), former member of Saddam Hussein's Baathist Party and leader of the Islamic State of Iraq from 2006 to 2010

Abu Ayyub al-Masri (given name Abu Hamza al-Muhajir), Egyptian explosives expert and Zarqawi associate who became the number two commander of the Islamic State of Iraq in 2006; killed in an air strike in 2010

Abu Bakr al-Baghdadi (given name Ibrahim Awad al-Badri),

Islamic cleric and ISI spiritual adviser who rose to leadership in 2010; declared himself "caliph" of the Islamic State of Iraq in 2014

Abu Wahib (given name Shaker Wahib al-Dulaimi), brutal, media-obsessed ISIS commander in Anbar Province notorious for killing Shiite truck drivers and other civilians

Haji Bakr (given name Samir al-Khlifawi), deputy to Abu Bakr al-Baghdadi and leader of ISIS's military council; killed in 2014

In Jordan

King Abdullah II, fourth sovereign of the Hashemite Kingdom of Jordan

Abu Haytham, senior counterterrorism official, General Intelligence Directorate (GID), Jordan

Abu Mutaz, GID case officer and later manager; expert in "flipping" Islamists into informants

Ali Bourzak, GID official and legendary interrogator known as the "Red Devil"

Laurence Foley, midlevel official at the U.S. Embassy in Amman, Jordan

Salem Ben Suweid, Zarqawi disciple who plotted Foley's assassination

Azmi al-Jayousi, Palestinian-Jordanian, trained at Zarqawi's camp in Herat, Afghanistan; plotted to explode chemical "dirty" bomb in Amman

Sajida al-Rishawi, would-be suicide bomber in 2005 terrorist attack on hotels in Amman, Jordan

In Iraq

Saddam Hussein, president of Iraq, 1979 to 2003

Charles "Sam" Faddis, CIA operative inside Iraq prior to 2003 invasion; urged preemptive strike on Zarqawi's camp

Nada Bakos, CIA officer and chief "targeter" responsible for tracking Zarqawi

Zaydan al-Jibiri, Sunni tribal leader from Ramadi, Iraq

General Stanley McChrystal, head of Joint Special Forces Command that led the hunt for Zarqawi in Iraq

Zaid al-Karbouly, Iraqi customs officer in the pay of al-Qaeda in
   Iraq
Nouri al-Maliki, Shiite prime minister of Iraq from 2006 to 2014

In Syria
   Bashir al-Assad, president of Syria
   Robert Ford, U.S. ambassador to Syria, 2010 to 2014
   Mouaz Moustafa, director of the Syrian Emergency Task Force, a
      nonprofit that offered a window into deteriorating conditions in
      Syria
   Abu Mohammad al-Julani, leader of Jabhat al-Nusra ("al-Nusra
      Front"), the Syrian branch established by the Islamic State of
      Iraq in late 2011
   Kofi Annan, U.N. secretary-general, 1997 to 2006, who sought to
      broker Syrian peace accord

In Washington
   Dick Cheney, U.S. vice president, sought the CIA's support in con-
      necting al-Qaeda to Iraqi regime
   Hillary Clinton, secretary of state, 2009 to 2013
   Michael V. Hayden, NSA director and director of National Intel-
      ligence during anti-Zarqawi campaign; CIA director, 2006 to
      2009
   Frederic C. Hof, special State Department adviser on the Middle
      East and Syria, 2009 to 2012
   Sen. John McCain, chairman, Senate Armed Services Committee
   Leon Panetta, CIA director, 2009 to 2011; defense secretary, 2011
      to 2013
   Robert Richer, the CIA's former station chief in Jordan, later chief
      of the agency's Near East Division and deputy director of opera-
      tions
   George Tenet, CIA director, 1996 to 2004

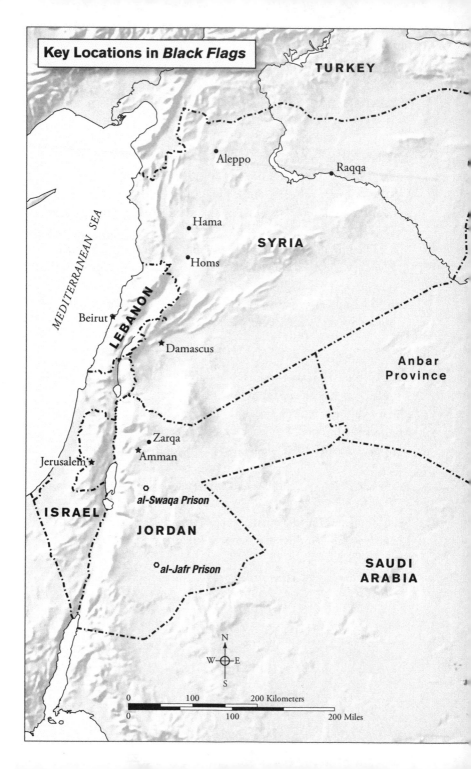

Key Locations in *Black Flags*

TURKEY

Aleppo

Raqqa

MEDITERRANEAN SEA

Hama

SYRIA

Homs

LEBANON

Beirut

Damascus

Anbar
Province

Zarqa

Jerusalem

Amman

○
al-Swaqa Prison

ISRAEL

JORDAN

○ al-Jafr Prison

SAUDI
ARABIA

N
W—⊕—E
S

0	100	200 Kilometers
0	100	200 Miles

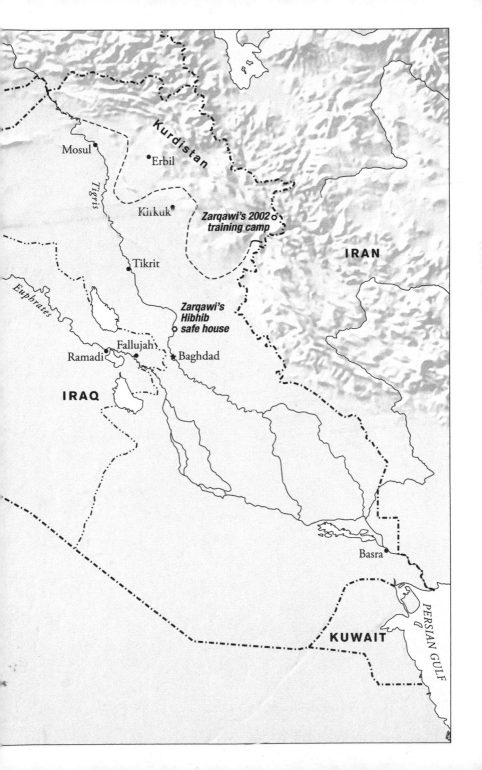

BLACK
FLAGS

PROLOGUE

Amman, Jordan, February 3, 2015

Just after nightfall, a warrant arrived at the city's main women's prison for the execution of Sajida al-Rishawi. The instructions had come from King Abdullah II himself, then in Washington on a state visit, and were transmitted from his private plane to the royal court in Jordan's capital. A clerk relayed the message to the Interior Ministry and then to the prisons department, where it caused a stir. State executions are complicated affairs requiring many steps, yet the king's wishes were explicit: the woman would face the gallows before the sun rose the next day.

The chief warden quickly made the trek to the cell where Rishawi had maintained a kind of self-imposed solitary confinement for close to a decade. The prisoner, forty-five now and no longer thin, spent most of her days watching television or reading a paperback Koran, seeing no one, and keeping whatever thoughts she had under the greasy, prison-issued hijab she always wore. She was not a stupid woman, yet she seemed perpetually disconnected from whatever was going on around her. "When will I be going home?" she asked her government-appointed lawyer during rare meetings in the months after she was sentenced to death. Eventually, even those visits stopped.

Now, when the warden sat her down to explain that she would die in the morning, Rishawi nodded her assent but said nothing. If she cried or prayed or cursed, no one in the prison heard a word of it.

That she could face death was not a surprise to anyone. In 2006, a judge sentenced Rishawi to hang for her part in Jordan's worst-ever terrorist attack: three simultaneous hotel bombings that killed sixty people, most of them guests at a wedding party. She was the suicide bomber who lived, an odd, heavy-browed woman made to pose awkwardly before TV cameras showing off the vest that had failed to explode. At one time, everyone in Amman knew her story, how this thirty-five-year-old unmarried Iraqi had agreed to wed a stranger so they could become a man-and-wife suicide team; how she panicked and ran; how she had wandered around the city's northern suburbs in a taxi, lost, stopping passersby for directions, still wearing streaks of blood on her clothes and shoes.

But nearly ten years had passed. The hotels had been rebuilt and renamed, and Rishawi had vanished inside Jordan's labyrinthine penal system. Within the Juwaida Women's Prison, she wore a kind of faded notoriety, like a valuable museum piece that no one looks at anymore. Some of the older hands in the state security service called her "Zarqawi's woman," a mocking reference to the infamous Jordanian terrorist Abu Musab al-Zarqawi, who ordered the hotel bombings. The younger ones barely remembered her at all.

Then, in the span of a month, everything changed. Zarqawi's followers, it turned out, had not forgotten Rishawi. The terrorists had rebranded themselves over the years and were now known in Jordan by the Arabic acronym Daesh—in English, ISIS. And in January 2015, ISIS asked to have Rishawi back.

The demand for her release came in the middle of Jordan's worst domestic crisis in years. A Jordanian air-force jet had crashed in Syria, and its young pilot had been captured alive by ISIS fighters. The group had broadcast photos of the frightened, nearly naked pilot being paraded around by grinning jihadists, some of them reaching out to embrace this great gift that Allah had dropped from the sky.

From the palace to the security agencies, the king and his advisers steeled themselves for even more awful news. Either the pilot would be publicly butchered by ISIS, they feared, or the terrorists would demand a terrible price for his ransom.

True to form, ISIS announced its decision in macabre fashion. Less than a week after the crash, the captured pilot's family received a call at home, from the pilot's own cell phone. On the other end, a stranger, speaking in Iraqi-accented Arabic, issued the group's singular demand.

We want our sister Sajida, the caller said.

The same demand was repeated, along with several new ones, in a constantly shifting and mostly one-sided negotiation. All the requests were routed to the headquarters of the Mukhabarat, Jordan's intelligence service, and all eventually landed on the desk of the imposing forty-seven-year-old brigadier who ran the department's counterterrorism unit. Even in an agency notorious for its toughness, Abu Haytham stood apart, a man with a burly street fighter's physique and the personality of an anvil. He had battled ISIS in its many incarnations for years, and he had famously broken some of the group's top operatives in interrogation. Zarqawi himself had taken several turns in Abu Haytham's holding cell, and so had Sajida al-Rishawi, the woman ISIS was now seeking to free.

Outside of Jordan, the demand made little sense. Rishawi had no value as a fighter or a leader, or even as a symbol. She was known to have participated in exactly one terrorist attack, and she had botched it. Hardly "Zarqawi's woman," she had never even met the man who ordered the strike. If ISIS hadn't mentioned her name, she would likely have lived her remaining years quietly in prison, her execution indefinitely deferred for lack of any particular reason to carry it out.

But Abu Haytham understood. By invoking Rishawi's name, the terrorists were reaching back to the group's beginnings, back to a time before there was an ISIS, or a civil war in Syria; before the meltdown in Iraq that gave rise to the movement; even before the world had heard of a terrorist called Zarqawi. The Mukhabarat's men had tried to keep this terrorist group from gaining a foothold. They had failed—sometimes through their own mistakes, more often because of the miscalculations of others. Now, Zarqawi's jihadist movement had become a self-declared state, with territorial claims on two of Jordan's borders. And Rishawi, the failed bomber, was one of many old scores that ISIS was ready to settle.

In summoning this forgotten ghost, ISIS was evoking one of the most horrifying nights in the country's history, a moment seared into the memories of men of Abu Haytham's generation, the former intelligence captains, investigators, and deputies who had since risen to lead the Mukhabarat. Once, Zarqawi had managed to strike directly at Jordan's heart, and now, with the country's pilot in their hands, ISIS was about to do it again.

Abu Haytham had been present that night. He could remember every detail of the crime for which Rishawi had been convicted and sentenced to hang. He could remember how the night had felt, the smell of blood and smoke, and the wailing of the injured.

Mostly he remembered the two girls.

They were cousins, ages nine and fourteen, and he knew their names: Lina and Riham. Local girls from Amman, out for a wedding party. They were both dressed in white, with small faces that were lovely and pale and perfectly serene. "Just like angels," he had thought.

They still wore the nearly identical lacy dresses their parents had bought for the party, and stylish shoes for dancing. Almost miraculously, from the neck up neither had suffered a scratch. When Abu Haytham first saw them, lying side by side on a board in those chaotic first moments at the hospital, he had wondered if they were sleeping. Injured, perhaps, but sedated and sleeping. *Please, let them be sleeping,* he had prayed.

But then he saw the terrible holes the shrapnel had made.

The girls would have been standing when it happened, as everyone was, whooping and clapping as the bride and groom prepared to make their entrance in the ballroom at Amman's Radisson Hotel, which was lit up like a desert carnival on a cool mid-November evening. The newlyweds' fathers, all big grins and rented tuxedos, had taken their places on the podium, and the Arabic band's bleating woodwinds and throbbing drums had risen to a roar so loud that the hotel clerks in the lobby had to shout to be heard. The party was just reaching its gloriously noisy, sweaty, exuberant peak. No one appeared to have noticed two figures in dark coats who shuffled awkwardly near the doorway and then squeezed between the rows of cheering wedding guests toward the front of the ballroom.

There was a blinding flash, and then a sensation of everything falling—the ceiling, the walls, the floor. The shock wave knocked guests out of their beds on the hotel's upper floors and blew out thick plate-glass doors in the lobby. A thunderclap, then silence. Then screams.

Only one of the bombs had gone off, but it cut through the ball-room like a swarm of flying razors. Hundreds of steel ball bearings, carefully and densely packed around the bomb's core, sliced through wedding decorations, food trays, and upholstery. They splintered wooden tables and shattered marble tiles. They tore through evening gowns and fancy clutches, through suit jackets and crisp shirts, and through white, frilly dresses of the kind young girls wear to formal parties.

Abu Haytham, then a captain, was winding down another in a string of long shifts on that Wednesday in early November 2005. It was just before 9:00 p.m. when the first call came in, about an explosion of some kind at the Grand Hyatt across town. The early speculation was that a gas canister was to blame, but then came word of a second blast at the Days Inn Hotel, and then a third—reportedly far worse than the others—at the Radisson. Abu Haytham knew the place well. It was an Amman landmark, glitzy by Jordanian standards, perched on a hill and easily visible from most of the town, including from his own office building, nearly two miles away.

He raced to the hotel and pushed his way inside, past the rescue workers, the wailing survivors, and the recovered corpses that had been hauled out on luggage carts and deposited on the driveway. In the ballroom, through a haze of smoke and emergency lights, he could see more bodies. Some were sprawled haphazardly, as though flung by a giant. Others were missing limbs. On the smashed podium lay two crumpled forms in tuxedos. The fathers of both the bride and the groom had been near the bomber and died instantly.

Abu Haytham assembled teams that worked the three blast sites through the night, gathering whatever remnants they could find of the explosive devices, along with chunks of flesh that constituted the remains of three bombers. Only later, at the hospital, standing over a wooden slab in a makeshift morgue, was he overwhelmed by the horror of the evening: The broken bodies. The scores of wounded. The smell of blood and smoke. The girls, Lina and Riham, lying still in their torn white dresses. Abu Haytham, a doting father, had girls the same age.

"How," he said aloud, "does someone with a human heart do a thing like this?"

Just two days later came the news that one of the attackers—a woman—had survived and fled. A day after that, Sajida al-Rishawi sat in a chair in front of him.

She would surely know something, tied as she was to such an obviously important and well-planned mission. Where would the terrorists strike next? What plans were unfolding, perhaps at this very hour?

"I don't know, I don't know," the woman would occasionally manage, in a soft mumble. She repeated the line slowly, as though drugged.

Abu Haytham pleaded with her. He threatened. He appealed to her conscience, to religion, to Allah. Hours passed—crucial hours, he feared.

"How brainwashed you are!" he shouted at one point. "Why do you protect the people who put you up to this?"

The woman would never offer a useful syllable, then or in the months to come, after she was convicted and sentenced to die. Yet, already, Abu Haytham knew who was behind the act. All the Mukhabarat's men knew, even before the culprit boasted of his responsibility in an audio recording made in his own voice. The signatures were all there: The coordinated blasts, all within ten minutes; the deployment of human bombers, each skillfully fitted with a device consisting of military-grade RDX explosive and enough loose metal to ensure maximum carnage. Most telling of all was the choice of targets—ordinary hotels where, on any given evening, Amman's middle class would pack a rented ballroom in their finest apparel to celebrate a union or mark a milestone. No intelligence operative or general was likely to pass through the lobby of the Radisson at 9:00 p.m. on a weekday night. But scores of Jordanians would be there, clinging to the rituals of normal life in a country bordering a war zone.

Such hallmarks, like the voice on the audio recording, unmistakably belonged to Zarqawi, a man the Mukhabarat knew exceptionally well. He was, at the time of the bombing, the head of a particularly vicious terrorist network called al-Qaeda in Iraq. But the Jordanians had known him back in the days when he was Ahmad the hoodlum, a high school dropout with a reputation as a heavy drinker and a brawler. They had watched him wander off to Afghanistan in the late 1980s to fight the communists, then return as a battle-hardened religious fanatic. After a first try at terrorism, he had vanished into one of Jordan's darkest prisons. This time he emerged as a battle-hardened religious fanatic who also happened to excel as a leader of men.

Abu Haytham had been among those who tried to alter Zarqawi's path after prison. He had been the last intelligence officer to meet with him in 1999, before Zarqawi was granted permission to leave the country for good, headed again to Afghanistan and a future that surely—so the Jordanians thought—offered nothing more than futility and a dusty grave.

Then, in the most improbable of events, America intervened. Few beyond the intelligence service had heard of Zarqawi when Washington made him a terrorist superstar, declaring to the world in 2003 that this obscure Jordanian was the link between Iraq's dictatorship and the plotters behind the September 11, 2001, terrorist attacks. The claim was wrong, yet, weeks later, when U.S. troops invaded Iraq, the newly famous and well-funded terrorist gained a battle-ground and a cause and soon thousands of followers. Over three tumultuous years, he intentionally pushed Iraq to the brink of sectarian war by unleashing wave after wave of savage attacks on Shiite civilians in their mosques, bazaars, and schools. He horrified millions with a new form of highly intimate terrorism: the beheading of individual hostages, captured on video and sent around the world, using the Internet's new power to broadcast directly into people's homes. Along the way, he lashed out violently at his native Jordan and helped transform America's lightning victory in Iraq into the costliest U.S. military campaign since Vietnam.

Yet his most significant accomplishment was not apparent until years later. Though some would cast his movement as an al-Qaeda offshoot, Zarqawi was no one's acolyte. His brand of jihadism was utterly, brutally original. Osama bin Laden had sought to liberate Muslim nations gradually from corrupting Western influences so they could someday unify as a single Islamic theocracy, or caliphate. Zarqawi, by contrast, insisted that he would create his caliphate immediately—right now. He would seek to usher in God's kingdom on Earth through acts of unthinkable savagery, believing, correctly, that theatrical displays of extreme violence would attract the most hardened jihadists to his cause and frighten everyone else into submission. His strategy shook the region as al-Qaeda never had.

But Zarqawi's excesses also deepened his adversaries' resolve. In the immediate aftermath of the hotel bombings, Abu Haytham and other Mukhabarat officers had a simple goal: to eliminate the man who had ordered them. And when they succeeded, in 2006, by providing the United States with intelligence that helped it track Zarqawi to his hideout, the terrorist and his organization appeared finished. Instead, his followers merely retreated, quietly gaining strength in Syria's lawless provinces until they burst into view in 2013, not as a terrorist group, but as an army.

This time, war-weary America would refuse to help until it was too late. There would be no serious effort to arm the moderate rebels who sought to deny ISIS its safe haven, and no air strikes to harry ISIS's leadership and supply lines. Twice in a decade, a jihadist wave had threatened to engulf the region. Twice, it seemed to the Jordanians, the American response had been to cut a fresh hole in the lifeboat.

Zarqawi's successors called themselves by different names before settling on ISIS—or simply the Islamic State. But they continued to refer to Zarqawi as the "mujahid sheikh," acknowledging the founder who had the audacity to believe he could redraw the maps of the Middle East. And, like Zarqawi, they believed their conquests would not end there.

In the prophetic passages of the Muslim holy texts known as the Hadith, Zarqawi saw his fate foretold. He and his men were the black-clad soldiers of whom the ancient scholars had written: "The black flags will come from the East, led by mighty men, with long hair and beards, their surnames taken from their home towns." These conquerors would not merely reclaim the ancient Muslim lands. They also would be the instigators of the final cataclysmic struggle ending in the destruction of the West's great armies, in northern Syria.

"The spark has been lit here in Iraq," Zarqawi preached, "and its heat will continue to intensify until it burns the Crusader armies in Dabiq."

The Mukhabarat's men had heard enough of such talk from Zarqawi back when he was their prisoner. Now the brazen claims were coming from his offspring. Thirty thousand strong, they were waiting just across the border, calling for their sister Sajida.

The charade of a prisoner swap ended abruptly on February 3, 2015, the day after Jordan's king arrived in Washingon for the official visit. For Abdullah II, it was the latest in a series of exhausting journeys in which he repeated the same appeal for help. His tiny country was struggling with two burdens imposed from abroad: a human tide of refugees from Syria—some six hundred thousand so far—and the cost of participating in the allied Western-Arab military campaign against ISIS. The trip was not going particularly well. Members of Congress offered sympathy but not much more; White House officials recited the usual pledges to bolster Jordan's defenses and struggling economy, but the kind of assistance Abdullah most desperately needed was nowhere in the offing.

The king's disappointment had long since hardened into resentment. During previous visits, President Obama had declined Jordan's requests for laser-guided munitions and other advanced hardware that could take out ISIS's trucks and tanks. On this trip, there was no firm commitment even for a meeting between the two leaders.

Abdullah was in the Capitol, making a pitch to Senator John McCain, the Republican senator and chairman of the Senate Armed Services Committee, when one of the king's aides interrupted him. The monarch stepped into the corridor and, on the small screen of a smartphone, watched ISIS deliver its final statement on the proposed prisoner swap. As video cameras rolled, masked jihadists marched the young Jordanian pilot into a small metal cage that had been doused with fuel. Then they lit a fire and filmed as the airman was burned alive.

By the time Abdullah returned to the meeting, McCain's aides had seen the video as well. The monarch kept his composure, but McCain could see he was badly shaken.

"Can we do anything more for you?" McCain asked.

"I'm not getting support from your side!" Abdullah finally said. "I'm still getting only gravity bombs, and we're not even getting resupplied with those. Meanwhile, we're flying two hundred percent more missions than all the other coalition members combined, apart from the United States."

The king continued with his scheduled meetings, but he had already made up his mind to return home. He was making arrangements when the White House phoned to offer fifteen minutes with the president. Abdullah accepted.

Inside the Oval Office, Obama offered condolences to the pilot's family and thanked the king for Jordan's contributions to the military campaign against ISIS. The administration was doing all it could to be supportive, the president assured the monarch.

"No, sir, you are not," Abdullah said, firmly. He rattled off a list of weapons and supplies he needed.

"I've got three days' worth of bombs left," he said, according to an official present during the exchange. "When I get home I'm going to war, and I'm going to use every bomb I've got until they're gone."

There was one other item of business to attend to before his return. From the airport, Abdullah called his aides in Amman to start the process of carrying out a pair of executions. On Jordan's death row, there were two inmates who had been convicted of committing murderous acts on orders from Zarqawi. One was an Iraqi man who had been a midlevel operative in Zarqawi's Iraqi insurgency. The other was Sajida al-Rishawi. Both should be put to death without further delay.

The king foresaw that Western governments would protest the executions as acts of vengeance, even though both inmates had been convicted and sentenced long ago as part of normal court proceedings. But he would not be deterred. As far as he was concerned, the appointment with the hangman had already been delayed too long, he told aides.

"I don't want to hear a word from anyone," Abdullah said.

The king was still airborne at 2:00 a.m. Amman time, when the guards arrived to collect Sajida al-Rishawi from her cell. She had declined the customary final meal and ritual bath with which devout Muslims cleanse the physical body in preparation for the afterlife. She donned the red uniform worn exclusively by condemned prisoners on the day of execution, along with the usual hijab for covering her head and face.

She was escorted outside the prison to a waiting van with a military escort for the drive to Swaqa, Jordan's largest prison, on a desert hill about sixty miles south of the capital. The vehicles arrived just before 4:00 a.m., as a full moon, visible through a light haze, was dipping toward the southwestern horizon.

Her last earthly view, before she was blindfolded, was of a small execution chamber with white walls and a row of tiny windows, and a few tired faces looking up from the witness gallery just below her. An imam prayed as a noose with a heavy metal clasp was secured, and a judge asked if Rishawi cared to convey any last wishes or a final will. She gave no reply.

She likewise made no audible sound as the gallows' trap opened and she plunged hard into the darkness. It was 5:05 a.m., nearly ninety minutes before sunrise, when the prison doctor checked for a pulse.

"Zarqawi's woman" was dead, her execution the closing scene in the worst act of terrorism in Jordan's history. But Zarqawi's children were pursuing the founder's far grander ambitions: the end of Jordan and its king, the erasing of international boundaries, and the destruction of the modern states of the Middle East. Then, with black flags raised above Muslim capitals from the Levant to the Persian Gulf, they could begin the great apocalyptic showdown with the West.

BOOK I

THE RISE OF ZARQAWI

1

"What kind of person can command with only his eyes?"

The most notorious of Jordan's prisons is the old fortress of al-Jafr, known for decades as the place where troublesome men went to be forgotten. It lies outside a Bedouin village of the same name, on a road that marks the outer boundary of human habitation in the country's fierce southeastern desert. Beyond the prison, the terrain flattens into a basin of baked mud that stretches to the horizon without a hill or rock or stubble of grass. The ancient sea that once stood here evaporated eons ago, leaving an emptiness like a missing limb, a void so unnatural that it stirs feelings of dread among the few travelers who pause for a look. "There's a terrible loneliness," wrote filmmaker David Lean, who shot parts of *Lawrence of Arabia* on the same mudflats in 1962 and pronounced the place "more deserted than any desert I've ever seen." His picture editor, Howard Kent, would describe al-Jafr as, simply, "a warning of what hell is like."

It was at this spot that British military overseers chose to build an imposing prison with limestone walls and high watchtowers for detainees regarded as too dangerous for ordinary jails. And it was here, years later, that the Jordanians began the practice of quarantining Palestinian militants and other radicals viewed as threats to the state. Hundreds of men, many of them held without formal charge, languished in stifling, vermin-infested cells where they endured temperature extremes, rancid food, and a catalogue of abuses later documented by United Nations investigators. Newly arriving prisoners were routinely beaten until they lost consciousness. Others were flogged with electric cables, burned with lit cigarettes, or hung upside down by means of a stick placed under the knees, a position the guards gleefully called "grilled chicken." Over time, the monarchy grew weary of the costs of running a prison so isolated from the country's population and so damaging to its reputation. In 1979, the last of its inmates were transferred to other jails, and al-Jafr was abandoned to the scorpions and its own ghosts.

Years passed, and then, in a sudden shift, the old prison was resurrected. Officials of the Public Security Directorate had grown worried about the behavior of a band of antigovernment zealots in the country's central Swaqa Prison, and in 1998 they decided to isolate the group to prevent the contagion from spreading. The officials reopened one of al-Jafr's dusty wings and dispatched an army of workers to sweep out corridors and prepare a large cell where all could be housed together. Twenty-five bunk beds were assembled and stacked in cramped rows, and a new door of latticed steel was bolted across the cell's entrance, the room's only opening other than air slits cut into walls at knee level. When the grounds were ready, the department appointed a warden and hired the usual complement of guards, laundrymen, and cooks. The inmates were too few to justify the hiring of a separate prison physician, and so it was that Basel al-Sabha, a recent medical-school graduate assigned by the Health Department to the local village, was pressed into service as the doctor of record for fifty of the most dangerous men in Jordan.

It was an unwelcome assignment for Sabha, a tall twenty-four-year-old with boyish good looks, and he complained bitterly about the posting. Prisons in Jordan were vile places, and this one exceeded all others, at least by reputation. Sabha's anxiety deepened on his very first day, as the warden, a middle-aged colonel named Ibrahim, sat him down to review a list of safety precautions. When dealing with inmates such as these, the warden cautioned, it was essential to stay on the other side of the bars at all times, even during medical examinations. And Sabha shouldn't be lulled into thinking that a metal door was protection enough, he warned.

"These people are very dangerous," Ibrahim said. "Even if they're not physically dangerous, they have a way of affecting you. Even I have to be careful that they don't affect me."

The warden went on to describe the peculiarities of the new arrivals, from their strange dress—most insisted on wearing an Afghan-style tunic over their jailhouse uniforms, because tight-fitting prison trousers were regarded as too revealing—to their ability to make converts out of hardened criminals and even prison employees. At Swaqa, so many guards had fallen under their spell that prison officials were forced to limit shifts to ninety minutes in any sector where the inmates might be encountered.

As the tour was ending, the warden repeated his warning about the prisoners. There was one inmate—the sect's apparent leader—whose seductive powers were extraordinary, he said. He was the one called Maqdisi, a religious scholar and preacher of considerable gifts, capable of infecting and twisting minds like a Muslim Rasputin.

"He is very smart, a walking library of Islamic knowledge," Ibrahim said. "You will know when you see him. A handsome guy, tall and slim, with light-brown hair and blue eyes. Don't be fooled."

Moments later, Basel al-Sabha was being escorted by guards into the prison's interior, past the watchtowers and armed guards, to the wing where the prisoners were kept. It was well past dark, and a dim light shone feebly through the bars of the doorway as the doctor approached. Drawing closer, he could make out the rows of bunks, followed by a jarring first glimpse of the prisoners themselves.

Forty-eight inmates sat upright on their bunks or prayer rugs, facing the doorway with rapt attention, like military conscripts awaiting inspection. Each wore the same peculiar uniform, a loose-fitting tunic worn over the standard blue prison shirt and trousers, just as the warden had said. All eyes appeared fixed on a figure near the doorway, and Sabha inched forward to see who it was.

At the front of the cell were two men. The first was tall and slender with scholarly glasses and a tangle of light-brown hair protruding from his prayer cap. Sabha guessed that this was the one the warden had called Maqdisi, the cell block's charismatic leader. Yet it was the second man who appeared to command the room's attention. He was darker and shorter but powerfully built, with a thick neck and shoulders that might have belonged to a wrestler or gymnast. Sabha, now only feet away, noticed an unusual scar on the man's right arm: a jagged gash across a patch of ink-stained skin the color of an old bruise. Around the wound the flesh showed the pulls and folds of amateur suturing.

The owner of the scar studied the rows of bunks for a long moment, then turned to lock his gaze on the visitor. The face was unremarkable, fleshy, with full lips framed by a thin beard. But the eyes were unforgettable. Deep-set and nearly black in the low prison light, they conveyed a cold intelligence, alert and probing, but lacking any trace of emotion. Neither welcoming nor hostile, his look was that of a snake studying the fat young mouse that had just dropped into his cage.

At last the warden spoke. He mumbled words of introduction for the new doctor, and then declared the start of clinic hours. *All prisoners with medical complaints can step forward to be examined,* he said.

Sabha edged closer to the door to await the inevitable rush. He had prepared for the moment and had brought along a supply of pills and salves to treat the rashes, minor wounds, allergies, and gastric ailments common to men living in close confinement. But, to his surprise, no one stirred. The inmates sat motionless, waiting for a sign from the scarred man, who at last turned his gaze on an inmate seated on a bed near the front of the cell. When he gave a slight nod, the seated prisoner stood and walked to the doorway without a sound. He nodded a second time, and a third, and, one by one, inmates took their place in line in front of the doctor.

Five men, and only five, were summoned, and still the man with the scar had not uttered a word. He turned to the doctor with the same reptilian stare, the look of a man who possessed, even in Jordan's harshest prison, absolute control.

Sabha felt an uneasiness, like a tremor welling up from somewhere deep in the foundation of the old fortress. "What kind of person," he wondered, "can command with only his eyes?"

Over the following days, the doctor scoured files for insights into his new patients and why prison officials had come to fear them. The group's core, he learned, consisted of about two dozen men who had been members of radical Islamic sects that sprang up in Jordan in the early 1990s. With the exception of the leader, Abu Muhammad al-Maqdisi—a firebrand preacher known for penning screeds against Arab leaders—their individual histories were unimpressive. Some had been street thugs who had gotten religion and found acceptance and purpose among the zealots. Others had been part of the Arab volunteer army that had fought against the Soviets in Afghanistan in the 1980s. Back home in safe, stable Jordan, these men had been drawn to organizations that offered a way to relive the glories of the Afghan campaign through perpetual holy war against the enemies of Islam.

Their efforts at jihad in Jordan had been anything but glorious. The leaders of Maqdisi's small band had been arrested before they could carry out their first operation, a planned attack on an Israeli border post. The other groups' targets had consisted of small-time symbols of Western corruption, from liquor stores to video shops and pornographic movie houses. One of the early attempts at a bombing had been a spectacular failure: A member of the group had volunteered to plant explosives inside a local adult cinema called the Salwa. After a few minutes in the theater, the would-be assailant had become so engrossed in the film that he forgot about his bomb. As he sat, glued to the screen, the device detonated under his feet. No patrons were hurt, but the bomber lost both his legs. Six years later, the double-amputee was among Sabha's charges at al-Jafr Prison. The doctor had noticed him on his first visit, propped up on his bunk, his pant legs neatly pinned at the knee.

By now, nearly all the men had been locked up for four years or more. But if prison was meant to break the jihadists and weaken their cause, the attempt was an utter failure. Confined mostly in the same communal cells, the men had been bound together by their privations and by the daily struggle to persevere as religious purists among drug dealers, thieves, and killers. They shared a common creed, an austere brand of Islam invented by Maqdisi and inculcated during endless weeks of confinement. They also possessed an uncommon discipline. The group behaved as a military unit, with clear chains of authority and unquestioned obedience to Maqdisi's handpicked enforcer, the scarred, thick-chested man who had made such an impression during Sabha's first visit to the prison. Maqdisi told the men what to think, but his number two controlled everything else: how the men spoke and dressed, which books they read and which television shows they watched, whether they accepted or resisted prison dictates, when and how they fought. The man's given name was Ahmad Fadil al-Khalayleh, but he preferred to be called "al-Gharib," or "the Stranger," a handle he had picked up during his days as a fighter in the Afghan civil war. Some, however, were already calling him "the one from Zarqa," the tough industrial town in northern Jordan where he grew up. The phrase in Arabic is "al-Zarqawi."

Sabha was able to observe both leaders up close. The Maqdisi he saw was mild and agreeable, more amiable professor than beguiling mystic. At just shy of forty, he had the weary air of an intellectual who felt he deserved better company than the few dozen backward men who shared his cell. He freely dispensed religious advice and the occasional fatwa, or religious ruling, but he preferred spending his time in solitary pursuits, writing essays and reading the Koran. On the printed page, Maqdisi was fearless: he gained renown throughout the Muslim world for inflammatory books with titles such as *Democracy Is a Religion,* in which he denounced secular Arab regimes as anti-Islamic and called for their destruction. His work eventually gained such resonance among Islamists that a Pentagon-commissioned study in 2006 would call him the most important new thinker in the jihadi intellectual universe.

Previous Islamist ideologues also had criticized leaders of the Arab world as corrupt and unfaithful to the religion. The same themes appeared in the writings of Sayyid Qutb, the influential Egyptian author whose works inspired the founders of al-Qaeda. But in Maqdisi's view, each Muslim bore a personal obligation to act when confronted with evidence of official heresy. It wasn't enough for the faithful simply to denounce corrupt rulers. They were compelled by Allah to slaughter them.

"His radical conclusion was that the leaders were infidels, and Muslims should kill them," said Hasan Abu Hanieh, a Jordanian writer and intellectual who was friendly with Maqdisi during the years when his ideas were beginning to congeal. "The 'killing' was the turning point. It was a message that resonated with Muslims who felt that the regimes were stupid and had allowed foreigners to occupy Arab lands. For these people, Maqdisi was not only validating their views but telling them they were obliged to do something about it."

Oddly enough, the man who called so bluntly for confronting Islam's enemies tended to shy away from conflict. As Sabha observed, whenever interrogators and agents of the intelligence services visited the prison, he would greet them politely and ask about their families, to the dismay of other inmates who had suffered at the hands of the same men. He would patiently explain to guards and prison officers why they and their government were heretics, buttressing his arguments with quotes from the Koran. But he would often retreat when challenged, allowing that less severe interpretations of scripture could also be valid.

"You can be a member of Parliament and still be a good Muslim," he told Sabha one day, offering a nuance that seemed to contradict his central thesis about the evils of nontheocratic governance. "If someone is elected because he wants to serve the people, that's being a good Muslim. But if he believes in democracy—if he believes in rules made by men—he is an infidel."

Maqdisi seemed fond of the young physician, who, though secular, was the only other person at al-Jafr with an advanced degree. Their relationship took a turn one day when the youngest of Maqdisi's wives fell ill during a visit to the desert prison. The woman suffered from unusual menstrual bleeding, and Sabha arranged to see her at his private clinic in the village. The gesture might have risked offense—many ultra-conservative Muslim men refuse to allow their wives to be seen by male doctors—but Maqdisi seemed genuinely grateful. After that day, the physician's visits to the cell block were greeted with wide grins.

But politeness and intellect are poor instruments for commanding men in such a hard place as al-Jafr. Maqdisi needed an enforcer. In Zarqawi, he had found the perfect helper: a man with the distinction of being at once slavishly devoted and utterly ruthless. "He is very tough," Maqdisi would say admiringly, referring to his number two, "and he is a Jordanian's Jordanian—a man of the tribe."

Their personalities could hardly have been more different. Zarqawi had no capacity for warmth or nuance. The man with the scar did not smile. He did not return greetings from prison employees, or engage in their small talk. When he spoke at all, it was with the street slang of a high-school dropout who had grown up as a brawler and petty criminal in one of Zarqa's toughest neighborhoods. His gruffness and refusal to conform to convention had marked him as a troublemaker since boyhood. They also helped burnish the legend that was already beginning to cement around Zarqawi in his thirty-third year.

Whereas Maqdisi preferred the ethereal world of books and ideas, Zarqawi was purely a physical being, with a compact, muscular frame that he chiseled through weight lifting, using buckets of stones as barbells. The whispered stories of his criminal past—the stabbings and beatings, the pimping and drug dealing—made him seem dangerous and unpredictable, a man of action, capable of anything.

He had fought bravely, even recklessly, in Afghanistan, and his reputation for impulsive violence had followed him into prison. He habitually defied authorities in the first of the jails where he and the others were confined, and he brutalized and humiliated inmates who crossed him, sometimes with fists or crude weapons and sometimes, it was widely said, sexually. Once, in a rage, he had grabbed a prison guard by his uniform collar and suspended him from a coat hook. Another time, he instigated a violent protest by inmates armed with crude clubs and swords fashioned from bed frames. "We have come to die!" the prisoners had screamed, and some surely would have, except for the timely intervention of a warden who acceded to many of the jihadists' demands.

Under Maqdisi's tutelage, Zarqawi's attacks subsided, but the violent energy simply shifted form. Zarqawi began memorizing the Koran, spending hour after hour reading, or staring blankly with the open volume in his lap. His diffuse rage took on a focus: a fierce, single-minded hatred for perceived enemies of Allah. The list started with Jordan's monarch, King Hussein, whom Zarqawi saw as the illegitimate leader of an artificial country, responsible for the unspeakable crime of making peace with Israel. It also included servants of the regime: the guards, the soldiers, the politicians, the bureaucrats, and countless others who profited from the current system. Even prison inmates he denounced as *kafirs*, or disbelievers. To Muslims the term is no mere epithet; if used in a fatwa, it implies that the person has lost the protection of Islamic law and can be killed with impunity. Within the prison, the guards began referring to Zarqawi and his closest followers as *al-takfiris*—"the excommunicators."

At the same time, Zarqawi began taking a stronger hand as a leader and an enforcer among the Islamist prisoners. He demanded the absolute obedience of the men, and he berated them whenever they skipped prayers or watched television news shows anchored by women who were not veiled. Despite his harsh manner, he won admirers because of his fearless defiance of prison authority. When official visitors came to al-Jafr, Zarqawi would often ignore them and refuse even to acknowledge their greetings. And he would order his men to do the same.

One day, after Jordan agreed to open its prisons to inspections from human-rights groups, a senior Interior Ministry official arrived at al-Jafr to check on conditions and implore the inmates not to say anything negative to the foreigners. The Islamists refused to answer his questions or even look at him.

The exasperated official first scolded the men, then tried to cajole them into cooperating with suggestions that their sentences could be reduced.

"God willing, King Hussein will pardon you!" he said.

Zarqawi stood suddenly and jabbed a finger just inches from the bureaucrat's nose.

"This master is not our master!" he snarled. "Ours is Allah almighty."

The visitor snapped. "I swear to God, you will not leave!" he shouted. "You will stay in this prison!"

"By Allah," Zarqawi replied coldly, "we will come out. Forcibly, if God wills."

There was another side to Zarqawi. Sabha would catch occasional glimpses of it during his prison visits. It was jarringly incongruous with Zarqawi's usual behavior, as though he suffered from a split personality.

Everyone at al-Jafr knew how Zarqawi worshipped his mother, how he became like a little boy whenever she visited. He would prepare for days, scrubbing his clothes in the sink and tidying up his corner of the cell. Some inmates knew about his love letters to her, and to his sisters. Scarcely a word was mentioned about Zarqawi's wife, Intisar, or their two young children. But to his mother and sisters he wrote gushing notes adorned with poems and hand-drawn flowers in the margins.

"Oh, sister, how much you have suffered on account of my imprisonment for the sake of my religion," he wrote to Umm Qadama in one carefully scrawled note with alternating blue and red ink. He closed with a poem:

I wrote you a letter, O my sister,
Which I made of my soul's desire.
The first thing I write is the fire of my heart,
And the second is my love and longing.

The other objects of Zarqawi's exaggerated attentions were the sick and injured among his men. When any of the Islamists fell ill, he put himself in the role of heroic caregiver, giving up his own blankets and rations to ensure their comfort. He hovered over Sabha and a second doctor who joined the prison staff, hectoring them whenever he felt his men were being shortchanged.

"Where's the medicine you promised for this one?" he would demand, according to Sabha's recollection. Once, when one of the inmates left al-Jafr for a few days of hospital therapy, he fretted like a nervous parent, nagging Sabha for news about the man's condition.

Sabha was particularly struck by the tenderness Zarqawi displayed toward the most fragile of the inmates, the double-amputee named Eid Jahaline, the unlucky bomber who flubbed the attack on the pornographic cinema. Jahaline, who suffered from a psychological disorder in addition to his physical disfigurement, had always bunked with the other Islamist inmates in spite of extreme disabilities. Zarqawi appointed himself as the man's personal valet, and assisted him with his bathing, changing, and feeding. Most days, he would simply scoop up the legless man in his arms and carry him to the toilet. Sabha suspected that the daily ritual had as much to do with Zarqawi's peculiar sense of propriety as with genuine compassion for his comrade. Under the Islamists' strict moral code, exposing the man's naked body to others would constitute both a humiliation and a sin.

One evening, while Sabha was visiting the cell, Jahaline suffered one of his occasional meltdowns, a screaming fit that usually required treatment with antipsychotic drugs. Sabha grabbed a syringe and was preparing to administer the shot when Zarqawi stepped forward to block him. Without a word, Zarqawi took a blanket from one of the beds and draped it over Jahaline's lower body. He held the blanket in place with one hand, and with the other he tugged at the elastic waistband of the disabled man's trousers, exposing a narrow crescent of skin. Then he motioned to the doctor.

"Just make sure it's in the right spot," he commanded.

Sabha felt for Jahaline's pelvic bone through his clothes and, satisfied, pushed the needle into the pale flesh.

When it was done and Jahaline was resting quietly, Sabha looked up to find Zarqawi watching him with a look of satisfaction. There was something different in the reptilian eyes, a quality that the doctor had not noticed before. He thought it might have been the stirrings of a smile.

The arrival of winter in 1998 brought freezing temperatures and scores of newcomers, as prison officials sought to relieve overcrowding elsewhere in the system. The Islamists remained cloistered together, as always, but now subtle cracks were beginning to show. Some of the jihadists were openly suggesting that Zarqawi should be the leader, replacing Maqdisi, whose professorial demeanor had begun to grate on some members of the group.

Zarqawi made no move against his mentor, but the feelings of many inmates were quite clear. Maqdisi's nuanced theological arguments were lost on the high-school dropouts and petty criminals who made up much of the group. These men preferred someone with tough-guy credentials, like Zarqawi, a brawler who talked plainly and refused to compromise. As he himself admitted, Maqdisi was no warrior. Even while living in Arab training camps in Afghanistan, he had given up on learning how to use a gun.

"He was not a fighter who lived between the bullets, the missiles and the tanks, even for a day!" one of the Afghan veterans later explained.

Zarqawi clearly liked being in charge, and he gradually took on a still more dominant role, with his mentor's blessing, leaving Maqdisi to oversee spiritual matters. For the first time, important people outside prison were beginning to hear his name. Maqdisi had many admirers within the Islamist movement's diaspora, from London to the Palestinian cities of the West Bank, and some of them were men with resources and extensive connections throughout the Middle East, North Africa, and Europe. Now they were learning through Maqdisi about his impressive assistant, an Afghan veteran of unusual courage and natural leadership ability.

Sabha, meanwhile, found himself working more frequently with Zarqawi, and their interactions became increasingly cordial, if not exactly warm.

One evening, as Sabha was making his rounds, Zarqawi pulled the doctor aside to make a request. It was the first time the man had asked for anything on his own behalf.

"I think I have high blood sugar," he began. "My mother has diabetes, so maybe it's in the family. Can you check?"

Sabha was happy to oblige, but it was complicated, he said. The test could not be performed in the prison—the risk of infection was too high to draw blood in al-Jafr's filthy, rodent-infested cells—so Zarqawi would have to be brought to the doctor's private clinic in the village.

There was another complication: obtaining the official approvals needed to allow such a dangerous inmate to leave al-Jafr. As expected, the warden protested vigorously. What if it was a ruse to help Zarqawi escape? What if his allies were waiting in ambush in the town? But eventually Ibrahim relented, and arrangements were made for the armed escort that would deliver the prisoner to the village clinic and back again.

On the day of the test, Sabha decided to wait at the village clinic for his patient to show up. It was well after dark when a convoy of ten vehicles arrived, with a complement of dozens of guards armed with assault rifles. It was the biggest military escort Sabha had ever seen, and he wondered at first if someone from the royal court had decided to call on the village. Instead, a solitary prisoner stumbled out of one of the vans and then disappeared again inside a moving cocoon of armed men.

Zarqawi was led into the doctor's office in his prison garb, still wearing his handcuffs.

"Please take those off," Sabha ordered, gesturing to the metal bracelets.

"Sir, the man is dangerous," one of the escorts protested.

"You have fifty soldiers watching his every move," the doctor replied. "I insist that the cuffs be taken off."

Having succeeded in freeing Zarqawi's arms, Sabha proceeded with his examination. He began to roll up one of the prisoner's shirtsleeves to draw a blood sample, but was stopped again, this time by Zarqawi.

"I'm sorry," the inmate apologized. Zarqawi lowered the sleeve back to its position before the doctor had touched it. Then he rolled it back up again, without help. Sabha had tripped on another of Zarqawi's indecipherable codes on the touching of naked flesh.

As the blood was being drawn, Sabha worked up the courage to ask, finally, about the nature of the mysterious scar on Zarqawi's arm.

"It was a tattoo. An anchor," he replied.

"What happened?"

Zarqawi began to recount how he had gotten the tattoo at age sixteen, at a time when, as he put it, "I wasn't very Islamic-minded." After he joined the jihadist movement, his tattoo became an embarrassment. He tried scrubbing it off in various ways, including with bleach. The skin turned an angry red, but the tattoo would not budge.

Finally, he turned to one of his Zarqa relatives, who was visiting the prison with a razor hidden in his clothes. As Zarqawi sat, the kinsman cut two elliptical lines around the tattoo. He then sliced away the upper layers of skin. When the tattoo was mostly gone, he closed the wound with crude stitches.

Sabha's face betrayed his horror at the story, but Zarqawi just shrugged, as though the act of hacking off an offending piece of flesh were as natural as squashing a cockroach. Islam—his brand of Islam—required it. This was an indisputable fact. The rest was a simple act of will.

"Tattoos," he explained impassively, "are *haram*. Forbidden."

Sabha finished his exam, and Zarqawi, who showed no signs of physical disease, returned to prison with his escorts. The doctor remained behind to ponder, in his small clinic by the road on the edge of a dead lake, dwarfed by the vastly larger Arabian desert just beyond it.

Seventy years earlier, an Islamic army had traversed the same road, riding north on horses and camels with the intention of wiping out the country known as Jordan in the name of Allah. These Bedouin raiders, who called themselves Ikhwan, or Brothers, had been armed and trained by Saudi Arabia's first monarch, Ibn Saud, to help him defeat his political rivals. But the Ikhwan had ambitions beyond the Arabian Peninsula. Bloodthirsty fanatics who regarded all Western inventions and practices as works of the devil, they saw themselves as divinely appointed to purify the region by slaughtering all who allied with foreigners or deviated from their narrow vision of Islam. From the harsh wastelands of the interior, they thundered into the newly formed countries of Jordan and Iraq in the early 1920s with the intention of toppling governments and creating a unified Islamic theocracy, or caliphate, spanning all of the Middle East. They hacked and slashed their way through entire villages that stood in their path, slitting the throats of every male survivor, to ensure that all traces of Western modernity were wiped out.

Despite vain attempts by the Saudi monarch to control them, an Ikhwan army of about fifteen hundred advanced to within ten miles of Amman, the Jordanian capital, before finally being stopped. British warplanes spotted the approaching column and cut them down with machine guns until all but about a hundred of the raiders were dead.

Small bands of militants continued to control parts of the Saudi interior at least until the 1950s, menacing and sometimes killing outsiders who wandered near their villages. Eventually they vanished, yet the fierce hatreds that animated the Ikhwan never went away.

The unwavering intolerance, the embrace of an extreme and pitilessly violent form of Islam as a kind of cleansing fire—these would find acceptance into the late twentieth century and beyond, from isolated villages in the peninsula's interior to the oil-rich cities of the Gulf Coast, and from the rugged hills of eastern Afghanistan to the crowded cells of an infamous Jordanian prison.

At al-Jafr, the contagion was contained within thick prison walls, at least for a time. Under the sentence handed down by the judge in Amman, Zarqawi's confinement was to continue for another ten years, until 2009, when the muscular and vital young man would be entering middle age. Yet, as Sabha well knew, prison terms in Jordan were rarely what they seemed on paper. A sentence could be drastically shortened because of a change in government, or a perceived need to curry favor with a religious party or tribe. If that happened, Zarqawi could find himself, and perhaps his army of followers, suddenly free.

2

"Here was a real leader"

Two weeks before King Hussein's death—in the calm before the deathbed farewells, the legions of mourners, and the lines of world leaders paying tribute to Jordan's greatest and longest-serving statesman—the monarch called his oldest son, Abdullah, to the palace to share a decision that would transform the young man's life and alter his country's destiny.

The king had just returned from a six-month hospital stay in the United States to treat an aggressive form of lymphoma, but the cancer had returned with a fury, and the doctors were warning that his time was short. On January 22, 1999, he phoned Abdullah, then a thirty-six-year-old army commander at the pinnacle of his military career, and asked him to come at once.

"I want to see you," he said.

Abdullah bin Hussein got into his car and drove up the steep road to the palace at Hummar, with its stunning hilltop vistas of the capital city. Inside, he found the king in the dining room, looking alarmingly frail. At sixty-three, he was bone-thin, and his skin was sallow from jaundice. The gray hair and beard that in earlier years had given him a vague resemblance to the actor Sean Connery had long since fallen away, from extensive chemotherapy.

The king excused his aides and shut the door. He then turned to Abdullah, pale fingers grasping his son's hands.

"I want to make you crown prince," he said.

The words were all but incomprehensible. For more than three decades, the title had belonged to Prince Hassan, the king's worldly and accomplished younger brother who had become heir apparent to the throne when Abdullah was still a toddler. The king's athletic and boyish-looking oldest son had spent his adult years driving tanks and helicopters and jumping from airplanes. He had shown little interest in politics or palace intrigues, preferring the military's cleaner lines of command. Now his father was seeking to propel him into a job whose perils included, among innumerable others, the near certainty of a clash with family members who had been waiting for years for a chance to run the country.

"What about my uncle?" Abdullah asked at last, according to his recollection of the meeting years afterward.

But the king had made up his mind. Days later, he would announce his decision publicly in the form of an open letter to Hassan, officially demoting him and hinting vaguely of his disappointment with greedy "climbers" in the royal family who he said were "meddling" and "disloyal." After his death, he said, the crown would pass from father to son—in this case, to a son who, among the monarch's brothers, nephews, and eleven children, was distinguished by his lack of ambition to be king.

Abdullah had been born a crown prince. Under Jordan's constitution as well as a centuries-old Hashemite dynastic tradition, the title automatically belonged to the oldest male child. But in the turbulent 1960s, with war clouds looming and the monarchy under constant threat of assassination or palace coup, Hussein made his brother the heir apparent, to ensure stability in the case of his death. Removed from the line of succession, Abdullah spent much of his youth and early adulthood outside Jordan. He attended American and British prep schools and universities, which gave him a worldly education but relatively little insight into the inner workings of his own country.

Back home, he had immersed himself in the culture of Jordan's lower and middle classes as a career soldier, sharing the same squalid barracks and dust-coated field rations as the other commissioned officers. He climbed the ranks to major general, but he retained his young man's passion for fast cars and motorcycles. He relished moments when he could personally lead his special-forces teams into operations against terrorists and criminals, as he had famously done the previous year, when his commandos stormed a gangsters' hideout in a street battle captured live on Jordanian TV.

But now the young commander sat in the dining room of the Hummar Palace, overwhelmed. With a single sentence, his father had upended his world and the stable, if privileged, life he had built for himself, his wife, and their two children.

The king also had acknowledged something he had never said aloud: the fact of his impending death.

"A cold sensation crept into my stomach," Abdullah would recall. "I think that was the first instant I felt truly alone."

He left the palace and returned home to find his wife, Rania, sitting on the floor of their living room with family photos spread out around her. Her eyes filled when he shared the news, as the magnitude of the changes awaiting both of them began to sink in.

"We would soon be thrust into the spotlight in a way that neither of us could have imagined," he later wrote in his memoir. "And there were a lot of wolves out there, waiting for us to stumble."

Those worries were soon shoved aside by more immediate crises. King Hussein had decided to try one more round of cancer treatment, which meant leaving Jordan for another bone-marrow transplant in the United States. Abdullah would effectively serve as regent during his absence, a role that would force him to plunge headlong into a sea of political and foreign-policy challenges, despite his limited experience. Though he did not yet know it, the list of urgent tasks would soon include preparations for a state funeral and his formal coronation as king.

On January 29, Abdullah drove his father to the airport to begin his journey to the Mayo Clinic in Minnesota. The king sat in the front passenger seat, looking quietly out the window as the car wound through Amman's affluent western district, with its high-rise hotels and office towers, and then onto the airport highway. They passed poorer suburbs and villages with their outdoor markets and small, neon-lit mosques. Then they were speeding through open country, past craggy hills and rock-strewn fields where sheep and Bedouin tents compete for space with satellite dishes and Toyota pickup trucks. Abdullah reached over to rest a hand on top of one of his father's, then kept it there as they rode in silence.

The farewells were going fine until they reached the airplane, when Abdullah, convinced he was seeing his father for the last time, briefly lost the steely composure he had vowed to maintain. Choking back tears, he helped his father onto the plane and then stood with him for a moment in the aisle to say goodbye. The king looked at his son directly but was clearly struggling with his emotions as well, Abdullah later recalled. Instead of a hug or parting instruction, he simply nodded, then turned to walk down the aisle alone.

Minutes later, the crown prince was on his way back to Amman and the duties awaiting him at the palace. He would never again see his father conscious. The king returned to the country he had ruled for nearly half a century, but this time there were no cameras on hand as the dying man was wheeled from the plane to a waiting ambulance and onward to Amman's King Hussein Medical Center, where thousands of ordinary Jordanians stood vigil in a cold rain, refusing to leave until the moment, shortly before noon on February 7, 1999, when television stations throughout the country abruptly went dark.

Abdullah sat by the hospital bed during the final hours, feeling even more alone for his inability to comfort his father, or to ask for a single word of advice on governing a country that seemed perpetually in crisis, beset by enemies within and without.

Not since the founding of the country had Jordanians seen an event as grand as the funeral of King Hussein bin Talal. Never had there been such crowds, as ordinary Jordanians—an estimated eight hundred thousand of them, or nearly a quarter of the country's population—clogged the sidewalks and spilled out of windows and rooftops along the route through which the flag-draped coffin would pass. They stood for hours, bundled up against a damp chill, to honor the only ruler most had ever known: the smiling monarch with the common touch who had led the country through wars and civil strife and then, in his later years, on a historic path to peace. Men and women openly wept, and some wailed and slapped themselves in a traditional Arabic show of mourning. Others ran alongside the funeral cortege and even lunged into its path in a frenzy of grief.

Nearly as impressive was the gathering of foreign dignitaries at Amman's Raghadan Palace. Less than twenty-four hours after the king's death, premiers and potentates from seventy-five countries had passed through the palace's arched limestone entrance to attend what commentators were already calling "the funeral of the twentieth century." Four U.S. presidents were among the visitors, including the White House's current occupant, Bill Clinton, who paused before boarding Air Force One to praise Hussein as a "magnificent man" whose nobility came "not from his title, but from his character." Britain's Prince Charles and prime minister Tony Blair rushed to Amman to attend, as did UN secretary-general Kofi Annan and the heads of state of Japan, France, Germany, and the other major European powers. Russian president Boris Yeltsin, looking pale and disoriented, arrived with a phalanx of security guards but left minutes later, complaining of illness.

The Middle Eastern guests invited the most stares. The contingent included a surprise visitor, Syrian president Hafez al-Assad, for years a bitter foe of Hussein, having fought his neighbor across their common border and tried repeatedly to undermine his government. Now the aging autocrat mingled with other emirs and strongmen who at various times had battled the Jordanians, or the Syrians, or each other. Israeli prime minister Benjamin Netanyahu, wearing a traditional Hebrew prayer cap over his graying locks, occupied a corner of the domed reception hall with an entourage that included generals, bodyguards, and a bearded rabbi. The Palestine Liberation Organization's Yasser Arafat, his five-foot-two frame dwarfed by an oversized military coat, made small talk with Egypt's president Hosni Mubarak. Perhaps the most anxious man in the room was Khaled Mashal, the leader of the militant Palestinian faction Hamas and a repeated target of Israeli assassination attempts. Two years earlier, agents from Israel's Mossad spy service had jabbed Mashal with a poison needle on an Amman street a few miles from where he now stood. He survived only after a furious King Hussein prevailed on the Israelis to provide his doctors with an antidote.

Greeting them all, looking slightly uncomfortable in his black suit and red-checkered keffiyeh, was the man whom visitors now addressed as King Abdullah II. The new monarch stood near the coffin in a royal receiving line of siblings and uncles, shaking hands with presidents and ministers who were mostly strangers to him. He was not yet officially king—the formal swearing in would take place before Parliament later in the day—but he had gone on Jordanian television moments after Hussein's death to signal the change to the nation. When he appeared on camera, reading from a paper script with his father beaming from a portrait over his shoulder, it was the first time most Jordanians had heard his voice.

"This was God's judgment and God's will," he had said.

Now he was taking his place at the head of the line of mourners, walking behind his father's coffin to the royal burial plot, flanked by his uncles and brothers and trailed by the late king's favorite white stallion, Amr, bearing an empty saddle. At the graveside, next to markers for the first two kings of Jordan, Hussein's body was removed from the casket and lowered into the ground, covered only by a simple white shroud.

Then all that remained was the formality of the swearing-in ceremony before the combined houses of Parliament. After administering the constitutional oath, the Senate president introduced the country's new sovereign.

"May God protect His Majesty King Abdullah and give him success," he said.

It was official, and yet not quite real. As the new king was leaving the ceremony, he was caught off guard when an aide called out, "Your Majesty, this way."

"Out of habit, I looked around for my father," he recalled later.

But the title now was his, and so was the country. Abdullah now owned the sagging economy, the fractious politics, the sectarian tensions, the regional disputes.

At one stroke, he had also inherited legions of enemies. Some were close to home, and covetous of his job. Others were foreign powers who saw an independent Jordan as an obstacle to their own designs for the region. Still others were religious extremists opposed to the very idea of a secular, pro-Western state called Jordan. In the early months of 1999, as the newest heir to the Hashemite throne settled tentatively into his perch, all were watching closely to see if he would fall.

To serve as ruler of a Middle Eastern country is to give up any expectation of dying of old age. It's especially true in Jordan, where the extraordinary perils of the job seem to generate a kingly appetite for dangerous hobbies.

Hussein survived at least eighteen assassination attempts in his lifetime. He was just fifteen on the summer day in 1951 when his grandfather—Jordan's first king, Abdullah I—was shot to death by a Palestinian gunman as the two royals were visiting Jerusalem's al-Aqsa Mosque. The young prince gave chase, narrowly escaping death himself when the assassin turned and fired a bullet that deflected off a medal on his uniform, according to the palace's version of events. Later, his enemies would try ambushes, plane crashes, and even poisoned nasal drops, which Hussein discovered when he accidentally spilled the dispenser and watched in horror as the frothing liquid cut through the chrome on his bathroom fixtures. The king dodged death so many times that he took on an aura of invincibility. Jordanians would often say that Hussein possessed *baraka*—Allah's favor. The prospect that one of his sons could be equally blessed seemed unlikely.

Hussein refused to be deterred by the attacks. If anything, they increased his appetite for risky pastimes: racing cars and flying helicopters and fighter jets. Once, famously, while entertaining Henry Kissinger, he had taken the former U.S. secretary of state and his wife on a gut-churning chopper tour of the country, zipping across Jordan's rolling terrain as the helicopter's skids shaved the tops off palm trees. Kissinger would later recall that his wife tried politely to ask the king to climb to a safer altitude.

"I didn't know helicopters could fly so low," she said.

"Oh! They can fly lower!" the king replied. Then he dropped below treetop level and skimmed along the ground. "That really aged me rapidly," Kissinger said.

In choosing Abdullah as his successor, Hussein picked a leader who resembled him at least in that respect. In contrast to the cerebral and cautious Prince Hassan, the king's brother, Abdullah shared his father's informal bearing and devotion to high-testosterone pursuits. As a young boy, Abdullah would squeal with delight whenever his father put him in his lap and took off for a spin through the desert in his roadster, the dust billowing behind them as the car blew down empty highways to strains of the cartoon theme song "Popeye the Sailor Man." His adrenaline addiction spurred a lifelong interest in motorcycles, race cars, airplanes, and free-fall skydiving.

Abdullah excelled at wrestling, track, and schoolboy pranks at his American prep school, and as a military cadet at Britain's prestigious Sandhurst academy, he turned down an infantry officer's commission for the speed and firepower of battle tanks. He liked driving the Fox, a nimble, tanklike armored vehicle with a thirty-millimeter cannon, and wheels instead of tracks. Once, he led a column of Foxes on an expedition along the M4 motorway west of London, squeezing every ounce of horsepower from the boxy vehicles until they were flying past the civilian traffic. After a few minutes at full throttle, he peered out of the turret to see a police cruiser racing alongside of him, lights flashing. The officer motioned the column to stop and then approached Abdullah in the lead vehicle, shaking his head.

"I have no idea how I'm going to write this up," the officer said. The cadets were eventually released with a warning.

The prince's reputation for daredevilry nearly scuttled his courtship with his future queen, Rania al-Yassin, even before it officially started. The stylishly beautiful Rania was a twenty-two-year-old marketing employee for Apple Inc. when the two met at a dinner party. Abdullah was instantly smitten, but Rania shunned his advances. Abdullah was then a thirty-year-old armored-battalion commander with perpetually sunburned skin and a bad-boy reputation, and Rania, the daughter of middle-class Palestinian parents, had no interest in being his latest conquest, Abdullah would acknowledge in his memoir years later.

"I've heard things about you," Rania had said.

"I'm no angel," Abdullah admitted. "But at least half the things you hear are just idle gossip."

The two finally agreed to date. Six months later, having mustered the courage to pop the question, he drove Rania to one of his favorite spots in Jordan: the summit of a small mountain that had been the setting for daring hill-climb car races for both Abdullah and his father. "I had hoped for a more romantic proposal," he acknowledged afterward. But this time, Rania did not push him away. They were married on June 10, 1993, just ten months after they were introduced.

Yet, in the weeks after he became King Abdullah II, all traces of the brash battalion commander and adrenaline junkie faded from view. The man who had plunged from airplanes hundreds of times moved quickly to eliminate risks, at least those that threatened his survival as monarch. He set out to repair his tattered relations with members of the royal family, offering the position of crown prince to his younger brother Hashem, son of Hussein's popular fourth wife, the American-born Queen Noor. But he fired or demoted top officials of the security services whom he suspected of having close ties to his uncle, his stepmother, or other royals. He then decreed that his own, decidedly nonroyal wife would become queen. After that, Queen Noor left Jordan for good.

Other risks beckoned from beyond the border, so the new king launched a diplomatic offensive aimed at mitigating the biggest ones. He traveled to Saudi Arabia and the other Gulf emirates to patch a nearly decade-old rift over Jordan's policy of neutrality during the first Iraq war. He invited Israel's prime minister, the notoriously pugnacious Netanyahu, to Amman for a get-acquainted luncheon. He even tried to improve ties with Syria, reaching out first to President Hafez al-Assad and then, after the autocrat's death, befriending his son, Bashar al-Assad, another Western-educated thirty-something who had been a surprise choice to succeed his father.

Then, finally, it was time to make peace with the Islamists. Or, at least, with some of them.

Jordan's kings have long sought to preserve stability in the country through an uneasy alliance with the country's religious fundamentalists, allowing them a voice in Parliament and moving cautiously with reforms to avoid causing offense in what remained a deeply conservative tribal society. King Hussein relied on the Muslim imams in the 1960s and 1970s to help him beat back threats from Marxists and Pan-Arab nationalists. Many of these same clerics were furious when Hussein made peace with Israel in 1994, yet the king managed to maintain cordial ties with the country's most prominent Islamist group, the Muslim Brotherhood, which he repeatedly praised as "the backbone of the country."

The new king would try a similar approach. A few weeks after taking office, Abdullah invited the leadership of the Muslim Brotherhood to an informal meeting at his hilltop residence. The clerics arrived at the palace, a gaggle of flapping robes and wagging beards, bearing a list of complaints about mistreatment of prominent Muslim activists. They groused about media censorship and the country's arcane election laws, which they said were tilted to prevent the group's political candidates from winning seats in Parliament. Abdullah listened politely, and then, as the meeting wound down, he offered his visitors an unexpected gift: the government would immediately free sixteen Muslim Brotherhood activists who had been jailed following a street protest. The visitors seemed charmed, telling journalists afterward that the new king was a friend to the Islamists.

"Your Majesty, we are with you, as one team, one body that trusts you," the Brotherhood's leader told Abdullah.

If only it were that simple. Despite the occasional rhetorical barb hurled at the monarchy, the Muslim Brotherhood was effectively part of the Jordanian establishment. Other Islamists would not be swayed by the release of a handful of detainees, or by vague promises to broaden electoral choices. The Muslims wanted a say in running the country, even if they were divided about where they would take it.

Abdullah was willing to yield, to a point. The young king had already spoken in interviews about his intention to see Jordan become a true constitutional monarchy, headed nominally by a king but governed by a prime minister chosen by the people's representatives in Parliament. But Abdullah's advisers insisted that reforms should come slowly. In a country with few democratic traditions, attempting too much change too quickly could backfire, they argued. The Islamists already commanded large numbers of supporters, and they were organized, motivated, and well funded. They could easily win a popular vote, putting the country's future in the hands of a movement whose leaders included men with a radically different vision for Jordan from that professed by the Muslim brothers.

The turbaned men seated around Abdullah's table could be reasoned with. But there were others in Jordan and the region who held no regard for reason, in the Western sense. They could only be fought.

Jordan already bore deep scars from previous struggles with Islamic extremists, dating back to its earliest days as a monarchy. Some saw the very existence of the state as anathema, an attempt by colonial powers to keep Muslims divided and weak. As they saw it, Jordan's royal family, the Hashemites—rulers of the holy city of Mecca for nine hundred years—had played a role in the betrayal.

It is true that no country called Jordan existed—and, likewise, no group of people called Jordanians—until the early twentieth century. For a thousand years, the arid lands east of the Jordan River were part of Islamic empires, or caliphates, that at times extended from North Africa to the Balkans and encompassed all of the Arabian Peninsula and the Levant. The first caliphs, who were viewed as successors to the Prophet Muhammad, ruled from Damascus and Baghdad. They were supplanted in time by the Ottoman Turks, who expanded the Islamic Empire and established an Ottoman Caliphate under the supervision of powerful sultans in Istanbul. The Turkish conquerors permitted limited self-rule in Mecca, allowing the Hashemites to retain control of the city's holy sites in a tradition dating back to the tenth century. Then, early in the twentieth century, came a Hashemite whose ambition and audacity would alter the family's destiny and redraw the boundaries of the Middle East.

Sharif Hussein bin Ali, the seventy-eighth emir of Mecca and the great-grandfather of Jordan's King Hussein, came to power as the Ottomans were lurching toward collapse. After the Turks sided with Germany at the outset of World War I, Sharif Hussein began secret negotiations with Britain with the aim of instigating a rebellion seeking Arab independence. In 1916, he agreed to help Britain and the Allied powers drive against the Turks in exchange for a promise of future British recognition of the new Arab-Islamic nation. Four of the sharif's sons—Ali, Faisal, Abdullah, and Zeid—would lead Arab armies in what became known as the Great Arab Revolt, at times fighting at the side of the British Army officer T. E. Lawrence, later immortalized by historians and filmmakers as Lawrence of Arabia.

The Arabs were victorious, but Britain's promises to Sharif Hussein expired even before the conflict ended. Britain and France preemptively divvied up the captured Ottoman lands into British and French protectorates under the secret Sykes-Picot Agreement of 1916. After the war, the maps were redrawn to create entirely new states, including the kingdoms of Iraq and Syria and, on the narrow strip of land between the Jordan River and the Mediterranean Sea, a Jewish homeland that would later become Israel.

On the eastern side of the river, home to Bedouin tribes and vast deserts, the British carved out an enclave for Sharif Hussein's third son, Abdullah I. The British had taken a small step toward honoring their promises to the ruler of Mecca, but their creation—initially called the Emirate of Transjordan, and later the Hashemite Kingdom of Jordan—seemed a few ingredients shy of a real country. No historical precedent existed for such a country, nor was there anything resembling a national identity among the scattering of tribes who lived in the region. The new state lacked significant reserves of oil or gas, or minerals for mining, or water for agriculture. Even its emir, Abdullah, had been imported from abroad. Many political observers at the time assumed that Transjordan would quickly collapse as an autonomous state, to be absorbed by one of its larger neighbors.

The first serious threat came from the Ikhwan hordes who invaded the country in the 1920s and were finally dispatched by Saudi intervention. Then, in the late 1960s, it was Palestinian guerrillas who threatened Jordan's sovereignty. A patchwork of militant groups, drawn from the four hundred thousand Palestinian immigrants and refugees massed in Jordan after three decades of wars, staged attacks on Jordanian troops and tried repeatedly to assassinate King Hussein. The monarch launched an offensive that became known as Black September, killing thousands of Palestinian militants and driving many more into Syria or Lebanon. Heavy clashes spilled into the largely Palestinian town of Zarqa, where the man who would become known as Abu Musab al-Zarqawi was then a boy of four years.

In the 1980s, it was regional unrest that threatened to spill across Jordan's relatively peaceful borders. Thousands of Palestinian youths clashed with Israeli troops in the first intifada, or uprising, while young Jordanian men volunteered by the hundreds to fight the Soviets in Afghanistan. Some returned to their villages and refugee camps with military skills and new ideas. A few, like Zarqawi, formed into groups and began looking for ways to continue the struggle against perceived enemies of Islam.

And yet radicals such as these were few in number, and notoriously disorganized. Like other Arab rulers, Jordan's monarchs sought to contain the threat by fostering powerful and ruthless intelligence networks to keep the extremists in check. At the same time, they would co-opt relatively moderate Islamists by granting them positions of privilege and offering limited political freedoms. Abdullah, like his father, supported the Muslim Brotherhood's role as a moderate opposition force in Jordan. And, like his forebears, he would look for ways to bolster the informal alliance, by granting occasional favors and concessions that would benefit the group's leadership politically and ensure loyalty to the crown.

Just such an opportunity arose in March 1999, as the country marked the end of the official forty-day mourning period for King Hussein's death. In a tradition dating back to Jordan's founding, new kings are expected to declare a general amnesty in the country's prisons, granting royal pardons to inmates convicted of nonviolent offenses or political crimes. It was a way to clean the slate and score points with important constituencies, from the Islamists to powerful East Bank tribes. To ensure the maximum political return, members of Parliament were given the task of nominating release-worthy prisoners and drafting the amnesty's legal particulars. Their list quickly grew to five hundred names, then a thousand, then two thousand. And still lawmakers pushed for more.

A debate over the names spilled into the open. Whereas the new law excluded anyone convicted of a violent crime or terrorism, some lawmakers wanted to free dozens of detainees convicted of draft dodging or of conspiring in attacks against Israelis. Others pushed for pardons for the so-called Arab Afghans, veterans of holy war against the Soviets in Afghanistan who had formed Islamist cells after returning home.

"Jordan is on the threshold of a new phase of its history, which means that the government should turn a new page, especially with political detainees," Saleh Armouti, president of Jordan's Bar Association, told the *Jordan Times* as negotiations dragged on. But some of the country's law-enforcement chiefs saw a disaster in the making.

"Most of them will be repeat offenders and we will see their faces again and again," a police official complained to the same newspaper. "Most of them are thugs who will harm people when they are free."

In the end, the list, now with more than twenty-five hundred names, was endorsed by Parliament and sent to the palace for the final approval. The king, then just six weeks into his new job and still picking his way through a three-dimensional minefield of legislative, tribal, and royal politics, faced a choice of either adopting the list or sending it back for weeks of additional debate.

He signed it.

Many months would pass before Abdullah learned that list had included certain Arab Afghans from the al-Jafr Prison whose Ikhwan-like zeal for purifying the Islamic faith should have disqualified them instantly. But by that time, the obscure jihadist named Ahmad Fadil al-Khalayleh had become the terrorist Abu Musab al-Zarqawi. And there was nothing a king of Jordan could do but berate his aides in an exasperated but utterly futile pique.

"Why," he demanded, "didn't someone check?"

On the evening of March 29, 1999, a caravan of prison vehicles arrived at al-Jafr to haul away the first of the Islamist prisoners granted freedom under the royal amnesty. Under the law, the state is obliged to deliver inmates to the town where they were first arrested, so Zarqawi and his mentor, Abu Muhammad al-Maqdisi, took seats on the van bound for Amman. They carried their few belongings, and freshly stamped release papers that reinstated their rights as free citizens, able to work, visit, associate, and travel just as any other Jordanian citizen. The Amman van's driver waited until dark, then eased the vehicle through the main gate, past the guards and machine-gun nests, past the drooping, parched palm trees planted along the driveway, and finally onto the rough asphalt of the highway leading to the capital. For the first time in five years, they were free men.

But not entirely free. Both men had wives and children they barely knew, families that had scraped by during their confinement, surviving on handouts from relatives. Both were subject to continued scrutiny and even harassment from the country's secret police. And both were bound to the Islamist brotherhood they had forged together in prison, though to differing degrees.

Maqdisi's detachment from the other inmates had deepened during the months in al-Jafr. As the day of his release approached, he talked about returning to his family and his writing; about expanding his audience throughout the Muslim world while taking care to avoid the kind of offense that could land him back in prison.

Zarqawi, on the other hand, was torn between two families: the one in Zarqa and the one he had gained in jail. His al-Jafr brothers were a cadre of men devoted to him personally and willing to follow him anywhere. With the amnesty, the survival of this family was suddenly in doubt.

Sabha, the prison doctor, was away on the evening when Zarqawi and the others departed for Amman. The release of so many prisoners under the amnesty meant a much lighter workload, and the prison staff was abuzz with rumors that the entire facility would soon be shut down for good. The morning after the release, Sabha arrived for his shift early and stopped by the warden's office for coffee and the latest news. Colonel Ibrahim greeted him with a strange look.

"Our friend has come back," he said.

The warden led the doctor through the courtyard toward the Islamists' cell, which now held only a handful of inmates who had committed violent offenses and were ineligible for the pardon. As they approached, Sabha could see a bearded man standing at the doorway, talking to the prisoners through the bars. It was Zarqawi.

"He has been here since five-thirty this morning," the warden said.

Zarqawi had traveled all the way to Amman, visited his mother in Zarqa for a few hours, then turned around and driven through the night in a friend's car to arrive at al-Jafr before daybreak. Now here he was, back inside the hated prison, ministering to other inmates like a field commander checking the morale of his troops.

Sabha watched for a moment in disbelief.

"Here," he said afterward, "was a real leader.

"I knew at that moment that I would be hearing about him," he said. "This man was going to end up either famous, or dead."

3

"A problem like that always comes back"

Six months after regaining his freedom, Abu Musab al-Zarqawi strode into the departures lounge of Amman's Queen Alia International Airport with a plan to escape Jordan for good. He carried a freshly minted Jordanian passport, No. Z393834, along with a Pakistani visa stamp and a serviceable cover story: Zarqawi, the war veteran and ex-convict, was going into business as an international honey merchant.

He had thought to bring along his mother, the fifty-year-old Dallah al-Khalayleh, a useful prop for someone trying to pass as a simple businessman looking for partners for his apiarist venture. Notably absent were his wife and his three children. Zarqawi's true destination was no place for a young family; besides, he already had plans for picking up a second wife once he had settled.

But he hadn't anticipated the reception the Mukhabarat had prepared for him.

As he approached the gate, several large men in dark suits grabbed Zarqawi by the shoulder and quickly hustled him into a side room, leaving his exasperated mother spluttering in the corridor. Minutes later, he was sitting in the spy agency's headquarters, visibly struggling to contain his rage.

"I didn't do anything!" he protested. "Why did you stop me?"

The man who sat opposite Zarqawi had by now interrogated the jihadist so many times he could practically deliver his lines for him. Abu Haytham, the intelligence-service captain then in his fifteenth year in the Mukhabarat's counterterrorism division, had followed Zarqawi's preparations for weeks and arranged for the predeparture "chat." He had never been impressed with Zarqawi, regarding him as another Islamist hothead, louder and more aggressive than most, but lacking in the kinds of intellectual or organizational talents that might make him exceptionally dangerous. But now Zarqawi was leaving Jordan through an obviously concocted scheme. What exactly was he up to?

Zarqawi had been right about one thing: he had committed no criminal offense, at least nothing of a magnitude that would warrant a dramatic scene in front of his mother and the scores of airport passengers. But the Mukhabarat wasn't about to let him slink away easily. His prison stint had only hardened his views and expanded his network of possible co-conspirators. And now he had a plane ticket to Peshawar, Pakistan, gateway to the Hindu Kush Mountains and, just beyond them, Afghanistan. Osama bin Laden was in Afghanistan. The Saudi terrorist had blown up two U.S. embassies in Africa in 1998 and declared war on the United States.

The captain had yet to divine Zarqawi's true plans, but he was certain they had nothing to do with raising honeybees in Pakistan's northwestern mountains. If Zarqawi were to link up with terrorists, it could come back to haunt Jordan.

"You can't just push him off on others," Abu Haytham would explain to colleagues. "Sooner or later, a problem like that always comes back."

Legally, Abu Haytham could detain Zarqawi for three days while the Mukhabarat's agents searched his belongings and quizzed his relatives and associates. In reality, the spy service could hold him as long as it wanted to. Zarqawi, still straining to keep his anger in check as he waited in the spy agency's interrogation cell, knew this as well as anyone. But Abu Haytham reminded him anyway.

"As the security service," he said, "it is our duty to know what you're doing."

—

Zarqawi had not always been so pliant. Abu Haytham's first encounter with the man then known as Ahmad Fadil al-Khalayleh was an adrenaline-infused struggle, and very nearly proved fatal.

On March 29, 1994, Abu Haytham was part of a team of fourteen heavily armed officers who raided an apartment where Zarqawi was staying. At the time, the intelligence service was rolling up a cell of Afghan war veterans connected to what appeared to be a serious terrorist plot. Members of the cell—all with ties to a radical preacher, Abu Muhammad al-Maqdisi—had acquired land mines and antitank rockets and were preparing to attack Israeli soldiers at one of the border crossings with Jordan. A known leader of the cell was Zarqawi, then a twenty-seven-year-old Afghan war veteran who worked as a video-store clerk and spent his free time meeting secretly with small groups of Islamic radicals. As other cell members disappeared into the Mukhabarat's prison, Zarqawi had moved from his house to the apartment to make arrangements to flee Jordan. He was finalizing his escape plan just as Abu Haytham and the other officers gathered in an alley behind the building to prepare for the assault.

The agents had watched the apartment throughout the day to see when Zarqawi would come home, and then waited for hours after the lights went out. At 1:00 a.m., using a key secured from the landlord, they quietly slid back the deadbolt and began creeping up the stairs. They found Zarqawi alone in a back room, dead-asleep.

The men had reached the foot of the bed when Zarqawi jerked awake. He swore at the strangers and thrust a hand behind his pillow, as if to grab something.

"Gun!" one of the officers shouted.

A wall of men fell on top of Zarqawi and struggled to pin him, while another in the raiding party snatched the weapon. It was then that one of the team's members noticed an odd stirring behind a drapery. He lunged instinctively and tackled a second man, an Egyptian who, fortunately for the officers, had not been armed.

"We didn't know there was another person in the house," Abu Haytham explained afterward. "We found him only because the curtain was moving and there was no window behind it."

The agents tossed the pistol—an M15 automatic, with three loaded clips—into their van along with the cursing suspects. Zarqawi—still "ready to kill," as one of them later described him—sat glowering at the agents from the backseat, with his tangle of matted hair and torn nightshirt, tattoos poking out below the sleeve.

"He was angry, just screaming curses: 'You are *kafirs*. You are infidels," the officer recalled.

Then it was back to the Mukhabarat's fortresslike headquarters for the interrogation. Among those looking in on the suspects was Samih Battikhi, the agency's worldly, silver-maned deputy chief. He watched as his men, working in a small, glaringly lit cell, tried in turns to wear the suspect down. Zarqawi was having none of it, he recalled.

"He just spouted ideology. His head was full of it," Battikhi said.

Battikhi, who would soon be named director of the spy agency, had been watching with growing unease the stream of Jordanian nationals returning home after fighting under the mujahideen army's Islamist banner in Afghanistan. At first, he recalled, the Jordanians who volunteered for duty in Afghanistan "were the good guys, fighting the communists," in ideological lockstep with the country's most important allies, including the Americans, the British, and the Saudis. Now they were returning home as combat veterans with radically different views, and even different ways of speaking and dressing. Zarqawi looked and sounded like the others, but with an aggressiveness that reminded Battikhi of a caged animal. It was widely known that Zarqawi had been a vicious brawler and petty criminal as a youth. Battikhi now wondered if the two parts of his personality had fused together—the gangster and the religious fanatic.

"He didn't fit the profile," Battikhi said. "Here's a guy who had been a thug and a drunk. His family had gotten worried and tried to steer him toward religious groups to straighten him out. But then it was like he went too straight. So now you've got the worst of both worlds."

In fact, the Mukhabarat knew a lot about Zarqawi, even in those early days before prison. Between his thick police file and the spy agency's legions of informants, the officers were quickly able to fill in the remaining blanks.

Ahmad Fadil al-Khalayleh, as the records showed, had been troubled since childhood, taking the hard path from vandalism to drugs and alcohol to more serious crimes. He was born October 30, 1966, to parents of working-class Jordanian stock: a civil-servant father who worked for Zarqa's municipal government, and a devoutly religious mother who doted on the young boy above his seven sisters and two brothers. The family lived in a modest two-story house perched on a hill above a large cemetery where Zarqa's working class buries its dead. The graveyard is a shambles, a few thousand crumbling, hand-lettered tombstones strewn across a sloping lot overrun with weeds and feral cats; it is also the closest thing in the neighborhood to a public park. The boy who would become Abu Musab al-Zarqawi spent countless hours playing in the cemetery as a child; later, when he was a teen, the graves became the backdrop for his first forays into delinquency and crime.

The Khalaylehs came from a large and respectable East Bank tribe, the Bani Hassans, a biographical fact that normally carried certain advantages for a young man looking to make connections and find work in a patriarchal society like Jordan. But Zarqawi had blown one opportunity after another. He dropped out of high school, despite above-average grades and test scores showing an aptitude for art. He skated through two years of compulsory military service, but then got himself fired from a city job his father had arranged for him. His criminal career began at age twelve—he had cut a neighborhood boy in a street fight—and progressed to pimping, drug dealing, and assault. By his late teens, he had acquired tattoos and a reputation as a heavy drinker and street tough who took pleasure in brutalizing his victims and opponents with fist or blade. His idea of a sexual conquest—according to security officials and to acquaintances who knew him at the time—was to force himself on younger men as a way to humiliate and assert his own dominance.

He was twenty-one when he married his cousin, Intisar, who quickly bore him a daughter. But Zarqawi's great love remained his mother. Dallah al-Khalayleh fretted over her troubled youngest son, but she never stopped believing in his basic goodness, or gave up her certitude that he would make something of himself. She also understood her son's intellectual limitations. Years later, when journalists would show up at her house to ask about Zarqawi's reported accomplishments as a terrorist commander and bomb maker, she would seem genuinely amused.

"He wasn't that smart," she told an American reporter. She allowed that her boy was "committed to Islam," but explained his decision to join a jihadist movement as the only option available to a young man who couldn't find a real job at home.

"My son is a good man, an ordinary man, a victim of injustice," she said.

It was his mother who nudged Zarqawi into joining the Islamists. She signed him up for religion classes at the local al-Husayn Ben Ali Mosque, hoping he would find better role models among the imams and pious youth, with their theological debates and fundraising drives to benefit Muslim holy warriors in Afghanistan. To everyone's surprise, Zarqawi plunged into Islam with all the passion he had once reserved for his criminal pursuits. He swore off drinking and became a regular at Koran discussions and Friday prayers. He devoured propaganda videos and audiocassettes on the sectarian wars being fought in Afghanistan, Bosnia, and Chechnya. And when the prayer leader at the local mosque asked for volunteers to fight against the communist oppressors of Afghanistan's Muslims, Zarqawi's hand shot up.

He arrived at the Afghanistan-Pakistan frontier in the spring of 1989, weeks after the last Soviet troops withdrew, but just in time to join the Islamist assault on the pro-Moscow Afghan government that was left to fend for itself after the Russians pulled out. One of the Afghan veterans who greeted him at the airport would later remember a wiry young man who seemed eager but also oddly self-conscious. He said little, explaining at one point that he was embarrassed to speak, fearing he would betray his inadequate schooling and thin grasp of the Koran. Although it was already hot, he insisted on wearing long sleeves to cover up his tattoos.

"We all knew who he was: he had been this notorious tough guy in Zarqa," said Hudhaifa Azzam, a fellow Afghan-fighter and son of the influential Palestinian cleric Abdullah Azzam, regarded by many as the father of the global jihad movement. "Now he had found religion, and he was very much ashamed of his tattoos. You could see him covering up his hands self-consciously."

Zarqawi's first assignment was to write articles for a jihadist magazine describing mujahideen exploits on the battlefield, a job that proved taxing for a young man of limited schooling. Among his first friends was Saleh al-Hami, a fellow journalist who had lost his leg to a land mine. Zarqawi spent long hours at the man's bedside as he recovered, becoming so impressed with his devotion that he arranged to have one of his own sisters flown to Pakistan to marry the man. His new brother-in-law would later move to Jordan to become Zarqawi's admiring biographer. Al-Hami remembered the young Zarqawi as highly emotional, and quick to cry whenever he read the Koran. Most of the Arab fighters tried to avoid such open displays, but not the Jordanian.

"Zarqawi was crying whenever he said prayers aloud, even when leading the prayers," al-Hami wrote.

During breaks in training, Zarqawi wandered around the Pakistani city of Peshawar, sometimes visiting a local mosque that had become a favorite for Arab fighters. Years later, the mosque's imam still vividly remembered the earnest young Jordanian who seemed preoccupied with past sins. One day, after the cleric mentioned his plans to travel to Mecca, Islam's holiest city, Zarqawi approached him with a request.

"If you are to go on pilgrimage," the youth said, "on your way there, pray to God that he may forgive Abu Musab."

Zarqawi's first taste of actual combat came in 1991, when mujahideen rebels launched an offensive against government-held towns in Afghanistan's eastern provinces of Paktia and Khost. Zarqawi fought with enthusiasm, and quickly gained a reputation for bravery bordering on foolhardiness, comrades remembered. Once, according to Azzam, he single-handedly held off a column of a dozen or more Afghan government troops during fighting in the eastern city of Gardez, allowing time for others in his unit to escape.

"He was so brave, I used to say he had a dead heart," Azzam said. As Azzam recalled it, Zarqawi's heroics appeared to go beyond mere risk taking. He seemed at times to be trying to purge himself of something.

"I was struck by the way his past seemed to affect him, as he always struggled with a sense of guilt," Azzam said. "I think that is why he was so brave. He would say, 'Because of the things I did in my past, nothing could bring Allah to forgive me unless I become a *shahid*'—a martyr."

Zarqawi would never be a martyr, but in the mountains of eastern Afghanistan he earned his credentials as a mujahid—a holy warrior. By the time he left Afghanistan in 1993, he was a combat veteran with a few years of battlefield experience. He had been steeped in the doctrine of militant Islam, learning at the feet of radical Afghan and Arab clerics who would later ally themselves with the Taliban or with Osama bin Laden. He had gained formal military training at a camp operated by Abdul Rasul Sayyaf, the Afghan rebel commander who would also mentor Khalid Sheikh Mohammed, the mastermind of the September 11, 2001, attacks on New York and Washington.

Like the other Afghan fighters, he had also drunk from the heady cocktail of battlefield camaraderie and the rebels' own improbable success. A ragtag army of Afghans and Islamist volunteers had humbled the Soviet superpower. How could such a thing be explained, except as an act of divine intervention?

"God granted the Muslim mujahidin in Afghanistan victory against the infidels," declared Sayf al-Adel, a deputy to Osama bin Laden, in a written account of the war. It was an opinion widely held among the veterans, and Zarqawi was utterly convinced of its truth.

In 1993, Abu Musab al-Zarqawi and hundreds of other Jordanian veterans returned home to a country they barely recognized. But it wasn't only Jordan that had changed. In four years, while Amman and the other big towns had grown larger and more modern, Zarqawi and his comrades had traveled backward in time by journeying to Taliban-controlled Afghanistan, a place that by almost every measure lagged centuries behind the rest of the world.

Now back in his hometown, Zarqawi had become his self-chosen nickname—"the Stranger." Even a trip to the local market was a reminder of the gulf between moderate, easygoing Jordan and the strict Islamic discipline Zarqawi had witnessed in Afghanistan. He complained to friends about immodestly dressed Jordanian women and the mixing of unmarried couples at cafés and cinemas. He griped about the liquor stores and pornography vendors, which, years earlier, he himself had patronized. Even his own family disappointed him: his mother and sisters refused to wear the burka-style veil commonly worn by Afghan women, and his brothers allowed their families to watch un-Islamic movies and comedies on their TVs. The news shows that Zarqawi occasionally watched were even more upsetting, bringing reports of progress by both the Palestinians and the Jordanian monarchy in negotiating treaties with Israel. The very idea of peace with the Jewish state was anathema to many Islamists. Some formerly steadfast supporters of King Hussein never forgave the monarch for this act.

Zarqawi would take a stab at a normal life, spending his days renting out Hollywood movies and Islamist propaganda tapes at the video store. But, inevitably, he was drawn toward the one thing that had given him a purpose. He read books about early Islamic heroes, and became particularly fascinated with Nur ad-Din Zengi, a warrior-prince who ruled from Damascus in the twelfth century. Nur ad-Din had famously destroyed a European Crusader army and sought to unify a patchwork of Muslim kingdoms under a single sultanate extending from southern Turkey to the Nile River. After his soldiers killed the French-born prince of Antioch, Nur ad-Din arranged for the sovereign's head to be placed in a silver box and sent to the caliph in Baghdad as a gift.

Years later, Zarqawi came to view himself as a modern incarnation of Nur ad-Din and would seek to emulate his military strategy. But for now, Zarqawi was prepared to start small. He tracked down an old acquaintance from Afghanistan, the preacher and scholar named Abu Muhammad al-Maqdisi, showing up at his house in Amman to say he wanted to "work on behalf of religion in Jordan," as Maqdisi later recalled. The two began a years-long partnership that began with Koranic study groups for other Afghan veterans and progressed to the organizing of small cells for more ambitious endeavors.

"We printed out some of my books and disseminated them among the people," Maqdisi would write later about his early days with Zarqawi. "Young men rallied around our call and circulated our books and messages."

Similar groups, also led by disaffected ex-mujahideen fighters, were forming simultaneously across Jordan, and some had carried out minor attacks against liquor stores and other symbols of Western vice. Soon Zarqawi, too, was pushing to do something more dramatic than photocopying religious tracts. He suggested ways to disrupt upcoming parliamentary elections in Jordan, talking excitedly about possible targets until others in the group became nervous.

"He wanted everything to be done quickly," remembered Muhammad Abu al-Muntasir, a Jordanian Islamist who attended some of the meetings in 1993. "He wanted to achieve all of his ambitions in a matter of months, if not hours." Because of hastiness, Zarqawi made decisions "unilaterally at the wrong time and place," he said.

"More tragically," al-Muntasir added, "the majority of brothers used to agree with him."

By early 1994, the group had a name: Bay'at al-Imam, or literally, the Oath of Allegiance to the Prayer Leader. They also had a small stock of weapons from an unlikely source. Maqdisi, who had lived in Kuwait at the time of the 1990 invasion by Saddam Hussein's army, had acquired a few mines, grenades, and artillery rockets left behind after the Iraqis' retreat in 1991, and hid them in his household furniture when he moved to Jordan after the war. The spark that finally propelled the group into action came on February 25, 1994, when a Jewish extremist opened fire on praying Muslims in a religious shrine in the West Bank town of Hebron, killing twenty-nine men and boys and wounding scores of others. Incensed by the murders, the group decided, with Maqdisi's reluctant support, to use their weapons in a coordinated attack on an Israeli outpost along the border. The plan called for striking the guard station with back-to-back suicide bombs followed by small-arms fire.

The plotters never had a chance. The Mukhabarat, with its vast network of informants, inevitably learned of the plan and moved quickly to squash it. Abu Haytham's team launched their raids, ending with the dramatic arrest of Zarqawi in his bed on March 29. He and twelve other members of the cell eventually signed confessions admitting to possessing illegal weapons and plotting an act of terrorism.

Maqdisi tried to turn the group's trial into a showcase for his radical views, at one point shouting at the military judge, "You are guilty!" The defendants yelled and banged the bars of the prisoners' box as they were being sentenced, while Maqdisi called out a warning:

"Your penalties only strengthen our faith in our religion!"

Perhaps it was so. But with Maqdisi and Zarqawi both drawing prison terms of fifteen years, the greater likelihood was that the men and their movement had been silenced for good. And if Jordan's prisons couldn't control them, the Mukhabarat had a variety of alternate methods that could deliver the same result, as Abu Haytham was fond of reminding Western visitors.

"The agency is not averse to using pressure," he would say, "if it's the only way to stop a bad thing from happening."

The truth was, the leaders of the Mukhabarat weren't entirely sure what to do with Zarqawi when he emerged unexpectedly from prison in the spring of 1999. The spy agency was still pondering the question six months later, right up to the morning he turned up at the airport with his mother and a pair of coach-class tickets for Pakistan.

As Zarqawi stewed in a holding cell during his three days of confinement, the Mukhabarat's men made a careful inventory of his belongings, looking for clues about his destination and how long he intended to stay. They found a handwritten letter in one of the bags, and pored over every line for possible coded messages, eventually concluding that it was a harmless greeting from one of Zarqawi's friends to a mutual acquaintance in Pakistan.

Abu Haytham tried quizzing Zarqawi directly, asking the same questions different ways. The detainee freely admitted that he hoped eventually to settle in Pakistan, once his honey business was doing well enough to support his family.

"I can't live here in this country," he told the captain. "I want to start a new life."

Zarqawi's discomfort was hardly surprising. For one thing, he missed prison. Harsh though it was, al-Jafr had given Zarqawi an identity and a community. Life on the outside just left him feeling anxious and disoriented, he told family members.

But it was the Mukhabarat that accounted for most of his stress. Deeply unhappy with the Islamists' early release, the service's counterterrorism chiefs endeavored to keep Zarqawi and his brethren in a state of perpetual agitation.

Abu Haytham and his colleagues were masters of the art. Indeed, getting into the heads of suspected terrorists and troublemakers was one of the many things Jordan's intelligence agency did exceptionally well. The service had always been relatively small, and it traditionally depended on the United States and other allies for surveillance technology and operating cash. But few in the world could rival its capabilities in developing informants, running spy operations, or penetrating hostile networks. In earlier times, its interrogation methods included physical cruelties so extreme that some Jordanians referred to the Mukhabarat's imposing prison as "the fingernail factory." But in later years, the service's directors adopted subtler techniques that achieved the same result.

To keep Zarqawi off balance, the Mukhabarat employed a strategy of regular harassing visits its men called "annoyances." A pair of officers would turn up at the Khalayleh house at odd hours, even late at night, and ask Zarqawi to take a ride with them. Invariably, they would end up at headquarters for "chats" that often went on for hours. A key part of the ritual would be a recitation of things the agency's informants had overheard Zarqawi say or do, just to remind their guest of how closely he was being watched.

Though Zarqawi clearly resented the visits, he had no choice but to submit. During one routine "annoyance" in late summer, the sight of the spy agency's black car sent him into a rage, as one of the officers later recalled.

"Oh, look who's here again—it's the Mukhabarat," Zarqawi boomed, with sarcasm that could be heard down the block. His mother, her plump face crimson against her dark head scarf, met the visitors at the door with a string of epithets, denouncing the intelligence service, the government, and even her troublemaker son. "I curse the day he was born!" she said.

At headquarters, officers took turns with Zarqawi in a kind of tag team of interrogators and techniques. Abu Haytham sometimes alternated with his boss, Ali Bourzak, the head of the counterterrorism section and one of the most feared men in the Mukhabarat. Bourzak's harsh manner and thin fringe of red hair earned him the nickname Red Devil among the spy agency's frequent visitors. Zarqawi loathed him. Years later, long after leaving Jordan for good, he twice sent operatives to Amman with explicit instructions to assassinate the Red Devil. Both attempts failed.

A third officer who took a particular interest in the case was a young counterterrorism specialist nearly the same age as Zarqawi. Abu Mutaz was part of a new generation of Mukhabarat officers: college-educated and traveled, with special training in intelligence analysis at institutions in Britain and the United States. But he was also a son of one of Jordan's desert tribes, steeped in the same culture as many of the jihadists and criminals he worked with. His close-cropped hair, jagged teeth, and leather coats gave him a streetwise look, but his warm brown eyes and easy laugh made him instantly likable, even among the Islamists.

When Zarqawi arrived, Abu Mutaz would grab a notebook and pack of Parliament cigarettes and make his way to the sparsely furnished office where informal interrogations took place. Zarqawi would sit opposite him across a small table, without handcuffs or restraints, maintaining his usual look of icy indifference. Abu Mutaz thought he seemed a bit shabby, with his loose Afghan clothes and patchy beard that he never groomed. His fingernails were unfailingly untrimmed and dirty, giving him the look of a rough field hand.

Abu Mutaz would offer sugary herbal tea and sweets, which were usually accepted, but not coffee or cigarettes. Zarqawi disliked coffee and, as a strict Islamist, he viewed smoking as a Western vice. Abu Mutaz would light up anyway.

"So, Ahmad," Abu Mutaz would begin, using Zarqawi's given name, "talk to me about your plans."

Abu Mutaz became adept at pushing Zarqawi's emotional buttons as a way of drawing him out. He found that he usually could provoke a reaction by bringing up religion or family, particularly Zarqawi's tribal roots. Tribal identity is a matter of profound importance among Jordan's East Bank communities, and Zarqawi's Bani Hassan lineage tied him to one of the biggest and most important tribes in the region, dating back to the time of Muhammad and beyond. A person's tribal affiliation defined his standing in society and incorporated elements of patriotism, filial duty, and family pride. Abu Mutaz would drop into the conversation that he had spoken to tribal elders about Zarqawi, and they were concerned about him. The defiance would briefly disappear from Zarqawi's expression, but he said nothing.

"The thing that you were doing," Abu Mutaz would say, "is something that could destroy your tribe. It could destroy the country."

When the subject turned to religion, Zarqawi became animated. He seemed to enjoy showing off his knowledge of the Koran and the Hadith, the collection of apocryphal sayings of Muhammad and his companions, extensively mined by jihadists to justify their beliefs. Abu Mutaz, accustomed to parrying with Islamists, quizzed him on his views about violence. Didn't Islam prohibit the taking of innocent life?

Apostates are not innocent, Zarqawi would argue. "It is not just *halal*"—permitted—Zarqawi said flatly. "We are commanded to kill the *kafir*."

Eventually, Zarqawi would weary of the conversation and shut down. "You didn't like me when I was a delinquent," he mumbled to Abu Mutaz one day. "Now I'm religious and you still don't like me."

As disturbing as his words were, Zarqawi was only mouthing standard jihadist rhetoric. Senior Mukhabarat officials regarded his partner, Maqdisi, as a truly dangerous thinker and proselytizer, and they would find reasons to keep him behind bars for most of the next fifteen years. Zarqawi clearly wasn't in Maqdisi's league, but what, exactly, was he? The agency's experts were perplexed.

Though Zarqawi talked like a religious radical, the agency's intensive surveillance showed that his behavior was filled with contradictions and carried echoes of his prereligious past. He would disappear for hours to the home of a Zarqa woman who was not his wife, and then he would head directly to an Islamist gathering or to the local mosque for evening prayers. Abu Mutaz observed that Zarqawi would habitually lie about the most insignificant things, and he would stick to the false story even after being confronted with contrary evidence. His behavior was so baffling that Mukhabarat officials hired private psychiatrists to review his files and make an assessment. Though inconclusive, their review suggested that Zarqawi could suffer from a kind of multiple-personality disorder, one in which the subject's deep insecurities and shattering guilt battled with an outsized ego convinced of its own greatness.

"He had a hero complex and a guilt complex," Abu Mutaz said. "He wanted to be a hero and saw himself as a hero, even when he was a thug. But it was the guilt that made him so extreme."

Some of his Islamist friends also noticed his increasingly strange demeanor. One recalled that Zarqawi would sometimes sit for hours in a favorite falafel shop in Zarqa in his Afghan garb without speaking to anyone. "He struck me as being like a Sufi, or a mystic," the friend said. "He would sit there, looking calm, pious. Slightly sad." At other times, he seemed nearly manic, prattling on about his ambitions to revive his old Islamist cell, either in Jordan or abroad.

"He visited me at home and asked me to open a new chapter with him, work together, and perhaps travel to Afghanistan," recalled al-Muntasir, the Amman Islamist who had been arrested and imprisoned with Zarqawi in 1994. "I welcomed him as a guest, but I refused to work with him again in any way in view of his narcissism, not to mention other traits."

But such talk did not constitute a crime. Abu Haytham acknowledged as much to Zarqawi on the last of his three days in Mukhabarat custody after the scene at the airport. The captain was questioning Zarqawi, for what would turn out to be the last time, when his subject began to complain bitterly about his limbolike existence at the agency's headquarters.

"Take me to court if you have something on me!" Zarqawi pleaded.

"If I had something on you, I would take you to court!" Abu Haytham acknowledged.

It was a rare moment of mutual candor. The captain explained again the necessity of keeping men such as Zarqawi on a tight leash. "It's nothing personal," he said.

"You have to understand how we look at you," he said. "You're an extremist."

"You have to understand how I look at you," Zarqawi retorted. "You are all infidels."

The next day, Zarqawi and his mother returned to the airport for a Pakistan-bound flight. There would be no interference this time, but the Mukhabarat would still be watching.

4

"The time for training is over"

On November 30, 1999, Jordanian investigators were running a wiretap on a twice-jailed Islamist militant when an ominous phrase turned up in one of the daily transcripts. The suspicious call came from a phone in Afghanistan, and the speaker appeared to be giving a kind of coded instruction.

"The time for training is over," the Afghan caller had said, speaking in Levantine-accented Arabic.

Though the words were maddeningly vague, Mukhabarat leaders decided to move quickly to head off whatever it was the Islamists were planning. It was soon clear that they had stumbled upon something huge. Within a few days, the Jordanians had arrested sixteen people, including the recipient of the call, Khadar Abu Hoshar, a Palestinian and veteran of the Afghan war with ties to several extremist groups. They seized bomb-making manuals and hundreds of pounds of chemicals hidden in a secret underground passage. They picked up key details from one of the suspects, including the intended date of the attack—New Year's Eve, 1999—and what the detainee said was the operation's slogan: "The season is coming; bodies will pile up in sacks."

A few days later, the agency's deputy director invited the CIA's Amman station chief, Robert Richer, to dinner. Sa'ad Kheir seemed unusually anxious and waited until he had consumed several drinks before blurting out the news.

"Rob, I have to tell you something, but you can't tell my boss," the Mukhabarat's number two commander said. "We just picked up some people who are planning major attacks against a number of targets in Jordan."

Kheir described how the Jordanians had stumbled on the plot and what was known so far about the intended targets. Topping the list was the Radisson Hotel, the Amman landmark that on any New Year's Eve was certain to be packed with Americans and other Westerners as well as hundreds of Jordanians. He said top Mukhabarat officials had decided against sharing details with U.S. counterparts until they were certain they had all the plotters in custody.

Richer cut him off.

"Sa'ad, I have to use this information," he told the Jordanian deputy. "I've got to see your boss and get this released."

Richer, a former marine on his second tour as the CIA's spy chief in Jordan, well knew the Mukhabarat's complex internal politics. But this time American lives were potentially at stake. The next morning he walked into the office of Samih Battikhi, now the Mukhabarat's director, to say that the CIA had learned independently of a plot to strike Jordan on the eve of the millennium. Battikhi, surprised, had little choice but to tell the Americans everything he knew.

Over the next two weeks, American counterterrorism teams would arrive to assist the Jordanians in reconstructing what became known to history as the Millennium Plot, following a trail of clues spread across at least six countries. Organized by an al-Qaeda associate in eastern Afghanistan, the Jordanian portion of the plan called for a wave of bombings and small-arms attacks targeting not only Amman's Radisson, but also an Israeli border crossing and a pair of Christian shrines popular with Western tourists. A separate plot to attack the Los Angeles International Airport was foiled when U.S. customs agents arrested the would-be bomber as he attempted to cross the U.S.-Canadian border in a car packed with explosives.

Seized documents and an expanded surveillance web identified still more alleged participants, raising the number of suspects to twenty-eight. Out of all the names on the list, one in particular evoked surprise: a Jordanian from Zarqa whose given name was listed as Ahmad Fadil al-Khalayleh.

Zarqawi was back.

When he left Jordan just two months earlier, Abu Musab al-Zarqawi had made it as far as western Pakistan and then appeared to have gotten stuck. The informant who briefly trailed him sent back word that he was attending daily prayers at an Arabic-speaking mosque in Peshawar and staying clean. Now, just weeks later, he had resurfaced with a bit part as a consultant to one of the biggest terrorist plots against Jordan in years.

Zarqawi appears to have played only a minor advisory role, but wiretaps that linked him to the plot were sufficient to earn him new criminal charges and a guilty verdict in absentia. He would also be featured in a report that landed on Robert Richer's desk at the CIA's Amman station.

"It was the first time," the American intelligence officer recalled later, "that we had heard Zarqawi's name."

In dismantling the plot, the Jordanians had saved lives while averting an economic and political disaster. The jihadists had deliberately targeted symbols of Jordan's vital tourist industry, at a moment when the country and its unexpected young monarch were still finding their footing after King Hussein's death. Nine months into his reign, Abdullah II was struggling to implement economic and political reforms in the face of heavy resistance from Jordan's old guard, including the army generals, security chiefs, and tribal leaders who had held positions of privilege under his father. A successful attack could have altered the face of Jordan, crippling its economy and weakening the new king's grip on the country.

For the Mukhabarat, there was little euphoria over the plot's disruption. The Islamists had signaled their determination to attack Jordan, and they had come close to succeeding. And even though some of the participants were now in jail, the key planners were in Afghanistan and Pakistan, where they were free to try again.

Among this group was Zarqawi, whose intentions were now clear. In September, Zarqawi had sat in the office of the Mukhabarat's Captain Abu Haytham, begging for a chance to put Jordan behind him and start a new life. Less than three months later, the spy service was bitterly ruing the decision to allow him to leave.

"Despite everything that happened," Abu Haytham would lament, "he had not forgotten about Jordan."

Indeed, Zarqawi's interest in his home country would never slacken, even as his focus shifted to bigger targets. "The way to Palestine is through Amman," Zarqawi often told friends.

The Mukhabarat would soon learn of other plots to attack Jordan. The next one to invoke Zarqawi's name would be organized and planned by him alone.

Zarqawi's sojourn in Pakistan had not gone as he planned.

He arrived in Peshawar in September with the intention of traveling onward to the northern Caucasus, where a new war pitting Chechen separatists and Islamists against the Russian Federation was just getting under way. If he could link up with Chechnya's volunteer Islamic International Brigade, Zarqawi would at last have a chance to fight Russians, something he had never managed to do during the Afghan civil war. But it was not to be. Pakistan's government, which helped bankroll the Afghan rebels in the 1980s, was far less tolerant of itinerant Arab jihadists in 1999, and Zarqawi struggled to obtain connections and travel documents. As he waited, most of the Islamist army in Chechnya was destroyed when Russian planes dropped massive fuel-air bombs into mountain passes on the Chechen-Dagestan border.

Then, six months into his trip, Pakistani officials notified him that his visa had expired and he would have to leave the country. Zarqawi was suddenly confronted with a choice of either returning to Jordan—with the near certainty of arrest and imprisonment for his role in the Millennium Plot—or heading across the mountains into Afghanistan, a destination that offered far less appeal than it did when he last visited. Not only had the country been devastated by six years of civil war, but the conflict's newest phase also lacked the moral clarity that had attracted Zarqawi and tens of thousands of Arab volunteers in the 1980s and 1990s. Now, instead of a struggle between Islamists and communists, the Afghan contest pitted a confusing array of Muslim warlords and Taliban generals against one another in ever-shifting alliances.

Still, Zarqawi chose Afghanistan. With a pair of friends, he made his way to Kandahar, eventually arriving at the headquarters of the one former Afghan Arab who might have been expected to welcome him: Osama bin Laden. But instead of getting a warm greeting from his old mujahideen comrade, Zarqawi was rudely snubbed. The al-Qaeda founder refused even to see Zarqawi, instead sending one of his aides to check out the Jordanians. Bin Laden's caution with visitors of any stripe was likely well founded: the deadly attacks on two U.S. embassies in Africa the previous year had landed Bin Laden on the FBI's most-wanted list. Bin Laden had good reason in particular to be wary of visitors who associated themselves with Muhammad al-Maqdisi, Zarqawi's former cellmate and mentor. Maqdisi had infuriated the rulers of Bin Laden's native Saudi Arabia with his essays calling for the violent overthrow of apostate Arab regimes. Bin Laden had his own problems with Saudi leaders, and publicly associating with Maqdisi would only make things worse.

Zarqawi was left to languish in a guesthouse for two weeks before Bin Laden finally dispatched a senior deputy, a former Egyptian army officer named Sayf al-Adel, to meet with him. Al-Adel, writing about the events years later, acknowledged that he also was leery of Zarqawi, a man who already had a reputation for being stubborn and combative.

"In a nutshell, Abu Musab was a hardliner when it came to his disagreements with other fraternal brothers," al-Adel would write. "Therefore, I had reservations."

After exchanging traditional greetings and hugs, al-Adel took a moment to size up the Jordanian. It was not an encouraging first impression.

"Abu Musab was a sturdy man who was not really very good at words," al-Adel recalled. "He expressed himself spontaneously and briefly. He would not compromise any of his beliefs."

Zarqawi's one big idea, it seemed, was "the re-establishment of Islam in society," and he had rigid views on what such a society should look like. But he had no handle on how to begin working toward that goal, al-Adel said. Moreover, in quizzing Zarqawi about events in his old neighborhood, the al-Qaeda deputy found the Jordanian curiously uninformed.

"He had adequate information about Jordan, but his information about Palestine was poor," al-Adel said. "We listened to him, but we did not argue, since we wanted to win him to our side."

Despite Zarqawi's many shortcomings, al-Adel gradually came to feel sympathy for his visitor, who, in his lumbering, inarticulate way, reminded al-Adel of a younger version of himself. Anyone as stubbornly opinionated as Zarqawi could never be part of al-Qaeda, and al-Adel never suggested that he should join. But the al-Qaeda deputy had an idea about a different way Zarqawi could be helpful to the organization. He raised it with Bin Laden the next morning.

By late 1999, al-Qaeda had built a powerful support network in Afghanistan, in North Africa, and across the countries of the Persian Gulf. But it lacked a comparable presence in the countries of the Levant. Al-Qaeda's great goal was the eventual destruction of Israel; yet it never managed to put its cadres in place in Jordan or the Palestinian territories to prepare the ground for such a blow, starting with the necessary step of overturning Jordan's pro-Western government. Perhaps Zarqawi, with his Jordanian roots and deep ties to Palestinian Islamists from his prison days, could help fill a critical gap.

"How could we abandon such an opportunity to be in Palestine and Jordan?" al-Adel asked. "How could we waste a chance to work with Abu Musab and similar men in other countries?"

Zarqawi's trustworthiness remained in question, so al-Adel proposed an experiment: Let the Jordanian run his own training camp, specifically catering to Islamist volunteers from Jordan and the other countries of the Levant as well as Iraq and Turkey. Al-Qaeda could provide start-up money, and then watch from a distance to see what Zarqawi could accomplish. The "distance" in this case would be a separation of some 350 miles: the camp for Levantine fighters would be "somewhat remote from us," al-Adel acknowledged, located near the Iranian border in Herat, a city on the opposite end of Afghanistan from al-Qaeda's base. Zarqawi would not be obliged to swear allegiance to Bin Laden, or to sign on to every point of al-Qaeda's ideology. But there would be plenty of cash from wealthy Gulf patrons, as well as what al-Adel described as full "coordination and cooperation to achieve our joint objectives."

Zarqawi considered the proposal for two days and decided to accept.

His first training base was initially made up only of a handful of close friends from Jordan, along with their families. But Zarqawi sent invitations to some of his old mujahideen comrades and prison contacts, and soon others were making the trek to western Afghanistan. When al-Adel stopped by weeks later to check on Zarqawi's progress, he counted eighteen men, women, and children. In another two months, the camp's population had swollen to forty-two people, including Syrians and Europeans. One of the Syrians, Abu al-Ghadiya, a trained dentist and comrade from Zarqawi's mujahideen days who spoke four languages, served as a kind of travel agent and logistics chief, in a preview of the role he would assume years later, when he ran the Zarqawi network's supply pipeline through Syria and into Iraq. For the moment, though, the most reliable route for recruits headed for Afghanistan passed through Iran. Although Zarqawi disliked Shiite Muslims and viewed Iran's leaders as heretics, he managed to link up with several helpful Iranians who ran safe houses and smuggled men and supplies to the Afghan border.

The camp's leader, meanwhile, had turned into an enthusiastic commanding officer. He had taken a second wife, Asra, the thirteen-year-old daughter of one of his Palestinian campmates, discomfiting some of his al-Qaeda sponsors, who viewed the marrying of children as unseemly. He spent his free time reading books, learning basic computer skills, and polishing his speaking ability, trading his habitual Zarqa slang for the classic Arabic of the Koran. He supervised his recruits' instruction in everything from firearms to Islamic history and religion.

"They were establishing a mini Islamic society," a proud al-Adel declared.

But it was not to last. Back in Kandahar, Bin Laden had given the final approval for the September 11, 2001, attacks that would draw the United States into war against al-Qaeda and its Taliban hosts. According to al-Adel, Zarqawi was kept in the dark about al-Qaeda's plans until after the strikes against New York and Washington were carried out. But Zarqawi's Herat base would be targeted by the Americans along with Bin Laden's in the weeks of fighting that followed.

Zarqawi's disciples and their families eventually organized a convoy of vehicles and traveled across Afghanistan to join al-Qaeda in the defense of Kandahar. The U.S.-backed Northern Alliance, supported by American commandos and air strikes, had already captured Kabul, the capital, and were preparing to march on the Taliban government's final stronghold. But soon after the Herat group's arrival in Kandahar, a U.S. bomber struck a house where senior al-Qaeda leaders were meeting, wounding several of them and burying others, including Zarqawi, under debris. The Jordanian was pulled from the rubble with serious wounds, including several broken ribs. He was still undergoing treatment when Bin Laden fled, deserting the Taliban and stealing away to his private sanctuary in the eastern mountains, the fortress known as Tora Bora.

Zarqawi collected his followers and a few al-Qaeda stragglers and made a dash in the opposite direction, toward Iran, where he sought safety in the border towns through which his recruitment network once ran. There the refugees huddled in small groups, as al-Adel recounted later, to consider their dwindling options. In eastern Afghanistan, Bin Laden's mountain redoubt had fallen under heavy U.S. bombardment. In Iran, government officials who had initially granted entry to the al-Qaeda refugees had shifted course, arresting dozens of the newcomers, including most of the Herat contingent. Where on earth could al-Qaeda's men find a haven that offered both physical safety and a chance for the organization's surviving members to rest and regroup?

In Iraq's northeastern mountains, there was one such place. Just a few miles from the Iranian border, a handful of Kurdish villages and towns had attained a precarious autonomy outside the writ of the Iraqi dictatorship. These Kurdish provinces were protected under the U.S. no-fly zone established at the end of the first Persian Gulf War in 1991, and within their boundaries a number of wildly disparate political factions had taken root. One of the Kurdish groups was a Taliban-like movement that included scores of Afghan war veterans and called itself Ansar al-Islam, or "Helpers of Islam." Its leaders were Sunni Muslim extremists who quickly imposed harsh Sharia law in the villages they controlled. They banned music in all forms, forced women to cover their faces in public, and outlawed schools for girls. They also developed a fondness for experimenting with poisons, building a crude lab in which they exposed stray dogs to cyanide and homemade ricin.

Beyond these charms, northern Iraq offered other advantages for a Jordanian on the run. Zarqawi could blend more easily with the local population than he did in Afghanistan, where he spoke none of the local languages. And the region's extreme isolation offered a chance to recuperate without interference.

After reaching the Ansar al-Islam base, Zarqawi moved into primitive quarters in the tiny village of Sargat, a cluster of stone hovels on a dead-end road leading up into the hills. With a handful of his Herat followers and a few thousand dollars of leftover al-Qaeda money, he set about re-creating the training camp he had established in Afghanistan. There would be important differences, starting with the absence, this time, of any significant al-Qaeda influence now that Bin Laden was in hiding more than two thousand miles away. He would have new allies and supporters, including sympathetic Islamists in Baghdad, who sheltered him when he traveled there in secret to obtain medical treatment for his broken ribs. In addition, Zarqawi was beginning to think more broadly about the targets of his jihad. Until 2001, Zarqawi's two great hatreds were Israel and the government of his own country, Jordan. Now the pain from his cracked ribs provided a constant reminder of his wish to inflict harm on the United States. He said as much to al-Adel one day shortly before leaving Iran to join Ansar al-Islam's forces. It was the last time the two men would meet.

"When he came to say goodbye before he left Iran," al-Adel recalled, "he underlined the importance of taking revenge on the Americans for the crimes they committed during the bombardment of Afghanistan, which he witnessed with his own eyes."

Zarqawi's rough character had been thrice remolded: by war, by prison and by the responsibilities of command at the helm of his own Afghan training camp. He had come to regard himself both as a leader and as a man with a destiny. And now, in al-Adel's view, his energy and thinking had been altered again, honed this time by "hatred and enmity against the Americans."

In the West, newspapers were beginning to speculate about whether America's government, under the leadership of President George W. Bush, was preparing for a possible second war against Iraq's Saddam Hussein. Zarqawi, for one, believed the stories. In conversations with disheartened Islamists in the bleak months of 2002, he talked of the epic conflict still to come, and how he had been steered by destiny to precisely the right place for engaging the great enemy of Allah, according to Fu'ad Husayn, a Jordanian journalist who met Zarqawi in prison and later penned a biography about the terrorist leader's early years. At that moment, Bin Laden was on the run in Pakistan, and the Taliban's rear guard was being chased by U.S. commandos across the eastern mountains of Afghanistan. Yet the real showdown still lay ahead, Zarqawi predicted, in a country that had had no history of serious religious militancy in at least a hundred years.

"Iraq," Zarqawi told friends, "will be the forthcoming battle against the Americans."

5

"I did it for al-Qaeda and for Zarqawi"

Laurence Foley was never a flashy man, but there were certain things about the Boston native that stood out, even in a city as cosmopolitan as Jordan's capital. He was big by Amman standards, with an ample midsection that had grown to accommodate the many diplomatic dinners and lunches required of a midlevel official at the U.S. Embassy. He wore a fringe of snowy hair that stood out like bleached cotton against his freckles and ruddy Irishman's complexion. He liked to take long strolls with his golden retriever, Bogart, in neighborhoods where the sight of a human walking any kind of pet still attracted stares. More striking, to friends, was his refusal to succumb to fretting over security, as so many Westerners did in the anxious months after the September 11, 2001, terrorist attacks. "Jordan is a safe place," the sixty-two-year-old assured family members who saw the reports about rising threat levels for Americans and became worried for him.

In the weeks and months after the attacks, as hostility toward Americans soared, some families retreated to gated enclaves near the embassy, which also sprouted new security fences and heavily armed military guards. But Foley, who had served in far more dangerous places during three decades of overseas work, elected to keep his two-story villa in West Amman, with its promise of an expat's version of Jordanian normality behind the wrought-iron window grills and rosebushes. In the evenings, he and his wife, Virginia, continued their walks with Bogart along Abdullah Ghosheh Street, greeting neighbors with a wave and a phrase or two in simple Arabic. Each morning, Foley rose early to drive himself to the embassy in his used Mercedes, a burgundy-red 280-Class with diplomatic plates, which he kept on a small carport behind an ornamental gate. He kept to his schedule—deliberately, defiantly—even as new warnings were quietly passed in the early autumn of 2002 of a plot to kidnap Americans in Jordan.

His job at the mission—arranging financing for clean-water projects and business partnerships for Jordanian entrepreneurs—was not particularly prestigious, but it was important, and Foley embraced it with energy and passion. He liked working in Amman's refugee settlements and drawing the residents into conversation. His endless questions about life in the camps prompted some to suspect that Foley was a CIA spy, though most were charmed by the portly American with the disarming grin. His bosses were so impressed that they decided to present him with a special award, and so, on the evening of October 27, 2002, the embassy honored Foley with a plaque and a dinner party that continued late into the evening. He came home tired but ebullient, as Virginia recalled afterward.

"I am where I want to be," he told her, "doing what I want to do."

The next morning, he rose at the usual time, dressed, and headed for the carport at 7:20 a.m. He was reaching for the door of the Mercedes when a figure rose suddenly from the far side of the car. The man's face was swathed in a black-and-white-checkered head scarf, or keffiyeh. His right hand held a small handgun tipped with a silencer.

Pip. Pip.

Foley staggered. The gunman stepped forward and emptied the entire clip.

Pip. Pip. Pip. Pip. Pip.

Foley crumbled to the pavement, shot in the face, neck, shoulder, and chest. The man in the keffiyeh scrambled over a low wall and sprinted toward a car and driver waiting a block away. The incident had played out in less than a minute, with so little commotion that no neighbor heard the shots or saw the body sprawled in a bloody pool between the Mercedes and the rosebushes.

But someone, many miles from West Amman, did happen to be listening in an hour later, when the gunman telephoned a contact somewhere in northern Iraq.

"Inform the sheikh," the gunman said. "Everything was done properly."

The snippet of intercepted conversation between the shooter and his contact had been a routine grab by the National Security Administration, or NSA, the spy agency that operates America's vast global surveillance network. Since the September 11 terrorist attacks, the NSA had been methodically sweeping up prodigious amounts of data, concentrating on regions of the world that might conceivably be harboring Osama bin Laden or any number of other al-Qaeda operatives. In the summer and fall of 2002, the northeastern corner of Iraq was one such place. Soon officials at the highest levels of the White House and Pentagon would be intently focused on a handful of mountain villages so remote they did not register on many maps of the region.

A United States diplomat had been assassinated—an exceedingly rare event, even in this turbulent part of the world. And the early suspicions, based on the initial analysis of the shooter's phone call, pointed to al-Qaeda, generally, and specifically to a man whose name still had not penetrated the consciousness of the majority of analysts in the CIA's counterterrorism center.

The one analyst who knew Abu Musab al-Zarqawi the best had reasons to be skeptical. Nada Bakos, a newly minted thirty-three-year-old officer who had just landed at the intelligence agency office two years earlier, was quickly becoming the CIA's top expert on the Jordanian. In later years, this rancher's daughter from central Montana would help lead the hunt for the terrorist, working for weeks at a stretch in dusty Iraqi military bases a few miles from where Zarqawi was presumed to live. She would track his known movements, interrogate his captured fighters, and even accompany U.S. soldiers on midnight raids on suspected safe houses. She dug into his personal history and habits with such intensity that co-workers teased her about her Jordanian "boyfriend."

But something about the rush to blame Zarqawi made her uneasy. It was conceivable that Zarqawi had ordered the hit, she allowed, but it would also be quite convenient. The Jordanians would be eager to show that the crime was a deliberate act by international terrorists, and not mere random violence of the type that could damage the country's reputation with the tourism industry. Moreover, the few officials in the Bush White House who knew Zarqawi's name had lately shown a strange fascination with the Jordanian. Bakos's division at the CIA was constantly fielding queries from Bush appointees about rumored connections between al-Qaeda and Saddam Hussein, the Iraqi president now at the center of the administration's crosshairs. If Iraq had played even a minor role in supporting al-Qaeda's September 11 terrorist attacks on New York and Washington, the case for an invasion would be clear-cut. The CIA was able to knock down most of the rumors about Iraqi links to 9/11, but the Zarqawi case was murkier. Hadn't the Jordanian been seen in Baghdad, getting medical treatment in one of the city's state-run hospitals? Wasn't he the same Zarqawi who had been given cash and land by al-Qaeda to set up his own training camp in western Afghanistan? After the start of the Afghan offensive, didn't he flee to Iraq instead of joining Bin Laden at Tora Bora? A still more disturbing question: did the Ansar al-Islam camp's rumored poisons laboratory suggest a link to Saddam Hussein, whose interest in chemical weapons in the 1990s was well documented?

Bakos and her colleagues dutifully fielded the questions and tried, within the confines of the limited intelligence on Zarqawi in late 2002, to answer them.

Now there would be many more questions. A U.S. diplomat had been shot, and the best evidence so far suggested that the deed had been ordered from Iraqi soil, by a man with clear connections to al-Qaeda.

To most Americans, and even to most CIA analysts, Zarqawi

remained an unknown figure in an obscure cul-de-sac of the global jihadist movement. But at senior levels of the Bush White House, he had just catapulted to the top of the terrorist heap.

There were times during Nada Bakos's tumultuous first two years at the Central Intelligence Agency when history seemed to hurtle straight at her, like random shrapnel, or a brick crashing through a windshield. One such moment came early on the morning of September 11, 2001, when Bakos and other young analysts crowded around a TV monitor in time to see the second airliner pierce the aluminum skin of No. 2 World Trade Center and explode out of the building's northern side. Amid the gasps and tears, a single name—al-Qaeda—rippled through the ranks of officers as they watched the black smoke billowing over Lower Manhattan. Co-workers began streaming out of the building under a general evacuation order, but Bakos, then a rookie analyst, with honey-blond hair and soft brown eyes, couldn't bring herself to leave.

"I kept wondering, 'What can I do?'" she said afterward. "I hope they ask us to do something." Indeed, minutes later, the CIA counterterrorism chief, Cofer Black, rallied a group of two hundred officers who had stayed behind, issuing what would become the first orders of the agency's years-long campaign to find, destroy, and defeat Osama bin Laden. "We're at war now," Black said, "a different kind of war than we've ever fought before."

Another moment came just over a year later, when Bakos found herself in a small conference room with the vice president of the United States. The country was edging closer to war with Iraq, and Dick Cheney, then the salesman-in-chief for the Bush administration's war strategy, had decided to pay a highly unusual visit to the CIA's Langley, Virginia, campus to query the agency's top terrorism experts in person. Cheney's office had been prodding the CIA for months over possible links between the September 11 attacks and Iraqi president Saddam Hussein. Zarqawi had emerged as an intriguing figure, but the CIA's reports on the man were far more cautious than those coming from the Pentagon's Office of Special Plans, the shadow intelligence service set up by Defense Undersecretary Douglas J. Feith, an Iraq hawk and a Bush appointee. What did the agency really know?

The vice president had arrived that morning with a handful of aides, all scowls and dark suits, for what was to be the second showdown with the agency over its Iraq files. The first meeting, chaired by CIA director George Tenet, had gone badly. The senior managers who attended had no ready answers to Cheney's questions about suspicious contacts between alleged al-Qaeda operatives and Saddam Hussein. His questions implied serious gaps in the agency's knowledge about the Iraqi leader and his support for terrorists, possibly including Bin Laden himself.

Tenet convened a second meeting to bring in the more junior officers who knew the file best. And so it was that Bakos, in her third year as a CIA officer, was invited to participate in the education of the second-most-powerful man in the country.

The meeting was in the headquarters building's seventh floor, near the executive suites, in a room overlooking the dense woodlands that provide an extra security buffer between the spy agency and Washington's crowded Virginia suburbs. Cheney and his advisers sat on one side of a long table, facing a row of midlevel managers armed with files and notes from a practice session—dubbed a "murder board"—the day before. Bakos, who was among the youngest intelligence officers in the room, took a seat behind her boss. Her job was to serve as the backup, fielding any questions that slipped past the front line. Nervous at first, she eventually relaxed and watched with fascination as Cheney personally led the questioning. He peered skeptically over his glasses at the CIA's experts, and his tone was polite but insistent, like that of a seasoned prosecutor breaking down a reluctant witness.

Nada Bakos sat silently in her chair against a far wall, listening but not entirely believing. There were plenty of good reasons for going after the man who helped facilitate the Millennium Plot in 1999. But a cabal including the radical jihadist and the fiercely secular Iraqi leader—a man who routinely tortured and killed Islamists in his country? Was Cheney serious?

Cheney was more than serious. In the weeks that followed, his aides would react furiously to a top-secret CIA report—which Bakos had helped write—all but demolishing allegations of operational ties between Saddam Hussein's government and al-Qaeda. The stories circulated by Bush aides about secret contacts between the two longtime foes "appear based on hearsay," the report said, with "no substantiating detail or other information that might help us corroborate them."

The answers Cheney sought did not exist; yet, the more the CIA pushed back, the more insistent the Cheney team became. At least once, a Bush aide telephoned Bakos directly at her desk to quiz her about a line in one of her reports. The call violated long-established protocols that barred political appointees from directly contacting individual analysts, a rule intended to protect CIA employees from political influence. Bakos quickly hung up and complained to her boss, who phoned the White House, incensed about the breach.

"They were asking us to prove a negative: to prove to them that Zarqawi wasn't part of al-Qaeda, and wasn't working with Saddam," Bakos said. "And even when we tried to do that, the answer would be: 'So what? All those people have the same agenda, so who cares?'"

It was hardly the role Bakos had imagined for herself when she applied to the spy agency just over two years earlier. The application had been a lark, a casual bet she had placed with herself. Long after she was hired, relatives back home still believed Bakos was an administrative assistant of some kind, answering phones and opening mail. No one from tiny Denton, Montana, had ever done anything as glamorous as tracking terrorists for the CIA.

Bakos once dreamed of being a veterinarian, work that seemed well suited for a young woman who grew up around horses and spent long summer days in solitude, roaming the ranch with a favorite stallion. Her horizons as a girl were framed by her tiny high school, with its graduating class of nine students, and the cop shows she loved to watch on television. But even then, Bakos knew she wanted more.

A car accident during her freshman year at Montana State nearly snuffed her ambitions. But Bakos was eventually able to return to college and channel her energy into a new major—economics—and a vague plan to work in international relations. She married, and worked briefly for a cement manufacturer and a mining company. Then, a few months before her thirtieth birthday, she packed her belongings into her Ford F-150 pickup truck and drove across the country to Washington, D.C. She was newly divorced, and had neither a job nor firm prospects, but she had been urged by her stepfather, a Vietnam War veteran, to try the intelligence service. He had seen an advertisement in *The Economist* and figured Bakos was as capable as anyone.

"They're never going to hire me," she had told him. "Why would they hire me?"

"Just apply," he said.

She couldn't shake the idea. She had been thinking about working as an economic analyst for a government agency, perhaps the State Department. The CIA sounded like an adventure.

"Why not?" she finally asked.

Bakos filled out an application and took an exam, and, to her amazement, an agency recruiter called back to set up an interview. Five months after that, she was walking through the agency's iconic entrance, past the sixteen-foot seal of inlaid granite bearing the agency's logo. She worked at first as a technical specialist, deep within the agency's bureaucracy, but quickly made the jump to intelligence analyst, a demanding job that combined sleuthing skills with an ability to process vast amounts of data from the CIA's electronic and human spy networks. Bakos's economics background landed her on a team that tracked Saddam Hussein's financial crimes, including his rampant cheating on UN trade embargoes. But soon the job was expanded to include other intelligence on Iraq, including the dictator's support for terrorist networks—which, in turn, led her to Zarqawi.

Slender and blond, she attracted notice in a workplace that remained predominantly male, particularly in the leadership ranks. But what stood out most was her astonishing command of the subject matter. Not only had she absorbed every scrap of available data about Zarqawi and his top deputies, but she also possessed a remarkable talent for picking out patterns from the mountains of seemingly random detail. One of her supervisors at the time called her "simply one of the best analysts I've ever met."

"She reminds me of someone who counts cards at Las Vegas," the now retired senior CIA officer said. "She understands all the permutations that come from each particular draw. That's something you can't teach."

Bakos would tell her friends that the job was the first that truly seemed to fit her. "It's the center of the action," she would say. Yet, for the first time, she also was being confronted with unpleasant truths. One of them, demonstrated repeatedly throughout her career, was that political leaders tended to choose selectively from a menu of classified material in order to present a skewed, self-serving version of reality to the voting public. All presidents had indulged in the practice, though some perhaps more than others.

And now the lesson was being learned again. The Cheney visit had ended with sour looks all around. The vice president and his team left for Washington without a single addition of consequence for their Iraq file. For some of the CIA analysts in the room, the visit was deeply dispiriting. The White House was clearly preparing for invasion, and Cheney and his team seemed unfazed that the available evidence undermined the administration's case.

"In my opinion, we didn't know nearly enough," Bakos said. "But I was completely naïve about the process for going to war."

Years later, Cheney would insist that his focus on possible Iraqi ties to terrorism was appropriate. "I asked tough questions," he acknowledged in his written account of his visits to the CIA. In surveying possible threats to the country in the wake of September 11, Cheney concluded that there was "no place more likely to be a nexus between terrorism and [weapons of mass destruction] capability than Saddam Hussein's Iraq."

"With the benefit of hindsight—even taking into account that some of the intelligence we received was faulty—that assessment still holds true," Cheney wrote.

Justified or not, the White House clearly wasn't finished with Zarqawi. The intense interest in the Jordanian's possible ties to Iraq would continue up to the start of the invasion, and, indeed—to Nada Bakos's dismay—for years after that. The murder of a U.S. diplomat in Jordan had only dialed up the pressure even more.

—

The daylight shooting of Laurence Foley in one of Amman's safest neighborhoods set off something akin to panic at senior levels of the Jordanian government. No American diplomat had ever been seriously harmed, let alone assassinated, in Jordan in the country's history. King Abdullah II took charge of the official response, meeting with CIA and State Department officials to coordinate the initial investigations. He and his wife, Queen Rania, paid a call on Foley's widow to offer sympathy and assistance in preparing her husband's body for return to the United States. Meanwhile, the police and the Mukhabarat began rounding up scores of Islamic radicals for questioning in Foley's slaying. Within forty-eight hours, more than one hundred people were jailed, and yet intelligence officials had no clue who was behind the killing, or why Foley, out of the thousands of Americans living in Amman, had been targeted. Who would go to the trouble of stalking and executing a midlevel bureaucrat whose main duty was improving Jordan's drinking-water supply?

On October 30, dual escorts of U.S. marines and Jordanian ceremonial guards carried Foley's casket to a military transport plane at an Amman airport, trailed by Virginia Foley and Bogart, the couple's golden retriever. Across town, at the Mukhabarat's headquarters, meanwhile, the interrogations ground on. An obscure jihadist group's claim of responsibility was investigated and dismissed. Detectives squeezed, threatened, and cajoled. Weeks passed, and not a single useful lead had been produced, other than the snippet of a phone call, apparently made from a cheap "burner" phone containing a stolen memory chip.

Then, in late November, one of the Mukhabarat's informants overheard whisperings about a strange Libyan man who had moved into an apartment in the Marka refugee settlement, on Amman's outskirts. The foreigner had arrived in September, ostensibly to help a friend open a women's clothing shop specializing in the black *abayas* and head coverings worn by the pious. The two had rented a small storefront and posted a sign that read "The Little Princess." They also rented a small warehouse, to the bafflement of neighbors, who wondered why a tiny clothing shop would require so much storage space.

The Jordanian partner was a Palestinian named Yasser Ibrahim Freihat, a struggling businessman with jihadist sympathies but lacking any known connection to radical groups or crimes. The Libyan looked much more interesting. After tracking him for several days, the Mukhabarat became convinced of his identity: he was Salem Ben Suweid, a veteran of the Afghan civil war who had been arrested three years earlier, after entering Jordan under a forged passport. Police at that time suspected that he had al-Qaeda connections and kicked him out of the country. If this was truly Suweid, he had managed to sneak into Jordan a second time without being detected.

After midnight on December 3, Mukhabarat agents raided the warehouse, the Little Princess shop, and then the apartments of the two men. They rousted Suweid and Freihat in their bedclothes and began a thorough ransacking of their belongings for anything suspicious. Suweid's house yielded a bonanza. Agents found gloves and masks, bulletproof vests, tear-gas canisters, and over ten thousand dollars in American currency. In a back room they found Suweid's weapons cache: five Kalashnikov assault rifles along with ammunition, a handbook on explosives, and a notebook with diagrams of potential targets. But there was no sign of a silencer or a seven-millimeter handgun that would match the shell casings found at Foley's villa.

At 4:00 a.m., the two men were delivered to the Mukhabarat's counterterrorism branch and into the hands of Abu Haytham, the counterterrorism section's deputy, and Ali Bourzak, the division chief and legendary interrogator known as the Red Devil. By 6:00 a.m., as the approaching dawn softened the clouds over the Judean Hills to a dull gray, Suweid was a broken man. He signed a confession, admitting to planning and carrying out the assassination of the diplomat Laurence Foley. Freihat, his business partner, had acted as his lookout and driver, he said.

It was quick work, even by the Mukhabarat's standards, and Abu Haytham knew the confession would invite suspicions. Jordanians and even Westerners would assume that the spy agency had used torture to produce a suspect in a murder case that had damaged the country's standing with its most important ally. So, with the ink on the confession still drying, the captain resorted to a tactic he often used when a suspect's credibility was in question: he organized a guided tour of the crime scene.

As a subdued Suweid sat in handcuffs in the backseat, Abu Haytham and his driver began heading toward West Amman, home to most of the city's embassies and diplomats.

"Take me to the place," he ordered.

Suweid directed the driver through a maze of side streets until the vehicle stopped in front of the carport where Foley's body had lain. The house was empty now; Virginia Foley had left Jordan with her husband's body and would never again live in the Middle East. All signs of the slaying had long since been scrubbed away.

The prisoner sat quietly in the backseat with his head bowed.

"Show me how it happened," Haytham commanded.

Suweid slowly recounted the story just as he had laid it out in his confession. He had slipped across the Jordanian border from Syria in September with orders to find American and official Jordanian targets to strike. After setting up the front company with Freihat, he sent his old friend back into Syria to retrieve a cache of weapons, including the Kalashnikovs and a handgun. Then, in October, he had begun cruising Amman's diplomatic district and wealthier neighborhoods popular with Westerners.

Foley had been a chance discovery, Suweid said. Open and gregarious, the American had made an impression during his frequent visits to Amman's refugee enclaves, where he had worked with Palestinians on water projects. His friendly questions about life in the camps had led some to suspect that he was an operative of some kind. Everyone knew about the red Mercedes with the distinctive diplomatic tags, which Foley continued to use even after other embassy staffers had switched to ordinary Jordanian plates.

Suweid found Foley's house and studied it for three days. He noticed Foley's white, thinning hair and late-middle-age paunch. He observed the absence of guards and security cameras, and the low wall that ran along the front and side of the house, offering both easy access and ample hiding places. He jotted notes on Foley's morning routine: the early risings, the dog walks, the set-your-clock regularity of his 7:20 a.m. departures for the office, always alone in the Mercedes's front seat.

Finally, on October 28, as the city's muezzins were sounding the call for dawn prayers, the Libyan and his partner climbed into a borrowed Hyundai and headed toward Amman's western side, with the pistol and mask hidden in a small satchel on Suweid's lap. Whether Foley was a spy, Suweid did not know. But he was looking to kill an American, and he now had his chance.

"I thought it would be easy, with just a few shots, to kill him," Suweid told Abu Haytham.

He showed the Mukhabarat officer the spot where he had breached the wall, and where he had crouched while waiting for Foley to emerge from the house. He recounted how he had shot the diplomat without a word, and then shot again to ensure that the wounds were fatal. He pointed to the place where Freihat had waited in the idling Hyundai, and described how the two had hurried back to the Marka neighborhood afterward, stopping at one point to toss the handgun into the polluted Zarqa River. They had returned home in time to change clothes and open the Little Princess store, precisely at 10:00 a.m.

Abu Haytham listened intently, and then asked, again, the question that had confounded him since news of the murder first broke:

"Why?"

"I did it," Suweid said, "for al-Qaeda and for Zarqawi."

Was Zarqawi truly involved?

Jordanian officials waited nearly two weeks before announcing the arrests and publicly linking Zarqawi to the crime, perhaps in the hope that the CIA would find additional evidence bolstering the connection between the shooter and the man who was rapidly becoming Jordan's most famous fugitive. As it was, many Jordanians were prepared to believe Suweid's lawyer when he told the Amman newspapers that the claim of a Zarqawi role had been induced through torture.

Investigators would counter by leaking details about the inter-

cepted call between Suweid and his contact in Iraq, a man they identified as Muammar Yousef al-Jaghbeer, a known Zarqawi disciple.
Jaghbeer himself was arrested years later in Iraq, and his statements
to his American captors supported the claim that Zarqawi had personally dispatched Suweid to Jordan with a budget of fifty thousand
dollars and instructions to find and kill Americans—any Americans.

Yet, oddly, Zarqawi never claimed responsibility for Foley's murder, even as he took credit for hundreds of other killings, including
those of numerous U.S. citizens. Islamists who knew Zarqawi during
his time in northeastern Iraq have insisted that he was not involved.

Nada Bakos, one of the CIA analysts who saw the intelligence in
real time, said some key questions were never fully answered.

"The evidence was ambiguous," she would later say. "We were
convinced of Zarqawi's role, analytically. Whether you could put
together a criminal case, that's a different story."

Still, the analytical case provided more than sufficient grounds for
action. A grave crime had been committed against a U.S. government employee on official duty overseas, and there were reasons for
believing that Zarqawi was at least complicit.

Justice would have to be served, and that meant capturing Zarqawi himself. Fortunately, the U.S. government knew, in those wan-
ing weeks of the autumn of 2002, exactly where he was.

6

"This war is going to happen"

The man who would become the CIA's chief spy in northern Iraq had barely heard of the suspected terrorist called Abu Musab al-Zarqawi when he arrived in the country in the summer of 2002. But within weeks, Charles "Sam" Faddis knew the Jordanian's home address, down to the square meter on his targeting grid.

The chances to go after Zarqawi would never be better than this.

Faddis, a six-foot-two navy captain's son from the Appalachian foothills of southwestern Pennsylvania, had slipped into Iraq with a team of CIA operatives to gather intelligence on Iraqi military units as well as Ansar al-Islam, the militant oddballs who lived on the Iranian border and maintained loose ties with al-Qaeda. Though already forty-seven and a lawyer, he had pushed hard for the assignment. Faddis had been anxious to find a way to get into the fight after the September 11 attacks, and his counterterrorism background, Middle East experience, and mastery of Turkish had made him particularly suited to lead the mission. Now he and his team were living in safe houses and conducting surveillance of Ansar al-Islam's base, home to Zarqawi and several dozen other refugee jihadis from Afghanistan. Donning Kurdish clothes, the officers sometimes crept so close to the base they could clearly see the perimeter guards with their long beards and slung AK-47s.

The target was remote in the extreme. Sargat, the hamlet where

Zarqawi had landed after his flight from Afghanistan, was the last stop on the rutted road leading to Iraq's border with the Islamic Republic of Iran. A few miles to the northwest was Halabja, a town forever associated with one of the great genocidal atrocities of the late twentieth century. There, on March 16, 1988, Saddam Hussein attacked Kurdish villagers with deadly nerve gas, killing as many as five thousand men, women, and children in history's worst chemical attack against a civilian population. The region never fully recovered; after the first Iraq war, in 1991, daily patrols by U.S. aircraft kept Saddam's planes and tanks out of Kurdish settlements, but the absence of a central authority gave rise to local militias and warlords that skirmished with Iraqi ground troops and with each other.

By the time Zarqawi arrived, the Ansar al-Islam militants had already carved out a small enclave that also included the town of Khurmal and several other small villages, which they administered with Taliban-like zeal. Officially at war with both the Iraqi regime and Kurdish nationalist groups, they built hillside defense works offering a commanding view of the mountain passes, as well as escape routes that led across the border into Iran. The main base in Sargat consisted of seven small buildings, without heat or electricity except for a single generator, encircled by earthen walls and bunkers festooned with black banners. A separate cluster of cinder-block dwellings served as housing and training facilities for Zarqawi's men, who mostly avoided blending with their Kurdish-speaking counterparts. Locals would remember them as a mix of Arab nationalities with uniformly stern views about behavior and dress. Some villagers grumbled afterward about the impracticality of some of the Islamists' rules in a community where both men and women spent long hours tending livestock and crops.

"They used to force women to wear the cover and a gown while going to the fields and gardens to work," one man complained to a TV interviewer a few months after the militants had left.

But the CIA's interest in the Islamists had little to do with religious codes. Now that al-Qaeda had been chased from Afghanistan, the Ansar al-Islam base represented the largest known gathering of militants with ties—albeit minor ones—to Bin Laden's group. Faddis's orders were to assess the strength of the combined force of Arab and local Islamists living in the Iraqi enclave. If possible, he was also to determine how, if at all, Ansar's militants were coordinating their operations with Iraqi government forces. Regardless of whether al-Qaeda and Iraq had colluded in the past, the White House worried that Saddam Hussein might use terrorists as proxies to strike a blow against the West. Friendly Kurds had reported seeing chemical weapons in Ansar's camp, deepening suspicions within the White House that Saddam was arming the Islamist militants for a future terrorist strike.

The CIA team leader was skeptical. Faddis had spent years in the region, and he understood the bitter hatred nearly all Kurds felt toward the Iraqi tyrant after years of genocidal policies that had wiped out two thousand Kurdish villages and nearly two hundred thousand ethnic Kurds in the 1980s. For Kurdish militants to unite with Saddam for any reason was nearly impossible to fathom.

Still, Faddis told his team to keep an open mind.

"Look, if we can produce solid intelligence that proves Saddam is in bed with al-Qaeda, that's fabulous," he recalled telling his men during a group huddle in the summer of 2002. "But we're not saying anything remotely like that until we get solid evidence that's happening. We're not going to pass off rumors and bullshit as the truth."

Faddis's group consisted of eight men, all of them with extensive military experience and two of them members of the CIA's secret paramilitary unit known as the Special Activities Division. Their base was a small house provided to them by friendly Kurds a few miles from the Ansar camp. It served as an operations center as well as living quarters for the men, who spent much of their days conducting surveillance and joining in the questioning of captured militants seized by friendly Kurds. Their access to Ansar and al-Qaeda prisoners was extraordinary; the Americans were able to interrogate dozens of prisoners, and they considered each new account against a growing database of intelligence gleaned from earlier detainees as well as their own surveillance of Ansar's camps. The findings were beamed to CIA headquarters in the form of hundreds of classified electronic messages, relayed to Langley via Faddis's satellite phone.

Faddis quickly grasped the stark differences between the Afghan exiles—mostly Arabic-speakers with at least rudimentary education and knowledge of the world—and the simple Kurdish farmers and goat herders who filled Ansar's ranks. Yet the two groups shared the same ideology and a common interest in the tradecraft of terrorism. Together they had set about creating a miniature Afghanistan in the Iraqi mountains, an Islamic theocracy whose harsh codes were enforced by the gun and the blade.

It was true, he learned, that the militants harbored a deadly secret: a stockpile of poisons they were testing for possible use in terrorist attacks abroad. Through the CIA's interrogations, and with additional help from well-placed spies, the nature of Ansar's poisons fixation became clear. The group had managed to acquire dozens of gallons of deadly chemicals, including cyanide, and a small supply of castor beans for making highly lethal ricin. Each of the ingredients could be purchased easily and legally—potassium cyanide is used in film developing—and there was no sign that Ansar's militants possessed the equipment or know-how for making real chemical weapons. Still, the experiments seemed serious enough. Inside their makeshift lab, amateur technicians mixed cyanide with skin cream and other cosmetics. Their rumored experiments on stray dogs were later confirmed in videotapes that were discovered in the fort's ruins.

"Their abilities are crude, but their aspirations are huge," Faddis remembered thinking at the time. "They are out for blood, and they are no joke."

The other question preoccupying the White House—whether Iraqi forces were somehow helping the Islamists—was even easier to unravel. Faddis's team picked up the trail of suspected Iraqi operatives in the area near the Ansar camp, and confirmed that the men were members of Saddam Hussein's feared intelligence service. But Faddis soon discovered that the Iraqis were doing exactly as he was: trying to collect intelligence on the militants. The Iraqis watched from afar and tried to recruit informants—a risky proposition, given Ansar's history of poisoning suspected spies and displaying their severed heads on stakes outside the fort. Far from colluding with the Islamists, the Iraqis appeared fearful of them.

Still, the Bush administration had promised to hunt down al-Qaeda-allied terrorists wherever it found them, and to Faddis, this bunch fit the definition perfectly.

The United States had a "golden opportunity," Faddis wrote in one of his cables to CIA headquarters in Langley. Ansar al-Islam was a terrorist organization with an ambitious international agenda. It was harboring dozens of Arab militants with known links to al-Qaeda. More disturbingly, it possessed chemical poisons that could potentially be used with horrifying effect in the cities of Europe or the United States. But the threat in its entirety could be erased, Faddis wrote, with a single well-placed blow.

"We knew exactly where every one of these Islamist terrorists slept," Faddis said afterward, describing his detailed accounts to CIA headquarters. "We knew where each gun was, literally down to every machine-gun position and mortar tube."

Best of all, he added, "None of them knew we were there."

As Faddis hoped, his cables created a stir in Washington. At Langley, and later at the Defense Department, a series of meetings was convened to discuss what to do. At the Pentagon, a forty-eight-year-old brigadier general named Stanley McChrystal—soon to rise to prominence as the head of special forces in Iraq—was asked to come up with options for attacking the base. One idea was to hit the Islamists with a missile barrage, followed by a helicopter assault by teams of American and Kurdish commandos, who would scoop up any evidence of biological or chemical weapons production.

The plan was deemed workable, but the Bush White House split sharply over whether to order the raid. Defense Secretary Donald Rumsfeld favored the strike, but other senior aides, including National Security Adviser Condoleezza Rice, advised against it. The administration was already deep into the planning for an invasion of Iraq, opponents said, and any strike on Iraqi soil carried the risk of an escalation that could start the war prematurely. Other critics of the plan simply worried that McChrystal's proposal was too sprawling. "It's big enough to be an invasion," one of the brigadier's superiors complained. "You were in special operations. Can't they do anything small anymore?"

Bush decided to nix the plan, for now.

"It was like getting punched in the gut," Faddis said later. "We were all putting ourselves at risk. When the mission was sidelined, you knew right then and there what it meant. We weren't going to pull the trigger now. And when the time came when we did pull the trigger, the important targets will no longer be here."

Faddis tried again, suggesting a less ambitious campaign that would rely on local Kurds to do most of the fighting. With a little air support, a few 150-millimeter mortars, and some logistical help from the CIA team, the local guys could destroy the base on their own, he argued.

"For the love of God, just give us two B-52s, or just the mortars, and we'll get it done," Faddis pleaded. "Give it to us tomorrow, and we'll get it done the day after. Al-Qaeda and Ansar al-Islam don't have a clue we are here. Total stealth."

The response from Langley was the same.

"I hear you, Sam," came the reluctant reply, according to Faddis. "All I can tell you is, that's the way it is. The last time I checked, the president outranked you."

Faddis and his team remained in northern Iraq with orders to continue their surveillance. Zarqawi, meanwhile, was free to build his network without fear of attack or interference. CIA officials at the time understood that the Jordanian was becoming increasingly dangerous. As Tenet, director of the spy agency, later noted, Zarqawi was clearly on the move in those prewar days, training his recruits at the Ansar al-Islam camp while dispatching envoys to Middle Eastern and European capitals, seeking money, volunteers, and allies. "He was able to forge ties between Algerians, Moroccans, Pakistanis, Libyans and other Arab extremists located through Europe," Tenet would write of Zarqawi in his memoirs. "Over several months of tireless links we identified Zarqawi-connected terrorist cells in more than 30 countries."

Apprised of this, the Bush administration held one final debate on the possibility of a strike against Zarqawi and the Ansar al-Islam camp. It happened in early January 2003, just two months before the start of the Iraq war, and weeks before then Secretary of State Colin Powell was to give his now famous speech to the UN Security Council, outlining the rationale for invasion. By then, White House officials were reluctant to take any action that might detract from the all-important battle for public opinion, according to an account of the meeting in *Days of Fire,* the journalist Peter Baker's acclaimed history of the Bush White House. A strike on the militant base now would undermine one of the pillars of Powell's upcoming speech: the existence of terrorist networks on Iraqi soil.

"That would wipe out my briefing," Powell said, according to Baker's account. Besides, he added, "We're going to get [Ansar al-Islam] in a few weeks anyway."

The administration was still debating a possible strike on Zarqawi's camp, when, on January 23, 2003, a delegation of U.S. generals arrived in Amman for a visit cloaked in unusual secrecy. Reporters were kept far away when General Tommy Franks, commander of the Pentagon's U.S. Central Command, landed at the airport, and the palace imposed a blackout on details of his meetings with Jordanian officials, including whether King Abdullah II had participated. Later, anonymous military sources revealed the purpose of the visit in carefully worded leaks to the Western press: with a war against Iraq just weeks away, the United States was preparing to offer Jordan its advanced Patriot missile-defense system, in hopes of securing the Hashemite kingdom's support when the shooting began.

"We are considering it," one of the members of the U.S. team told a Jordanian journalist during the visit. In fact, the missile batteries would be shipped to Jordan within days, along with six new F-16 fighter-bombers, bolstering Jordan's defenses in preparation for a possible war next door.

But the U.S. assistance came at a price. For months, the Bush White House had been pressuring Jordan to get behind its plan to topple Iraqi president Saddam Hussein. The squeeze had begun in the late summer, when the king met with Bush and his top deputies during an August 2, 2002, visit to the White House. The usually charming Texan was cool and stiff, as Abdullah recalled later. Aides warned the monarch that the president was upset over comments he had made to a British newspaper, accusing the Bush team of being "fixated on Iraq" and determined to start a war that would "really open a Pandora's box in the Middle East."

Bush, crunching on ice cubes as the two men sat in the Oval Office, said he hadn't yet decided whether to invade Iraq. "When I do, you will know," he said. He called Iraqi president Saddam Hussein a "thug" who had to be challenged. "I don't want people to think, 20 years from now, that I chickened out on confronting him," he said.

Later that day, Bush brought up Iraq again, this time framing the standoff with Saddam as a moral, even religious obligation.

"You and I have two great fathers, and we both believe in God," Bush said, as Abdullah later recalled. "We have an opportunity to do the right thing."

Abdullah was stunned. He despised Saddam, and he knew America's vast military could quickly destroy the Iraqi dictator's army. He had offered, without public acknowledgment, support for the U.S.-led assault on the Taliban in Afghanistan, and even volunteered Jordan's help in tracking down Osama bin Laden. Yet he was convinced that war against the Iraqi tyrant would be a colossal mistake. An attack by U.S. troops on an Arab leader—even one as unpopular as Saddam—would inflame the region, putting Jordan at risk. But it was clear that Bush had made up his mind. Back in Amman, the monarch told his aides to get ready. "This war is going to happen," he said.

Through the late summer and fall, the war drums grew increasingly urgent, and so did the appeals to Jordan to back the administration's war plan. A steady stream of American politicians and generals visited Amman, pressing the king to allow U.S. forces to stage along the country's border, or to fly sorties through Jordanian airspace. Vice President Dick Cheney phoned Abdullah personally to ask for permission to use Jordan as a springboard for the assault on Baghdad. Against the intense wrangling over war preparations, the shock over the Foley assassination quickly faded.

Abdullah ultimately claimed a middle ground. His father, Hussein, had famously opposed the first Gulf War, a stance that set back the country's relations with both Washington and key Arab allies. Abdullah likewise would maintain a posture of opposition to a conflict that Jordanians overwhelmingly rejected as unjust, and he refused to allow significant numbers of U.S. troops into the country. But he did agree to offer the Americans behind-the-scenes support, mostly in the critical arena of covert operations involving small groups of U.S. commandos.

The decision to accept the Patriot missile batteries was a last-minute concession. Publicly, the monarchy could claim that the missile-defense system would shield Jordanians from any errant Iraqi SCUDs that might threaten Jordanian territory. In reality, the Americans wanted an additional safeguard against a possible Iraqi attack on Israel in retaliation for the invasion. It was yet another sign that war was coming.

"I tried to walk the tightrope of opposing the war and staying out of it," Abdullah acknowledged afterward. "But I was certain of one thing: the longer the war lasts, the more terrible the consequences would be."

7

"Now his fame would extend throughout the Arab world"

The world's introduction to Abu Musab al-Zarqawi came on February 5, 2003, in the sixty-first minute of Colin Powell's speech to the UN Security Council making the case for war against Iraq. It began with a declarative sentence that, like many others in the seventy-five-minute presentation, was technically true but widely off the mark.

"Iraq today harbors a deadly terrorist network headed by Abu Musab al-Zarqawi, an associate and collaborator of Osama bin Laden and his al-Qaeda lieutenants," Powell began, just before Zarqawi's bearded image appeared on a large screen behind the council's circular table.

Nada Bakos, watching on a TV monitor at work, heard the line and cringed. Yes, Zarqawi lived in the remote mountains of northeastern Iraq—in an area off limits to Iraq's military. To suggest that Saddam Hussein was providing sanctuary to him was contrary to everything that Bakos, the Zarqawi expert, knew to be true. It was like claiming that America's twenty-second president, Grover Cleveland, had "harbored" Geronimo, the famed Apache chieftain of the frontier West who attacked settlers and Blue Coats from his base along the U.S.-Mexican border.

She continued watching, transfixed.

"Iraqi officials deny accusations of ties with al-Qaeda. These denials are simply not credible," Powell continued. "Last year an al-Qaeda associate bragged that the situation in Iraq was, quote, 'good,' that Baghdad could be transited quickly."

True enough. But were the terrorists gaining passage through official Iraqi complicity, or because of weaknesses in the country's notoriously corrupt and inefficient border security?

To those who knew the subject matter best, the speech was an extraordinary performance, an artful rendering of a selective set of facts that favored invasion. Powell later described the presentation as one of the biggest blunders of his career, a mistake he would attribute to sloppy intelligence and wishful thinking at senior levels of the Bush administration. In reality, every word of the Zarqawi portion of the speech had been written by senior officials of the CIA after weeks of rancorous debate with White House officials over what should and should not be left out. To his credit, Powell rejected out of hand an earlier script written by White House aides, one that included much stronger claims about terrorist links gleaned from untested informants and unconfirmed rumors picked up by the Pentagon's Office of Special Plans.

Still, there were lines in the speech that baffled Bakos and her CIA colleagues. Powell acknowledged at the beginning that Zarqawi and his Ansar al-Islam allies operated in an area outside Saddam Hussein's control. But he then asserted that "Baghdad has an agent in the most senior levels of the radical organization," suggesting that Iraq effectively controlled the group. Nothing in the CIA's vetted reports confirmed that such a relationship existed.

Powell paused at one point to mention the assassination of Laurence Foley, the diplomat killed in Amman three months before, a "despicable act" that he credited to Zarqawi. After the slaying, he said, the State Department had contacted Iraqi intelligence through a third country—it was Jordan, officials later confirmed—demanding that the terrorist leader be turned over for trial.

"Iraqi officials protest that they are not aware of the whereabouts of Zarqawi or of any of his associates," Powell said. "Again, these protests are not credible. We know of Zarqawi's activities in Baghdad."

The assertions were coming faster than Bakos could mentally counter them. It was becoming painful. This was not how intelligence analysis was supposed to work. When Cheney had made similar claims on Sunday talk shows, Bakos often found herself yelling at the television screen, as though she were contesting a referee's blown call in a football game. Now Powell, like Cheney, was "asserting to the public as fact something that we found to be anything but," she later said.

Ultimately, the speech would tarnish Powell's reputation and further undermine the credibility of the Bush administration with key allies, particularly after claims that Iraq harbored weapons of mass destruction turned out to be false.

The other painful side effect would not be fully appreciated until much later. With one speech, the White House had transformed Zarqawi from an unknown jihadist to an international celebrity and the toast of the Islamist movement. The image of the mysterious Zarqawi glowering at world leaders from the UN Security Council's screen sent hordes of reporters scurrying to their computers to figure out who he was. Newspaper reporters and TV crews flocked to Jordan to write profiles and interview people who claimed to know him. Zarqa, the gritty industrial town of the terrorist's youth, now had a new favorite son.

Watching the transformation with special bitterness were the Jordanians who had tried for so long to keep Zarqawi on a leash. Samih Battikhi, then chief of the Mukhabarat, erupted in a rage when he saw Zarqawi's photo behind Powell at the UN Security Council.

"This is bullshit!" Battikhi shouted.

Abu Mutaz, the young counterterrorism officer who had once sought to influence Zarqawi's behavior, was sitting with a colleague in a Dead Sea hotel bar when Powell appeared on the TV screen talking about his former case.

"We were sick about it," Abu Mutaz said, recalling his reaction that day. "I kept asking, 'How could they do this? How can they think this way?' Eventually, I decided it must be politics. Just politics."

Even some of Zarqawi's old friends and allies in Amman were amazed by the turn of events. On Web sites that promote jihadist causes, Islamists swapped stories and gossip about Zarqawi's exploits, and bloggers wrote paeans to his courage and manhood, recalled Hasan Abu Hanieh, who knew Zarqawi in the 1990s.

"With that speech, Colin Powell gave him popularity and notoriety," said Abu Hanieh, the Islamist-turned-author from Amman. "Before anyone knew who he was, here was the secretary of state of the world's most powerful government saying Zarqawi was important. Now his fame would extend throughout the Arab world, from Iraq and Syria to the Maghreb and the Arabian Peninsula. People were joining al-Qaeda because of him."

It was one of the great ironies of the age, Abu Hanieh said. In deciding to use the unsung Zarqawi as an excuse for launching a new front in the war against terrorism, the White House had managed to launch the career of one of the century's great terrorists.

"And Zarqawi responded," Hanieh added, "by turning all their warnings about terrorism into reality."

Sam Faddis was in another part of Iraq in March 2003, when, more than a week after the start of the U.S. invasion, the Bush administration finally authorized an attack on Ansar al-Islam's camp. Dozens of Tomahawk missiles slammed into the compound at Sargat, leveling the buildings and destroying the equipment the Islamists used to mix their poisons. U.S. commandos, backed by hundreds of Kurdish militiamen, chased the remaining Islamists into hills, where some managed to scurry to safety across the Iranian border. From the dead and captured, the soldiers recovered passports and identity cards from more than a dozen countries, from Algeria to Yemen. But there was no sign of Zarqawi. Other CIA operatives later confirmed that the Jordanian had by then already moved to Baghdad to await the arrival of the U.S. troops.

Among the first Americans to enter the shattered Ansar camp was a CIA operative who had been among the eight members of Faddis's surveillance team. In his description to Faddis, the man described a ruined base and his sinking feeling that an opportunity had slipped away.

"Everybody who mattered left before we got there," the CIA officer told Faddis. "All that was left were the foot soldiers. The cannon fodder.

"It was better than nothing," he said. "But we missed our shot."

BOOK II

IRAQ

8

"No longer a victory"

The Iraqi officer was crying, again. He sat at the far side of the table, head cradled in shackled hands, sobbing with such abandon that he could be heard outside the small trailer that served as an interrogation cell. He cried until it was impossible to make out his words, if indeed there had been any.

Nada Bakos paused to see if the man could compose himself. The room was stifling and smelled of stale clothes and sweat, and a solitary air conditioner struggled vainly against the 110-degree Iraqi heat. Bakos was exhausted, mentally and physically, yet she resolved to keep her own emotions in check.

She tried the question again, calmly.

"Were you aware that Zarqawi was in the country?"

More sobs. Hasan al-Izbah, until recently a senior manager in Saddam Hussein's intelligence service, was a broken man, and it was unclear whether fear or humiliation had brought him to his current state. He would not look at the Iraqi translator, who politely repeated Bakos's questions, or the American MP who watched from the doorway. He could not bring himself to look anywhere near Bakos, as though being in the presence of an American CIA interrogator—and a female officer, at that—was a fate too embarrassing to contemplate.

Bakos tried a different angle.

"What kind of contact was there between Zarqawi and the Mukhabarat?"

Silence. This wasn't working.

Everything within Bakos's line of vision was steeped in dreariness: drab trailer walls, the salvaged furniture, the mottled greens and browns of the soldiers' desert-camo uniforms, the graying stubble of the prisoner's quivering chin. It was weeks after the fall of Baghdad and less than a month after her first face-to-face encounter with U.S-occupied Iraq. Now she spent her days in a bombed-cratered air base north of Baghdad, using whatever combination of charm, guile, and menace she could muster to glean secrets from men who until recently had been running spy operations for Iraq's intelligence service.

It was frustrating work, and not only because of the unrelenting grimness of the task, or because Bakos—who had never served in the military or in law enforcement—felt underqualified. What grated her most were the scripted questions from Washington and Langley, pushing her ever harder to find something that Bakos knew did not exist.

The mood in Baghdad was changing. Bakos and her fellow CIA officers could sense the shift during their still-unconstrained travels into the city's neighborhoods to meet contacts or visit a favorite ice-cream place. The smiles and shy waves of the early weeks of the occupation had long since been replaced by sullen stares and drawn shades. Iraq was rapidly tiring of occupation, while the Bush administration's attention seemed permanently fixed on settling the score with its political rivals in Washington. The moral underpinnings of the White House's war effort were collapsing like rotten timbers, and aides to the president were working furiously to control the damage. The weapons of mass destruction that had loomed so threateningly in Bush's speeches had not been found after four months of searching. Likewise, Americans had seen nothing of Saddam Hussein's supposed links to al-Qaeda and other terrorist groups. Congress was beginning to push for answers, and so, in the summer of 2003, the White House ratcheted up the pressure on the CIA's analysts to find some.

Washington was particularly interested in any gleanings from conversations with former senior security officials who would know about the Iraqi intelligence service's secret dealings with foreigners and might be persuaded to talk in exchange for money or special favors. "What are you learning about terrorist links?" Langley wanted to know.

"It doesn't stop," Bakos thought to herself, astonished and perplexed. Indeed, the questions continued throughout the rest of 2003 and the following year, and the next.

Occasionally, there would be a breakthrough of a sort: a statement from a detainee, or a recovered document that seemed to offer something definitive. Bakos witnessed one such moment, when a homesick Iraqi official was persuaded for a brief moment to reveal what he knew.

The question was, was anyone at the White House listening?

Bakos had volunteered for Iraq, despite her own misgivings about the war.

"We had invaded, and now it was all hands on deck," she remembered afterward.

She landed in May 2003 in a country that struck her as wild and chaotic and more than a little sinister for a young intelligence officer on her first war posting. The country itself was in better shape than she had imagined. Even after two wars and a decade of economic sanctions, Baghdad was largely intact, and certainly better off than some of the other Middle Eastern capitals she had visited. She drove to appointments on broad, palm-tree-lined avenues and well-engineered freeways with green directional signs that reminded her of the ones back home.

Life at work during the early months was a succession of long days in the interrogation trailer with breaks for meals and sleep. U.S. forces now held dozens of Saddam Hussein's generals and intelligence chiefs, some of whom would surely know the locations of any secret WMD stashes, or possess insight into terrorist plots that had been engineered with Iraqi support.

American officials hoped that some of them could be persuaded to cooperate if offered the right inducement, such as emigration papers or cash. Among these men, none appeared more promising on paper than the weeping Hasan al-Izbah. The Iraqi was not only a high-ranking intelligence official; he also happened to be Iraq's official liaison to Palestinian militants regarded by the West as terrorists. Saddam Hussein had openly backed violent groups such as the Abu Nidal Organization, in part to shore up his anti-Israel credentials with fellow Arabs. Someone within Saddam's spy agency could illuminate the murky world of Iraqi terrorist links, and perhaps it could be Izbah—if Bakos could persuade him to talk.

Bakos had sat across the table from numerous Iraqi officials during her first weeks in the country, but she had never met with one quite like this. He was surprisingly young, perhaps in his late thirties, and he bore little resemblance to the thuggish operatives who seemed to make up the bulk of Saddam's intelligence arm. Clean-shaven except for his prison stubble, and lacking even the standard-issue mustache worn by nearly all Iraqi government officials, he had the polished look of a Western business executive. But whatever confidence he might have had before the invasion had collapsed into soggy mush. When he wasn't crying during interrogations, he mostly shut down.

Bakos could see the man was frightened, and she leaned on her translator to try to discover why. Izbah's story was complicated, but more than anything he was afraid for his family, especially a young son. Saddam's Baath Party and its intelligence service had killed and tortured thousands of Iraqis over the decades. Now they were out of power, and survivors and relatives would be seeking revenge. What would happen to his children, especially with Izbah in prison?

Bakos thought briefly and offered a small gesture.

"If you help me," she said, "I can let you contact your family."

Izbah softened, thinking about the offer. Then he nodded his assent. The old regime was finished, and he had nothing to lose and potentially much to gain if he talked. Here, finally, was a chance to shine a torchlight into one of the deepest dungeons of Saddam's security network, guided by a man who knew every crevice.

Bakos guided Izbah through a web of Iraqi terrorist connections, letting him describe in detail the Palestinian and Iranian operatives that Saddam had supported over the years, at least until he grew weary of them and ordered them killed. But when the subject turned to al-Qaeda, Izbah shrugged. There was nothing to talk about, he said. Perhaps there had been a low-level meeting years earlier, a discreet encounter intended to size up the other side. But nothing had come of it. Iraq's secular regime persecuted and killed Islamic extremists, and al-Qaeda's leaders abhorred the Iraqi dictator. The distrust was too great to allow even the most rudimentary cooperation.

"What about Zarqawi?" Bakos finally asked.

"We had heard of him," Izbah said. "But there was no relationship."

Nothing at all? Bakos pressed further to see if Izbah would hedge his answer.

"If you had met him," she asked, "is he the kind of person you would have tried to recruit?"

The answer was simple and emphatic: "No."

Izbah had kept his promise, and now Bakos fulfilled hers. A phone was brought in, and the former spy chief was allowed to call his wife for the first time since his capture, weeks earlier. Bakos stayed in the room for a moment to make sure the call went through. When a voice came on the other end of the line, Izbah again broke down in a geyser of tears.

Leaving the Iraqi in the care of the American MP, she edged toward the door and slipped away.

The line of visa applicants outside the Jordanian Embassy was small for a Thursday, even one in scorching early August, when temperatures routinely top one hundred degrees before 10:00 a.m. Only a few dozen Iraqis had arrived by midmorning on August 7, 2003, forming a queue that hugged the shade of a concrete wall that ran along the front of the building. Dusty taxis and ancient sedans rolled to the curb to discharge passengers as the Iraqi guards, their uniforms already stained with sweat, gestured and barked with more than the usual gusto, evidence of a jitteriness that had infected the staff in the past twenty-four hours. A day earlier, someone had tossed a handwritten note over the wall, warning that the compound was about to come under attack.

The embassy's security detail had taken the note seriously, yet they were mystified by the strange threat. The kind of carnage that would soon become so familiar—the car bombs and suicide assailants that blew up outside mosques and marketplaces—was still unknown in Baghdad. And why would the embassy be singled out? Jordan, after all, was a brother Arab state that had deep historic and cultural ties with its Iraqi neighbor, and the embassy itself, a handsome two-story villa in one of Baghdad's most fashionable districts, served mainly to assist Iraqi travelers. Amman, so stable and so affordably close, had long been a preferred destination for middle-class families looking for a shopping holiday or simply an escape. The high demand for visas was the main reason the Jordanians erected the embassy's high wall, built not for security but to control the daily crowds that had become as much a part of the scenery as the palm trees along Arbataash Street.

And so the sudden appearance of a shabby green passenger van at the embassy's front gate stirred concern, but not panic. As the sentries watched, the young driver pulled to a spot within a few feet of the concrete barrier, then hopped out of the vehicle and began walking away from the embassy building at a fast clip. In the seconds before the guards could make their way over to investigate, the bomb hidden inside the van's cargo bay was detonated by remote control.

The blast was so powerful it sent the van's front section spiraling skyward to land on a rooftop two buildings down. It tore a thirty-foot hole in the embassy's barrier wall, killing guards and visa applicants and crumpling the frames of passing cars. The explosion shook a nearby children's hospital so violently that some doctors thought the hospital itself was under attack, until the waves of wounded began flooding the emergency ward. Seventeen bodies were recovered—all of them Iraqis—including entire families with children who were incinerated inside passing cars. The severed head of a young girl, her long hair scorched and tangled, lay in the street, discovered by passersby who covered it with cardboard and then, amid the horror and confusion, began frantically digging in the hard dirt to try to bury it.

Never, since the start of the U.S. invasion, had anyone deliberately attacked such an overtly civilian target. Across the capital, enraged Iraqis flailed at phantom suspects. Some blamed the Americans, citing rumors about a U.S. helicopter that had been seen firing a missile at the time of the explosion. Others faulted the Jordanians themselves, arguing that the monarchy had brought trouble to their country by secretly working against Saddam—or maybe, according to an opposing theory, by secretly working *with* Saddam. The crowd that gathered outside the wrecked embassy compound grew increasingly agitated until, at last, dozens of men surged into the building, smashing portraits of King Abdullah II and his father, King Husseln, and chasing embassy workers down the street.

At official levels, the reaction to the bombing was equally confused. Jordan's information minister speculated that the bombing was the work of an Iraqi political faction with grievances against the Jordanian monarchy. A Pentagon spokesman saw al-Qaeda behind the attack, though the Bush administration's security expert in Baghdad ruled out any role by the terrorist group. The most prescient observation came from L. Paul Bremer III, the Bush-appointed head of the Coalition Provisional Authority, who thought the blame might lie with foreign fighters connected with Ansar al-Islam, the Islamist extremist group that had operated in Iraq's remote northeastern mountains before the invasion. U.S. intelligence operatives were seeing evidence that some of Ansar's fighters had migrated into Iraqi cities to prepare to carry out attacks like this one.

"We may see more of this," Bremer said of the car bombing, in one of several interviews granted to American reporters that week. "We have seen a new technique for Iraq that we have never seen before."

Regardless of who was behind it, the attack deepened the unease that Iraqis and some Americans were beginning to feel. For U.S. soldiers, routine patrols through Iraqi neighborhoods were becoming ever more hazardous, with near-daily ambushes and sniper fire. Within hours of the embassy bombing, a buried bomb detonated as an American Humvee rolled past, killing two GIs and sparking a firefight that continued into the evening. Another soldier was fatally shot as he stood guard duty.

For ordinary Iraqis, the killings of innocents outside the embassy reinforced a sense of abandonment, a feeling that the American occupiers cared little about Iraqi self-governance and were unwilling or unable to provide basic security. "When Saddam was in power we could protect the embassies. Now there are no procedures to do that,"

Gatia Zahra, a young Iraqi police lieutenant told American journalists as he watched rescue workers pick through the embassy debris for body parts.

In Washington, U.S. officials promised to assist in the investigation while making clear that they regarded the bombing as an internal police matter for Iraqi authorities, and one of many inevitable bumps on the road to building a stable democracy. President George W. Bush felt compelled to interrupt his August vacation to reassure the country that his administration's Iraqi venture was on track.

"We've made good progress," he told White House pool reporters at his Crawford, Texas, ranch. "Iraq is more secure." Asked about comments by one Pentagon official suggesting that American forces might have to stay in Iraq for as long as two years, Bush declined to answer directly. "However long it takes to win the war on terror, this administration is committed to doing that," he said.

Bush's national security adviser, Condoleezza Rice, also brought up the bombing while speaking to a group of African American journalists that evening in Dallas. She suggested that the turmoil in Iraq was not unlike the birth pains experienced by Germany as it was refashioned into a democratic state after World War II.

"Remnants of the regime and other extremists are attacking progress—just as they did today with the bombing of the Jordanian Embassy," she said. "And coalition soldiers continue to face mortal dangers. But democracy is not easy."

This day had surely been one of the hardest. More people had died than on any single day since the war's combat phase had ended, and a new type of terrorism had emerged, one that targeted civilians with powerful explosives hidden in cars. It was all so contrary to the image presented by the White House—that of a reborn Iraq striding confidently toward stability and democracy—that Rice seemed to go out of her way to lower expectations.

"The road is hard," she said.

In fact, it was far harder than anyone at the White House had dared to imagine. Before August ended, Baghdad would see two more car bombings, each more destructive than the last. By the time the president returned to Washington in September, the nature of the conflict had radically, and permanently, changed.

—

The target of the second blast was perhaps the only foreigner in the Iraqi capital whom everyone genuinely liked. Sergio Vieira de Mello, the dashing Brazilian who headed the United Nations mission in Iraq, was a diplomat's diplomat, a savvy and experienced peacemaker who could be elegantly charming in five languages. Officially neutral on the war itself, he was the face of the international effort to put Iraq back together after the shooting ended. He was a tireless advocate for Iraqis, overseeing delivery of food and medicine while refereeing squabbles among Iraqi factions and between the Iraqis and the Americans. In the late summer of 2003, as temperatures and tensions soared, the man everyone knew as "Sergio" was the embodiment of dignified calm, as crisp as one of his trademark silk ties that never seemed to wilt or sag even on the hottest days.

Vieira de Mello was a frequent presence at the heavily fortified bases and converted palaces that served as command centers for the generals and civilian appointees who ran U.S.-occupied Iraq. Once, he stopped by the intelligence operations center where Nada Bakos worked, introducing himself to the CIA officers and getting into polite but pointed arguments with senior managers just beyond the earshot of the American analysts. But the diplomat insisted that UN offices be kept free of the symbols of military occupation. He set up his own command post in Baghdad's Canal Hotel, a low-slung building with arched windows used by UN agencies since the 1990s. A perimeter wall was hastily built after the fall of the Iraqi government, but visitors streamed through the compound gate without frisking or questioning by the mostly Iraqi guards. UN officials insisted that the Americans remove a military observation post that had been set up on the hotel's roof, as well as the U.S. Army truck that barricaded the narrow street that ran along the rear of the compound. "The presence of coalition forces does intimidate some of the people we need to speak to and work with," one of the mission's senior managers explained to reporters.

At 4:30 p.m. on August 19, 2003—twelve days after the Jordanian Embassy bombing—Vieira de Mello sat at his desk on the hotel's third floor, oblivious to the large flatbed truck racing its engine at the entrance to the same narrow alley that had until recently been blocked. Two foreign visitors and a handful of UN aides had arrived in the diplomat's suite for a meeting on Iraq's refugee crisis, and they had just finished introductions when an explosion sheered away the building's front side. The truck's driver had detonated a monstrous bomb rigged from old aircraft munitions, obliterating the vehicle and cleaving through three floors of UN offices like a knife through a layer cake.

"The explosion went off and we were thrown into the air," one of the foreign visitors, Gil Loescher, a Notre Dame University professor, said afterward. "Immediately the ceiling of the third floor collapsed upon us and we were thrown down, catapulted down, two floors to the first floor."

Loescher regained consciousness to find himself lying upside down with his legs crushed beneath ceiling debris. Vieira de Mello lay buried in rubble a few feet away, but he had managed to reach his cell phone to call for help. As the rescue team burrowed their way toward him, the diplomat slowly bled to death, becoming one of twenty-two people to die in the bombing. It was the deadliest attack ever on a United Nations facility.

The discovery of the young suicide bomber's body in the wreckage removed any doubt that the attack was the work of terrorists and not, as some U.S. officials initially suggested, an attempt at score settling by loyalists to the former Iraqi regime. Bush, in one of his first public statements on the bombing, acknowledged that "al-Qaeda-type fighters" appeared to be infiltrating the country. "They want to fight us there because they can't stand the thought of a free society in the Middle East," the president told reporters at a campaign fund-raiser three days after the Baghdad attack.

But which fighters?

While FBI teams combed the shattered UN building for bomb fragments to analyze, experts from the NSA and CIA began digging backward through vast troves of intercepted phone calls and texts, looking for any that might be linked to preparations for the bombing or to conversations between operatives after the deed was carried out. Nada Bakos, then in the home stretch of her first deployment to Iraq, was put in charge of sifting through preliminary findings and preparing reports for senior CIA and White House officials back in Washington.

A few of the calls picked up by the NSA's eavesdroppers made an immediate impression. They were brief, with limited small talk, clearly intended to relay messages. There were no names or place-names used, just vague references to a deed, along with what sounded like a congratulatory message.

"Brother," one of the callers said, "Allah was merciful today."

At the CIA, the agency's telecom sleuths traced the calls as far as they could, through digital signatures embedded in electronic phone records. The callers, it turned out, had used cell phones equipped with prepaid SIM cards stolen from a vendor in Switzerland. Who ultimately came to possess them, and how they ended up in Iraq, was anyone's guess.

It would be another ten days, and another gruesome bombing, before Bakos and the other analysts caught a break. The next strike was far worse than the others, and occurred not in Baghdad but in Najaf, a Shiite provincial capital and home to one of the most important shrines for the country's majority Shiite Muslim population.

August 29, 2003, was a Friday, the Muslim holy day, and huge crowds had jammed the city's gold-domed Imam Ali Mosque to hear a sermon by Ayatollah Mohammed Bakir al-Hakim, a highly influential Shiite cleric who had returned from exile in Iran in the weeks after the U.S. invasion. A moderate whose family had been persecuted by Saddam Hussein, the grandfatherly Hakim was regarded by U.S. military officials as a potential partner, a man who preached a message of unity and patience and seemed open to working with Iraq's U.S.-appointed interim council. On this day, the portly cleric climbed the mosque's minbar in his robe and turban to deliver a blunt critique of the occupation forces, decrying their failure to bring security to the country, and specifically mentioning the bombings at the Jordanian Embassy and UN headquarters. Iraqis should take responsibility for their own security with the support of the full population, the imam said. "We should join efforts in order to return full sovereignty to the Iraqi people by forming an Iraqi government," he said.

Hakim had just finished his sermon and was walking toward his motorcade when a car bomb exploded, followed quickly by a second. The blasts killed at least eighty-five people who had crowded the plaza for a glimpse of the cleric, and wounded more than five hundred. Thousands of worshippers and pilgrims fled the shrine in a panic, trampling over the dying and injured as they rushed the gates. Of Hakim, a man who had embodied the hopes of so many Iraqis as well as Americans, nothing identifiable was found except for a hand bearing the imam's wedding ring.

The shock from the assassination quickly reverberated across the country, igniting protests in several cities and dampening hopes for uniting Iraqis behind an interim governing council. In Baghdad, tens of thousands of people from the city's Shiite slums marched through Sunni neighborhoods, chanting "Death to Baathists!" and "No to America! No to Saddam! Yes, yes to Islam!" U.S. cable news stations interposed images of enraged protesters with video of an ill-timed visit to Iraq by Defense Secretary Donald Rumsfeld the same week. The Pentagon's top official repeated his now familiar line attributing the violence to "dead-enders" from Saddam Hussein's deposed regime, perhaps with help from Iranian-backed Hezbollah militants from Lebanon. Aside from these distractions, progress in Iraq had been "extraordinary," Rumsfeld insisted.

"Baghdad is bustling with commerce," he said.

At the battered shrine, meanwhile, yet another search for bomb fragments and other clues was beginning to yield results. Strewn across the vast debris field were pieces of old aircraft munitions and homemade wiring remarkably similar to those found after the bombings at the Jordanian Embassy and UN headquarters. The evidence increasingly pointed to a single actor: someone with significant bomb-making skills and a determination to wreak havoc.

The NSA's antennas again strained for signals, and now the Americans' surveillance bore important fruit. An intercepted phone call contained another congratulatory message: Allah had been "merciful" again. But this time the phone numbers lit up as a match in the CIA's database: the recipient of the call had also been telephoned after the bombing of the UN building. Moreover, the CIA now knew more about the batch of SIM cards from Switzerland. One of the electronic chips had been found on a Syrian man arrested a few days earlier. The man, a self-described Islamist, had admitted to traveling to Iraq to wage jihad. He claimed to be the disciple of a Jordanian holy warrior, one whom foreign fighters called Zarqawi.

Bakos, back at Langley recovering from her first Iraq tour, followed the reports of foreign fighters moving in Baghdad and wondered if Zarqawi was among them. Now it was clear: the intercepted calls linked him not only to the Najaf carnage but also to the UN attack, and perhaps the embassy bombing as well. Somehow, just five months after the destruction of the Ansar al-Islam training camp, Zarqawi had managed to move his network into a strange capital and build an operation with sufficient intelligence-gathering, firepower, and logistical support to carry out a chain of sophisticated, large-scale terrorist attacks in close succession. Zarqawi was not only part of the worsening violence in Iraq, he was helping direct it.

Bakos studied the reports and prepared to write the summary that would be included in the next day's briefing papers for the White House. By now the essential conclusion looked solid: Abu Musab al-Zarqawi was behind the attacks. The terrorist the Bush administration had cited as a reason for attacking Saddam Hussein had in fact become empowered by the Iraqi leader's defeat. A minor worry before, when he was confined to a remote corner of Iraq's northern mountains, now he had been set loose in the Iraqi heartland and was becoming more menacing by the day.

Much later, intelligence officials and terrorism experts who studied the early war years marveled at Zarqawi's strategic cunning. Whether deliberately or by coincidence, he picked targets that would confound U.S. ambitions for Iraq and ensure that the occupation of the country would be long and painful. The opening salvo against an Arab embassy would effectively discourage other Muslim nations from participating in Iraq's rebuilding in a way that might give the Americans legitimacy. That blow was followed by two others that, in sequence, showed "brilliant strategy," said Bruce Riedel, a senior CIA terrorism analyst who went on to advise two U.S. presidents.

"By attacking the UN, he drove out all the nongovernmental organizations and discouraged anyone from opening an embassy," Riedel said. "Then he went after the Shia-Sunni fault line with attacks on the Shiite mosques.

"So first he isolated us in Iraq," Riedel said, "then he put us in the midst of a civil war."

It was too early to draw such conclusions in August 2003, so Nada Bakos simply wrote what she knew, trying to avoid thinking about the trouble her report would surely cause at senior levels of the Bush administration.

Bakos's supervisors pressed her repeatedly on the details. No one was anxious to break the news to the White House that Zarqawi was responsible for the killings, Bakos recalled later.

"Take another day," she was urged by one of her supervisors. "We're not writing this unless we're absolutely sure."

The edits and rewrites continued through the day and well into the night. It was after midnight when the draft was finished, and nearly 3:00 a.m. by the time Bakos returned to her apartment for a few hours' sleep.

Hers was just a single report, but it ran contrary to the administration's official narrative for the war. Some in the White House would find it threatening, she knew, and perhaps would try to bury it. But it was the truth.

"It's why we were being so cautious," Bakos said. "We knew there would be push-back, because what we were telling them meant that this was no longer a victory. It was a freaking nightmare."

9

"So you guys think this is an insurgency?"

A few days after the bombing of the UN building, Robert Richer was driving home from Canada after a long-deferred family vacation when his CIA phone rang. On the line was one of the agency's brief ers, working on detail to the White House, anxious to know about an alarming document that had just made its way to the president's desk.

The president wants to know if the agency stands by this report—the one about the beginning of an insurgency in Iraq, the briefer said.

Richer, who happened to be crossing the Ambassador Bridge from Windsor, Ontario, to Detroit at the time, waited until he was on the American side to pull over. Yes, he knew the report, he said. He had personally signed off on it just a few days before.

"It's factual," said Richer, the CIA's former station chief in Jordan, who had now risen to become chief of the agency's Near East Division. "It's the chief of station's view. We stand behind the analysis."

The tension on the other end of the line was palpable, even from five hundred miles away. The White House did not like the use of the word "insurgency" in conjunction with a war that President George W. Bush had declared essentially won. Anyone with a casual interest in the news could see that violence in Iraq had grown dramatically worse since the early summer. Besides the string of spectacular car bombings, American soldiers were dying at a rate of more than ten a week from snipers' bullets and hidden roadside bombs. But "insurgency" was a dangerous word, conjuring up images of Vietnam and endless guerrilla warfare. At National Security Council meetings, the Pentagon's civilian managers ran PowerPoint presentations highlighting provinces in Iraq that were relatively peaceful. The attacks elsewhere in the country were isolated and scattered, the work of a few Baathist holdouts loyal to Saddam Hussein, who was then still in hiding. "How important are these?" asked an aide to Defense Secretary Donald Rumsfeld at one such meeting attended by Richer.

How important? Richer, who made frequent visits to Baghdad's CIA station, was incredulous. Real important, he thought to himself. "We're seeing it every day," he told colleagues.

That Iraq harbored terrorists was beyond dispute. But no one had dared used the word "insurgency" to describe the conflict until August 30, 2003. On that day, the CIA's Baghdad station chief, Gerry Meyer, dashed off a cable to headquarters just hours after the double explosions that killed the Shiite cleric Ayatollah Mohammed Bakir al-Hakim and scores of worshippers at the mosque in Najaf. The secret cable was called an "aardwolf," spy-speak for a kind of formal assessment for headquarters from one of the agency's field stations. Meyer, having witnessed the effects of August's trio of car bombings, warned that the conflict was rapidly entering a perilous new phase. Foreign jihadists were beginning to pour into Iraq, drawn by the prospect of a fight against Americans, and aligning with shadowy groups intent on unleashing mayhem to destabilize the country and discredit the U.S. occupiers and their Iraqi supporters. The emergence of this insurgent army could potentially reverse the progress of the past five months, Meyer wrote. Moreover, with the new arrivals, waves of future suicide bombers were already in the country, poised for attacks that would be carried out regardless of whether Saddam Hussein was caught.

The report's stark tone caught White House officials by surprise and drew a loud dissent from the administration's point man in Baghdad, L. Paul Bremer III, the diplomat who ran the Coalition Provisional Authority. Bremer complained that the report's conclusions were overdrawn and excessively negative, and it was his reaction that prompted the CIA to track down Richer on his vacation.

"There was a firestorm," recalled Richer, who retired from the agency in 2005. "The CIA is saying that an insurgency is developing, and now the White House is pissed off." In effect, he said, two versions of reality were colliding in Iraq: the one witnessed by the agency's spies, and another that sought to reinforce the message communicated so dramatically by Bush in May on the deck of the aircraft carrier USS *Abraham Lincoln*

"The problem for the White House," Richer said, "was that the president had just landed on a ship to say that we had won."

For now, Meyer's report would simply be ignored. It would be another ten weeks and scores of additional deaths before the president's top national security aides sat down again to debate whether the use of the word "insurgency" was appropriate in describing the conflict in Iraq. More months passed before the White House acknowledged that there actually was one.

If Abu Musab al-Zarqawi could have dictated a U.S. strategy for Iraq that suited his own designs for building a terrorist network, he could hardly have come up with one that surpassed what the Americans themselves put in place over the spring and summer of 2003.

Countless articles and books have documented the Bush administration's missteps, from the refusal to halt massive looting after the invasion to the wholesale dismantling of the Iraqi military and security structure by Bremer's CPA. But no Americans appreciated the magnitude of the blunders more than the intelligence officers and U.S. diplomats in Iraq who were watching Zarqawi's organization gain momentum.

Years later, CIA officials who were brought into the final planning for the March 2003 invasion expressed astonishment at the lack of forethought on how the country would be managed after Saddam Hussein's deposal. Junior officers were pressed into service at the eleventh hour to draft papers on possible risks U.S. soldiers could face in attempting to preserve order in occupied Iraq. But by then it was already too late to affect the outcome.

"Right before the invasion, I asked the Pentagon, 'Is anyone writing policy on force protection?' The answer was no, so I said I'd do it," said one former CIA analyst who was enlisted to help. "I was doing military analysis because they had literally no one doing it on the inside."

Weeks later, as Baghdad skidded into lawlessness, a brief window of opportunity slammed shut. One State Department official, who was among the first to arrive in the Iraqi capital after the city fell, said the initial greeting from Iraqi citizens was not so different from the exultant reception the Bush administration officials had predicted before the war.

"The thing is, people really were glad to see us," said "Mike," a retired diplomat whose employment as a security contractor excluded him from using his real name. "No actual flowers were thrown, because that culture doesn't throw flowers. But every night there was celebratory gunfire, and as I would travel around Baghdad, everyone was delighted to see us."

But Iraqi views hardened after weeks of frenzied looting of everything from government offices to priceless museum artifacts to the rebar on newly constructed buildings, Mike said. Having neither the mandate nor the military-police brigades to restore order, U.S. forces came across as both impotent and indifferent to Iraqi perceptions of injustice and suffering. More Iraqis began viewing the occupying troops with a suspiciousness bordering on contempt.

"We had created a black hole," he said.

The failure to provide security after the invasion had been a sin of omission: U.S. officials had not anticipated the breakdown in civil authority that would follow the invasion. By contrast, the decisions to dissolve the Iraqi army and ban Baath Party members from positions of authority were as deliberate as they were misguided. In Saddam Hussein's Iraq, anyone seeking a management job—from school principal or police captain to the head of the intelligence service—was obliged to join the Baath Party. So were applicants for Iraq's universities. Overnight, tens of thousands of professional workers and experienced bureaucrats were out of work, and U.S. officials in Iraq found themselves confronting two mammoth problems. One was an absence of the kinds of local security agencies best equipped to preserve order and root out illicit networks. The other was a large contingent of embittered and well-connected Iraqi officials who now had to fend for themselves without salaries or pensions.

"We put these people out on the streets—people who had the tools and knew how to use them," Richer said, recalling his exasperation over the de-Baathification decision—the CPA's "Order No. 1" issued on May 16, 2003. "We put them out there without paychecks. Some of them had fifteen or twenty years in the military, and we didn't even let them collect their pensions."

It was in this reordered Iraq that Zarqawi would find both freedom to maneuver and powerful allies willing and able to support his cause. Captains and sergeants who once served Saddam Hussein now enlisted in Zarqawi's army, and some rose to leadership positions. Others offered safe houses, intelligence, cash, and weapons, including, investigators later concluded, the aerial munitions and artillery shells that provided the explosive force for Zarqawi's biggest car bombs.

Except in the CIA's classified reports, Zarqawi's role in the Iraq insurgency was still largely unknown. The agency's analysts disagreed on key details, including whether the terrorist was in Iraq or perhaps directing events from Syria or some other foreign city. But throughout the fall of 2003, as officials in Washington debated whether an insurgency existed in Iraq, the run of spectacular attacks continued.

On September 22, the UN headquarters in Baghdad was struck for a second time, though by this date many of its employees had already left the country. A security guard was killed, and nineteen people were wounded.

On October 12, a Toyota Corolla barreled past security barriers and exploded outside the lobby of the Baghdad Hotel, a luxury high-rise in a neighborhood of pharmacies and doctors' offices. Six people were killed and more than thirty wounded, including three U.S. soldiers.

Most dramatically, on October 27, terrorists launched a wave of coordinated suicide bombings across Baghdad, striking the headquarters of the International Committee of the Red Cross and four police stations. At least thirty-six people were killed, including an American GI, and two hundred people were wounded.

On November 10, the CIA's Baghdad station chief sat down again to describe the unraveling security situation in a formal report to headquarters. The images Gerry Meyer sketched this time were even more dire. The insurgency he described was not only real, it was winning. The terrorists, with help from Baathist allies, were well supplied and appeared capable of moving freely, with little fear of either American troops or the hastily reconstituted but ineffective local police departments. In the eyes of ordinary Iraqis they appeared to be powerful and "largely unchallenged," he wrote, eroding any lingering hope that American military might be able to stabilize the country.

"The ease with which the insurgents move and exist . . . is bolstering their self-confidence further," Meyer wrote, according to a version of the "aardwolf" obtained by American journalists soon after it was transmitted to Langley. As for the terrorists' supporters— disaffected Sunni Muslims and former officers of Saddam Hussein's security establishment—they had been handed a perfect opportunity to regroup, the station chief said. "The continued sense of isolation in the Sunni heartland, the complete dissolution of the army and other institutions of security, rigid de-Baathification, and the lack of economic opportunities or political direction gave these regime elements the confidence they needed to repair their networks and reestablish themselves," the report said.

Meyer's brutal candor caused some of his colleagues to fear for his job, and, sure enough, the new report infuriated senior Bush aides, prompting accusations that the CIA was trying to undermine the president politically, with an election year just getting under way.

On November 11—the Veterans Day holiday for government employees—the White House convened a second meeting to kick around Meyer's latest report and its implications. Robert Richer was again summoned, this time in person, along with CIA director George Tenet and his top deputy, John McLaughlin, Defense Secretary Donald Rumsfeld, and other national security aides. The president began the meeting with a blunt question to the CIA contingent.

"So you guys think this is an insurgency?" he asked.

McLaughlin began a prepared briefing framed around the question "Who is the enemy?" But when he used the word "insurgent," a skeptical Rumsfeld interrupted.

"Define 'insurgency,' " he demanded.

McLaughlin and other CIA officials began ticking off a list of components of a classic insurgency from a standard Pentagon field manual. Iraq, they said, was facing an organized resistance movement that sought to overthrow central authority through subversion and armed conflict. They described the collusion between domestic opponents and foreign terrorists and highlighted what was known about the movement's leadership, tactics, and weapons. According to one participant, the Defense Department's representatives were unmoved.

"The military wasn't interested in hearing this," the official recalled years later. "They were hoping they were done with the war, and they didn't go in for any talk about insurgencies."

Bush, by contrast, was thoughtfully quiet. His parting comment as the meeting ended suggested that he had accepted the turn of events in Iraq, even if he wasn't ready to talk about it publicly.

"I don't want any commentary," he said.

One month later, the White House enjoyed a brief respite from the tide of grim news with the announcement of the capture of Saddam Hussein during a December 13, 2003, raid on a remote farmhouse near his hometown of Tikrit. But the former dictator's arrest brought no relief from the now daily attacks on coalition troops and Iraqi civilians. Zarqawi, after months of fighting from the shadows, was gaining confidence as the de-facto leader of a full-blown insurgency in Iraq. His movement, now supported by thousands of embittered Iraqis and sympathetic Islamists from across the Muslim world, would soon pose the greatest single threat to American ambitions in Iraq.

Gerry Meyer, the man who had warned of the growing insurgency in two CIA reports, did not survive in his post as Baghdad station chief long enough to see the uprising come to full flower. Within weeks of his November 10 report, he was relieved of command and ordered back to Washington.

For years afterward, when CIA officials would dissect the mistakes of the war's early months, some would marvel at the improbable confluences that enabled Zarqawi to achieve so much so quickly. Like a seed stirred up by a vile wind, the Jordanian had landed at precisely the right time in a patch of soil that had been perfectly prepared to enable him to take root.

"The fertile soil was Iraq after de-Baathification," Richer said. "The rain and sunshine were the ineptitude of the provisional authority and U.S. misunderstanding of Iraqis and their culture.

"All of that," he said, "allowed Zarqawi to blossom and grow."

The lushest swath of Iraqi soil for sprouting an insurgency turned out to be a band of dusty towns and villages north and west of the capital. Within the boundaries of the region that became known as the Sunni Triangle, anxiousness about the American invasion turned quickly to resentment and then, for some, to open hostility.

Zaydan al-Jabiri, a tribal leader with a large sheep ranch near Ramadi, vividly remembered the day he lost faith in the Americans as liberators, or even as an improvement on Saddam Hussein's police state. It was April 28, 2003, nearly three weeks after Baghdad fell, and three days before U.S. president George W. Bush's "mission accomplished" speech. The forty-year-old sheikh had been watching closely for clues about how the occupation forces would manage commerce—prolonged curfews and travel restrictions could be disastrous for a man who traded in wool and fresh mutton. Like many in his Dulaim tribe, he had been willing to give the newcomers a chance. Then came the event that changed everything.

Until that day, a Monday, Zaydan had seen little of the Americans invaders. The columns of tanks with their coffee-stain desert camouflage had deliberately avoided the provincial cities during the early phases of the campaign, but now they were backtracking, clearing out any lingering resistance and consolidating their lines. On April 23, soldiers from the Eighty-second Airborne Division and Third Armored Calvary Regiment had rolled into the nearby city of Fallujah and set up camp inside government buildings and a school. On the evening of April 28, a crowd of about two hundred protesters defied a citywide curfew and gathered outside the school building, chanting and yelling at U.S. paratroopers inside. The Americans would later say that some in the crowd had brandished weapons, and shots were fired. In any case, the GIs opened up with a volley that killed seventeen demonstrators and wounded seventy. Investigators from Human Rights Watch later found no evidence of bullet damage to the school where the troops were staying. Iraqis were outraged, but Zaydan was among the tribal officials who counseled restraint. "We tried with all our might not to create problems with the Americans," he would say years later. After gathering informally to discuss a solution, the heads of the major clans from central Anbar Province picked emissaries to meet with the U.S. commanders in Fallujah.

"We went to them and we said, 'We are tribes, and we can have a tribal solution: you pay *diyya*—blood money,'" Zaydan recalled. "'These [victims] had families, some had kids. Pay the families money to guarantee their future, so their kids won't be part of the resistance.'"

The reply came days later. Yes, the United States was willing to compensate the victims' families. The rate was set at three thousand dollars for each dead Iraqi.

Zaydan was furious. "Three thousand dollars? That's what you pay to replace one of your police dogs!" he fumed.

"After that, we realized that the Americans had no good intentions," he said.

It was the first of a series of unhappy encounters for Zaydan, a man who might have seemed a likely ally to any army that toppled Saddam Hussein. He had been barely thirty years old when members of his tribal family decided to back a coup attempt, organized by an Iraqi air force general from a prominent Anbar clan, against the dictator. When the plot was discovered, Saddam rounded up and executed more than 150 army officers and detained more than a thousand other Iraqi Sunnis, including Zaydan and one of his brothers. Zaydan, condemned to die with the others, was granted clemency at the last minute, in a general pardon intended to repair relations with the powerful Sunni tribes that had long helped Saddam stay in power.

Yet, even after the death sentence, and despite his deep antipathy for many of the dictator's policies, Zaydan settled into an odd ambivalence toward the Iraqi leader. He admired Saddam's toughness. He privately cheered his fearless defiance of the West, which for many Sunnis evoked a glorious past when Iraq was part of a mighty empire, and Baghdad was a global center of science and learning. For all their technology, the Americans were arrogant upstarts, with little appreciation for the cultural richness of a land that had given birth to written language, mathematics, astronomy, and the law. Iraq was not a mere product of lines drawn on a colonial map, whose value lay in the oil buried beneath its sands. It was a country of tribes that traced their lineage to the beginning of civilization itself.

"The Americans and their media made us imagine that Iraq would never be Iraq until Saddam Hussein went away," Zaydan said. "Iraq is seven thousand years old. America is only two hundred years old. It's like comparing a Mercedes to a Hyundai."

Still, Zaydan saw little point in opposing the American invasion, even after the killings in Fallujah, just forty miles from his ranch. "We're not an army," he said, "and we didn't want to look like we were defending the regime." But as the occupation neared its first anniversary, his concerns about U.S. intentions multiplied. It was clear to Zaydan's mind that the Americans intended to stay indefinitely. Worse, they had stripped power from Iraq's long-dominant Sunni tribes and handed it over to Shiites, leaders Zaydan viewed as "thieves and bandits" whose true allegiance lay with Iran. In Baghdad, Sunnis were being targeted by roving bands of Shiite militiamen. Zaydan watched with conflicted emotions as other members of his tribe formed secret cells, initially for self-defense but later to engage in hit-and-run attacks against American troops. Stories began to circulate about a mysterious Jordanian who paid hard cash to any Iraqis who joined his movement. Zaydan would never swear allegiance to the jihadist who called himself Zarqawi. But others in the Dulaim clan did.

The sheikh tried to meet once more with American military commanders in Fallujah. It was on July 4, as he later remembered, and he showed up unannounced with other tribal leaders, bearing a gift: flowers to commemorate the American holiday. The marine officer who met with the Iraqis struck Zaydan as agitated and suspicious, perhaps with good reason: Iraqi leaders generally visited the base to make a request, usually for compensation for some kind of injury or damage. Years afterward, Zaydan could not recall the reason for the meeting, but he still remembered the argument that ensued.

At one point, the American commander managed to insult his visitors with a comment that seemed to lump together Iraqis and terrorists. One of the sheikhs, angered, accused the Americans of being dupes of Ahmad Chalabi, the exiled Shiite politician who provided the Bush administration with faulty intelligence about weapons of mass destruction.

"We know you were deceived by Chalabi into coming to Iraq!" one of the sheikhs declared.

Zaydan tried to smooth things over, but it was clear that the meeting was over. More insults followed, and one of the Iraqis banged the table loudly.

As he got up to leave, Zaydan was struck by the impossible gulf between the man in the camouflage and the Iraqis in their tribal dress. Even when they used the same vocabulary, somehow the words were not the same.

As the Iraqis were leaving, Zaydan managed a parting word to the marine commander.

"You'll never be able to stay in Iraq," he said.

A conflagration had begun, Zaydan saw, and he would do nothing to stand in its way.

"This," he said later, "is when the real battle started."

10

"Revolting is exactly what we want"

In January 2004, some ten months after his arrival in Baghdad, Abu Musab al-Zarqawi sat at a keyboard to compose a letter to Osama bin Laden. It had been two years since his departure from Afghanistan, and almost four years since the al-Qaeda founder had refused to meet him in person at his Kandahar compound. But now Zarqawi was ready to offer a truce.

He opened with a sentimental flourish.

"Even if our bodies are far apart, the distance between our hearts is close," he wrote to the author of the September 11, 2001, terrorist attacks.

A lot had happened since their last communication, and Zarqawi felt compelled to account for his time in Iraq, as though Bin Laden had somehow missed the news of the insurgency. The situation in Iraq was different from anything the two commanders had experienced in Afghanistan, he said, both in good ways (Iraqis spoke Arabic) and bad (awful terrain, with few hiding places). Zarqawi maintained that he was making good progress in the campaign he had started, and he hoped that Bin Laden might be willing to help. But first he would offer a jihadist's view of the battlefield and a sketch of the major combatants, including his own small army.

He started with the Americans. For all their firepower, he said, they were "the most cowardly of God's creatures," uninterested in a real fight and preferring to remain on their bases. But they'd be gone soon enough, he predicted, leaving the country and the war to others.

As for Iraqi's Sunni minority—the group most likely to be sympathetic to his cause—Zarqawi was equally scornful. The Sunnis were leaderless and divided, "more wretched than orphans at the tables of the depraved," he said. Even the Iraqi soldiers who joined the jihadists lacked real experience in fighting and preferred lobbing grenades or firing occasional mortar rounds to confronting the enemy directly.

"The Iraqi brothers still prefer safety and returning to the arms of their wives, where nothing frightens them," Zarqawi wrote. "Sometimes the groups have boasted among themselves that not one of them has been killed or captured. We have told them in our many sessions with them that safety and victory are incompatible, that the tree of triumph and empowerment cannot grow tall and lofty without blood and defiance of death."

Turning to the country's Shiite majority, Zarqawi launched into a bile-spewing screed that continued for pages.

"The insurmountable obstacle, the lurking snake, the crafty and malicious scorpion, the spying enemy, and the penetrating venom," he wrote, straining with his metaphors. He dismissed Iraq's majority religion as worse than paganism, having "nothing in common with Islam except in the way that Jews have something in common with Christians under the banner of the People of the Book." Shiites had designs on destroying the Sunni faith, and they had craftily allied themselves with the U.S. occupiers.

"They have been a sect of treachery and betrayal throughout history and throughout the ages," Zarqawi declared.

Bin Laden was an odd choice to receive such a rant. Though Sunni himself, the al-Qaeda founder saw himself as a unifier of Muslims and had never expressed interest in attacking Shiite innocents. In fact, he had condemned it, as Zarqawi doubtlessly already knew. Perhaps the Jordanian believed he could change Bin Laden's mind, for he proceeded to the heart of his message: a plan for a coming battle that called for killing Shiites in even greater numbers. Such a campaign, he argued, would simultaneously achieve three objectives: destabilizing Iraq, eliminating a hateful apostasy, and, most important, forcing Sunnis to take up arms in a war that would lead to their liberation—a war that he would ignite—an "awaking of the slumberer and rousing of the sleeper."

> The solution that we see, and God the Exalted knows better, is for us to drag the Shi'a into the battle because this is the only way to prolong the fighting between us and the infidels. . . . The only solution is for us to strike the religious, military, and other cadres among the Shi'a with blow after blow until they bend to the Sunnis. Someone may say that, in this matter, we are being hasty and rash and leading the [Islamic] nation into a battle for which it is not ready, a battle that will be revolting and in which blood will be spilled. This is exactly what we want.

Now Zarqawi had a favor to ask: His organization, though small, had been behind nearly all the major terrorist attacks in Iraq, excluding the far-northern cities—twenty-five strikes in all, according to his count. But he could accomplish much more with al-Qaeda's official endorsement and global resources, he argued. "All that we hope is that we will be the spearhead, the enabling vanguard, and the bridge on which the Islamic nation crosses over to the victory that is promised," he wrote. If Bin Laden agreed with Zarqawi's strategy—"if you adopt it as a program and road, and if you are convinced of the idea of fighting the sects of apostasy"—then Zarqawi was prepared to swear allegiance. "We will be your readied soldiers, working under your banner, complying with your orders," he said.

If the alliance was not to be, there would be no hard feelings, Zarqawi assured Bin Laden. But either way, the al-Qaeda leader would be hearing from him. Very soon, he said, he would step out of the shadows and publicly announce himself to the world.

"We have been waiting until we have enough weight on the ground," he said. Now, at last, "the decisive moment approaches."

On a chilly February night a few weeks after Zarqawi composed his letter, Brigadier General Stanley McChrystal rested on the staircase of a darkened townhouse in Fallujah, in the violent heartland of the Iraqi insurgency, listening to his soldiers as they swept from room to room, searching for fighters and hidden weapons caches. At that very moment, the object of his search also waited in darkness, straining to interpret sounds: the low rumble of idling diesel engines, the banging of metal against wood, the shouts in American English, the barking dogs, the crunch of heavy boots against glass.

By sheer luck, the commander of U.S. special forces in Iraq had delivered a team of commandos to the very housing block where Iraq's most dangerous terrorist had lain sleeping. The two men were less than 150 feet apart, separated only by a couple of thin concrete walls and the blackness of a city that had been mostly without electricity since the U.S. invasion nearly a year before.

"I was likely standing less than a block from Abu Musab al-Zarqawi," McChrystal acknowledged afterward.

It had been just another in an endless string of raids that winter, targeting an insurgency that even the most optimistic in Washington could no longer deny. The Pentagon had established teams of special-forces operators with responsibility for rooting out cells of the local and foreign fighters behind Iraq's worsening violence. The man now in charge of the mission was widely regarded as a soldier's soldier, the kind who occasionally went along on dangerous midnight raids in hostile territory. Now forty-nine, McChrystal had himself been one of the army's elite soldiers, a member of the storied Seventy-fifth Ranger Regiment, known for its "further, faster, harder" credo and a history of achievement stretching from Normandy's beaches to the Battle of Mogadishu, depicted in the book and film *Black Hawk Down.* A distance runner known for his legendary self-discipline—he regularly ran seven to eight miles a day, ate a single meal, and slept no more than four hours a night—McChrystal had landed the job as chief of the U.S. Joint Special Operations Command, or JSOC, barely four months earlier. Now he was channeling his prodigious energy into the search for the terrorist gaining renown among Iraqi Sunnis as the fiercest foe of the American occupation.

On this night, the plan called for a perilous house-to-house search in one of the most dangerous neighborhoods in all of Iraq. In just over a month, Fallujah would become forever associated with the deaths of four American security contractors who were ambushed and then dismembered, dragged through the streets and burned, with their bodies left dangling from a Euphrates River bridge. But for now the night's destination was just another GPS coordinate on McChrystal's battle map, a location that had been flagged by military intelligence and needed to be checked and crossed off the list. The general strapped on his pistol and climbed into a Humvee with the others in the team, intending not to fight but to observe.

This was to be no stealth raid. Rather than swooping into the village by helicopter, McChrystal and his team made the journey from Baghdad in a convoy of Humvees and armored trucks, lumbering noisily along on unlit streets and then to the Highway 1 expressway that heads west toward Jordan and Syria. They rode for an hour on nearly empty freeway, pulling off at the point where the desert gives way to the flat roofs and scrawny palms of Fallujah's outer suburbs. Finding the first target house in the dark, the Delta Force soldiers tossed flash-bang grenades through the door and blitzed from room to room with wordless precision.

McChrystal stepped through the doorway of one house as a weapon search was under way. The lights were on here, so the commander flipped up his night-vision goggles and watched as his soldiers interrogated a group of Iraqi men who had been rousted from sleep. In the next room were the women and children, most of them sitting up on futons swaddled in blankets to ward off the cold. The children looked up at the lanky American with obvious curiosity. But in the eyes of the women he saw something else—an intensity of emotion that would stick with him for years.

"It was pure, unadulterated hatred," McChrystal said.

This was the first time McChrystal had lingered inside an occupied house as his men worked through it. There would be many such encounters to come, and they left an indelible impression. Once, during a raid in Ramadi, the GIs rounded up several men from a suspected safe house and forced them to lie facedown on the concrete with their hands behind their heads. From inside the house appeared a small boy of about four years. Seeing his father lying on the ground, the boy walked between the rows of prostrate men and, without a word, lay down next to his father, placing his tiny hands behind his head.

"We're still thinking of ourselves as liberators," McChrystal said afterward. "But you've got these big guys—huge, in their body armor—carrying weapons, turning over mattresses. We weren't trashing furniture. We weren't tossing the place. But you can imagine someone coming into your house, with your wife and kids there, and going through your drawers. I remember thinking, 'What if this was my house?' It's a memory you would keep with you forever." The searchers finished their work, and the crashing and shouting moved farther down the block.

As the commando teams progressed to the next house, a solidly built figure in dark clothes slid open a second-floor window and dropped into the dark alley below. Picking himself up, he felt his way to a back street and vanished, perhaps heading north over the railroad tracks, or hiding in the shadows to wait the Americans out. Only later, after finding his cast-off belongings, did the Americans learn how close they had come to capturing Zarqawi.

It was an opportunity missed, one that might have altered the history of the war. It would be more than a year before American troops would again come this close.

Zarqawi's escape was disappointing to the new special-forces commander, even though he and other American generals had not yet imagined how destructive the Jordanian would become. Later, in his memoir, McChrystal recalled his first Fallujah mission as a relatively tranquil time, "before Iraq became truly hellish as it turned into a civil war."

"The bloody consequences of our failure were not immediately apparent," he wrote. "On that night, Zarqawi was not yet Iraq's bane."

Yet McChrystal could see the contours of battles to come. In the eyes of an Iraqi family, he had glimpsed the raw emotion that Zarqawi—or someone like him—could exploit in raising money and volunteers. The raids on civilian houses, though necessary, were only deepening the rage that many Iraqis felt after months of blackouts, sewage overflows, and chronic job shortages, all of it "producing fury, most understandably directed at us," he wrote.

"With calculated barbarism, Zarqawi was already at work exploiting our failures, making us look powerless or sinister, or both,"

McChrystal said. "His disappearance into the dark that night was troubling, but I was consumed with this Iraqi family. Watching them watch us, I realized this fight was going to be long and tough."

But to begin such a fight, McChrystal had to build a force equal to the task of rooting out an insurgent network hidden across a province the size of New York State. Not since Vietnam had an American army faced a challenge like this one, and the army and marine units spread across Iraq in early 2004 were nowhere near prepared.

McChrystal was himself learning the job on the fly. In his rapid ascent through the ranks, he had gained a reputation as something of a troubleshooter, an innovative thinker who excelled at spotting dysfunction within an organization and was never shy about shaking things up.

Born into an army family—his father was a major general, and all five of his siblings either served or married into the military—McChrystal had been a brilliant underachiever as a youth, earning admission to West Point but also racking up a hundred demerits for drinking and insubordination. His decision to enter Special Forces School had seemed at best a detour for an officer looking to climb the promotional ladder. But McChrystal repeatedly impressed his superiors with his extraordinary drive and his penchant for challenging the status quo. His self-discipline—and an insistence on high standards for those under his command—earned him a nickname that would stick: the Pope.

McChrystal was promoted to brigadier general a few months before the September 11, 2001, terrorist attacks, and he briefly helped direct the U.S. military campaign in Afghanistan before being tapped as vice director of operations for the Pentagon's Joint Chiefs of Staff. When the Iraq war began, he was chosen to do the daily televised briefings from the Pentagon for the news media. He stood at the podium on April 14, 2003, when the Pentagon formally announced the Iraqi government's capitulation. "I would anticipate that the major combat engagements are over," he said.

Just six months later, he was in Iraq, commanding a hybrid force of elite commandos and intelligence officers in a military campaign that was only getting started. Indeed, as McChrystal and his team made their first visits to key command posts over the late fall and winter, the entire country appeared to be slipping into disarray. Even in Mosul, the ethnically divided northern city once championed as a model for effective U.S.-led reconstruction, the army's grasp of security was weakening. The city had been seized and occupied by 101st Airborne Division troops under the command of then Major General David Petraeus, who moved quickly to reopen government facilities and schools, rebuild the local security force, and repair infrastructure. But soon after Petraeus turned over the city to a smaller American garrison in January 2004, insurgents moved in. Gunmen even shot down one of the helicopters in McChrystal's entourage during one of his visits to the region.

So much had gone wrong, so quickly. Yet, as he settled into his first headquarters at the Baghdad International Airport, McChrystal was startled by the near absence of any organized strategy for the kind of war the Americans suddenly found themselves fighting. Even the special-forces unit created to battle the insurgency—most commonly dubbed "Task Force 6-26" but assigned other names as the war continued—lacked basic procedures for handling intelligence collected from the battlefield or gleaned from informants.

Some of the lapses were jaw-dropping. One day, as McChrystal was visiting a holding facility for new detainees, he passed by a small office that had become the drop-off point for evidence collected during raids. In the room was a waist-high pile of documents, notebooks, computers, cell phones, and other detritus, much of it shoved into trash bags or empty sandbags and never examined.

"What is that?" McChrystal asked an aide.

"That stuff was sent down here with detainees," came the reply.

"Well, that's raw intelligence," the general said. "What are we doing with it?"

"When the interpreters have free time, we have them come in here and look through it," the aide said.

McChrystal was furious.

"It was unbelievable," he said, recalling his reaction. "Of course, the interpreters didn't have free time. And they wouldn't know what they were looking for. So this stuff was just sitting there, literally like ripe fruit rotting."

A few months into the job, McChrystal decided to gather his JSOC commanders from Iraq and Afghanistan for a two-day conference to talk about the unfolding insurgencies in both countries. He issued reading assignments—including *Modern Warfare,* the 1961 French classic treatise on counterinsurgency—and arranged for a screening of *The Battle of Algiers,* a fictionalized but historically accurate 1966 portrayal of the French army's bloody efforts to subdue Algeria's National Liberation Front insurgency in the 1950s. After the film ended, he prompted a debate about two troubling themes. The first was the use of torture, and how it ultimately undermined France's position, tactically and morally. The other was what McChrystal described as the French army's cluelessness about Algerian culture, including why the insurgency's message held such potency for so many of the country's ordinary citizens. The similarities to the current conflict were strikingly obvious, but McChrystal gestured toward a wall to drive home the point.

"We fundamentally do not understand," he said, "what is going on outside the wire."

Equally striking to McChrystal was the fact that Zarqawi, a foreigner, had managed to build such an impressive network after less than a year in the country. Clearly, the Jordanian was getting help from Iraqis. But he also was displaying undeniable skill as an organizer and a strategist.

Zarqawi's own intelligence-collection ability was remarkably effective, judging from his ability to strike many miles from his presumed base. His personal security showed surprising sophistication, including a knack for flying just below the Americans' electronic surveillance nets. Operationally, he was audacious yet careful, picking relatively easy targets and powerful but simple bomb designs. Most impressive of all was his ability to think strategically: Zarqawi was not merely seeking to wage war. He was changing the battlefield itself, using terrorism as a brutal forge for creating new enemies and allies as it suited his purposes. Just now, it suited Zarqawi to stir hatred between Iraq's Sunnis and Shiites.

This sectarian resentment was woven into the country's fabric, a legacy of massacres and pogroms that dated back to Islam's founding generation. And yet, particularly in the later decades of the twentieth century, Iraqis had come to share a common national identity and a uniquely Iraqi sense of patriotism, one that had been made stronger by an eight-year war against Iran's Shiite-led theocracy. Before Saddam Hussein's overthrow, Sunnis and Shiites mingled easily in Iraqi schools and universities and often lived side by side in mixed neighborhoods. Now, thanks in large measure to Zarqawi, the country was segregating itself into armed enclaves. Soon the nights belonged to Shiite and Sunni gangs who carried out reprisal killings and dumped mutilated bodies in alleyways and irrigation canals.

"Zarqawi aimed to get Iraqis to see each other as he saw them," McChrystal wrote. "And to him they were not countrymen or colleagues or neighbors or in-laws or classmates. They were either fellow believers or an enemy to be feared and, in that fear, extinguished."

While Zarqawi hoped to create problems for Iraq's interim leadership and American occupiers, the sectarian violence he instigated quickly developed its own momentum. Shiite self-defense militias, some of them just as vicious as Zarqawi's thugs, seized control of entire neighborhoods and waged running duels with U.S. troops as well as rival Sunnis. Some, like the Badr Brigade, turned to Iran's security service, the Revolutionary Guard, for weapons, training, and money. In short order, Tehran, seeing an opportunity to bedevil America—a bitter foe since the 1979 revolution that brought the Shiite Ayatollah Ruhollah Khomeini to power, and had even armed Saddam in his war with Iran—was running its own proxy armies inside Iraq. Soon the country's highways were seeded with sophisticated, Iranian-designed IEDs, specially engineered to penetrate the shells of American Humvees.

Zarqawi had essentially created a three-sided war, with U.S. forces drawing fire from the other two sides at once. His embrace of "revolting" violence, so passionately described in his letter to Bin Laden, had been distilled into a book, titled *The Management of Savagery*. The volume, which began circulating on jihadist Web sites in early 2004, urged unflinching cruelty in order to achieve the Islamists' ultimate objectives.

"If we are not violent in our jihad and if softness seizes us, that will be a major factor in the loss of the element of strength," writes the book's author, an al-Qaeda theorist who called himself Abu Bakr Naji. "Dragging the masses into the battle requires more actions which will inflame opposition and which will make people enter into the battle, willing or unwilling.

"We must make this battle very violent," he said, "such that death is a heartbeat away."

Less than two weeks after his letter to Bin Laden, Zarqawi's bomb makers prepared to deliver another such blow, an attack on Shiite civilians far bloodier than any since the start of the war.

On March 2, 2004, millions of Shiites around the world would commemorate the martyrdom of one of the religion's great icons, Husayn Ibn Ali, grandson of the Prophet Muhammad, on the holy day known as the Day of Ashura. For Iraqi Shiites, the date was especially meaningful as the first observance of the holiday since the toppling of Saddam Hussein and his government's policy of strict controls on religious pilgrimages.

By midmorning, huge crowds—unofficial estimates topped a million people, including tens of thousands of visiting Iranians—swarmed Shiite religious shrines in Baghdad and in Karbala, the city in central Iraq where Husayn Ibn Ali was said to have been killed. Among the pilgrims in both cities were several young men who quietly worked their way through the throng, wearing heavy vests concealed under their coats. At 10:00 a.m., near-simultaneous explosions ripped through the crowds, hurling shrapnel and body parts. As the panicked crowds began to flee, mortar shells fired from several blocks away fell into the courtyard, killing dozens more. Investigators later confirmed a dozen explosions and nearly seven hundred casualties, including nearly 180 dead.

This time, U.S. officials quickly pointed to Zarqawi as the likely culprit. In less than twenty-four hours, the top U.S. military commander in the Middle East, General John Abizaid, told a congressional panel that he possessed "intelligence that links Zarqawi" to the Ashura bombings.

"The level of organization and the desire to cause casualties among innocent worshippers is a clear hallmark of the Zarqawi network," Abizaid testified on March 3.

Many Iraqis looked elsewhere for blame. The country's leading Shiite cleric, Ayatollah Ali al-Sistani, condemned the American occupiers for allowing the collapse of security in a country that, despite its problems, had been mostly stable. Others were convinced that the Americans themselves were behind the massacre, refusing to believe that Muslims could commit such atrocities.

Some lashed out at journalists, who, for many, represented the closest tangible symbol of the West. Near Baghdad's bomb-damaged Imam Musa al-Khadam shrine, an Iraqi woman, draped from head to toe in a black *abaya,* trailed a pair of American reporters, screaming insults.

"Why," she shrieked, "have you Americans done this to us?"

Barely a year had passed since Zarqawi arrived in central Iraq, armed with only a few weapons, some cash, and his own ambitions. His stated goals were to isolate and harass the American occupiers and ignite conflict between Iraq's Shiite and Sunni communities. He had managed to achieve both, and, what's more, Iraqis had come to blame the Americans for the violence that he himself had sparked.

As he had hoped, Iraq was sliding into chaos, and Zarqawi would soon unveil new tactics to deepen the misery in the country and horrify the Western world. But first he had unfinished business to resolve. He had not forgotten his first object of loathing—Jordan.

11

"It would surpass anything al-Qaeda did"

On February 29, 2004, Dallah al-Khalayleh, the revered mother of Abu Musab al-Zarqawi, died after a long battle with leukemia. Jordanian agents had been watching the house for weeks as she lay dying, and monitored the funeral service to see if the woman's doting son would show up. He did not.

Zarqawi likewise stayed far away when, on April 6, a Jordanian court sentenced him to death in absentia for the murder of the American diplomat Laurence Foley. Instead, he prepared a gift, a reminder to the monarchy's leaders that he had not forgotten about them. It would be, in Zarqawi's mind, a gesture on an epic scale, greater than anything he had accomplished so far in Iraq. With one awesome blow, he would seek to eviscerate Jordan's security establishment, paralyze the monarchy, and eclipse Osama bin Laden as the most audacious Islamist warrior of his time.

The man he selected for the mission was a Jordanian of Palestinian descent named Azmi al-Jayousi. A stocky thirty-five-year-old with thinning auburn hair and light, European features, Jayousi had been with Zarqawi since his Afghanistan days. He picked up explosives-making skills at the Jordanian's Herat camp in western Afghanistan, at some point losing a finger for his troubles. When Zarqawi moved to the mountains of northern Iraq, Jayousi went to work at Ansar al-

Islam's chemical lab, tinkering with combinations of simple toxins and testing the results on dogs. Now Zarqawi sat down with him to sketch out a plan for a device that would draw on all of Jayousi's talents: a massive bomb, powerful enough to level buildings, that would simultaneously release a large cloud of poison gas in the heart of the Jordanian capital. Similar to a radioactive "dirty bomb" that uses conventional explosives to spread radiation, this would be a true terror weapon, unleashing panic as invisible toxins wafted through the city. With a favorable wind, his "suicide chemical attack," as his followers called it, could potentially kill thousands.

But first the bomb maker would have to find a way to get to his target. Jayousi, like Zarqawi himself, was well known to Jordan's Mukhabarat, having been arrested and imprisoned for his links to radical causes in the 1990s. He might be recognized at the border, even with a fake passport. Zarqawi took no chances. With the help of his Syrian logistics chief, the polyglot dentist Abu al-Ghadiya, a scheme was devised for moving Jayousi and an accomplice across the Jordanian border inside a gasoline tanker truck. Ghadiya arranged for the terrorists to hide inside the fuel tank itself, in a compartment outfitted with breathing tubes so the stowaways would not be overwhelmed by fumes during the two-hour trip through customs and across the Syria-Jordan border. The men would bring no supplies with them other than an explosives recipe and thick wads of Jordanian dinars and euro notes, the first installment on a budget that eventually topped a quarter of a million dollars.

Once he was safely across the border, Jordanian friends whisked Jayousi to a safe house from which he could begin his preparations. Jayousi bought a used Opel, then went on a shopping spree. He assigned aides to rent warehouse space in three towns in northern Jordan, and purchased four other vehicles from different vendors. One was a Chevy Caprice, which, with its powerful V8 engine and Detroit-steel frame, contained sufficient muscle for punching through a security checkpoint. Then he bought three trucks, two of them to be converted into giant bombs, and a third to hold vats of chemicals. Finally, he put teams of helpers to work on a dozen different tasks, from welding reinforced bumpers onto the trucks to buying and stockpiling chemicals—pesticides, potassium cyanide, hydrogen peroxide, glycerin, acetone—in batches just small enough to avoid raising suspicion. The supplies, twenty tons in all, soon lined the walls of a small warehouse in the northern city of Irbid, in jugs and crates marked with orange warning labels. Among his workers were twelve who were slated to serve on the mission itself, with no expectation of ever returning home.

Jayousi oversaw the work like a malevolent maestro, steering his Opel from one warehouse to the next to avoid having to communicate over a telephone line that might be tapped. Between visits, he cruised through Amman to gather intelligence personally on potential targets: the Mukhabarat headquarters; the monarchy's royal court complex with its palaces; the U.S. Embassy; the new Mecca Mall, with its five floors of shops and restaurants.

Jayousi found that he could travel around Jordan without interference, and, with weeks to go before his mid-April deadline, he began to relax. A man with a notorious sweet tooth, he visited pastry shops to buy kanafeh, a cannoli-like tube of sweetened cheese in a pastry crust of long noodle threads. Then he began to contemplate a riskier outing: a visit to his old neighborhood to see his wife. The woman had no idea that her husband was in Jordan, but Jayousi, anxious as he was for a reunion, was savvy enough to know that any attempt to contact her would likely be noticed and reported to the Mukhabarat.

In the end, for the lonely Jayousi, love trumped prudence. One day in early April, he sent one of his deputies to watch the family's house. When the lookout spotted Jayousi's wife walking home from a visit with her parents, he drove his car next to her and introduced himself. The two spoke for a moment; then the woman disappeared into her house. When she emerged again, she had her bags and three children in tow.

Jayousi's plans were coming into shape, and now he had his wife to help him while away the hours until everything was ready.

The target date for delivering Zarqawi's mighty bomb was less than two weeks away.

—

The tripwires began firing off almost at once, starting in the outlying towns and far suburbs of the capital and pulsing through invisible networks that led to the Mukhabarat's operations center. The agency's sensors at first picked up odd puzzle pieces, such as the disappearance one day of the entire family of a well-known Zarqawi associate, the Palestinian called Jayousi. The jihadist himself had not been seen in Jordan in years. Had he smuggled his family to Iraq to join him?

A bigger clue landed on the desk of Abu Mutaz, the youthful counterterrorism officer who had tried to turn Zarqawi after he emerged from prison with the 1999 amnesty. Nearly five years later, Abu Mutaz was a captain with subordinates and responsibilities that extended to regional offices across the country. Now one of those offices, in Irbid, a city near the Syrian border, was picking up multiple reports about strangers with large amounts of cash and a highly specific shopping list: a small number of used but sturdy cars and trucks, and warehouse rentals located away from houses and pedestrian traffic.

Abu Mutaz pressed for details. The mysterious shoppers had behaved strangely enough to pique local interest, and since then, the suspicions had deepened. Routine queries about their identities ran into dead ends. In fact, it soon became clear that the buyers were not the real buyers.

"They're using middlemen," Abu Mutaz concluded. "We don't know anything about who's behind this."

The Mukhabarat's men picked up one of the intermediaries, a local car broker in his forties who had gotten into trouble for shady dealings in the past. Since his earlier scrapes with the law, he had gone straight and even become religious, though not a zealot. When the Mukhabarat came for him, he grew exceedingly nervous, quickly blurting everything he could remember about the men who had hired him to buy a Chevy Caprice.

"I didn't even take a commission!" the broker protested.

But the names the broker supplied turned out to be fakes, and the phone numbers he had scribbled down no longer worked. Now the only firm leads the Mukhabarat had were descriptions: details about the vehicles—including the Chevy and a large yellow truck of German make—and vague accounts of the mysterious men who had bought them. Everything about the transactions, from registration papers to licenses plates, had been stolen or fabricated.

Meanwhile, more disturbing reports were landing on Abu Mutaz's desk. Several hardware stores in the area had reported large cash purchases of certain chemicals closely tracked by the intelligence service because of their potential use in explosives. Alarmed, Abu Mutaz appealed to his supervisors. Soon agents throughout the country joined the now urgent search for the Caprice and the yellow truck.

"We had been patiently gathering information, until we heard about these chemical supplies," he remembered afterward. "The amounts suggested that this was no longer a search for a few terrorists trying to make a weapon. This appeared to be a much bigger project."

So far, the Mukhabarat's leaders had seen no reason to bring American officials into the case. There had been no mention of specific targets, and no suggestion of involvement by al-Qaeda or Zarqawi in whatever was unfolding in Irbid. Practically speaking, there was little the CIA could offer. The skills essential for solving such a case were ones that the Jordanians already possessed, in abundance. In the gritty art of human intelligence-gathering, they were wired in a way that the Americans, for all their money and technical wizardry, were not. And Abu Mutaz was widely regarded as one of the best.

Abu Mutaz hailed from tiny Tafilah, a three-thousand-year-old East Bank town where ancestral roots matter more than schooling or wealth. He used his good grades and tribal connections as a ticket to an overseas education in Qatar, where he had studied journalism and envisioned a career in newspapers or television. Instead, he was offered an entry-level post in the Mukhabarat after scoring high on an entrance exam. His writing skills quickly earned him a spot drafting reports for the director on counterterrorism cases. But Abu Mutaz was a natural as a field intelligence officer, showing real talent for recruiting informants among the jihadists. Though not especially religious himself, he had an open, authentic manner that made people trust him. "For every person, there's a key that will get you inside—you just have to find it," he often said.

But cracking an Islamist almost always required a second key: a way to penetrate a religious code designed to keep outsiders away. Abu Mutaz knew the Koran as well as almost any jihadi, and sometimes he sat for hours with a single detainee, matching him, verse for verse, in endless theological debates. More than once during these sessions, he would excuse himself for a few hours on the pretense of attending prayers at the local mosque. Instead, he would skip across town to fortify himself with a beer or two at a hotel bar.

The job also required extraordinary patience, a quality with which Abu Mutaz was naturally gifted. Once, he worked for four months to win over a single jihadist, a young radical who showed promise as a potential informant. The youth appeared to be a fence straddler: he had trained as a militant in Afghanistan, yet he remained attached to his family and secular life in Jordan. Abu Mutaz decided to pressure the young man through his parents, so he staked out the neighborhood to learn all he could about the man's mother, including the stores she visited. He found the woman's favorite grocery store and then began cultivating a friendship with the shop owner. One morning, he arrived at the shop with a basket of squabs—domestic pigeons, a delicacy in Jordan—and asked the grocer to host a special luncheon, inviting the jihadist, his mother, and Abu Mutaz himself as guests. As lunch was ending, the Mukhabarat agent took the mother aside and asked for help in keeping her obviously bright, talented son from ending up in the spy agency's prisons. The two became friends, and the son, ever dutiful, became one of Abu Mutaz's best informants.

Now Abu Mutaz called in every chip and leaned on every neighborhood gossip on the payroll to come up with something concrete about what he had come to fear was a major terrorist plot. The entire Mukhabarat, with its plodding, low-tech efficiency, was now engaged in the search. Word spread through tribal networks and village councils that the agency's men were desperately seeking information to head off a possible attack.

The big break came from a walk-in, an Irbid businessman who showed up at the local police precinct with a possible tip. The man had heard about the Mukhabarat's search, and wondered if his newest tenants might be somehow linked. He had recently rented a garage and warehouse on the main Irbid-Amman highway to strangers who paid in cash and were oddly vague about their plans. No customers ever came around, and the renters were oddly secretive, covering up the road-fronting windows and erecting a fence around the property at their own expense. Once, during a visit to his property, the man had managed a quick peek through a gap in the window coverings.

"There is a large truck inside," the man told police.

Police swooped into the warehouse, surprising a small handful of workers, who gave up without a struggle. In an interior storage room, lined up like stacks of paint cans, were barrels of chemical precursors, enough, the Mukhabarat's men figured, to level a large swath of central Amman. Sacks of cumin seed—an explosives enhancer—lay in another corner. And in the garage, as promised, was a truck: a yellow German-made MAN, matching precisely the description of the vehicle on the Mukhabarat's search list. The workers had just finished welding to the front of the truck a frame of hardened steel, the same kind of barrier buster used by Iraqi insurgents to drive truck bombs deep into a targeted building before detonating. The delivery system for Zarqawi's bomb was fully operational.

Other raids followed in quick succession. At separate locations a few miles from the warehouse, investigators found other vehicles, as well as Jayousi's laboratory. For the latter, the bomb maker had picked a rural site next to a livestock ranch, where no neighbor would likely notice if odors escaped from the mixing of chemicals.

By now, between interrogations and scraps of recipe notes from the laboratory, Abu Mutaz knew with near precision what the plotters intended. This was to be a suicide bombing like none other: a "dirty chemical bomb" that blended conventional explosives and poisons, creating a toxic cloud that would kill as it settled over the capital. The epicenter was to be the Mukhabarat's own headquarters, with the main detonation to take place at a fueling station for the spy agency's vehicles, not far from where Abu Mutaz worked.

"By the time we found them they were nearly ready," Abu Mutaz recalled afterward. "The plan was to start with an attack on the main gate, using RPGs and small arms to kill the guards. Then the main truck—the MAN—would destroy the fuel station, followed by the other trucks carrying explosives and poison chemicals in layers. After the explosion the place would become so toxic that not even the ambulances would be able to enter. It would surpass anything al-Qaeda did, anywhere in the world."

But there was still a missing piece: the bomb maker had not been found.

Jayousi had been careful. Few in the Irbid cell knew his real identity, and none of them knew where he was staying. He used only prepaid calling cards and switched mobile phones every few days to thwart any effort to track his movement. When the raids began, he disappeared into a safe house in Marka, a Palestinian enclave outside Amman, apparently intending to wait out the Mukhabarat before fleeing or trying again. But by now the Jordanians had a name—a familiar one, at that—along with a photograph they could broadcast on state-run television. They also possessed what turned out to be a critical piece of intelligence: Jayousi's wife and children were with him. Precisely how they traced the family to the Marka hideout—an errant phone call, perhaps, or a relative's indiscretion?—is unclear. But as night fell on Monday, April 17, 2004, commando teams moved into position around the apartment building with high confidence that the bomb maker was inside.

At 2:10 a.m. on April 18, a dozen soldiers crouched with guns drawn as an officer banged loudly at the door.

"Police!" the lead officer shouted.

The reply was a burst of submachine-gun fire through the door, showering the hallway with bullets and splinters. One of the soldiers fell, wounded in the shoulder. The others blasted their way into the apartment. They shot and killed the first defender, and then raced through darkened rooms looking for others.

They found Jayousi huddled in a bedroom with his wife and children. The man who specialized in designing bombs capable of killing large numbers of innocents made no move in his own defense, clinging instead to the wife he had brought along, at great risk. Even as the police moved in, he insisted on keeping his family close, bunking his kids amid boxes of C-4 military explosives and the fuses and detonators that were to have been the final ingredients in Zarqawi's history-making bomb.

Later that morning, Abu Haytham, the intelligence captain who had been the last to meet with Zarqawi before his flight to Pakistan in 1999, peered into an interrogation room to see another face from his past. The suspect sat in his chair, alone now, his hair matted and his eyes puffy from a lack of sleep. But it was the same Jayousi he remembered from years before, clean-shaven and a little stouter, this time facing accusations that all but guaranteed that he'd never again live with his wife as a free man.

Abu Haytham walked into the cell with a small tray and sat down. The bomb maker looked up briefly, but his expression registered only exhaustion and defeat. This would be easy.

The captain slid the tray across the table, putting the honey-drenched cheese pastries directly under Jayousi's nose.

"Have a kanafeh," he said.

Two days later, Abu Mutaz sat next to Jayousi as the bomb maker retold his story, this time with video cameras rolling. Throughout the capital, Jordanians were waking up to news reports about the disrupted terrorist plot, which, according to official estimates, carried the potential for killing up to eighty thousand people in central Amman. But Jayousi, answering questions from a Mukhabarat officer, spoke in the flat monotone of a mechanic explaining a transmission overhaul. He described the stealthy border crossing, the financing, the faking of documents, the hiring of welders, and the crafting of special canisters designed to hold corrosive toxins. Then he talked about the attack itself:

> The men in the Caprice would have RPG weapons, and their task was to strike the obstacles and kill the guards. Then the big MAN truck would break through. There was a bumper installed on the truck to allow it to remove any barrier. It was even designed to go through a wall and continue until it came to the center of the General Intelligence. I think the administration of the General Intelligence was in the center. That's where the truck would explode.
>
> Any guards not killed in the explosions would either be in shock or so injured they couldn't fight back. Then the other cars

would enter the location slowly, one at a time, and each would slowly park wherever it wanted. There would be no resistance. Being an expert in explosives, it was my understanding this would destroy the General Intelligence and everything around it, with even distant sections being destroyed.

Only when he was asked about the reasons for the attack did Jayousi become animated. All of it, he said, had been done under the orders of a man he described as his commander and mentor since the day he had turned up at the Herat training camp in western Afghanistan.

"I promised my loyalty to Abu Musab al-Zarqawi," he said, as the video camera rolled. "I agreed to work for him—no questions asked." To be killed in such an operation was to have been an honor, he said.

"If I die, I become a martyr," he said, "and those I kill will go to hell."

No one followed the details of the plot with greater foreboding than the man who, in the fantasies of the radicals who dreamed it up, might have been the chief victim. For King Abdullah II, the events of April 2004 had been much more than a close call. In seeking to explode a toxic bomb in central Amman, Jayousi had officially delivered the Iraq war to the Jordanian capital.

Abdullah had warned that the violence unleashed in Iraq could never be neatly contained. He had expressed his deep misgivings prior to the invasion to senior U.S. officials, including the president himself. Even after the lightning victory over Saddam Hussein's army, Abdullah predicted to friends in the region that the war would lead to "unforeseen negative consequences that we would be dealing with for decades." But he had not imagined that it would be as bad as this.

The monarch had also lodged compaints with U.S. officials about the aftermath of the invasion. In July 2003, before Iraq spiraled into chaos, Abdullah met with L. Paul Bremer, the White House–appointed head of Iraq's provisional government, and urged him to reconsider decisions to disband the Iraqi army and blacklist members of Saddam Hussein's Baath Party. Pulling Bremer aside during a meeting at an economic forum in Jordan, the king warned that the decisions "would blow up in all of our faces," according to his account of the conversation.

"I said I hoped he understood that if he was going to de-Baathify across the board, he would be setting himself up for major resistance across the board, and would create a power vacuum that someone would have to fill," Abdullah wrote in his 2011 memoir. As for disbanding the army, "it was crazy . . . a recipe for anarchy and chaos," he said.

Bremer's reply was brusque, as he recalled it.

"I know what I'm doing," the American diplomat said. "There's going to be some kind of compensation. I've got it all in hand, thank you very much."

To the king, it was no surprise to see how quickly security unraveled. As a Sunni himself, he could empathize with Iraq's minority Sunnis, who, after decades of privileged status, saw themselves as increasingly isolated and threatened. Those anxieties would drive some Iraqis toward radical Islamists, who in turn would open the door to foreign jihadists. Of course al-Qaeda and its allies would leap at a chance to establish a base in a strategically important corner of the Middle East.

"They could shift their operations from Afghanistan to the heart of the Arab world," he said.

Soon another American stumble would give the extremists a powerful boost. In the same month the chemical plot was disrupted, U.S. television networks carried images of GIs abusing prisoners at Iraq's notorious Abu Ghraib prison. Arab anger boiled over at photos of naked inmates wearing dog collars and being sexually humiliated by female soldiers. Abdullah, during a visit to Washington that spring, urged President George W. Bush to apologize to Iraqis for the degrading treatment of prisoners, which Bush did, with Jordan's king standing by his side.

But other officials showed little interest in views that clashed with the administration's official narrative of a steadily improving Iraq. A few months after the Abu Ghraib scandal erupted, Abdullah was queried about conditions for ordinary Iraqis during a private New York dinner party attended by prominent journalists and government officials. Even with the upsurge in terrorist attacks, surely women's lives had improved since the dictator's removal, one of the dinner guests suggested.

"They're ten times worse," the king replied. "When you had a secular regime under Saddam, men and women were pretty much equal."

Abdullah's candor did not sit well with some Bush appointees in the room. Liz Cheney, the vice president's elder daughter, then a senior official in the State Department's Near Eastern Affairs section, turned to one of the king's aides with a word of unsolicited advice, according to the king's memoir: Abdullah should avoid making such discordant statements in public. The aide initially wondered if the comment was meant as a joke, but the next day, Cheney telephoned him again to reinforce the message. She said she had discussed the king's remark with Paul Wolfowitz, the Defense Department official who had been one of the architects of Bush's Iraq policy, and both had agreed that Abdullah should keep his views to himself.

The monarch was exasperated.

"What I said over dinner was true," he wrote afterward. "I was shocked that some members of the administration and their supporters seemed to feel that there could be no dissent on Iraq—and that in America, a country that prides itself on opinionated self-expression, they would try to muzzle inconvenient news."

The reality that was becoming painfully clear to Abdullah was an Iraq engulfed in flames and seeding the entire region with dangerous sparks. Jayousi and his poison bomb had drifted into Jordan on a fire whirl, and Jordan's Mukhabarat had only narrowly managed to stop them. Meanwhile, the man who directed and financed the plot remained free inside Iraq to try again.

The Mukhabarat prepared one more blow against the sponsors of the chemical plot. To discredit the jihadists and expose the barbarity of the crime they had nearly succeeded in carrying out, the intelligence directorate aired excerpts from Jayousi's videotaped confession on state-run television. All of Jordan would be able to watch the Palestinian coldly recite his plans to level a portion of the capital. Arab news channels broadcast the performance to a wider audience across the Middle East, including in Iraq, where Jayousi's puffy face filled a screen in the safe house in which Abu Musab al-Zarqawi was staying.

Zarqawi surely knew what had happened to Jayousi and his other soldiers. But after watching the video, he decided to make an equally public response.

"Yes, there was a plot to demolish the Jordanian General Intelligence Directorate [GID; the Mukhabarat] building," Zarqawi said, speaking into a microphone for an audio recording posted to Islamist Web sites.

The terrorist tried to deflect the accusations about toxic weapons as a Mukhabarat fiction. "God knows," he said, "if we did possess [a chemical bomb], we wouldn't hesitate one second to use it to hit Israeli cities such as Eilat and Tel Aviv." He insisted that his targets were military—the apostate regime and its security forces—and that the arrest of Jayousi and his aides was a temporary setback.

"The battle between us and the Jordanian government has its ups and downs," he said. To the monarchy, he warned: "Terrifying events are awaiting you."

In fact, the collapse of his plan sent Zarqawi into a funk, Mukhabarat officials discovered much later, in piecing together a larger narrative of the plot from informants and captured jihadists. He disappeared for days, refusing to talk to aides about the bomb plot and what had gone wrong.

"This was supposed to be his 'shock and awe,' the thing that would give him a global reputation," said a Jordanian intelligence official who participated in the agency's review. "Zarqawi really did want his own name to precede Bin Laden's. And more than that, he really wanted to hurt the GID."

But Zarqawi's moodiness was short-lived. Already, in the final days of April 2004, an unexpected opportunity had fallen his way. He began to see a path to jihadi stardom that required only a single spectacular death.

12

"The sheikh of the slaughterers"

The camera's recording light flicked on. Abu Musab al-Zarqawi clutched a script in both hands and began to read. He was dressed in black, from his baggy trousers and tunic to the ski mask that concealed his face, and he towered over the pale figure in the orange jumpsuit who sat on a blanket in front of him. The seated man shifted uncomfortably, his legs and arms bound with ropes.

"Nation of Islam, great news!" Zarqawi began in Arabic, with exaggerated inflection. "The signs of dawn have begun and the winds of victory are blowing."

Zarqawi was flanked by four of his men, also hooded and dressed in black. The men carried rifles and wore ammunition pouches and fidgeted like athletes loosening up for a contest. Most fixed their attention on the prisoner as Zarqawi spoke, as though the young man might somehow throw off his ropes and try to flee. Everyone in the room behaved as though acutely aware of the video camera except for the man in the jumpsuit, who stared straight ahead as though in a daze. Whatever his thoughts, Nicholas Evan Berg gave no sign of awareness of what was about to happen to him.

Before the hooded men came into the room, Berg had been made to sit on a plastic chair before the same camera and answer questions about himself. He appeared relaxed, his hands resting in his lap, and he spoke as calmly as though interviewing to open a bank account.

"My name is Nick Berg," he began. "My father's name is Michael, my mother's name is Susan. I have a brother and sister, David and Sarah. I live in West Chester, Pennsylvania, near Philadelphia."

His eyeglasses were missing, and he had grown a scruff of beard that made him seem younger than his twenty-six years. But he sounded confident and friendly, very much the same Nick Berg who had traveled alone to Iraq two months earlier with outsized notions about starting a business repairing communication equipment. Zarqawi had seized him because he was looking for an American, any American. But in Berg he had found an American archetype: a young man bursting with ambition and big plans, trustful of others, and possessing an unshakable faith in his own ability to succeed, in a country and culture unknown to him, through sheer persistence and the logical power of his ideas. How a would-be entrepreneur from suburban Philadelphia came to play a starring role in Zarqawi's grotesque coming-out video involved a journey as improbable as any that occurred during the war.

Berg had come to Iraq uninvited, and against the advice of nearly everyone he knew. But whereas others saw only danger, he saw in Iraq's ruins an opportunity to fulfill two of his most pressing needs in the early months of 2004: jump-starting his struggling business, and being part of something noble and important, specifically the transformation of a country benighted by decades of dictatorship. Berg had made a similar attempt two years earlier in Africa, prospecting for business opportunities in Kenya while also helping with humanitarian causes. On the last day of his Kenyan visit, he had famously given away the entire contents of his suitcases, to return home with only the clothes he was wearing. Now he would redirect his energy and resources toward a country whose "liberation" he heartily supported, hoping to help open a new world of opportunities for Iraqis, and also for himself.

"I am reasonably confident we can score some work out of this," Berg wrote in a January 2004 e-mail to friends, during his initial scouting visit to Iraq. "It is treacherous, though."

Berg's reasons for being in Iraq mystified U.S. and Iraqi officials and virtually everyone else, except those who knew him personally.

A self-described inventor and adventurer, Berg was never known to hold more than a passing regard for convention. As a boy, growing up amid the split-level houses and boutique shopping centers of West Chester, he was regarded as mildly eccentric, the kind of kid who grew a yeast colony for fun and kept a ready supply of wires and duct tape with him in a small toolbox. He amused friends with an ever-changing array of homemade gadgets, from an electric "truth detector" to a battery-powered alarm that was rigged to shout "Get out of here!" whenever intruders entered his cabin at summer camp. High-school classmates remembered the brainy prankster with the piercing blue eyes and unusual hairstyle, cropped extremely short except for a tuft of dark-blond curls that tumbled over his forehead. He played the sousaphone in the marching band, competed in science fairs, read obscure philosophy texts, and tested his physical limits with cross-country bicycle treks of a hundred miles or more. Even at home he hewed sharply against the grain: a religious conservative, an exuberant capitalist, and an unapologetic interventionist in a family of secular Jews whose liberal political leanings bordered on pacifism.

"He went where no one else did," Peter Lu, a high-school friend, said of him. "If there was a path, you could bet Berg wouldn't be on it."

Berg was assured admittance to a good college, but he dropped out of Cornell University just shy of a diploma. He drifted through a succession of schools and jobs, never earning a degree but gaining experience as a volunteer relief worker in Africa and as a service technician for radio towers, discovering, in the latter role, that he possessed both the talent and steely nerve to make a living fixing transmission equipment while dangling from atop a six-hundred-foot metal spire. Gradually, he began to formulate a vision for a business that would incorporate all his eclectic interests. At age twenty-four, with support from his family, he formally launched Prometheus Methods Tower Service, naming himself as president. His business plan called for helping developing countries build radio towers out of Lego-like clay blocks that he designed himself, using cheap, local materials. The idea was unorthodox and improbably ambitious, and it suited him perfectly.

Now he needed a market, and Iraq, with its ruined infrastructure and open spigots gushing with U.S. contractor dollars, seemed to be just the place.

"There are so many parties involved in this work and they all sub-contract to people, and none of them are specialists like us," he wrote home in another e-mail. "It's unheard of for a company to actually have skilled specialists here—I think this gives us an advantage, but we have to get past the 'I have a friend' stage. I'm hoping a good business manager will move this along."

Berg's initial scouting visit to Iraq was sufficiently encouraging that the young entrepreneur returned in March 2004 to try to land his first real clients. Working on his own, he drove around the countryside, looking for communications towers, and offered to inspect and repair any that were damaged or broken. He climbed rickety steel masts, created prospect lists, and wrote more cheerful e-mails to friends at home. It was slow going, but Berg's enthusiasm never flagged, right up to the day when Iraqi police in the city of Mosul noticed a strangely dressed foreigner prowling around a radio tower outside of town.

The Iraqis had no idea what to make of the bespectacled young man with his tool kit and notebooks filled with sketches of communications equipment. Convinced that Berg was a spy—Israeli, perhaps, if not Iranian—the officers arrested him. He was taken to a Mosul police station on March 24, 2004, and placed in detention, ending abruptly the young businessman's Iraq adventure. Or so it seemed.

The plight of a solitary American civilian who runs afoul of Iraqi authorities is normally a matter for junior consular officers at the U.S. Embassy in Baghdad. But the strange case of Nicholas Berg soon commanded the attention of more senior officials at the State Department and the Pentagon. Eventually, queries about the businessman made their way to the CIA's counterterrorism division in Langley, where Nada Bakos was then the principal analyst in charge of the Zarqawi file.

Reports afterward showed that the Iraqi police quickly deposited Berg with U.S. forces in Mosul, who were just as baffled as the Iraqis by the earnest young man and his story about traveling across Iraq prospecting for business opportunities. By chance, Bakos happened to know one of the American military policemen who were present when Berg was taken in.

What are you doing here? Berg was asked. And asked again.

"No one could figure out what his deal was," Bakos recalled. "Why was he wandering around Iraq by himself, looking for something to do? No one could believe he was just going around looking for a job."

Meanwhile, background checks turned up another oddity. Three years earlier, a suspected al-Qaeda terrorist had used an e-mail address and Internet password that had belonged to Berg. There was an explanation, albeit a bizarre one: The ever-trusting Berg had once loaned his laptop computer to a stranger during a bus trip, and when the man had trouble accessing his e-mail, Berg had given him his personal log-on information. The stranger turned out to be a friend of Zacarias Moussaoui, the so-called "20th hijacker," who was arrested while undergoing pilot training to fly one of the planes in the September 11, 2001, terrorist attacks.

With so many questions swirling around the young businessman, army officials in Mosul were reluctant to let him go. In the end, they had no choice: Berg's family in Pennsylvania had been anxiously telephoning State Department officials, asking them to investigate their son's disappearance. When they learned, in an April 1 e-mail, that Berg was being held by American forces against his will, they were furious. The family filed a lawsuit accusing the military of false imprisonment, and a day later, on April 6, 2004, Berg was released.

Berg spurned an offer for a seat on a military plane back to the United States, opting instead to travel to Baghdad to sort out his own arrangements. He checked into a hotel on the day of his discharge and made a few phone calls. Then, on April 10, he vanished completely.

Again the family pressed for answers, and again the U.S. Embassy sent out queries to detention centers and military posts. But there was not a scrap of news about Berg all that week, or the next.

Finally, on May 8, a military patrol spotted an object hanging from a highway overpass. Pulling closer, they were horrified to see a human torso in loose orange clothing, dangling from a rope, with its hands and feet bound. Beneath the corpse, on a bloodstained blanket, was the severed head of a young white man with a scruffy sandy-blond beard.

Nicholas Berg had been found.

Two days later, the video containing one of the Iraq war's most disturbingly iconic images began streaking across the Internet. Bakos had no desire to see it, but in the end she forced herself. The viewing took place in a CIA conference room with two other analysts present.

On the screen was Berg, trussed and seated on the ground in his orange jumpsuit, his expression blank. Five hooded men in black stood behind him against a light-colored wall, and the man in the middle was reading from a script. She knew the voice and recognized the familiar stocky build, even with the mask. It was Zarqawi.

Bakos noted the orange jumpsuit, so familiar to anyone following the still-unfolding scandal over the abuse of Iraqi prisoners by American military guards. Zarqawi had never been accused of subtlety or sophistication in his few previous attempts at public statements. Was he sending a message to Muslims, inviting them to witness an act of symbolic revenge for the humiliation of inmates at Iraq's most notorious prison?

He was.

"Is there any excuse left to sit idly by?" the man with the script was saying. "How can a free Muslim sleep soundly while Islam is being slaughtered, its honor bleeding and the images of shame in the news of the satanic abuse of the Muslim men and women in the prison of Abu Ghraib. Where is your zeal and where is the anger?"

The screed continued for several minutes, with more appeals to Muslim pride and numerous Koranic references, including a nod to the Prophet Muhammad as "our example, and a good role model," for having ordered the beheadings of prisoners after a revolt by Jewish merchants in the city of Badr. Then, addressing the U.S. president directly, he delivered a warning:

Hard days are coming to you. You and your soldiers are going to regret the day that you stepped foot in Iraq and dared to violate the Muslims. . . . We say to you, the dignity of the Muslim men and women in the prison of Abu Ghraib and others will be redeemed by blood and souls. You will see nothing from us except corpse after corpse and casket after casket of those slaughtered in this fashion.

With that, Zarqawi then pulled a long knife from a sheath and pounced on Berg who, tied as he was, toppled onto his side. As the other men held the prisoner, Zarqawi grabbed Berg's hair with one hand and with the other began to cut at his throat. There was a brief, terrible scream, and then a frenzy of movement as the other hooded men held Berg's legs and shoulders while Zarqawi continued to struggle with his grisly task. More seconds passed of thrusting and sawing, as the camera wobbled and jerked. And still more seconds.

Bakos felt the nausea starting to build.

"Just get it over with," she found herself thinking. But it wasn't stopping.

Bakos finally excused herself and left. "There's no utility in watching this," she thought.

She missed only the final frames, in which one of Zarqawi's companions, a tall figure in a white hood, lifted the head, now free of its body, and held it aloft like a trophy, then set it gently on the victim's back.

Zarqawi's message to the world was five minutes and thirty-seven seconds of grainy video shot with a shaky, handheld camera, depicting an almost unimaginable act of cruelty. It was an instant global hit.

Countless thousands of computers downloaded the images, from North America to South Asia and across the Middle East. Some viewers cried out in disgust. Others reacted with sadness, despair, or rage. But they watched.

To ensure proper credit for the deed portrayed, the video helpfully included a title: "Abu Musab al-Zarqawi shown slaughtering an

American." The man who had longed to eclipse Osama bin Laden as the Islamist world's daring man of action had done just that, at least for the time being.

Other terrorists had beheaded their victims. Two years earlier, the *Wall Street Journal* reporter Daniel Pearl had been murdered by al-Qaeda operatives in a similarly public fashion. But Pearl was a seasoned journalist who had traveled to Pakistan looking for a story about al-Qaeda. Nick Berg was targeted and killed simply because he was an American. And the video of his execution hit at the very time when millions of Americans were connecting to broadband, and when support for the Iraq war was plummeting.

Even the White House, which earlier in the month had been promoting business opportunities in Iraq, was forced to confront Zarqawi's brutal deed.

"Their intention is to shake our will. Their intention is to shake our confidence," President Bush said, speaking to journalists in Washington about the terrorist act witnessed by so many Americans, in such excruciatingly intimate detail. He defended progress in Iraq but declined to take reporters' questions.

Other U.S. politicians, including some in the president's Republican Party, could sense the shift in the public's mood, even before opinion polls confirmed it. The Abu Ghraib scandal had, for many, ripped away the last tattered remnants of moral rectitude underpinning America's war with Iraq. The popular image of a high-tech U.S. military machine delivering shock and awe to Iraqi forces had also been tarnished, replaced by video clips on the nightly news of IED attacks and flag-draped coffins. And now Americans were witnessing in their living rooms a new kind of savagery.

"If you had your thumb on the pulse of America, that pulse beat changed when Americans heard about the beheading of Nick Berg," Representative Roy Blunt, a Missouri Republican, told *The New York Times* in an interview. "It jolted everybody's memory again about why we were there in Iraq and who we're dealing with."

But whom, exactly, were the Americans dealing with? To many viewers, the men in the video were al-Qaeda, one black hood indistinguishable from another. Three days after the release of the video, another message seemed designed to answer the question.

On May 13, 2004, jihadist Web sites posted a message announcing a new terrorist organization that called itself "al-Tawhid wal-Jihad," or Unity and Jihad. It was to be a kind of Islamist super-group: a merger of smaller factions of Iraqi insurgents and foreign fighters under a single umbrella, with Zarqawi as leader. The statement referred impressively to a "decisive historic turning point."

"This merger is a strength for the people of Islam, and blazing flames for the enemies of God, where they shall burn until the retrieval of the stolen rights, and the establishment of God's religion on the Earth," the message read. "It is a ticket and an inducement for the groups and sects to rush for the fulfillment of this legitimate duty and factual necessity. We give our word [to] the Islamic Nation that we shall not betray or retreat, and we shall keep our promise until we reach either one of two aspired outcomes: victory or martyrdom."

The communiqué listed two co-leaders, with Zarqawi—the "sheikh"—taking top billing. Just over three months earlier, in a letter to Bin Laden, Zarqawi had asked for a partnership with al-Qaeda and said that, in any event, the world would soon be hearing from him. That moment had arrived. With the release of the Berg video and the announcement of a pan-insurgent group with himself at the helm, Zarqawi had staked out a spot at the forefront of the global jihadist movement. No longer was he merely the leader of a particularly violent terrorist faction in Iraq. He was now a rival to Bin Laden himself as the terrorist that the West feared and young Islamists most wanted to emulate. Yes, Bin Laden had his videos, too: the Saudi appeared in his golden robes and dye-blackened beard, delivering ponderous sermons from behind a desk. Zarqawi's showed a vital, charismatic young man in ninja garb, killing an American with his own hands.

CIA analysts studying the video and communiqué wondered if the young Jordanian had overreached. Zarqawi was an upstart who lacked formal education and had never been regarded as having the vision or brainpower to run a large organization. He also lacked the kind of institutional support that had helped make Bin Laden successful, including backing from recognized Islamic scholars whose fatwas gave spiritual cover to such violent deeds as killing unarmed civilians or employing suicide tactics. Zarqawi sought no such approvals, and he had taken upon himself the responsibility of deciding how jihad against U.S. forces would be waged.

Nada Bakos wondered if Zarqawi's main achievement had been to elevate himself as a priority target, and not just for the Americans. "Zarqawi jumped the shark," she mused afterward. "Even al-Qaeda tried to abide by principles, using its theologians to interpret Sharia law. But Zarqawi interprets the law however he wants. He creates his own rules, like a cult," she said. "He is becoming the megachurch."

There would be a backlash, surely. The high priests of al-Qaeda and the other established jihadist networks would not look favorably on such exuberantly heterodox behavior, especially when it offended the sensibilities of the wealthy and pious Arabs who supplied the organization with most of its cash.

But many ordinary Muslim men lined up to join Zarqawi's swelling congregation. In Iraq and elsewhere, admirers had begun to refer to the Jordanian by a new nickname that had come into use in the days after the Berg video first aired.

Bin Laden would remain the respected figurehead, the man who years ago had fought the Soviets and planned the attacks on New York and Washington. But Zarqawi was now hailed as the "sheikh of the slaughterers," a terrorist for a brutal new age when broadcasting butchery on the Internet would be used as a tactic to win support among hardened jihadists and to sow fear among everyone else.

13

"It's hopeless there"

On June 23, 2004, diplomat Robert S. Ford tossed his bags onto an armored airport bus and took his place for the final leg of a journey he had tried to avoid. In twenty-five minutes he would be in the Green Zone again, navigating its mazes of blast walls and trailer villages, breathing in the city's hot, sweaty air with its accents of diesel fuel and rotting garbage. Six months after swearing off Baghdad for good, he was back, just in time to see the country's fortunes careen sharply toward the worst.

Signs of Iraq's unraveling lay scattered along the airport road. Barriers and checkpoints now dotted the ten-mile highway in a vain attempt to stop the daily shootings and bombings along what U.S. soldiers dubbed "Route Irish" and Iraqis called "Death Street." A year earlier, getting from the airport to the international district had been as simple as catching a shuttle. Now a ride into town meant booking a secure taxi, outfitted with armed escorts and bulletproof glass, that might cost as much as a thousand dollars per trip. Or, for a senior member of the U.S. diplomatic corps, it meant a seat on the steel-plated embassy van that raced between the terminal and the Green Zone at terrifying speed.

"Not a good sign," Ford thought to himself.

By every measure, Iraq was a more sinister place, especially for Americans. Though Ford, at forty-six, was one of the State Department's top Arabists, his light brown hair and blue eyes marked him as a Westerner. During his last assignment in Iraq, Ford had been held at gunpoint for two hours by a group of Shiite militiamen. This stint, he suspected, would be even more eventful.

Ford's earlier tour had been his own idea. Weeks after the fall of Baghdad, the State Department had issued an urgent appeal for Arabic-speaking volunteers to help the struggling U.S.-led interim government. Ford was then a veteran Middle East diplomat with near-flawless language skills and a comfortable post as the number two official at the U.S. Embassy in Bahrain. Like many of his colleagues, he had been dubious about the Bush administration's Iraq adventure. Still, the need appeared genuine. He raised his hand, and soon afterward he was boarding a military transport to Iraq, arriving in August 2003 in a capital city still reeling from the UN headquarters bombing that killed Sergio Vieira de Mello. His first assignment landed him in the Shiite holy city of Najaf as a diplomatic liaison to a contingent of U.S. marines in charge of securing the town. But the marines he met were mostly interested in getting out of Iraq as quickly as possible, and local leaders were caught up in a bloody feud between rival Shiite militias the Americans were seeking to disarm.

The encounter with the Shiite militiamen occurred in his first week on the job. Ford had a habit of plunging headlong into challenges, and in Najaf he set out at once to meet community leaders and build relationships away from the marine base. One Saturday afternoon, as he was meeting with one of the city's prominent clerics, a group of twenty-five militiamen burst into the house with guns drawn and clustered around Ford and a marine major who had accompanied him on the visit. The gunmen grabbed a young Iraqi translator and dragged him outside, where they savagely punched and kicked him.

Ford grasped for the only weapon available to him: a bluff. He pulled within a few inches of the man who seemed to be in charge.

"I'm Robert Ford, the coalition's representative here from Baghdad," he began in Arabic. "I have a meeting with your militia leader at midnight tonight. You can tell him I'm going to be late because you're holding me."

It worked. The Americans were released, and the militants scurried to their vehicles, first releasing the Iraqi translator, whose injuries were severe enough to warrant hospitalization. Minutes later, Ford, undaunted, was pressing his marine escort to call on the militia group's commander immediately to try to leverage the episode into an agreement on disarming.

The marine glared at Ford, this hyperenergetic diplomat with an apparent death wish.

"Goddamn nut!" he swore. The Americans returned to their base.

Ford's attempts at bridge building resumed the very next day, but the disappointments and frustrations piled up quickly. Months later, when he was formally asked to return to Iraq for a second stint, it wasn't the physical danger that compelled him to say no. Nor was it the awful weather, the Spartan living conditions, the freezing-cold showers, or the impossibly complex, constantly shifting nature of Iraq's sectarian and tribal rifts. It was the sense of waste and futility that hovered over nearly every endeavor like a toxic cloud.

"Oh, no, no, no, no. I already volunteered for Iraq once, and I don't want to go back," Ford told his boss over the telephone when the new request came. "It's hopeless there. It's not a serious effort. I want nothing to do with it."

And yet back he went. Back to the Green Zone, with all its surreal contrasts: the palaces and palm-lined swimming pools, and the dreary barracks, with walls of sandbags that offered scant protection from the mortar shells that fell randomly from the sky, like exploding lawn darts flung by a giant. Back, despite his wife's anger and his own personal misgivings about losing another chunk of his life—and possibly more—to what was surely a hopeless cause. Back, because he felt he had no choice.

"You can't say no unless you quit," he said afterward. "And we didn't have enough money to quit."

In fact, Ford's transfer orders had come from the very top of the State Department. The newly appointed U.S. ambassador to Iraq, John Negroponte, had asked Secretary of State Colin Powell to appoint Ford to the prestigious post of political counselor in the U.S. Embassy. Though relatively junior for such an assignment, Ford had won admiration at Foggy Bottom for his internal memos and e-mails candidly assessing the Iraq war's impact on the region. He had also earned admiration from colleagues for his bravery after years of unflinching service in some of the Middle East's roughest neighbor-hoods. A former Peace Corps volunteer conversant in five languages, he spent most of his professional life in provincial towns from the Moroccan interior to coastal Turkey, working like a journalist to gain local knowledge and build a source network. Nothing seemed to intimidate him, friends remembered.

"He spent his entire career in dangerous places," Robert Neumann, the former U.S. ambassador to Afghanistan, said of Ford. "He's not someone who stays in the [embassy], but someone who gets out and develops a very broad range of contacts. If you constantly have to feel totally safe, you're basically useless in those jobs."

This time, Ford's role would be different. The Bush administration, sensing its Iraq experiment slipping out of control, had moved to expedite the installation of an interim Iraqi government that would quickly assume primary responsibility for securing the country and organizing elections. The insurgency that U.S. officials had been so slow to acknowledge was now an indisputable fact, and the costs—financial, political, and human—were soaring. With a U.S. presidential election looming, Ford later recalled, "there was a drive, full speed ahead, to turn over sovereignty to the Iraqis and get us out."

To that end, the Coalition Provisional Authority would go out of business to make way for an Iraqi interim government headed by a new interim prime minister named Iyad al-Allawi. The transition officially occurred on June 28, 2004, less than a week after Ford arrived in the country. The Americans pledged to stick around only until Iraq was strong enough to stand on its own. How long would that take? Months, surely; perhaps even a year? No one knew. The Sunni towns north and west of Baghdad were sliding rapidly into lawlessness, and parts of Fallujah and Ramadi were effectively controlled by insurgents, some of them foreigners who had traveled to Iraq for jihad. The new Iraqi leadership and its U.S. backers desperately needed Sunni allies: respected, credible Sunnis who could help pacify the region and lead the Sunni tribes through a democratic transition that included elections and a unity government that shared power equally among Sunnis, Shiites, and Kurds.

One of Ford's assignments was to identify such allies and try to win them over. In his first month on the job, he traveled to Fallujah and arranged meetings with U.S. military commanders and Arab diplomats to get a sense of the task ahead of him. It was worse than he imagined. In Fallujah, the capital of the insurgency and traditionally the most rebellious city in Iraq, townspeople were in no mood to negotiate. The marines picked off occasional targets from their base on the outskirts of town, but most of the city remained a "denied area" to Americans in the weeks after the killing of the four American security contractors, officers told Ford.

"Insurgents and foreign fighters largely operate without constraint within the city," read a classified State Department cable describing Ford's meeting with the marines. "Coalition forces are still seeking to disrupt insurgents and foreign jihadists with surgical strikes against Abu Musab al Zarqawi–related targets within the town in order to prevent Fallujah from operating as a safe-haven for extremists."

A Jordanian diplomat with extensive contacts within the Sunni tribes described the situation as all but hopeless. Sunnis remained bitterly opposed to the American presence in Iraq, and though some were conflicted about the presence of foreign insurgents, others welcomed them as a bulwark against persecution by Shiite militias seeking to settle scores after decades of Sunni rule. Out of desperation, some tribal elders had even taken up the idea of restoring the Iraqi monarchy that had been overthrown in the 1958 coup, the Jordanian said.

"Sunnis are hostile, divided, leaderless, and unable to envision a political solution acceptable to others," the diplomat told Ford, according to a cable that bore eerie echoes of Zarqawi's own analysis of the country's Sunni minority.

There was still another obstacle, much harder to gauge from diplomatic interviews. Somewhere in the western desert, Zarqawi was also making his own plans for Iraqi's Sunni heartland. He, too, was gathering intelligence, recruiting allies, and laying the groundwork for future governance, though his vision differed from the Americans' in every conceivable way.

Ford's decades of diplomatic experience had shown that political solutions existed for almost every conflict. Eventually, even Sunnis and Shiites would weary of killings and destruction and grope toward a solution that would allow the sides to peacefully coexist as Iraqis. But Zarqawi was no Iraqi, and he had no interest in coexisting. Zarqawi's objective was to raze and tear down, leaving a scorched terrain too depleted to support the return of a secular country called Iraq.

The Iraqi city of Ramadi was not yet the "capital of the Islamic state of Iraq," as Zarqawi's followers would soon call it. But already, in the early summer of 2004, there was little doubt about who controlled the town.

A sprawl of low-rise concrete buildings and palm trees on the Euphrates River an hour west of Baghdad, Ramadi had the post-apocalyptic feel of a city that had been a free-fire zone between powerful armies. Decapitated buildings lined an abandoned market street strewn with broken concrete and shattered glass. People and cars darted and weaved as though pursued by invisible assailants. From behind walls of sandbags and Hesco barriers on the city's outskirts, the local U.S military commanders proclaimed Ramadi to be under U.S. control. In reality, the Americans' jurisdiction extended only to their bases and outposts and the range of their heavy machine guns. Marine patrols into the city's neighborhoods invariably sent insurgents scurrying through the alleys like cockroaches.

Zaydan al-Jabiri watched them run, and said nothing. The rancher and Sunni tribal leader who had once tried to mediate disputes between Iraqis and Americans had long since given up on peacemaking. It wasn't merely a frustrating occupation; it was dangerous. One of the sheikh's oldest friends, a physics professor at Anbar University, had taken a risk by agreeing to meet with visiting Coalition Provisional Authority officials to talk about ways to control the spasms of violence that had turned so much of Ramadi into rubble. The day after the meeting, the professor was pulled from his car at an intersection and shot dead in the middle of the street.

In many more instances, death was frighteningly random. In the weeks after sixteen U.S. marines had been killed in a series of ambushes around the city, the Americans were in a vengeful mood.

Firefights erupted daily in residential neighborhoods, and bullets tore through bedrooms where families slept. Checkpoint sentries reflexively shot at motorists who approached too quickly or failed to heed warnings shouted at them in English. In the desert outside Ramadi, forty-five Iraqis had died when American warplanes stuck a building that U.S. officials insisted was an insurgent safe house. Iraqis said the jets mistakenly struck a wedding celebration. Amateur video showed bodies of women as well as children and infants.

Outraged and humiliated, Ramadi's Sunnis initially welcomed the resistance fighters, including the foreign Islamists who poured into the city promising to drive away the invaders. Compared with the local insurgents, the Islamists were organized, disciplined, and fearless. But it was soon clear that their plans included more than fighting Americans. The foreigners commandeered houses and forcibly collected "taxes" and supplies from shopkeepers. Declaring themselves in charge, they rolled into residential neighborhoods armed with heavy weapons and a harsh moral code that banned drinking, smoking, female education, and Western fashion and hairstyles. One Ramadi man defiantly lit a cigarette in front of such an Islamist patrol and was shot dead on the spot.

Businesses suffered as well, despite the insurgents' crude attempts at establishing courts and maintaining essential services. It was quickly clear that the rebels had neither aptitude for nor interest in running anything. Their checkpoints and roadside bombs made transportation a high-risk enterprise, even when the cargo consisted, as in Zaydan's case, of cows and sheep. In town, the hallmarks of modern civilized life slipped away, one by one: garbage collection, phone service, electricity. Shopkeepers who tried to stay open found themselves subjected to arbitrary and occasionally bizarre regulations. In some neighborhoods, grocers were threatened with punishment if they displayed cucumbers and tomatoes in the same stall. The jihadists maintained that the vegetables resembled male and female body parts and should not be permitted to mingle.

Despite the hardships, some merchants chose to back the Islamists anyway, hoping at least to enjoy a measure of protection. Zaydan demurred. The presence of foreign troops in his city irritated him. Yet he was equally resentful of what he saw as the Islamists' impertinence in challenging the traditional authority of the tribes. He was appalled by the Islamists' tactics and disdainful of their thuggish, swaggering behavior. He complained to friends about the personality cult that seemed to be developing around the Jordanian named Zarqawi, the black-clad phantom whose exploits were already legendary in some of the city's neighborhoods.

"He surrounds himself with the scum of Anbar," Zaydan complained. "The people accept him because they are sheep without a shepherd. But the men close to him are lowlifes, people with no conscience. And they are drawn to Zarqawi because he has a lot of money."

Zarqawi himself was rarely seen in the town, but his Iraqi deputies quickly earned notoriety as colorful butchers. Most famous was a religious zealot called Omar the Electrician, a stocky tradesman with chipped teeth who, in his twenties, had shot a police officer in Saddam Hussein's government in an act of revenge over the killing of a relative. He sought refuge with Ansar al-Islam, the Islamist group that had sheltered Zarqawi in Iraq's northeastern mountains. When Zarqawi entered Baghdad, Omar the Electrician came along, and rose to become the leader of Zarqawi's brigade in Fallujah. His band became among the most notorious in Iraq, staging hit-and-run attacks on American patrols and running kidnapping-for-ransom operations to raise money. Hostages who couldn't pay up were killed, though not by Omar himself. He "swore he'd never personally beheaded a hostage," one of his comrades told journalists. "He said he chose men who don't have hearts to do the actual killing."

Zarqawi eventually began to solicit pledges of support—*bay'at,* a loyalty oath—from Anbar tribal leaders and elders. In the summer of 2004, word was passed to Zaydan through a cousin that Zarqawi was looking for a declaration of allegiance from him. The question was relayed over coffee, the first of two occasions when Zaydan would receive such a request. "Will you publicly pledge your support to Zarqawi?" the cousin asked.

How to respond? Inside, Zaydan was furious. The arrogance of this foreigner—this criminal—who dared to presume that he could assert authority over tribal traditions that had held sway for centuries! For all he knew, Zarqawi was an American agent, sent by Washington to stir unrest so the Westerners and Iranians could have an excuse to destroy Iraq utterly and divide the spoils among themselves. But even Zaydan dared not utter such opinions aloud. He chose to deflect the question, for now.

"Who is Zarqawi?" he shrugged. "I never met him."

In July 2004, the Bush administration announced that it had increased the reward for information leading to Zarqawi's capture, from ten million to twenty-five million dollars—identical to the bounty offered for Bin Laden's head.

Zarqawi celebrated his rise in the most-wanted rankings with a video, posted to jihadist Web sites. In it, he was introduced under his new favorite moniker—"the sheikh of the slaughterers"—and his voice boomed with confidence. He talked about famous Muslim warriors such as Musa Ibn Nusayr, a hero of the Islamic conquest of Spain, implying his own place in the chain of great men. Then he made an impassioned plea for Muslims from across Iraq and around the world to join him.

"This is a call for help from the depths, to the lions in Baghdad and al-Anbar, and to the heroes in Diyala and Samarra, and to the tigers in Mosul and the north: Prepare for battle," he said.

His intended audience by now knew exactly the kind of battle he meant. Since Berg's savage murder, Islamist media were awash in Zarqawi-inspired gore. The Jordanian's men carried out dozens of executions, many of them videotaped, including the beheadings of a Bulgarian truck driver, a South Korean translator, and an Egyptian contractor. Scores of others would follow, including Americans, Britons, Japanese, Austrians, and Italians. Lebanese kidnapping victims who were freed through ransom told stories of torture and unimaginable cruelty in makeshift prisons; of poor immigrant laborers who lacked money for ransom being killed slowly with electric drills; of other victims being held down while their tongues were hacked out. Young foreign-born Islamists who answered Zarqawi's call to jihad most often ended in suicide-bomber school. Some would be called upon to sacrifice their own lives to destroy targets with no discernible gain other than to kill a few innocent Iraqis who happened to be in the wrong place.

In recruiting volunteers for suicide bombings, Zarqawi was knowingly defying a Koranic commandment that strictly forbids Muslims from taking their own lives. Some Islamic scholars have held that military suicide missions might be permitted under extreme circumstances, and jihadists have argued for decades over exactly where the lines fall. Zarqawi seized on a small loophole in Islamic law and stretched it to absurd proportions, using hand-picked clerics to sanction the use of "martyrdom operations" for any purpose that suited him. The result was a torrent of suicide attacks unrivaled in the history of the jihadist movement, scholars later concluded.

As Zarqawi himself later wrote, such operations were the most "deadly weapons we have in our possession: weapons with which we can inflict the deepest wound upon our enemy." He added, somewhat cynically: "All of this is notwithstanding the fact that these kinds of operations are of little effort for us; they are uncomplicated and are the least costly for us."

In the videotape appealing for new recruits, Zarqawi offered the usual platitudes about heavenly rewards. More appealing, perhaps, was his invitation to be part of a movement that transcended history itself. The liberation of Muslim lands was a worthy goal, but it was only the start. Zarqawi promised nothing short of a reshaping of the global order. "You shall overcome America, by Allah. You shall overcome America, though it may be after a while," he said. "It shall remain a mole of shame on the cheek of time."

For the first time, Zarqawi also revealed a conviction regarding his own destiny as a midwife for the new golden age of Islam. He referred to apocalyptic passages in the Hadith describing the end-times struggle that would lead to Islam's ultimate triumph. According to the ancient prophecies, mankind's final battle would be fought in northern Syria, near a village called Dabiq. The story echoes early Christian teachings about the epic contest between forces of good and evil at Armageddon.

Jihad's "flames will blaze," Zarqawi said, "until they consume the Armies of the Cross in Dabiq."

A young Ahmad Fadil al-Khalayleh—
the future Zarqawi—poses with his
mother and a younger sibling in an
undated family photo. (Hashemite
Kingdom of Jordan)

Zarqawi as he appeared around the time
he left Jordan for Afghanistan in 1989
to join the mujahideen. (Hashemite
Kingdom of Jordan)

A foiled terrorist plot landed Zarqawi in
a Jordanian prison in 1994, but he was
released in a general amnesty in 1999,
around the time this photo was taken.
(Hashemite Kingdom of Jordan)

A young Prince Abdullah in army uniform presents a gift of cermonial daggers to his father, Jordan's King Hussein. (Royal Hashemite Court)

Jordan's king and Queen Rania pose for an official portrait in 2010. (Royal Hashemite Court)

King Abdullah II meets with President George W. Bush at the White House a month after the September 11, 2001, terrorist attacks. Though relations are cordial, Abdullah warns that the coming U.S. invasion of Iraq would open a Pandora's box in the region. (White House photo; Courtesy of George W. Bush Presidential Library)

The United Nations Iraq headquarters lies in ruins after a devastating suicide bombing that kills the mission chief and twenty-two others. The August 2003 attack is among the first linked to Zarqawi. (Defense Department photo)

Zarqawi, masked, stands behind seated American hostage Nick Berg, a Pennsylvania businessman captured in Iraq in 2004. The videotaped beheading of Berg becomes Zarqawi's signature act, and the first of many such executions. (SITE Intelligence Group)

Zarqawi cradles a light machine gun for a publicity video in 2006. Despite widespread revulsion over his brutal tactics, Zarqawi's reputation for fearlessness draws thousands of Islamist volunteers to Iraq. (SITE Intelligence Group)

Nada Bakos, pictured here in 2014, was the CIA's chief "targeter" for Zarqawi during the early years of the Iraq war. (Courtesy of Nada Bakos)

Diplomat Robert S. Ford tried to encourage Iraqi Sunni politicians to run for office despite threats from Zarqawi. Later, as U.S. ambassador to Syria, he sounded the alarm about the growing presence of Islamists among the country's rebel militias. (State Department photo)

General Stanley McChrystal inspects troops during a 2010 ceremony. As commander of U.S. special forces in Iraq, McChrystal helped devise the strategy that led to Zarqawi's death in 2006 and the near destruction of his organization in the years that followed. (Defense Department photo)

Would-be terrorist Sajida al-Rishawi displays the suicide vest that failed to explode during Zarqawi's 2005 attack on Western hotels in the Jordanian capital. (*The Jordan Times*)

Soldiers searching through rubble of Zarqawi's safe house after the building is flattened by a U.S. fighter jet. (Defense Department photo)

Zarqawi was pulled alive from the rubble of his safe house but died minutes later from blast injuries, surrounded by U.S. troops. His body, pictured here, was taken to a U.S. military base so his identity could be confirmed. (Defense Department photo)

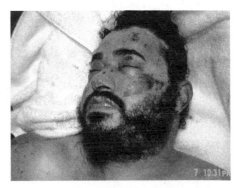

Huge crowds protest against the Bashar al-Assad regime in Hama, Syria, in July 2011. Intervention by U.S. diplomats delayed, but did not prevent, a bloody assault by government security forces. (Shaam News Network)

Future ISIS leader Abu Bakr al-Baghdadi is photographed at the U.S. military detainee facility Camp Bucca in February 2004. (Defense Department photo)

ISIS soldiers march through the streets of Raqqa, the western Syrian city captured by the terrorist group and claimed as its capital in 2013. (SITE Intelligence Group)

ISIS leader Baghdadi proclaims himself leader of Islamic caliphate at the Great Mosque of al-Nuri in the Iraqi city of Mosul. (SITE Intelligence Group)

ISIS terrorizes captured Iraqi and Syrian cities with public executions, from beheadings to crucifixions, such as this one in Raqqa's main square. (SITE Intelligence Group)

A convoy of ISIS vehicles crosses the Iraqi desert in early 2014. With crucial support from sympathetic Iraqi Sunnis, the terrorist group is easily able to capture Iraq's second-largest city, Mosul, and much of Anbar Province. (SITE Intelligence Group)

ISIS propaganda video shows captured Jordanian pilot Muath al-Kasasbeh before he is burned alive on video. (SITE Intelligence Group)

King Abullah II embraces the father of slain pilot al-Kasasbeh outside the family home in southern Jordan. (Royal Hashemite Court)

Jordanian fighter jets return home from a bombing mission in Syria after Jordan's monarchy vows revenge for the execution of its captured pilot. "They will be hit hard," the king declares. (Jordanian Armed Forces photo)

—

The claim was audacious. Around the world, other Islamist leaders and religious scholars argued furiously about Zarqawi.

Among his harshest critics were a number of fellow jihadists, including some who knew Zarqawi well. One of the sharpest rebukes came from the terrorist leader's old cellmate and mentor from Jordan, the man who was first to recognize Zarqawi's leadership potential within al-Jafr Prison. Abu Muhammad al-Maqdisi had been in and out of detention during the years when Zarqawi was away, and the differences that emerged between the friends during their last weeks in jail had widened in the years since. Now Maqdisi watched in disapproval as his former protégé killed Muslim men, women, and children who had nothing to do with overthrowing a corrupt leader.

"I hear and monitor the chaos that rages today in Iraq, by means of which they seek to blemish the Jihad and its honorable image by blowing up cars, planting bombs in the roads, and firing mortars in the streets, markets, and other places where Muslims congregate," Maqdisi wrote in a letter he posted on his personal Web site, assuming—accurately—that Zarqawi would see it. "The hands of the Jihad fighters must remain clean, so as not to be sullied with the blood of those whom it is forbidden to harm, even if they are rebellious sinners."

Maqdisi had no qualms about using violence, but he was a stickler for the rules, as he understood them. Zarqawi, the pupil, had somehow missed some of the nuances.

"An example of this," he wrote, "is when the fighter crosses the lines of Sharia by abducting or killing a Muslim for non-Sharia reasons—such as claiming he worked for the infidels when the work doesn't reach the level of giving aid to the infidels."

And there was another thing: suicide bombing. Islam forbids it, he declared, except in rare cases where there are no other means of waging the struggle. Zarqawi's men had compounded the sin by using suicide bombers to kill the innocent, he said. That the intended victims were Shiites was no excuse.

"Even if our Sunni brothers in Iraq have many justifications, this does not justify blowing up mosques," Maqdisi said. "Permitting the [spilling of] blood of the Shiites is a mistake in which Jihad fighters had best not become entangled."

A religious backlash to Zarqawism stirred among mainstream Muslims as well. The most significant repudiation of Zarqawi's ideology came from his native country, organized by the man whose amnesty decree in 1999 had inadvertently given Zarqawi his chance.

In 2002, King Abdullah II had been scolded by American officials for warning that an invasion of Iraq would "open Pandora's box," and he was taking no pleasure in seeing his predictions coming true. Sickened by the bombings and beheadings carried out in Allah's name, the monarch began a series of private meetings with religious scholars to talk about a way to draw a line between Islam, the ancient faith, and the hateful *takfiri* creed used by Zarqawi to justify the killing of those he regarded as apostates.

It was no easy assignment. Unlike Shiites or Roman Catholics, Sunni Muslims lack a centralized religious hierarchy that settles theological debates. Muftis, Sunni clerics of a certain rank, can issue religious edicts called fatwas, but any two can disagree wildly on the same topic: what is a damnable sin to one scholar may be regarded as permissible or even obligatory behavior to another. Since his arrival in Iraq, Zarqawi had become a master at exploiting the contradictions in the system, surrounding himself with like-minded clerics who issued fatwas to condone suicide bombings and the killing of Muslim innocents, actions that would be regarded as anti-Islamic under almost any reasonable interpretation of Koranic texts.

The best antidote, Abdullah felt, was a strong denunciation that carried the moral weight of all branches of Islam, everywhere in the world. It must be a statement of clarity and universality, equally acceptable to mainstream Sunnis and Shiites from Cairo to Kabul, and from Tehran to Timbuktu. To begin the task, Abdullah deputized one of his cousins, a Cambridge-educated Islamic scholar named Prince Ghazi bin Muhammad, and pulled together the country's top clerics and religious experts to draft a declaration that sought to address three key questions:

Who is a Muslim? Who is empowered to issue fatwas? And under what circumstances can one Muslim brand another as an apostate?

On November 9, 2004, the king took a seat next to Jordanian Chief Justice Iz al-Din al-Tamimi as the judge read a short declaration that Abdullah hoped would serve as the template for Muslim rejection of *takfiri* beliefs.

"We denounce and condemn extremism, radicalism and fanaticism today, just as our forefathers tirelessly denounced and opposed them throughout Islamic history," al-Tamimi read. "On religious and moral grounds, we denounce the contemporary concept of terrorism that is associated with wrongful practices, whatever their form may be. Such acts are represented by aggression against human life in an oppressive form that transgresses the rulings of God."

The statement drew little notice in the West. In Washington, the news media and political establishment were busily dissecting President George W. Bush's narrow reelection victory over his Democratic rival, John F. Kerry, the previous week. Within thirty-six hours of the declaration, the spotlight would shift to France, where the Palestinian leader Yasser Arafat would die while receiving treatment for the flu, sending much of the Arab world into spasms of mourning.

Still, Abdullah continued to lobby Muslim leaders to support his declaration. Months later, more than two hundred Islamic scholars—representing more than fifty countries, from Saudi Arabia and Egypt to Iran and Lebanon—gathered in the Jordanian capital to craft a more expansive statement that carried the same blanket rejection of religion-inspired violence. Over the following year, a total of five hundred Islamic scholars and seven international Islamic assemblies would formally endorse what came to be called "the Amman Message."

"It is neither possible nor permissible to declare as apostates any group of Muslims who believes in God," the statement said.

It was the first time scholars and religious leaders from across the Islamic world had come together to denounce *takfiri* ideology collectively, in a consensus statement considered legally binding for observant Muslims. No one expected an immediate halt to the bloodshed in Iraq, and, indeed, the killings continued as before. Yet Abdullah, reflecting on the effort afterward, said there had been no choice but to speak out. Even though Zarqawi might be fighting Americans and Shiites, his chief targets were ultimately the minds of young Muslims he hoped to win to his cause. Each bombing shown on the nightly news, each grotesque video uploaded to the Internet, brought Zarqawi closer to his goal. And until now, the rest of the Muslim world had offered nothing substantial in reply.

"The ability of a few extremists to influence perceptions through acts of barbarity places greater responsibility on the moderates, of all religions, to speak up," the king said. "If the majority remains silent, the extremists will dominate the debate."

Another contender for the sympathies of young Muslims was beginning to see Zarqawi in a more charitable light. Osama bin Laden had never tried to disguise his personal dislike for the Jordanian. But three years after the attacks of September 11, 2001, Zarqawi offered the potential for something that Bin Laden desperately needed: a win.

The al-Qaeda founder was trapped in an exile of his own making, able to do little more than pass along instructions and advice by courier to operatives hundreds of miles away. By co-opting Zarqawi, al-Qaeda could share the credit for his successes and draw in new energy from his suddenly white-hot celebrity. Over time, perhaps it could also rein in some of Zarqawi's worst excesses.

The partnership was officially confirmed by Bin Laden in an audiotape broadcast on Arab cable-news channels. In his usual low-key manner, he announced a new branch of the al-Qaeda movement, and an impressive promotion for the man he designated as the leader.

"It should be known that mujahed brother Abu Musab al-Zarqawi is the emir of the al-Qaeda for Jihad Organization in the Land of the Two Rivers," Bin Laden said. "The brothers in the group there should heed his orders and obey him in all that which is good."

The statement from Zarqawi's side—a choreographed response, Western analysts believed—gushed with enthusiasm. It heralded a historic merger, the details of which would bring "great joy to the people of Islam, especially those on the front lines."

"It was with good tidings of support during this blessed month that Tawhid wal-Jihad's leader, Abu Musab al-Zarqawi (God protect him) and his followers announced their allegiance to the Sheikh al-Mujahideen of our time, Abu Abdullah Osama bin Laden, God protect him," the posting stated.

More than a mere partnership, this merger marked a new beginning, the birth of a movement that would cleanse Muslim lands of "every infidel and wicked apostate" and pave the way for a restoration of the Islamic caliphate, it said.

"This is undoubtedly an indication that victory is approaching, God willing, and that it represents a return to the glorious past," Zarqawi's statement continued. "We shall, with great fury, instill fear in the enemies of Islam."

Zarqawi promised Bin Laden that he would obey him, "even if you bid us plunge into the ocean." Yet he could not resist pointing out that it was Bin Laden who had come around to accepting Zarqawi's plan for running the insurgency. "Our most generous brothers in al-Qaeda came to understand the strategy," he wrote, "and their hearts warmed to its methods and overall mission."

Al-Qaeda now officially had a franchise in Iraq, and the rough-talking thug from Zarqa had a new title: *emir*. Or, in English, "the prince." The marching orders for al-Qaeda's newest franchisee came courtesy of Osama bin Laden himself: Stop the Iraqi elections.

14

"Are you going to get him?"

Iraq's historic first vote for a National Assembly was set for January 30, 2005, and Bin Laden, in the same audio statement that welcomed Abu Musab al-Zarqawi into the fold, denounced the polls as sinful. "An apostasy against Allah," he said. In fact, Zarqawi was already hard at work to ensure that the elections failed. He didn't have to stop all voting; he needed only to keep enough of Iraq's Sunnis away from the polls to discredit the results. His campaign to make Iraq unsafe for democracy seemed designed to frustrate the efforts of the U. S. Embassy's chief political officer, whose impossible mission that winter was persuading Sunni politicians to run for office.

Robert Ford was seeking something that was, in the minds of many of the Iraqis he canvassed, tantamount to a death warrant for them and perhaps their families. It was hard to argue otherwise. Over the past year, Sunni government officials and candidates had been shot, stabbed, kidnapped, blown up at home, and blown up in their cars. Most distressing to Ford were the cases involving Iraqis he had gotten to know personally, like the nervous Anbar governor he met in Ramadi on one of his first trips outside the Green Zone. This man, Karim al-Burjas, a former army general, confided to Ford that he was thinking about quitting his job in fear for his safety. Five days later, gunmen from Zarqawi's organization attacked his house and kidnapped his three sons, the youngest of whom was only fifteen. Burjas resigned immediately to secure their release. His hastily appointed replacement was forced to double as governor and mayor of Ramadi, because no one in the city wanted the post.

"Local government is in a state of crisis," Ford's office wrote in a confidential cable to Washington after the Ramadi visit.

Ford continued his search. As he often did during these months, he paid a visit to the one Iraqi Sunni official who could be counted on for frank, if occasionally harsh, advice. Tariq al-Hashimi was a former army colonel whose English accent and tailored suits betrayed his affinity for the West. He often infuriated other senior Americans at the embassy with his long diatribes about the U.S mishandling of the occupation. But he possessed an agile mind, a strong grasp of Sunni political currents, and fearlessness in expressing his views. Ford listened respectfully, and the two men eventually became friends.

In his thirties, Hashimi had become involved in underground Iraqi politics as part of the Muslim Brotherhood, the conservative religious organization with branches across the Islamic world. He rose to prominence in what became known as the Iraqi Islamic Party, while also pursuing an advanced degree as an economist. After Saddam Hussein's overthrow, the party emerged by default as the strongest and most organized political faction for Iraqi Sunnis, with Hashimi as its leader. When the Americans scheduled January elections for a National Assembly to draft Iraq's constitution, Hashimi's party initially embraced the idea and offered a slate of candidates. But then, a few weeks before the voting started, it abruptly shifted course and withdrew completely.

Ford made the journey from the Green Zone to Hashimi's villa to ask him to reconsider. The retired colonel, ruggedly handsome with close-cropped silver hair and a trim beard, was gracious, as always, addressing the diplomat by his first name. Then he invited Ford and his American compatriots to get lost.

"We're not going to put candidates in the election, because we're not going to get ourselves killed," he said flatly.

Hashimi had a long list of complaints that he recited for any American who would listen. It usually began with the grievance shared by most of Iraq's Sunnis: Since the overthrow of Saddam Hussein, Sunnis had been politically marginalized—and in many of Iraq's ethnically mixed neighborhoods, brutalized—by Shiites seeking revenge after decades of oppression. Sunnis had been evicted from Shiite neighborhoods in Baghdad and Basra, and some had been tortured and murdered by Shiite gangs and even Shiite police officers. The killings happened on both sides, of course, but many Sunnis, after decades of comparatively privileged status under Saddam, were incensed that U.S. forces were failing to stop the attacks. Rather than providing security, American troops raided Sunni houses at night to search for weapons and insurgents, destroying property and violating Arab cultural taboos against allowing strange men inside the private chambers where women and children slept.

"You target us with arrests, left, right and center," Hashimi complained. "Frequently, you get it wrong, and then you embarrass people like me."

But aren't Sunnis shooting at American soldiers and blowing up their Humvees? Ford wondered. And what about Sunnis who provide sanctuary to terrorists like Zarqawi?

Hashimi, as Ford well knew, was equally unhappy about Zarqawi and other foreign fighters who had taken over whole villages and urban neighborhoods across western Iraq. Weeks earlier, U.S. troops had waged a brutal block-by-block battle to drive them out of the city of Fallujah, only to see them slip away to Ramadi and other cities. Zarqawi had turned Sunni residential neighborhoods into war zones, and innocent Iraqis were being killed in car-bomb attacks. Still, Hashimi refused to concede the point.

"Of course they're fighting you," he replied. "You're making their lives hell."

Despite the bluster, it was clear to Ford that Hashimi wanted Sunnis to have a proper voice in the future Iraqi government. But it wasn't going to happen now, not with Zarqawi regularly broadcasting messages promising death to any Iraqis who ran for office or lined up to vote. Hashimi could not in good conscience ask his fellow Sunnis to take such a risk, he said.

"They'll be murdered by hard-line Sunnis in places like Ramadi and Fallujah," he said. "In places like Mosul, if they're not murdered, there will be a boycott anyway, so they'll lose, under your stupid proportional representation system, to the Shiites and the Kurds."

Over the following weeks, Ford and his embassy colleagues sent reports to the Bush administration urging that the election be postponed until Iraq's security improved and Sunnis could be persuaded to participate. The United States should not serve as guarantor for a vote that would be seen by a third of the country's population as illegitimate, the diplomats warned.

"We told Washington this," Ford said later. "Shiites will vote, Kurds will vote, but the Sunnis will not vote. You'll get a heavily lopsided Shiite-Kurdish government, without any Sunnis. And that will make the problem worse."

It was a message that few at the highest levels of the Bush administration wanted to hear. Some administration officials suggested introducing alternate ways of voting so Sunnis could cast ballots at home, without exposing themselves to violence at a polling booth. One proposal would have allowed Iraqis to vote over the Internet or by cell phone, but that option was quickly ruled out as impractical. Even assuming that computers could be found, many parts of Anbar Province had only sporadic electric power, and often none at all. When Ford pointed out the impracticalities, a White House aide scolded him for being "unhelpful."

In any case, President Bush was adamant about keeping on schedule. Under the White House's plan, there would be elections for a constitutional assembly, then a new Iraqi constitution, then a second round of voting for a new Parliament, and, finally, a legitimately chosen Iraqi government that would assume responsibility for the country and its myriad problems. Even a single day's delay would mean postponing the moment when the United States could symbolically hand over the keys and move on.

"The president," Ford recalled, "would not hear of it."

On January 30, 2005, millions turned out to cast ballots in the country's first democratic election. TV news programs showed smiling Iraqis holding up fingers dyed with purple ink to signify that they had cast their votes. True to Zarqawi's warnings, insurgents carried out scores of attacks, mostly on polling stations in Sunni areas. At least forty-four people died.

U.S. and Iraqi officials declared the election a success. Despite the violence, Zarqawi had failed in his threat to "wash the streets in blood."

Yet, by another key measure, the leader of al-Qaeda in Iraq had achieved exactly what he wanted: throughout the country, from the Syrian border to the Persian Gulf, Sunni voters stayed home. In Anbar Province, the participation rate among Sunnis was a mere 2 percent. Over the next ten months, other Iraqis would approve a draft constitution that would decide how power and oil wealth would be divided among the country's three major sectarian groups and thirty-six million people. But Sunni voices would be muted during those discussions, and the Sunnis' despair about their diminished status—a disenfranchised and persecuted minority within a country they once owned—would only deepen in the years to come.

Still, with Ford's patient prodding, Hashimi eventually agreed to enter politics, rising to become Iraq's vice president and one of the country's most prominent advocates for Sunni concerns. But just a week after his swearing in, gunmen from Zarqawi's network ambushed Hashimi's brother and sister in separate, targeted attacks on Baghdad's streets. A second brother, a senior military adviser to the Iraqi government, was shot and killed five months later inside his house.

Two days after his sister's funeral, Hashimi consented to a televised interview with the BBC. The usual swagger was missing, and a slight quaver in his voice betrayed the strain of a man who had just buried two siblings, both killed in an attempt to frighten him into resigning. But Hashimi insisted he would not quit.

"We are satisfied that our course is sound," he said. "The blood that was shed and the martyrs who have fallen are the price that we pay."

As the body count grew, so did the ranks of Zarqawi's enemies. Even in Anbar Province, where so many had welcomed the foreign fighters when they were killing U.S. soldiers and Shiites, some now would deliver the terrorist to the Americans if they could. Almost daily, tips came in: to police stations, to military patrols, to informants who spoke to other informants along a chain that terminated in the CIA's ever-expanding operations center in Baghdad.

One such tip, in February 2005, almost netted Zarqawi. It unfolded as the CIA officer Nada Bakos watched—mesmerized, anxious, then furious—from monitors streaming live video from a surveillance drone flying overhead.

The morsel of intelligence that had fallen to the Americans was this: One of Zarqawi's top lieutenants would be traveling on the highway from Fallujah to Ramadi on February 20 on his way to an important meeting. The circumstances suggested better-than-even odds, U.S. officials believed, that Zarqawi would be making the journey as well. A surveillance drone and teams of commandos were positioned along the route to watch.

Sure enough, in midafternoon, the drone picked up the deputy's car and began trailing it as it sped west. Two other vehicles, including a small truck, followed the first at a discreet distance, racing along a flat desert road lined with irrigated farms and groves of date palms.

The sudden appearance of a military roadblock brought the tiny convoy to a screeching halt. The first vehicle was quickly swarmed by soldiers, but the others veered off the road into the desert, spun around, and tore off in different directions. The drone overhead locked its camera on the pickup truck as its driver, either from intuition or alerted by the aircraft's high-pitched whine, began swerving violently in an apparent attempt to avoid any missiles heading his way. The pickup skidded and jerked, narrowly missing abandoned cars and road signs in the driver's futile effort to outmaneuver the drone.

Bakos watched, transfixed. What incredible luck if Zarqawi's career were to end inside a hulk of twisted metal on the road to Ramadi, she thought.

"Just wreck!" she said, shouting at the silent images on the screen. "Die in the car, already!"

But Zarqawi would not die, not on this day. The speeding truck cut sharply again and flew down a dirt road toward a small farmhouse surrounded by dense palm groves. One figure leapt out of the truck, but the driver pressed onward, finally coming to a halt under a canopy of palm fronds.

Zarqawi still might have been caught, but for a technical glitch that occurred at the worst possible moment for the Americans. The surveillance drone's camera chose to reset itself just as Zarqawi was making his escape through the palms. When American soldiers arrived, they were forced to work slowly through the groves, moving carefully to avoid ambush or a booby trap. By then, the fugitives had long since disappeared, leaving the truck wedged against a date palm. Searching the truck, the soldiers made an extraordinary find. Resting on the seat was a laptop computer—Zarqawi's computer—next to a sack containing a hundred thousand dollars in mixed currencies. The truck's occupants had been in such a panic that they had not paused to grab even these treasures.

It took two weeks to break the computer's encryption, and far longer to translate and analyze the entire hard drive fully. By then, most of the immediately usable details—addresses of safe houses, operational plans, cell-phone numbers—were obsolete. Yet the laptop held something of inestimable value: it was the closest that American analysts had come to being able to peer inside Zarqawi's brain.

One file contained dozens of photographs, including a series of passport images showing Zarqawi trying on different looks and disguises, from clean-shaven businessman with wire-rimmed glasses to Arab sheikh with a mustache and checkered kaffiyah. Another held Zarqawi's medical files, with more photos and notes about therapy for various war injuries. There were memos and e-mails laying out the terrorist group's changing structure, in which Zarqawi carved out an "operational commander" role for himself while allowing Iraqis more visibility as the nominal leaders of al-Qaeda in Iraq. Still other folders contained long e-mails to al-Qaeda leaders, including Bin Laden himself, as well as PowerPoint presentations and priceless video recordings of meetings of Zarqawi's leadership council, in which the Jordanian discussed strategy and plans. While a few of the individual documents were already familiar to U.S. counterterrorism experts, others were new.

"There was a PowerPoint briefing that was as good as any given by one of our commands," said a military analyst who was among those who pored through the computer's contents. "His organization, as a line-and-block chart—all of it was laid out there. Kind of a who's-who."

One video captured an entire war-council session, with fly-on-the-wall intimacy that was at once fascinating and chilling. Here were hardened killers sitting on a circle of blankets like schoolchildren, listening with rapt attention as one of their members sang a song and another recited poetry. Zarqawi, when it was his turn, told jokes and stories. Then he talked about his vision for Iraq and the region, and how, from rubble and ash, the jihadists would lay the foundation for something that was utterly new, yet as old as Islam.

Here Zarqawi departed from the usual jihadi rhetoric. Other radical Islamists spoke vaguely of the restoration of the caliphate from Islam's golden age, when all Muslims lived under a single religious authority that erased the national boundaries imposed by the West. But Zarqawi wasn't talking about the distant future. He spoke of the caliphate in the present tense, with himself as the leader of a liberation army that was already on the march.

"He was already building it," said the military analyst who studied the laptop's contents. "His thinking was strategic and very long-term."

Bakos, too, was struck by Zarqawi's performance. Back at CIA headquarters in Langley, she studied the laptop's trove. The images deepened her conviction about the pathologies that drove the Jordanian and his core followers: the cultish behaviors and messianic thinking that distinguished them as different from Bin Laden and his aides. A formal analysis by CIA psychologists reached similar conclusions: A classic narcissist, Zarqawi truly appeared to see himself as the incarnation of one of the ancient Islamic warriors he so admired. Now his belief in his own greatness was swelling like a tumor. Long-settled doctrinal issues, such as the prohibition against killing innocents, no longer mattered, because Zarqawi's opinions trumped centuries of Islamic scholarship.

"There are some who study the Koran and understand it," Bakos later said of the evolving thinking on the Jordanian terrorist. "Zarqawi can recite parts of the Koran—he couldn't read it for the longest time, because he was barely literate—and he's just going to interpret it however he wants, even though he lacks the education and background."

The study of Zarqawi was now Bakos's full-time pursuit. Just a year earlier, fed up with the constant requests to chase phantom al-Qaeda connections to Saddam Hussein, she had tried to quit the CIA in an angry pique. She gave her boss notice and didn't return to work for four days, until a senior manager phoned to try to talk her into coming back. As a sweetener, she was promised a new job as a targeting analyst, focused solely on Zarqawi. "Targeters," as they are known in CIA-speak, are the agency's super-sleuths, assembling the trail of evidence that would lead to the capture or killing of a single terrorist regarded by the agency as a threat to the country. Some, like Bakos, lived divided lives, shuttling between the frenetic world of the CIA's counterterrorism office and dangerous outposts overseas. Often they stayed on the case until their quarry was removed from the CIA's list, usually by death. Bakos, as a newly minted targeter, would be able to dip into intelligence streams from across the U.S. government's vast networks to find the clue or security stumble that could put Zarqawi out of business for good.

Between Iraq deployments, Bakos returned to what, for her, passed as a normal life. She moved into Washington's Cleveland Park, a charming neighborhood of late-nineteenth-century homes and stylish cafés, dropping off her bags in a house that was a few blocks from the National Zoo. The extreme secrecy of her job—her family still had only a vague idea of what she did for a living—limited her socializing mostly to work friends. Though Bakos was no crafter, she joined a "knitting and wine" club made up of other female CIA analysts, just for the companionship.

"We could talk openly, and it was just nice," she said. "It was more about the wine drinking than the knitting."

But the next morning, it was back to the hunt.

One July day, five months after the near miss in the desert outside Ramadi, a fresh piece of the Zarqawi puzzle turned up in the daily cables from Baghdad. The surveillance net had snagged a singular piece of correspondence: a letter to Zarqawi from al-Qaeda's number two leader, Ayman al-Zawahiri. Bin Laden's deputy had authored a six-thousand-word performance appraisal that sought to express the organization's concern about its newest subsidiary. The CIA's acquisition of the letter was a closely guarded secret, so Bakos was only allowed to view it from inside a secure chamber that analysts call "the vault." She read, her fascination growing with every line.

The problem, which Zawahiri outlined in restrained prose, was simply this: Zarqawi's bloodthirstiness was beginning to damage the al-Qaeda brand among Muslims. It was fine to kill Americans and Iraqi soldiers, Zawahiri wrote, but the car bombings, the attacks on Shiite mosques, and the gory execution videos were sending the wrong messages. To ordinary Muslims, images of dead Shiite children and beheaded Bulgarian truck drivers were not inspiring, they were repulsive. "The mujahed movement must avoid any action that the masses do not understand or approve," Zawahiri warned.

> Among the things which the feelings of the Muslim populace who love and support you will never find palatable are the scenes of slaughtering the hostages. You shouldn't be deceived by the praise of some of the zealous young men and their description of you as the "sheikh of the slaughterers," etc. They do not express the general view of the admirer and the supporter of the resistance in Iraq, and of you in particular by the favor and blessing of God. And your response, while true, might be: Why shouldn't we sow terror in the hearts of the Crusaders and their helpers? And isn't the destruction of the villages and the cities on the heads of their inhabitants more cruel than slaughtering? All of these questions and more might be asked, and you are justified. . . . However, despite all of this, I say to you: that we are in a battle, and that more than half of this battle is taking place in the battlefield of the media. And that we are in a media battle in a race for the hearts and minds of our [Muslim community]. And that however far our capabilities reach, they will never be equal to one thousandth of the capabilities of the kingdom of Satan that is waging war on us. And we can kill the captives by bullet. That would achieve that which is sought after without exposing ourselves to the questions and answering to doubts. We don't need this.

The admonition was accompanied by praise for Zarqawi's courage and military accomplishments, and Zawahiri closed the letter by asking for some cash ("If you're capable of sending a payment of approximately one hundred thousand, we'll be very grateful to you"). Still, the intent was unmistakable. Here was evidence of a serious disagreement between the main branch of al-Qaeda and its Iraqi franchise.

Zarqawi replied in a fashion, though not to al-Qaeda directly. Two weeks after Zawahiri's reprimand, he penned an open letter to his old mentor and cellmate, Abu Muhammad al-Maqdisi, rebuking him and all Islamists who would question his methods. Maqdisi might be a respected Islamic scholar, but he didn't know everything, Zarqawi wrote.

"He does not and should not have a monopoly on knowledge, and not everything he says is correct, especially when it comes to Jihad and the current state of affairs," he said.

Zarqawi declared that everything he did—from killing Shiites to sending suicide bombers to their deaths—had been sanctioned by "righteous, truthful, Mujahideen scholars." But he couldn't name them, he said, because some were in prison and might be harmed.

A second rebuttal came in the form of an audiotaped message posted on jihadist Web sites in September 2005. Two months after al-Qaeda's number two leader cautioned him against killing Shiites, Zarqawi announced a new military offensive, specifically targeting the Rafidha, or "those who refuse"—a pejorative term for members of the Shiite faith.

"The al-Qaeda Organization in the Land of Two Rivers is declaring all-out war on the Rafidha, wherever they are in Iraq," Zarqawi said in the recorded message. He warned that other Iraqi groups would also be targeted unless they publicly renounced the Iraqi transitional government that had come to power after the January 2005 elections.

"You must choose between the good side and the bad side," he continued. "Any tribe . . . whose allegiance to the crusaders and their agents is proven will be targeted by the mujahedeen in the same way the crusaders are."

Such open defiance of al-Qaeda's leadership was mystifying, coming from a man who had worked so hard to obtain Bin Laden's approval. Bakos and other counterterrorism officers picked apart the letters and transcripts from inside their classified "vault," wondering whether Zarqawi was making a conscious play for global leadership of the jihadist movement, or just being boneheaded.

"We kept reading the letters over and over, just astonished at his tone," Bakos recalled afterward. "He was not deferential. He was emboldened, arguing with Zawahiri on what he thought was the right strategy to wage jihad in Iraq."

Bakos tried to imagine how it looked from Zarqawi's perspective, at the head of an army of thousands of fighters, all devoted to him and willing, even eager, to sacrifice their lives. Zarqawi had achieved something no mujahideen force had accomplished since the Afghan war: humbling a global superpower by miring it in bloody guerrilla war. He had plenty of money, weapons, and volunteer fighters. Unlike al-Qaeda's leaders in their self-imposed exile, he was fighting Americans and their Iraqi allies on a daily basis. As measured by plummeting U.S. support for the war in opinion polls, he was succeeding. Why should he take advice from Zawahiri?

His brutal tactics were offending some Muslims, it was true, but were they hurting Zarqawi's cause? Bakos was no longer sure. The hard-core jihadists—the ones willing to fight and die on Zarqawi's orders—were streaming into Iraq at a rate of 100 to 150 a month to join "the sheikh of the slaughterers." Zarqawi had embraced the emerging power of the Internet to craft a reputation as a fierce warrior who killed Allah's enemies without mercy. The images he posted, though repulsive to most people, made him an icon and a hero to many thousands of young men who saw him as avenging the Muslim nation for centuries of perceived humiliations and defeats. Here was evidence that Zarqawi no longer believed he needed Bin Laden's stamp of approval. Some analysts had begun to describe his organization as a local chapter or franchise, but it was clear that Zarqawi didn't see it that way. This was no al-Qaeda offshoot. This was al-Qaeda 2.0.

"People think he's hurting al-Qaeda's brand," Bakos said. "The truth is, he's helping his own brand, because he's winning."

—

That same summer, as Zarqawi and al-Qaeda sparred over the permissibility of hacking the heads off of hostages, President George W. Bush convened the first White House security meeting devoted primarily to the Jordanian terrorist.

It took place on the morning of June 29, 2005, in the cramped confines of the Situation Room. Bush, now six months into his second term, settled into his leather chair at one end of a polished wooden table as the other places filled up with familiar faces: Vice President Dick Cheney, Secretary of State Condoleezza Rice, Defense Secretary Donald Rumsfeld, National Security Adviser Steve Hadley. The morning's presenter was Michael V. Hayden, the four-star air force general and future CIA director, who was then the principal deputy in the office of the director of national intelligence.

Hayden opened with a quick sketch of the life of Iraq's most infamous terrorist. He talked about Zarqawi's upbringing in gritty Zarqa, his early delinquency, his adventures in Afghanistan, his religious conversion, and his jail time. He described the Herat camp, the flight to Iraq's eastern mountains, the assassination of the diplomat Laurence Foley, and links to the Millennium Plot. Then he began to outline Zarqawi's early terrorist forays in Iraq, including the mix of cunning and "dumb luck," as Hayden put it, that enabled him to land well-aimed blows against Iraq's leading moderate Shiite cleric and the head of the United Nations mission in Baghdad.

Bush looked up.

"He killed Sergio?" the president asked, referring to the diplomat Sergio Vieira de Mello, killed in Zarqawi's spectacular bombing of the UN building during the war's first summer. Bush had met the dapper Brazilian and liked him. "I didn't know that."

For the operations briefing, Bush turned to Rumsfeld, who in turn introduced a newcomer to the group. Stanley McChrystal, the Joint Special Operations Command chief and the officer in charge of the hunt for Zarqawi, happened to be on a visit to the United States and was tapped to update the president in person.

"Stan's going to tell you what we are doing to get Zarqawi," Rumsfeld told Bush.

McChrystal, now a major general, ran through a slide presentation as Bush asked occasional questions, according to the officer's written account of the meeting. When he finished, Bush studied the general for a long moment.

"Are you going to get him?" the president asked.

McChrystal summoned up all the conviction he could muster.

"We will, Mr. President," he said. "There's no doubt in my mind."

Later in the meeting, Bush turned to McChrystal again. "Do you want to kill him or capture him?" Bush asked.

"I'd like to capture him, Mr. President."

"Why don't we just kill 'im?" Bush asked, to nervous laughter around the room.

"Well, Mr. President, to be honest, I want to talk to him. He knows things we want to know."

Bush appeared satisfied. He smiled.

"Good point," he said.

In fact, McChrystal *was* confident, though there was no hard proof that he was any closer to capturing Zarqawi. McChrystal's Task Force 6-26 had zeroed in on several of the terrorist's lieutenants, killing some and interrogating others inside Balad Air Base, which served as the unit's headquarters. With each capture, the Americans' intelligence network grew stronger. And still it wasn't enough.

Better intelligence raised McChrystal's estimation of his adversary's ability. Educated or not, Zarqawi had repeatedly shown himself to be an able field commander, capable of transforming waves of untrained recruits into soldiers and suicide bombers who struck with purpose and discipline. From captured operatives, a portrait emerged of a leader with quiet, understated charisma and personal fearlessness. "This guy is the real deal," one of McChrystal's deputies said during a strategy session.

It was hard to disagree. Zarqawi possessed a "jihadist mystique—a potent mix of violence and real charisma, perfumed by thick propaganda efforts," McChrystal would later write. And now it was "wafting outside of Iraq's border."

Records seized by McChrystal's men also shed light on a remarkably sophisticated system for recruiting, transporting, training, and deploying suicide bombers from across the Middle East and beyond.

Often the initial contact was one of Zarqawi's propaganda videos, available to anyone with a computer and Internet connection, and handily supplying an e-mail address for communication. After the opening e-mail exchange, an army of handlers stood ready to guide the potential recruit through screening and indoctrination and then along a chain of safe houses and, finally, a perilous journey by foot across the Syria-Iraq border. Once inside Iraq, the volunteer would be relieved of any cash he had brought along, and then shunted to a kind of holding cell for further indoctrination in near-complete isolation.

"By design, often the first time a suicide bomber saw Iraqis in the flesh was in the moments just before he killed them," McChrystal said.

Recruits such as these rarely, if ever, saw Zarqawi, whose intense personal security tightened further as U.S. troops and CIA operatives stepped up their search. As McChrystal's men discovered in interrogations, Zarqawi kept his whereabouts secret to all but a small handful of top aides. He never used a cell phone, and he remained constantly on the move. He had acquired a third wife—an Iraqi, believed to be in her midteens—and his entourage now included two children from his second marriage. But Zarqawi hid them so well that the American search teams never saw a trace of them.

The hunters were improving, too, however. By mid-2005, McChrystal's Zarqawi team had expanded to include some of the best counterterrorism operatives and experts from across the U.S. government, from veteran special-forces soldiers to CIA analysts to techno-wizards from the NSA. To ensure that they meshed as a unit, he placed them together around plywood tables in a large "Situational Awareness Room," or SAR, surrounded by banks of video monitors carrying live feeds from a fleet of drones in constant orbit overhead.

McChrystal set out to neutralize what he perceived as Zarqawi's greatest single advantage: an ability to control the tempo of the fight. Zarqawi's nimble command structure allowed him to strike quickly and shift course to adjust to his enemy's movements. To defeat Zarqawi, the Americans would have to be even quicker.

"If we could apply relentless body blows against AQI [al-Qaeda in Iraq]—a network that preferred spasms of violence followed by periods of calm in which it could marshal resources—then we could stunt its growth and maturation," he said afterward, summarizing what became his strategy for the group the Americans now called by its new name. "Under enough pressure, AQI's members would be consumed with trying to stay alive and thus have no ability to recruit, raise funds, or strategize."

To keep the blows coming, the Americans needed to "operate at a rate that would exhaust our enemy but that we could maintain," he said. For Task Force 6-26, that meant keeping up with McChrystal's brutal personal regimen of sixteen-hour days with few diversions other than eating and fitness training. The general routinely worked through the night, catching a few hours' sleep beginning around dawn, followed by a daily run in Balad's 120-degree midday heat.

The night-owl schedule allowed the analysts to stay in sync with the commandos who conducted nightly raids on suspected insurgent hideouts. Captured fighters were immediately evaluated in an interrogation building next door to McChrystal's operations center. Other specialists quickly sorted through the night's "pocket litter"— cell phones, paper notes, maps—for scraps of information that might point the way to the next night's raids. The NSA's surveillance experts, arrayed around the same wooden tables as the commandos and CIA officers, added an additional layer of data from the day's video footage and cell-phone intercepts. The numbers of airborne cameras steadily grew, until much of the country was under twenty-four-hour scrutiny—an "unblinking eye," as McChrystal termed it—with the added advantage of being able to run the tape backward to retrace the movements of insurgents planting roadside bombs.

By the fall of 2005, the impact of the new strategy was unmistakable. McChrystal's teams were slowly eviscerating Zarqawi's command structure, removing scores of midlevel operatives responsible for everything from logistics and communications to recruitment and training. The list of Zarqawi lieutenants killed or captured grew to one hundred names, then two hundred. Of twenty-one known senior deputies, those closer to Zarqawi in the command chain, twenty were crossed off the wanted list, either dead or in prison. From Balad and Baghdad came a steady flow of confidential military cables reporting disrupted terrorist plots and vast stores of weapons and explosives seized and destroyed. One report dispatched to the Pentagon in late September described the discovery of a letter, signed by Zarqawi himself, authorizing an attack on the infamous Abu Ghraib prison outside Baghdad, where many of Zarqawi's men were being held. The strike was to be carried out by "AMZ elements"—the military abbreviation for Zarqawi's forces—in October or November, during the annual Ramadan observance, a time when an act of martyrdom is said to carry special rewards in the afterlife.

That plot having been exposed, Ramadan was relatively quiet by Iraqi standards. But five days later, on November 9, 2005, the TV monitors in McChrystal's operations center flashed urgent news. Across the border, in the Jordanian capital, three hotels were struck by suicide bombers in coordinated attacks. Scores had been killed.

McChrystal was at work that night, and he watched with his aides as news reports showed the Amman Radisson Hotel's shattered lobby and the covered bodies lined up in the driveway. There was little question about who was behind the attack. In McChrystal's mind, there was also little doubt that Zarqawi had made a grave, and possibly fatal, miscalculation.

"That," McChrystal said to a deputy sitting near him, "was a screw-up."

15

"This is our 9/11"

On the morning of the attack, Sajida al-Rishawi awoke for dawn prayers with the certain knowledge that the new day would be her last on earth. She idled away the hours in an empty rented apartment, killing time until her partner returned with the package that would allow them to start the final preparations. Finally, Ali arrived, and within minutes he had carefully begun to unwrap the bombs that had led them to make the perilous journey across the Iraqi desert to Amman. At last they lay side by side: his-and-hers suicide vests, tailor-made for the couple and constructed to be powerful, yet slim enough to go unnoticed under their street clothes.

Rishawi had not seen the vests until now; suddenly the time was nearly at hand. She picked up her vest, felt the surprising weight, touched the pouches bulging with steel bearings. It was impor-tant, she knew, to familiarize herself with the cables and detonating switch, and to make the little adjustments to ensure a proper fit around her shoulders and belly. Even a suicide vest should fit comfortably.

"He put one on me, and wore the other," the thirty-five-year-old Ramadi woman would say. "He taught me how to use it, how to pull the trigger and operate it."

Captain Abu Haytham listened quietly, careful to avoid any reac-tion that might halt the torrent of words. It was the second day of Rishawi's interrogation, and he was relieved that the woman was finally talking. All around Amman, memorials were still under way for the victims of the worst terrorist attack in Jordan's history: three simultaneous bombings at three hotels that had killed sixty people and shaken the country to its foundation. Abu Haytham, the senior deputy in the Mukhabarat's counterterrorism division, was now deep into a guided reconstruction of the crime, led by the suicide bomber who had lived.

The interest in Rishawi extended far beyond her role in the plot. The attack's principal author had quickly claimed responsibility, and the Mukhabarat had concluded from other evidence that Abu Musab al-Zarqawi was behind the deed. The question now was whether this hollow-eyed, emotionally distraught Iraqi woman could help point the way to Zarqawi himself. A suicide bomber could never have been part of Zarqawi's inner circle, but this woman had been selected for an unusually complex mission, one that required forged travel documents and an international border crossing. Someone had regarded Sajida al-Rishawi as worthy of a role in al-Qaeda in Iraq's first mass-casualty terrorist strike outside of Iraq. She might know the names of her recruiters, or perhaps the identities of the men who had trained her, or acquired the fake passports, or assembled the bomb. She might know of other operatives who were even now preparing for future attacks inside Jordan.

Others from the intelligence service were simultaneously playing out different strands. With a renewed urgency, the spy agency's teams arrested and interrogated Jordanians and foreigners suspected of having connections with the terrorists. Newly assembled undercover teams were moving into western Iraq to troll for snippets of information that might offer forewarning of Zarqawi's next strike. Yet the best hope for stopping Zarqawi lay in finding an insider, someone who could guide the Jordanians through the elaborate layers of the terrorist's security cocoon.

Inevitably the Iraqi woman would talk. With Rishawi, there would be no cause for anything more coercive than the captain's own voice.

The outlines of the woman's unhappy life emerged slowly, between bouts of quiet sobbing. Rishawi came from the volatile heartland of Iraq's Sunni tribal region, the sister of two men who had joined Zarqawi's insurgent movement in the early weeks of the American occupation. One of her brothers had become a midlevel officer with AQI before being killed by U.S. troops in the town of Fallujah. The Americans had also killed a second brother and a brother-in-law. The woman had been distraught over their deaths, and she felt a tug of obligation: according to tribal custom, Sunni Iraqis are obliged to avenge the killings of family members. The fall of 2005 brought a painful anniversary—one year since the first brother's death—along with the news of the first use of women as suicide bombers in the Iraqi capital. The authorities had been taken by surprise; females were usually waved through security cordons, and their loose-fitting *abaya*s, together with Iraqi taboos against searching women, made it easy to conceal explosives.

So Rishawi volunteered.

"I want to kill Americans," she told Abu Haytham, describing her pitch to the AQI contact she had met through her brothers.

Zarqawi's plan would unite the unmarried Rishawi with Ali, a man she knew from her hometown, as husband-and-wife suicide bombers, an ordinary middle-aged married couple who could walk into any public building without drawing a second look.

In early November, the couple met with two other Iraqi volunteers and their AQI contact to finish preparations. Rishawi and her partner were handed fake passports identifying them as a married couple, and told, for the first time, that they were participating in a critical mission across the border in Jordan, one that would target U.S. and Israeli intelligence officials. They also were given a realistic-sounding cover story: they were traveling to Amman for infertility treatments to help them conceive. As a final step, they were brought before one of Zarqawi's hired clerics for a hasty and legally dubious marriage ceremony. It was done not for the couple's sake—presumably, they would never live to consummate a marriage—but to avoid violating one of Zarqawi's strict religious codes. To the Islamists, it is forbidden for a woman to travel unless accompanied by her husband or a close male relative.

They waited for the Eid al-Fitr holiday, with its traditional feast marking the end of Ramadan, and the next morning they began the daylong trek across the desert to Jordan. Their travel documents passed scrutiny at the border crossing; finally, wearily, they arrived at the rented apartment arranged for them in one of Amman's predominantly Iraqi neighborhoods. The bombing was still four days distant: November 9, a date that Jordanians, like Europeans, abbreviate as 9/11.

When the day came, Ali produced the vests and helped her with the fitting. He secured the twenty-pound band of RDX explosive and shrapnel around her waist and, to ensure that everything was firmly anchored in place, wrapped layers of duct tape around the outside. Then they climbed into a rented car and made their way to the Radisson Hotel, where they arrived a little before 9:00 p.m.

The festive sight and sounds that greeted them in the hotel's grand Philadelphia Ballroom confused Rishawi, according to her account to Abu Haytham. Instead of English-speaking intelligence operatives in Western suits, she saw something far more ordinary and familiar.

A wedding.

Peering through the ballroom door, Rishawi saw families with small kids, and young girls and women wearing the formal gowns of a bridal party. Men were lined up along one side of the room, and women on the other, for the dabke dance that is traditional at Arab weddings. She watched, unsure what to do.

A hotel clerk approached the couple. Were they looking for someone? Rishawi's partner murmured something about wanting to see an authentic Jordanian wedding. Now they were forced to move.

Inside the ballroom, the two Iraqis separated and worked their way toward opposite corners, with Rishawi taking a spot near the women and girls. With one hand she reached into her overcoat and began to fumble with the detonator switch on her bomb. Why it failed to explode was never clear—was it a mechanical fault, or faltering nerves?—but the woman began motioning to her partner that there was a problem. With an agitated look, he pointed toward the ballroom door.

As she turned to leave, she could see him begin to climb onto a table. Then came the awful explosion.

"I didn't know what to do and I couldn't get rid of the belt," she would later say. "So I ran."

Rishawi fled through the lobby with the panicked wedding guests, stepping over the wounded and dying. When she finally stopped, gasping for breath, she was far from the hotel, still wearing the suicide vest and the black overcoat, now flecked with blood.

Later, in a taxi, she became agitated and confused, unable to remember addresses or landmarks. Shop owners and passersby would remember the strange woman in black who climbed out of the cab to ask for directions, speaking nervously with an Iraqi accent, and then walked with an odd, stooping gait. One who encountered her remembered that the woman was "just not normal." Rishawi remembered stumbling up to the home of her sister-in-law and collapsing onto the bed, where the Mukhabarat's men eventually found her.

Now, after days of replaying the events in her head, the confusion had turned to despair. Where were the American intelligence officers she had been sent to kill? Surely this had not been Zarqawi's intention.

"They told me I would be killing Americans," she complained repeatedly to Abu Haytham. "All I wanted was to avenge the deaths of my brothers."

She had been duped, and yet she clung, childlike, to the belief that something had gone wrong with the planning of the operation. Though she had never met Zarqawi, she could not grasp that the leader of AQI had really wanted her to sacrifice her own life to kill mothers and children at a wedding party. The fault was probably hers, she said, for, deep down, she had never been sure that she would be capable of pressing the detonator when the moment came, with her future and that of so many strangers balanced on a tiny metal pin.

"I didn't want to die," she said softly.

The questioning continued for days, but the limits of Rishawi's helpfulness were already becoming clear. She had never met any of the senior leaders in Zarqawi's organization. She was not a foreign recruit who might possess knowledge of safe houses or smuggling routes. Nor was she an Iraqi insider who might have insights into Zarqawi's patterns of movement. She was not, in fact, very bright. But for Zarqawi and his men, Rishawi had been perfect: a grief-stricken woman who could be persuaded to carry out a revenge mission against a target that did not exist. Even at that, she had failed.

Abu Haytham could not bring himself to feel pity; the horrific images from the Radisson ballroom were still too fresh. He left Rishawi in her cell and went back to his office, back to the task that now mattered more than any other: finding Zarqawi.

For Abu Haytham, the quest would become an obsession. Within the Mukhabarat, the counterterrorism deputy's stamina was legendary; everyone knew he often slept and showered at the office so he could work longer hours. Now, days would pass before he went home at all. Joining him on the case were scores of officers detailed from other divisions. Even translators and file clerks were pulled in to work the search.

"Everyone got the call," one officer remembered. "It was just, 'Get your weapon and come to work.'"

Zarqawi had searched for a way to spur his five million Sunni countrymen into action, and by that measure he had succeeded. Jordanians throughout the country were enraged and united—against him.

Within hours of the blast, thousands of people swarmed Amman's streets. Large crowds gathered in a square near Amman's oldest mosque, many chanting, "Burn in hell, Zarqawi!" Others marched somberly behind a woman in a black mourning dress who wore a sign expressing sympathy for "the brides of Amman." Religious leaders denounced the deed and its perpetrator from the minbars of the country's mosques during Friday prayer services. In the terrorist's hometown of Zarqa, his brother and fifty-six other relatives posted an ad in a local newspaper publicly renouncing their kinship with him.

Since the widely reviled U.S. invasion of Iraq two years earlier, Jordanians had been mostly quiet about the terrorist campaign under way next door. Though disturbed by the images of Iraqi car bombings and executions, some took satisfaction in witnessing the crumbling of the Bush administration's plans for reshaping the Middle East. In some of Amman's poorer neighborhoods, Zarqawi had been regarded as a kind of folk hero, protecting Iraq's tribal brethren from persecution by Shiites and Americans.

Now, and for years to come, Jordanians would speak of Zarqawi with contempt.

"This was a criminal cruel act that Islam has nothing to do with," one of the Amman protesters, a shopkeeper named Jamal Mohammad, told the city's English-language newspaper as he twirled a large Jordanian flag.

"Zarqawi is a delirious criminal. He has lost his mind," spat another.

Other Muslim voices echoed the refrain, from Internet chat rooms to newspaper op-eds to university campuses. In Iraq, Zarqawi had claimed that U.S. troops were his enemy, yet he killed innocent Iraqis. Now, in Amman, he railed against the monarchy and its servants, but he chose to slaughter women and children attending an ordinary Sunni wedding ceremony. Even the conservative Muslim Brotherhood denounced the bombings as "ugly and cowardly terrorist acts that cannot be justified under any logic or pretext."

The news of the bombing sent King Abdullah racing back to Jordan from Kazakhstan, where he was on a state visit. He flew all night, receiving updates and fielding sympathetic calls from other leaders, before finally arriving in Amman at 5:00 a.m.

Later that day he toured hospitals to visit the wounded survivors and appeared on national television to calmly assure Jordanians that the monarchy would "pursue these terrorists and those who aid them." Inwardly, he was seething, he acknowledged afterward.

"We're going on the offensive," he told a hastily called meeting of the heads of Jordan's security establishment. "What Zarqawi did was reprehensible. The gloves are off, and I want you to get him."

What Abdullah meant was not entirely clear at the time, perhaps even to him. But that day marked the beginning of a shift in Jordan's security policies. The Mukhabarat prided itself on keeping Jordanians safe, and the monarchy was seen as a reliable partner in sharing information about suspected terrorists with other countries, including the United States. But now Jordan would take a much more aggressive posture against al-Qaeda. Breaking with a long reluctance to work directly with U.S. troops, the monarchy began to deploy specially trained Mukhabarat teams to help American special-forces operators break up terrorist cells inside Iraq.

The change in tone was already clear a day after the attack, during a brief conversation between the king and Robert Richer, the former CIA station chief in Amman, who had become friends with the monarch during his two stints in Jordan. Richer, who now held the number two post in the CIA's clandestine Directorate of Operations, called the king to express condolences and ask about the investigation.

"This is our 9/11," Richer recalled the king saying. "This changed our optic."

Abdullah had known one of the wounded victims personally, and his visit to the hospital both moved and infuriated him. "They attacked innocent civilians," he fumed. "They killed the bride's father. They killed her husband's father."

The demonstrations faded in the weeks that followed, but Jordanian resolve appeared to hold. Even Islamists who had previously defended Zarqawi seemed ready to see him go, one longtime undercover operative said.

"People who would have never worked with the Mukhabarat were coming forward," the operative said. "Everyone wanted to talk about him now. Zarqawi had crossed a line."

So fierce was the outcry over the bombings that Zarqawi felt compelled to offer excuses. In the weeks that followed, he staged a remarkable retreat from the swaggering, supremely confident persona so familiar to millions of people around the globe.

Stung by the protests in his hometown, Zarqawi tried at first to claim a media distortion, as he did after the failed chemical plot. Just hours after acknowledging responsibility for the blasts, he issued a second audiotaped message, claiming that the dead wedding guests had been collateral damage from an attack on foreign intelligence operatives elsewhere in the hotel. Any Muslim deaths were due to an "unintended accident," Zarqawi said, resulting perhaps from falling debris from the real attack elsewhere in the building, or even from a separate bomb planted by the Americans themselves.

"Our brothers knew their targets with great precision," he said. "God knows we chose these hotels only after more than two months of close observation showed that these hotels had become headquarters for the Israeli and American intelligence."

But not even al-Qaeda was buying it. In July, Osama bin Laden's top deputy had gently reprimanded Zarqawi for his gratuitous use of violence. Now arrived a much sharper rebuke from one of Bin Laden's closest advisers. Atiyah Abd al-Rahman, a Libyan who had been a close ally of the al-Qaeda founder for two decades, ordered Zarqawi to stop defiling al-Qaeda's image among Muslims. He scolded the Jordanian for acting without permission in the case of the "recent operation of the hotels in Amman." From now on, he said, Zarqawi should seek approval for any major operation.

"Let us not merely be people of killing, slaughter, blood, cursing, insult, and harshness," Atiyah wrote. "Let us put everything in perspective. Let our mercy overcome our anger."

A veteran of Algeria's grisly civil war between radical Islamists and the state, Atiyah cautioned Zarqawi against mistakes that had brought down other jihadist movements that alienated themselves from local populations. "They destroyed themselves with their own hands, with their lack of reason. Delusions. Their ignoring of people. Their alienation of them through oppression, deviance and severity, coupled with a lack of kindness, sympathy and friendliness," he wrote. "Their enemy did not defeat them, but rather, they defeated themselves, and were consumed and fell."

For once, Zarqawi made no efforts to defend his actions. In January, two months after the Amman bombings, Zarqawi announced that he was giving himself a kind of demotion. Al-Qaeda in Iraq would have new Iraqi leadership and broader Iraqi representation as part of a new organization that called itself the Mujahideen Shura Council. Zarqawi would take a less prominent role as a strategic adviser, a move intended "to dismiss all the differences and disagreements," according to a statement issued by the new group in January 2006.

Zarqawi appeared to experience a rare moment of self-doubt. In a memo written after the Amman attacks, he refers to the group's predicament as "this current bleak situation" and acknowledges that things would likely worsen.

"In Iraq, time is now beginning to be of service to the American forces and harmful to the resistance," Zarqawi wrote in this memo, later found in one of his safe houses. He described Iraq's growing national army as "an enormous shield protecting the American forces," and he lamented the toll from the mass arrests of his fighters and disruptions in the money supply from abroad. He began thinking aloud about unconventional ways to knock the Americans off balance and restore AQI's momentum. What if the United States could be somehow drawn into a war with Iran? he wondered. Well aware of the intelligence debacles behind the U.S. decision to invade Iraq, Zarqawi mused about his chances of planting false evidence that could provoke U.S. fury against Tehran. Perhaps he could launch a terrorist attack against the West and plant evidence that would implicate Shiite agents backed by Iran. Or maybe he could disseminate "bogus messages about confessions showing that Iran is in possession of weapons of mass destruction," he wrote.

Perhaps Zarqawi understood the improbabilities of pulling off such a scheme, as there is no evidence that he ever tried. There were more practical steps that he could take to improve his chances against the Americans, and he listed them as well. One was to try even harder to incite sectarian conflict: between Shiites and Sunnis, Shiites and Kurds, Shiites and just about everyone.

The last step listed on the memo was an admonishment that had the feel of a self-directed critique.

"Avoid mistakes that will blemish the image of the resistance," Zarqawi wrote.

Then, suddenly, he was back.

After weeks of relative quiet, Zarqawi prepared an attack that would eclipse, at least temporarily, his blunder in Amman. His plan showed ambition, strategic cunning, and a theatrical flair rarely seen in Iraq's meat-grinder insurgency. More than anything Zarqawi had done to this point, this act would extinguish the American administration's hopes for an orderly end to the war.

Before dawn on February 22, 2006, five armed men in military uniforms walked into the courtyard of the thousand-year-old al-Askari Mosque, a revered shrine in the heart of the ancient Iraqi city of Samarra. The morning was moderately cool, and a crescent moon, penetrating through thin clouds, reflected off the mosque's iconic gold dome, one of the most celebrated structures in all of Shiite Islam. Moving quietly, the gunmen managed to subdue the mosque's guards and proceeded to plant explosive charges along the mosque's roofline.

At 6:44 a.m., two huge blasts shook the city awake. Residents poured into the street to see a rubble pile where the dome had stood. An entire outer wall had collapsed, and the dome cratered inward, leaving a concrete stump and a tangle of twisted rebar.

The bombs themselves injured no one—there would be no accusations this time that Zarqawi had murdered innocent Muslims. But destruction of the shrine touched off waves of killings and reprisal killings as rival bands of Shiites and Sunnis shot and hacked their way through the town, sometimes wiping out entire blocks. Days later, the body count at the city morgue had surpassed thirteen hundred, and the entire country appeared to be teetering. At the U.S. Embassy, the diplomat Robert Ford's office convened a series of urgent meetings with Iraq's political and religious leaders, pleading for calm. A confidential memo dispatched to the White House that evening bore the ominous heading "Sectarian Nerves on Edge."

"In public and private our contacts are speaking with genuine concern about the possibility of civil war," the memo read.

Bush administration officials quickly concluded that Zarqawi was to blame, and they watched in growing dismay as the toll from sectarian killings grew to surpass anything the Jordanian might have accomplished with explosive powder and shrapnel. Senior White House officials came to view the Samarra bombing as one of the tipping points of the war. Some credited Zarqawi for having "lit the match" that set the nation's sectarian tensions fully ablaze.

Bush took the news of the Samarra massacres particularly hard.

"I don't think anything disturbed him more than the sectarian violence that occurred in the wake of the Samarra mosque bombing," Peter Baker quoted John Negroponte, the former U.S. ambassador to Iraq, as saying of the president. "I think it looked to him like the whole game was going down the drain. He was really bothered by that."

From then onward, Negroponte said, when Bush's aides would brief him about the events in Iraq, "it was almost as though he was pleading with us not to give him any more bad news."

Zarqawi, on the other hand, was exultant. In the Samarra bombing's aftermath, he celebrated his success by doing something he had studiously avoided until now: he commissioned a photo session.

The Jordanian had made a number of resolutions during the weeks following the Amman debacle, and one of them was to improve his media game. Zarqawi had practically pioneered the use of Internet violence as a weapon and a recruiting tool, and he had personally starred in the Nicholas Berg execution video, though his face had been concealed by a mask. He now concluded that he, Zarqawi, should play the lead part in al-Qaeda in Iraq's public rebranding. He would no longer be the masked "sheikh of the slaughterers," nor would he consent to being filmed reading long sermons from behind a desk, in the fashion of Bin Laden and his deputy Ayman al-Zawahiri. Instead, Zarqawi would project himself as a kind of jihadist action figure.

The new video was shot over several days during the weeks following the Samarra bombing, and was edited and mixed to give the final product a professional gloss. The content would be all Zarqawi: Zarqawi meeting with his military council; Zarqawi studying a map; Zarqawi walking with other fighters through the desert; Zarqawi blasting away with a light machine gun.

Every scene conveyed the image of an outlaw warrior in his prime. In al-Qaeda's videos, Bin Laden sometimes sat next to his gun, or posed awkwardly while firing a few shots from a Kalashnikov, a gaunt, turbaned figure with a gray beard surrounded by much younger men. By contrast, Zarqawi moved with the confidence and vigor of a man who relished a fight. He dressed fully in black, from his beard and gangsterlike skullcap to his ninja's black pants and tunic. The only color contrast came from the green ammo pouch strapped to his chest and his jarringly white Made in the USA New Balance sneakers.

His narration bristled with the old Zarqawi swagger, but with fewer taunts and insults, other than the usual rhetorical blasts against the "crusader" army and its allies. Instead, he addressed Iraqis as "my treasured nation" and spoke in a poetic cadence.

"Your enemy is uncovered, by the will of Allah, weakened, unprotected, and broken in pieces," he said. "Do not give him a chance to take its breath, continue your stabbings one after the other. O flag holders, stand."

There was little need for bluster; the sectarian fire that Zarqawi had tried to ignite was sweeping through Iraqi provinces on its own momentum. Within days of the hotel bombs in Amman, U.S. soldiers in Baghdad discovered a secret underground prison where Shiite police officers systematically beat and tortured Sunni detainees. Inside the converted bomb shelter, the soldiers found nearly two hundred malnourished Sunni men, many of whom later described a daily regimen of beatings and electric shocks.

The bunker was located less than a block from the residence of Iraq's Shiite interior minister, Falah al-Naqib, who would later acknowledge that "there were some mistakes made." The discovery offered proof that the random sectarian attacks initiated by Zarqawi had prompted organized campaigns in response, supported in some cases by institutions of the Iraqi government. Even jihadists who questioned Zarqawi's war against the Shiites began to believe that the Jordanian's strategy was succeeding.

16

"Your end is close"

The border towns along Iraq's western frontier were already considered Zarqawi country in the early months of 2006. But, more practically, they were the domain of another man: an Iraqi customs officer who kept a self-interested eye on the stream of commerce flowing from Jordan and Syria into Iraq's western desert.

Zaid al-Karbouly nominally worked for the state, but he had long been in the pay of al-Qaeda in Iraq, a client who offered a far better salary, and other perks besides. Over time, Karbouly had been rewarded with ever-higher positions of authority within the terrorist organization, as befitted a man who regularly delivered intelligence on incoming shipments available for plunder. Sometimes he would perform shakedowns on his own.

Karbouly's stature in Zarqawi's criminal network and his reputation for personal avarice inevitably drew the attention of Jordanian spies who worked the border towns. So it was that, amid the soaring interest in Zarqawi following the Amman bombings, the Mukhabarat set a trap for the man who was known in the border towns as Zarqawi's personal customs agent.

It was now spring, five months since the hotel bombings, and fears inside Jordan of a second wave of Zarqawi-led violence had mostly ebbed. Extraordinary new restrictions were now in place throughout the country, from tighter controls at the border crossings to the concrete barriers and metal detectors that appeared overnight outside every major hotel and government facility. Still, the country was awash in Iraqi refugees, as well as visitors who crossed the border for medical treatment or to purchase Western goods that were hard to find in Iraq. One of the regulars was Karbouly, who was known to enjoy spending his illicit takings in Jordan's shopping malls and boutique stores. The Mukhabarat's officers simply waited for him to cross and, at the right moment, whisked him away. Soon he was in the spy agency's notorious holding cell, feeling the impatient stares of two of its top interrogators: Captain Abu Haytham and his boss, Ali Bourzak, the Red Devil.

Karbouly talked. Eventually, he even agreed to make a confession on videotape, admitting to a string of crimes including the shooting of a Jordanian truck driver during a shakedown and the kidnapping of two Moroccans who were turned over to Zarqawi's men for ransom. But the Jordanians were far more interested in what Karbouly could tell them about the network itself, and on that subject the details came surprisingly easily. It was as though Karbouly had been eager for a chance to unburden himself.

"He seemed almost relieved," said a former senior intelligence official who closely followed the case. "He didn't turn himself in. But once we had him, it was clear that he wanted out of that world."

Assured that the Jordanians would protect him, "he just started spewing," the official said. Suddenly the agency's interrogators were filling notebooks with rare insider accounts of AQI's command structure and tactics. One of Karbouly's jobs, according to the former senior intelligence official, was to oversee incoming supplies for Zarqawi's bomb factories—a job that gave him broad familiarity with terrorist cells around the country.

"He wasn't a bomb maker, but he understood how to get the material to the right places so it all came together," the official said, "He was sort of like a project manager."

Abu Haytham had spent time with dozens of men on the fringes of the Zarqawi network, and he recognized Karbouly's type. A Sunni tribesman from the Iraqi border town of al-Qa'im, he was in his early forties, much older than the typical foreign radical who crossed into Iraq to perform jihad. Though sympathetic to Zarqawi's cause and adamantly opposed to the U.S. occupation, he was also a career bureaucrat who looked out for himself and knew how to adapt to changing currents. Yet, somehow, a flicker of conscience had survived under the tough exterior. Karbouly was congenitally corrupt and inured to the daily violence around him, but he found himself gagging on Zarqawi's cruel excesses. The hotel bombings had been the worst, but there were other examples as well, including acts that Karbouly himself had witnessed.

Abu Haytham was puzzled. Killing innocents was Zarqawi's specialty, he noted. How could Karbouly avoid it? But the man was emphatic. The slaughtering of innocents was wrong. It was un-Islamic.

As the Mukhabarat continued probing, a story emerged about the Jordanian truck driver Karbouly had killed. The trucker had been stopped just inside the Iraqi border with a trailer filled with goods that, according to the cargo manifest, were intended for one of the American bases farther south. Drivers who were caught carrying such supplies were often executed as a way to discourage others. From Zarqawi's men came orders to kill this one.

Karbouly still remembered the man's name—Khalid—and the fear in his voice after he was handcuffed and blindfolded.

"He said, 'What will you do?' I said, 'I will kill you,'" Karbouly said in his confession. "He started to beg me: 'Please, do not kill me,' and so I said, 'I must kill you.'"

"He kept on begging me, and I pulled my personal pistol and said to him, 'Say your prayers,'" Karbouly said. "He said them as he was begging."

Karbouly shot the driver twice in the head and left the body, along with the man's passport and papers, next to the road. As an afterthought, he took his victim's cell phone with him.

When the trucker's phone rang a short while afterward, Karbouly reflexively answered. It was the dead man's brother. The customs agent made up an awkward story and said Khalid was fine, then hung up.

Moments later, looking at the phone still in his hand, he began scrolling through the personal files where the driver kept photos. He stopped on an image of four young girls, clearly Khalid's daughters.

"I had a kind of reaction," he said.

After that, each death that he witnessed felt like a reopened wound. In the second year of the insurgency, when Zarqawi had declared war on Shiites, Karbouly was at first sympathetic, having been incensed by stories of ethnic cleansing in Shiite neighborhoods in Baghdad and Basra. But now it was too much. Once, he had watched the grisly spectacle of a Shiite captive being beheaded by a gang of Zarqawi's thugs, for no discernible reason other than the fact that he was Shiite.

As the bodies piled up, Karbouly began to see clearly who Zarqawi was, and what Iraq was becoming.

"We didn't know the difference between Sunnis and Shiites until Zarqawi came," he said. "Now, every day, there is a killing."

By his own accounting, Karbouly was a peripheral player in the terrorist group: a sergeant, perhaps, not a general. But for the Jordanians, the arrest of a midlevel Zarqawi soldier—and a talkative one—was a breakthrough. Soon Karbouly was generating volumes of detailed reports about Zarqawi's operations in the border towns through which the group's supply lines passed. He knew dozens of other operatives like himself, and he knew the names of more senior commanders, including some who were high enough in the organization to take orders from Zarqawi's carefully guarded inner circle.

Karbouly did not know the location of Zarqawi's safe house. But with his help, the Jordanians were coming closer than they had ever been.

Throughout the spring of 2006, U.S. reconnaissance aircraft kept an unusually close watch on an Iraqi village called Yusufiyah, a cluster of bungalows and small farms built along a Euphrates River irrigation canal just south of Baghdad. The surrounding region had long been regarded as a staging ground for insurgent attacks on the capital. But in early April, an informant fingered the town as an occasional venue for high-level AQI meetings. Sure enough, on the morning of April 8, a drone assigned to Major General Stanley McChrystal's Task Force 6-26 caught sight of an unusual convoy of vehicles entering the town. Within two hours, an assault team of elite army Delta Force operators was on its way.

The helicopters swooped into Yusufiyah at 1:56 p.m., and minutes later the commandos crashed through the door of what they believed was a terrorist safe house. A wall of small-arms fire erupted from inside. One defender, wearing a large suicide belt, rushed the Americans, followed by a second, but both were shot dead before they could blow themselves up. A third would-be bomber detonated prematurely, splattering an interior wall with body parts but injuring no one else. After the shooting stopped, the soldiers found six bodies and rounded up five survivors, one of them wounded. They also seized caches of assault rifles, ammunition, and grenades and, from one room, some homemade videotapes.

The cleanup was still under way when surveillance cameras picked up other vehicles converging on another farmhouse, a few miles up the road. Again the helicopter rotors turned, and again the Delta team stacked around a locked door with blasting charges ready. But this time the occupants gave up without a fight. Twelve Iraqi men were handcuffed and squeezed onto the helicopters for the flight back to Baghdad.

At McChrystal's operations center, analysts reviewed the day's takings with bafflement. Task Force 6-26's counterterrorism experts came up mostly empty in their attempts to find background files on the twelve men arrested in the farmhouse. Yet everything about the Yusufiyah meeting suggested that the group was important. Several of the men were older and were treated by the others with obvious deference. Oddly, out of twelve adult Iraqi men, only one was arrested carrying a cell phone, suggesting the others had been savvy enough to get rid of theirs at the first sign of the approaching commandos.

The Yusufiyah detainees were quickly transferred to McChrystal's Balad Air Base, where the general tasked his best interrogators and analysts with breaking down their stories. The Americans were already convinced that several of the detainees were Zarqawi network officers of some stature, and these received special focus. Most interesting of all was a thickset former wrestler in his thirties whom McChrystal code-named Mubassir. The man spoke surprisingly good English, and he seemed to delight in making wisecracks and lecturing the Americans in their own language. During his first interrogation, he affected a posh British accent and feigned impatience at having to sit through hours of questioning.

"How long do you think this will be? Because I do need to get back to my family," Mubassir said, according to McChrystal's written account. The man claimed he was a video consultant who had been hired by other detainees for a one-day assignment, and he knew nothing about terrorism. As with the others in the group, his initial interrogation yielded nothing useful.

A separate team tore through the physical evidence obtained in the Yusufiyah raid. Here they made a remarkable discovery: on one of the videotapes seized in the first house, investigators found extensive unedited footage of a man in a ninjalike black costume and white sneakers, firing a machine gun from the hip. The significance of the find was soon clear: the occupants of the Yusufiyah house, whoever they were, were senior enough to own the raw outtakes from Zarqawi's propaganda reel.

McChrystal's men were getting closer, yet they still had no idea of the location of Zarqawi's base. They spent hours studying the video outtakes, looking for clues. Some of the scenes were inadvertently comical, showing Zarqawi struggling to figure out how to work the machine gun. After finally emptying his ammo clip, he handed the weapon to an aide, who grabbed it by the barrel and then dropped the gun with a howl of pain. The man appeared to have had no idea that the metal would be scorching-hot. These "blooper" moments would later be publicly released by the Americans in an attempt to undercut Zarqawi's propaganda image as a savvy street fighter. In a further slap, McChrystal also persuaded White House officials to reduce the reward for Zarqawi's capture from twenty-five million to five million dollars. The symbolic demotion would do untold damage to Zarqawi's towering ego, he reasoned.

Still, the Americans were grasping at shadows. In the weeks that followed, they continued searching the region near Yusufiyah, and added several new areas of northern and western Iraq to the priority list, based on an analysis of the terrain that served as the backdrop for the propaganda video. The interrogations of Mubassir and the other Yusufiyah detainees dragged on day after day, producing nothing. In the nearly three-year-old hunt for Zarqawi, the Americans appeared to have hit yet another dry hole.

But the searchers had important new allies. The Jordanians were proving to be invaluable partners. Jordanian operatives now working with U.S. special-forces teams excelled at picking up clues that Americans often missed, such as subtle differences in accents that could distinguish local Iraqis from out-of-towners.

Meanwhile, the Mukhabarat's interrogations of Karbouly and other captured Zarqawi operatives were yielding important insights. Karbouly, from his years as a customs officer, knew the major routes or "rat lines" that Zarqawi used to smuggle supplies and recruits. Two major arteries crossed the Syrian border near al-Qa'im, then ran to Sunni strongholds in the south, in Anbar Province, and northward to the city of Mosul; a third terminated in Baqubah, an ethnically mixed town northeast of Baghdad. Karbouly also knew enough about Zarqawi's past travel to sketch out a list of towns where the terrorist likely stayed. The Jordanian spy agency forwarded the new findings to the Americans, along with scores of tips ranging from possible Zarqawi sightings to the locations of weapons caches.

Impressed, McChrystal decided to meet personally with some of the Mukhabarat's team. First the general's top intelligence aides huddled with Jordanian counterparts at their headquarters in Amman. Then a small entourage led by Ali Bourzak arrived in the middle of the night at McChrystal's command headquarters at Balad, the first non-British foreigners ever allowed inside the highly sensitive operations center.

"We were just trying to learn everything we could from the only guys who had ever sat down with Zarqawi," explained one U.S. official involved in the meetings.

At one point, the Americans put up a map of Iraq and asked Bourzak where he believed Zarqawi was hiding. The Mukhabarat official thought for a moment and then rose from his chair.

"He walked up to the map and he put his finger right in the middle of Baqubah Province," the official recalled.

"If I were Zarqawi, I would be here," Bourzak said.

The Americans were mystified. Most of Zarqawi's support base and the bulk of the reported Zarqawi sightings were in the Sunni strongholds of Anbar Province and northern Iraq, between the Syrian border and Mosul. Baqubah, a city of half a million, was a restive mix of Sunnis, Shiites, and Kurds, barely sixty miles from the Iranian border.

McChrystal's team welcomed the input, but the Baqubah theory struck some of the Americans as a wild guess. There had been earlier reports of Zarqawi sightings near Baqubah; none had ever checked out.

"We never discounted it," the U.S. official said. "We just added it to our calculations."

Then, in May, another intelligence morsel arrived from Jordan that appeared to offer more immediate promise. At the Balad Air Base, the interrogation of the Iraqi detainee called Mubassir had stalled completely, frustrating the Americans and spurring Mubassir's hopes that he might soon be released. But now from the Mukhabarat came records of the man's past travels to Jordan, including several suspicious trips right around the time of the Amman hotel bombings the previous November. There also were hints of possible links between Mubassir and the family of Sajida al-Rishawi, the female suicide bomber whose vest had failed to explode.

None of it directly tied Mubassir to the bomb plot, but the Americans suddenly had a powerful new lever for prying open the Iraqi's lips. Two of McChrystal's most gifted interrogators marched into Mubassir's cell to lay out the new evidence and deliver an ultimatum: Help us, or we'll be forced to hand you over to the Jordanians for prosecution.

"We're trying to hold on to you, but if word gets out that you're tied to this, it could be really bad," the interrogators said, according to McChrystal's notes on the exchange.

Mubassir protested. "I can't give you anything because I don't have anything," he said. But then, just as the two Americans were leaving, he stopped them.

"I have something to tell you," he said.

—

Mubassir's new confession took up eight pages of typed notes. The highlight, by far, was a remarkable revelation about Zarqawi that had entirely eluded the Americans until now: the Jordanian had a spiritual adviser, an Iraqi imam called Sheikh Abd al-Rahman, who lived with his young family in Baghdad. And the two met regularly, about once every week to ten days.

For Zarqawi's hunters, it was the biggest break since the search began nearly three years earlier. If the information was true—and assuming McChrystal's team could find the right imam—they had just been handed a map to Zarqawi's hideout. Indeed, Mubassir's story was so good, some of the senior officers at Balad suspected that the Iraqi was bluffing or even leading them into a trap. The doubts grew after the Americans checked out an address for a Sheikh al-Rahman in Baghdad and found a house in a predominantly Shiite area—certainly the last place anyone would expect to find a Zarqawi confidant.

U.S. and Jordanian officials raced to gather whatever they could on Zarqawi's supposed father confessor. Drones hovered over the expensive house where the man known as Abd al-Rahman lived, and trailed his silver sedan when he rode around town with his chauffeur. Undercover agents in traditional Arab clothes waited near his mosque to snap secret photos of the young cleric with the close-cropped hair and trim beard. Finally, the images were shared with the Mukhabarat's new star informant, who cinched the case with a single glance. It was widely known within the terrorist network that Zarqawi had a young spiritual adviser, Karbouly said, but the man was known only by a fake name, a nom de guerre. The cleric in the photographs was the same adviser, the former customs agent said. He was sure of it.

Now came the wait. For two weeks, airborne cameras watched the house and followed the silver sedan on its mundane trips to markets, schools, and social outings. Each morning, the chauffeur waited in front of the house, and each evening, the cleric and his family returned home. At the Balad Air Base, the analysts watched their video screens and wondered if something had gone wrong. Had Rahman been tipped off? Should they simply arrest the cleric and try to get him to talk?

Then, around noon on a stifling hot Wednesday—June 7, 2006—McChrystal's team watched from their monitors as the sedan made a sudden break from its usual orbit. It meandered through residential neighborhoods and then turned to enter Baghdad's main freeway, heading to the northeast. On the on-ramp, the car abruptly stopped. Rahman got out of the car and began speaking on his cell phone. A few minutes later, a small blue truck pulled up behind the sedan, and Rahman climbed in. It was a classic car swap, the kind used for decades by spies to throw pursuers off track.

The truck sped through Baghdad's outer suburbs and then headed north, away from the city, and into open countryside. McChrystal was in his private office in another part of the operations center when one of his aides knocked on the door. Rahman was on the move and heading away from the capital, the general was told. But where to? McChrystal had guessed south, toward Yusufiyah. Instead, to his surprise, the car continued north for thirty miles, then veered east. Rahman's destination was now unmistakable: he was heading straight toward Baqubah, just as the Mukhabarat's counterterrorism chief had predicted.

The vehicles occupants made yet another attempt to shake off any pursuers. Just inside Baqubah's city limits, the truck pulled into a parking lot where a different vehicle—a white pickup with a red stripe—was waiting. Rahman got out to speak to the pickup's driver; then, for the second time in an hour, he switched vehicles. Soon he and the white pickup were heading north again.

About three miles from town, outside a tiny village called Hibhib, the pickup turned onto a small dirt road lined with thick groves of palm trees, and then proceeded down a driveway leading to a beige two-story house with a carport. The dwelling was all but obscured by a canopy of palms and dense shrubs, and it was protected at ground level by a wall and a metal gate. The Americans watched as the driver spoke to someone inside the compound, who opened the gate to let the truck inside. Rahman climbed out of the passenger seat, and then the driver backed the vehicle down the driveway and drove away.

It was 4:55 p.m., Baghdad time. Every eye in the operations center was now fixed on the grainy image of the small house under the palms. CIA analysts and military operators in the room had been waiting nearly three years for such a moment. Was this really the one?

McChrystal studied the images thoughtfully as one of his deputies replayed the frames of a white pickup entering the driveway. "I'm not going to promise you that's Zarqawi," one of McChrystal's deputies said, as the general recalled afterward. "But whoever we kill is going to be much higher than anybody we've killed before."

As they stared at the screen, a solidly built figure emerged from the building.

"We watched a guy dressed in all black come out and meet [Rahman] and take him in the house," McChrystal said. "And we watched that same guy, in all black, walk back out. He walked the length of the driveway to the main road and back."

McChrystal had seen dozens of images of the man he had been pursuing since 2003. The resemblance to the black-clad figure was unmistakable.

"Wow, that's Zarqawi," he told his deputy.

"That's right," came the reply. "That's what we think."

A team of Delta commandos was on standby in Baghdad, forty miles away, and now the command came for them to board their chopper. To the consternation of all, one of their helicopters was having engine trouble. Agonizing minutes passed. What if Zarqawi were suddenly to flee through the palm trees and escape? Could there ever be another opportunity like this?

At that moment, two American F-16 fighter jets were on routine patrol over central Iraq, under a policy that required twenty-four-hour coverage in case U.S. troops needed immediate air support. One of the jets was being refueled and was effectively out of commission, but the other was redirected toward Baqubah. An air-traffic controller read a set of coordinates, and the fighter was soon screaming toward tiny Hibhib, less than five minutes away.

McChrystal hoped the day would end with Zarqawi in his custody. "I really want to capture this guy," the general remembered thinking as the minutes dragged by. The truth is, no one could say with certainty that the man on the video was Zarqawi. McChrystal reckoned the odds at 80 to 90 percent.

The deputy interrupted his thoughts.

"I don't think we can wait," he said. "I'm going to bomb it."

"All right," the general said.

It was nearly 6:00 p.m. when the command came over the F-16's radio: "Drop the bomb."

The fighter swooped over the house, but, to the surprise of those watching the screens at Balad, the building did not explode. The pilot made a second pass, this time releasing a GBU-12 Paveway, a five-hundred-pound guided bomb. From the center of the F-16's video screen came a brilliant flash followed by three jets of smoke and dust, one shooting skyward and the others billowing through the palm trees. About a hundred seconds later, a second bomb hit in the same spot.

When the smoke finally cleared, the two-story house with the carport was gone.

It took the Delta team another twenty minutes to arrive by helicopter. The commandos raced up the driveway on foot, just in time to see Iraqi police loading a stretcher into an ambulance next to a rubble pile that had been Zarqawi's hideout.

The Iraqis backed away at the sight of heavily armed American commandos, and soon the soldiers were staring into the bloodied face of the man on the stretcher. He wore a thin beard and dusty black clothes, and he was bleeding from a deep gash on his left cheek. If the soldiers looked closely, they might have noticed an odd scar on his right arm, the legacy of a long-ago surgery to remove a tattoo.

Gravely wounded but alive, Zarqawi opened his eyes to see a ring of American faces looking down at him. Startled, he mumbled something unintelligible and tried to roll off the stretcher to get away, only to be stopped by American hands, some of them tattooed.

Years later, some of the soldiers present at Hibhib would claim that the commandos delivered the final blow, squeezing the life out Zarqawi as he lay on the stretcher. An autopsy found no evidence of it, concluding that Zarqawi had only minutes to live in any case, his lungs and other internal organs having been crushed by the intense pressure wave from the exploding GBU-12 bomb. A medic at the scene noted that Zarqawi's carotid artery had already collapsed from internal bleeding, and blood seeped from his nose and ears as he wheezed through a few last breaths.

One thing that appears incontrovertible is that Zarqawi was conscious long enough to look into American eyes.

The other certainty is that he died at 7:04 p.m. Iraqi time, as a fading sun cast long shadows over the palm grove that had sheltered him and his tortured dream of a resurgent Islamic state.

Major General Stanley McChrystal's first and only personal encounter with Zarqawi occurred that same evening, in a makeshift morgue in the Balad Air Base's detainee screening center. Zarqawi's body was laid out on a table so specialists could run through DNA tests to confirm the Jordanian's identity.

Minutes earlier, McChrystal had ordered a series of raids throughout the country in an effort to preempt possible retaliatory strikes by Zarqawi's AQI followers. He was still in the operations center when one of his men came up to him with word that Zarqawi's body had arrived.

He walked to the detainee facility to find the corpse laid out on a poncho. One of the Delta team operators, an army Ranger whom McChrystal knew well, was standing guard. A trickle of blood was drying below a gash on Zarqawi's left cheek, but otherwise the body showed no signs of serious trauma. McChrystal studied the face for a moment.

"He looks just like Zarqawi," he said, "like out of a poster." He turned to the Ranger.

"What do you think?" he asked.

"It's him," the Ranger said.

Zarqawi's death was not formally announced for another day, but the news was already being toasted in Washington, from the White House to the Pentagon to the CIA's leafy campus along the Potomac.

Bush's initial reaction was subdued. Just minutes before the news arrived from Baghdad, the president had been meeting at the White House with several members of Congress from both political parties. Illinois Republican representative Ray LaHood, a staunch supporter of the Iraq war, offered a word of unsolicited advice: "We really got to get rid of Zarqawi," he said.

Bush chuckled quietly, and Representative Steny Hoyer, a Maryland Democrat, leaned over to make a private joke at LaHood's expense. "Why didn't we think of that?" Hoyer whispered.

The first report of Zarqawi's possible death came minutes later, at 3:45 p.m. EDT, but the confirmation was delayed for another five hours. Members of Bush's national security team reacted ecstatically, but Bush could barely muster a smile.

"I don't know how to take good news anymore," he said.

The CIA officer Nada Bakos was traveling when the news broke. Just a few months earlier, the spy agency's top Zarqawi expert had returned to Washington for good, after angling for a new assignment that had nothing to do with the Jordanian. Now thirty-six, she had been the longest-serving member of the agency's Zarqawi team, and she felt frustrated and more than ready for a change. She had met a man she liked—someone far removed from the intelligence world—and they had recently gotten married. Their low-key wedding took place on an evening after work, and Bakos, overwhelmed by the daily demands of her job, showed up late for the ceremony.

She was with her new CIA colleagues on June 7 when the call came from a Langley friend that Zarqawi was finally dead. She remembered feeling slightly numb. What was the proper way to react to such news?

"I was happy," she remembered afterward. "But I guess I was disappointed that I wasn't with people who understood what it meant."

In Jordan, celebrations in the capital were counterbalanced by scenes of ugly protest in the terrorist's hometown of Zarqa, where some locals had begun reasserting their support for the town's most famous son in the weeks before his death. Near the family homestead, relatives and local Islamists erected a tent and announced a "martyrdom" celebration, lauding Zarqawi in television interviews before police arrived to shut the revelers down.

Abu Haytham, the Mukhabarat counterterrorism deputy who would soon rise to become the department head, expressed annoyance at the outburst but refused to let it darken his mood.

"I long had this mental image of Zarqawi bragging," he said, remembering his early encounters with the terrorist. "He always said that someday he would find a way to hurt us, to do something that would cut to the heart. To me, that was the hotel bombing—the image of those two little girls. Now, this is justice served."

But there was not justice in Iraq, not yet. Zaydan al-Jabiri, the rancher and tribal sheikh from Ramadi, watched the news of Zarqawi's death with indifference. The Jordanian might be gone, but the foul strain he had helped to unleash was stronger than ever, Zaydan told friends. Zarqawi's foreign-led terrorist network had morphed into something more insidious and homegrown. There were scores of Iraqi jihadists standing ready to take up Zarqawi's mantle.

In some parts of Anbar Province, the tribes were beginning to reclaim their rightful place, pushing aside the jihadists with threats and sometimes with arms. Zaydan would join them, eventually helping launch a movement that Americans called the "Anbar Awakening." It was an all-Sunni force that proved capable of driving the Zarqawists out of the streets and back into underground cells, at least for a time.

But for now, with Zarqawi dead, there were scores to settle with neighbors and relatives who had chosen the wrong side. One of them was Zaydan's very own cousin, the man who a year earlier had asked Zaydan to swear allegiance to the Jordanian criminal who aspired to be Iraq's leader.

"I told him, in our last meeting: 'Your end is close,'" Zaydan said. "We don't want to lose members of the tribe, but the crimes these people committed are too big for forgiveness."

Days later, the cousin was found shot to death.

"We killed him. My tribe killed him," he said. "It was treason, and he was killed, the way that we kill."

BOOK III

ISIS

17

"The people want to topple the regime!"

The trouble arrived in buses. Embassy officers spotted at least four of them, all big ones, such as the tour companies use, chartered by God-knows-who and packed with sweaty, agitated men armed with poles and sticks. The small caravan rolled into Damascus's posh al-Afif district at midmorning and parked a block away from the American diplomatic mission to discharge its jeering contents: a made-to-order Syrian mob.

Robert S. Ford, now the U.S. ambassador to Syria, stared from a chancery window at the sudden throng outside the embassy gates. Throughout this morning—July 11, 2011, four months into Syria's "Arab Spring" uprising—there had been reports of a similar gathering at the French mission, five blocks away. Now they were here, a small army of men in civilian clothes, with more arriving by car and on foot. Some were young with military-style haircuts; others had the paunches of middle age and scruffy beards and carried professionally printed portraits of Syria's autocratic president, Bashar al-Assad. An organizer wearing an ID card on a lanyard barked orders, while a handful of police officers stood idly in clusters farther up the block. From his top-floor perch, Ford watched as the street darkened with bodies like the thickening clouds of a summer storm. These were the regime's goons, without a doubt, and their presence here was anything but spontaneous. Ford ordered his staff behind thick walls and waited to see how far Assad would go.

For a time, it was just the usual chants and a few rotten melons lobbed over the gates. The attack, when it came, unfolded with surprising speed. First came the louder thumps and bangs of rocks striking the chancery walls and bouncing off shatterproof glass. Then a dozen men were being hoisted over the embassy's cement-and-steel fence, the one the contractor had called unscalable. Now intruders were running across the embassy grounds, shouting at one another, pounding on doors and windows, looking for weaknesses. Some of them clambered up a brickwork façade to the chancery roof, where satellite dishes and radio antennas were kept. Soon they were beating on the metal rooftop door that was the only remaining barrier between the protesters and the frightened embassy workers inside.

Ford stood near the battered door with two marines, both young recruits in their twenties assigned to the embassy's security force. The guards fingered their rifles as Ford mentally prepared himself for what might happen if the door burst open. Where were the Syrian police?

The awful banging continued, and Ford could now see the intruders' feet through a gap in the doorframe. One of the marines spoke:

"If they get through that door, we're shooting."

Ford thought quickly. Assad must have intended only to scare, not to harm. But why was he letting his goons get this far?

"No. You are not shooting," he insisted. "If they get through the door, you tell them to stop. If they see your guns and they charge anyway, then you may fire."

More banging. The wait continued, giving Ford ample time to second-guess himself. Surely the protesters would back away in the face of guards with rifles, he thought. Or would they?

Perhaps more than any other American, Ford understood the temperament of the autocrat who would have had to sign off on any decision to unleash mobs on two Western embassies. Assad was usually smart enough to avoid a needless provocation, but he also was famously short-tempered and vindictive. Ford had personally witnessed one of the president's mood swings, and the experience had made a lasting impression. An angry Assad could be unpredictable, and right now Assad was furious—at him. The assault could be called off at any moment, or the door could suddenly fly open to whatever combination of aggression and zealotry stood on the other side. In the broiling hot midsummer of Syria's civilian uprising, almost any outcome seemed plausible.

The pounding grew louder. The marines waited, rifles pointed at the door.

For a time, it seemed that the Arab Spring contagion might bypass Syria altogether. By mid-March 2011, tyrants and their security forces had been routed in Tunisia and Egypt, and others were falling in Libya and Yemen. But Syria was different. The country's economic and political elite lined up solidly behind the ruling Assad family, and the government's officially secularist policies and brutal secret police kept ethnic and sectarian tensions bottled up. As protests erupted in capitals from North Africa to the Persian Gulf, the tumult in Damascus's ancient passageways was limited mostly to the honking taxis and the cries of street vendors in the souks downtown.

The president himself was hardly the type to inspire protests. Mild-mannered by the standards of Middle Eastern autocrats—including his ruthless father, former president Hafez al-Assad—Syria's forty-five-year-old leader once had ambitions to be a physician. He studied in London as a young man and chose ophthalmology as his specialty, because he disliked the sight of blood. But his plans for a career in medicine derailed when his older brother, Bassel, died in a car accident, thrusting the tall, soft-spoken Bashar onto the leadership track. The death of Hafez in 2000 fueled hopes for political reform in Syria, and the new president at first seemed up for the challenge. Bashar al-Assad liberalized the country's economic policies and loosened restrictions on the Internet during his first months in office. More dramatically, he closed the country's infamous Mezzeh penitentiary, and declared an amnesty that released hundreds of political prisoners, including members of the banned Muslim Brotherhood organization.

U.S. officials watched the developments closely, sensing potential in the young Western-educated leader. What if Syria—so accustomed to playing the part of agitator and rogue—could be persuaded to take a more constructive role in the region? It was a distant hope, at best. Syria under Bashar al-Assad remained a chief supplier of arms and cash to Lebanon's Hezbollah militants, and a conduit for jihadists headed for Iraq. Damascus also possessed one of the world's largest stockpiles of illegal chemical weapons, including deadly sarin gas. And yet there were hopeful signs. Assad's security forces sometimes cooperated with the United States on counterterrorism cases, and the country's intelligence service occasionally made a show of arresting terrorist recruits at the airport and border crossings. Moreover, Syria's first family cultivated a public image that suggested a desire for closer ties to the West. Unlike his father, who preferred lectures and insults when entertaining Western guests, the younger Assad could hold a finely nuanced conversation on regional politics in flawless English. His wife, the elegantly beautiful Asma, was a British-raised economist who wore Christian Louboutin heels and promoted women's rights and educational reform. Massachusetts senator John F. Kerry, the future U.S. secretary of state, was among a parade of American officials to pass through Damascus and pronounce Assad to be someone the U.S. government could work with.

"My judgment is that Syria will move; Syria will change, as it embraces a legitimate relationship with the United States and the West and the economic opportunity that comes with it," Kerry, then the Senate Foreign Relations Committee chairman, said after a 2009 visit.

By late 2010, the Obama administration was ready for a bold step: it would appoint a U.S. ambassador to Syria for the first time since 2005, when relations between the countries hit a new low over alleged Syrian support for terrorism. To fill such an important post, the White House settled on a candidate with an impressive record for managing Middle East crises: Robert Ford.

The appointment had legions of doubters. So many senators opposed the notion of upgraded diplomatic relations with Syria that the White House dared not risk subjecting its candidate to the usual confirmation hearing. Instead, President Obama waited until Congress adjourned for the Christmas recess to name Ford as the fourteenth U.S. ambassador to Syria on December 29, 2010.

The president's choice for the job had misgivings of his own. Ford's distinguished service in Iraq had earned him his first ambassadorship in 2006, as the chief U.S. diplomat to Algeria, but two years had passed, and he was eligible for a new assignment. Ford considered Tunisia and Bahrain, both regarded as interesting but quiet postings. Syria, by contrast, was a notoriously brutal police state that openly supported anti-Israel militants. The job description there would consist of delivering regular scoldings to the regime over its support for terrorism.

"I don't want to go to Syria," Ford told his boss. "All I'll be doing is fighting with the Assad government all the time."

But he went. Just three weeks after his appointment, Ford was on his way to Damascus. A week after that, he was presenting his letters of credence to Assad in the presidential palace.

At the ceremonial meeting in Assad's hilltop residence, Ford watched the Syrian leader carefully for clues about the personality behind the charcoal suit. Seated in a powder-blue chair in a reception hall, Assad was affable and charming, showing no trace of the condescension so common among the region's palace-bred autocrats. He was tall and narrow-shouldered, with pale-blue eyes, and a trim mustache offsetting a weak chin; he spoke with the quiet self-assurance of a man who had grown into middle age without having to raise his voice. The meeting was going pleasantly enough until Ford gently broached the subject of the State Department's most recent report on human rights, with its lengthy catalogue of Syrian abuses, including official repression, torture, and murder. No sooner were the words uttered than the host's entire countenance changed. The volume never varied, but Assad was enraged.

"The last country in the world that I'm going to take advice from is the United States," he said in a low snarl. "Not on human rights. Not after what you've done in Guantánamo, Abu Ghraib, and Afghanistan."

Ford listened politely, summoning up as much diplomatic reserve as he could.

"Mr. President, the issues you just raised are perfectly legitimate," he said. "We should have to explain ourselves. But we're going to raise our concerns with you, too. And if we're going to make any progress on this bilateral relationship, we're going to have to have frank discussions about it."

Historic events would ensure that no such discussions would take place. Within two weeks of the meeting, Egyptian president Hosni Mubarak was driven out of office. Four days after that, Libyan security forces fired into a crowd of protesters in Benghazi, setting off a civil war that would topple the Libyan leader, Muammar Qaddafi. In early March, rioters clashed with police in the capitals of Yemen and Bahrain. And at last Syria, having seemed impervious to sparks from the revolutions south of its borders, caught fire in the span of a single turbulent week. On March 18, violent protests broke out in the southern city of Dara'a after police arrested and tortured local teens for writing antigovernment graffiti. On March 20, a mob torched Baath Party buildings in Dara'a, and police fired back with live ammunition, killing fifteen. On March 25, huge crowds poured into the streets there and in other cities, from Hama and Homs in the west to Aleppo, Syria's largest city, in the north. The House of Assad, so brutally efficient at keeping the peace at home, faced its worst domestic crisis in three decades, and the window for fruitful diplomatic engagement with the United States, its longtime adversary, slammed shut.

In Washington, State Department officials, scrambling to stay atop a half-dozen simultaneous meltdowns in the world's most turbulent region, watched to see which path Syria's uprising would take. Would Assad implement political reforms to try to stay ahead of the protesters, as the sovereigns of Jordan and Morocco had done? Would he share the fate of Egypt's Mubarak, jettisoned by his own generals in a bid to preserve peace and their own skins?

Syria's president quickly made his choice clear. From the beginning, Assad signaled a resolve to avoid the concessions that, in the minds of many of Syria's elite, had directly precipitated the fall of Mubarak in Egypt. There would be no serious effort to accommodate protesters' demands for political and economic reforms. Instead, Assad would seek to bludgeon, gas, and shoot his way out of the crisis. In the first week alone, at least seventy protesters were killed, and hundreds of others were thrown into makeshift holding cells.

The international watchdog Human Rights Watch later confirmed reports of twenty-seven interrogation centers set up by Syrian intelligence, where detainees were beaten with clubs, whips, and cables and given electric shocks. Yet the protests continued to grow.

The suffering by ordinary Syrians was, in the view of many U.S. officials, not only tragic but also wholly avoidable, if Assad were a more capable leader. Syria's biggest problems in 2011 appeared to be mostly economic: high unemployment, worsened by a prolonged drought that had sent rural villagers into the cities looking for work. The country's myriad ethnic and sectarian divisions had mostly been subdued after decades of secular Baathist rule. Many of the early protesters in Aleppo and Hama were angry not at Assad per se but at corruption within the president's inner circle. Frederic C. Hof, a former army expert on the Middle East who was appointed as special envoy to the region in 2009, wondered in the early weeks if Assad might still try to buy himself some goodwill by reining in some of his more extravagant relatives and dealing leniently with those protesting police brutality.

"The country's problems were being exacerbated by a general impression that Damascus elites were literally making out like bandits," said Hof, recalling his thinking at the time. "The president had spoken about reform and so forth, and people thought, *inshallah*, maybe he'll do something.

"If he had handled reform and protests smartly, he could have had himself crowned emperor of Syria," Hof said.

Instead, with brutal displays of force—nearly all of it captured on cell-phone cameras—the Syrian leader managed to unite much of the country against him. He still controlled considerable assets. Of twenty-one million Syrians, Assad could reliably depend on members of his minority Alawite sect, which controlled the country's elite army divisions and the security services. The remaining 87 percent of the population would have to be bought off or subdued. But how long could that last?

Not long. That was the consensus view of White House officials who watched Syria implode in the spring and summer of 2011. By April, Assad was deploying army troops against unarmed civilians.

By May, tanks barricaded the main squares of Hama, and snipers picked off individual protesters from rooftops. The demonstrations cooled for a while, then roared back to life in the early summer, seemingly unstoppable.

"The early intelligence was that Syria's 'spring' was not likely to go anywhere—it would be killed in the crib, and in a vicious way," said a senior U.S. official who monitored the daily cable traffic from Damascus. "Then the conventional wisdom shifted quickly. It went from 'Nobody could get rid of Assad' to 'There's no way to stop these people.'"

Robert Ford could not sit still. In twenty years of assignments in the Middle East, he had never failed to find a path to the turbulent center of whatever crisis happened to be unfolding in his host country. It was about to happen again in Syria, this time in a way that would capture the attention of millions of people and put the United States clearly on the side of the demonstrators—or so it seemed to the Syrians themselves.

Ford would admit to no particular bias, but in fact he owed a debt to ordinary citizens of Syria for kindnesses shown to him nearly three decades earlier. In 1983, Ford, then a skinny twenty-five-year-old student of Arabic with a mop of curly brown hair, made his first trip to Syria during a break in classes at the American University in Cairo. He and a schoolmate traveled by bus from Amman to Damascus and arrived in the Syrian capital very late, after most of the shops were closed. The city was packed with Iranian visitors on holiday, and the two Americans were turned away by one hotel after another. Just as they were resigning themselves to a night on the street in a strange city, a friendly hotel clerk called them over.

"You'll never find a hotel this late at night," the man said to the two dirty, road-weary foreigners. "Sleep at my house tonight, and I'll bring you back here early tomorrow."

Minutes later, the two youths were in the modest apartment where the man lived with his family. Though it was past midnight, the Syrian prepared a small supper, and the three stayed up talking for hours. When it was time to sleep, the host apologized for not inviting the Americans to stay longer. "If you stay more than tonight, I will have the secret police knocking at my door tomorrow," he explained. Other Syrians Ford encountered were equally warm. Just days before, an American warship had shelled a Syrian troop position in the hills above Beirut. Yet, when Ford found himself on a bus filled with Syrian soldiers, he was treated with a graciousness that still stuck with him decades later. "Welcome!" the troops said after discovering two Americans on the crowded bus. Some gave up their seats for the foreigners, and others peppered them with questions about dating rituals and whether all American women were like the ones on the hit TV show *Baywatch*. In a more serious moment, one of the officers in the group pulled Ford aside to make a request.

"When you get back to America," the officer said, "tell them we are not *barbar*"—barbarians.

Some twenty-eight years later, the government's *barbar* were loose in cities throughout Syria, snuffing out ordinary lives. The working-class Syrians whom Ford had admired when he was a young man were organizing into neighborhood defense committees, the precursors of rebel militias. For now, nearly all the killing was being committed by one side, and it was hard to be dispassionate, even for a neutral diplomat whose job was to appeal to both sides for restraint. Whatever his personal feelings, Ford could not stray beyond the script approved by Washington, which, in the midsummer of 2011, was sharply divided over what to say. President Obama had not yet called on Assad to resign, as he had done more promptly in the cases of Mubarak and Qaddafi. Among some of the president's aides arose new worries that the Syrian regime could suddenly collapse on itself before the U.S. administration could take a stand. The timing was critical: During Egypt's uprising, Arab leaders lambasted Obama for symbolically abandoning Mubarak, a longtime U.S. ally, while he remained the country's legitimate head of state. On the opposite side were Egyptian protesters who accused the White House of acting cowardly, waiting until Mubarak was all but finished before publicly breaking with him.

There were, however, ways to show support for peaceful protest without uttering a word. Since the early weeks of the uprising, Ford's senior staff had held low-key meetings with opposition leaders and posted carefully worded encouragement on the U.S. Embassy's Facebook page. But Ford's big gesture—the one that would infuriate the Assad regime and symbolically ally Washington with the protesters—grew out of a bid to prevent a massacre in Hama, a city in northwestern Syria where anti-Assad rallies were regularly drawing huge crowds. After weeks of clashes and scores of deaths, Assad fired the provincial governor on July 3, 2011, and deployed tanks and troops in rings around the city's suburbs. An uneasy calm prevailed for three days, with large numbers of protesters occupying Hama's center while Assad's heavily armed security forces waited on the outskirts.

Ford watched the standoff from afar before making his move. He dispatched to Hama one of his aides, a twenty-six-year-old woman who passed easily between the capital and the outlying cities, for a personal assessment of the demonstrators and their intentions. She came back with photos and an impressive report: tens of thousands of people were gathering in the city's main plaza daily, and—contrary to Syrian media accounts of looting, vandalism, and kidnapping—the crowds were as well behaved as anyone could hope. Ford relayed the reports back to Washington.

"They're releasing doves in the air and selling flowers," Ford said. "It's entirely peaceful."

But from the suburbs came ominous signs of preparations for battle. Intelligence reports suggested that Assad had decided to send his tanks into the city with the intention of smashing the opposition movement and turning Hama into an example for the rest of the country. Until now, Assad had simply ignored U.S. and European entreaties to exercise restraint. But as he watched the preparations, Ford wondered: would the Syrian leader risk an attack if he knew that a sitting U.S. ambassador was in the city to witness the outcome? Traveling uninvited to the uprising's bloody epicenter would be seen as a provocation, so Ford resolved to keep the visit as stripped down as possible. There would be no events or speeches, just the silent witness of an American diplomat whose mere presence would attract attention far beyond the city's borders.

"I would just be there to watch," Ford would later explain. "I'd have to be there myself, because otherwise it wasn't going to have any credibility."

On the morning of July 7, without a word to the Syrian authorities or his own bosses, Ford climbed into an SUV with three of his staff and headed north in a tiny convoy that included Ford's friend the French ambassador, Éric Chevallier. They crossed the ridge of stark brown hills above the capital and pushed onward through the lush farmland and ancient cities of the country's northwestern heartland, heading toward Hama and what was certain to be a confrontation, though when it would occur or how it would unfold was anyone's guess. It was far from clear whether they would even make it to their destination. All along the 130-mile highway—and particularly on the approach to Hama—were security checkpoints, and at each one, police would want to know why two foreign diplomats were passing through their territory without prior clearance from Damascus. Even if Assad's men allowed them to pass, there were no guarantees that Hama's demonstrators would welcome a pair of uninvited emissaries from Western governments that many Syrians viewed with suspicion and even hostility.

Yet the startled guards simply waved the travelers through. Hours after setting out, Ford's tan SUV pulled safely into central Hama and past large crowds milling around the city's Assi Square. The city's center had a jubilant feel, as though liberation had already occurred. Someone had hung a huge purple banner from the town's clock tower with the words "Long Live Free Syria—Down with Bashar al-Assad!" The troops, tanks, and even police remained behind their cordons in the suburbs; in central Hama, there was not a baton or uniform in sight.

As planned, the two ambassadors checked in to a Hama hotel that would serve as a base during their visit. They visited a hospital to talk to workers caring for protesters injured in earlier clashes with police. Then they held a series of discreet meetings with opposition leaders, away from the glare of TV cameras. Ford, in his meetings, took pains not to overpromise, he recalled later. The important thing, he stressed, was to avoid violence.

"If you become violent, we will not support you," Ford said. Western intervention in Libya notwithstanding, no U.S. troops would be coming to the rescue if the Syrian opposition got itself into a war, he explained. "After the Iraq war, the last thing we're going to do is send the military to Syria. It will never, ever happen."

The next day, a Friday, was the week's big protest day. As Ford and Chevallier set out in their SUVs, they found the central plaza packed with people—one hundred thousand or even more, according to later estimates. The crowd was exuberant but orderly, until someone happened to recognize the diplomatic license plates on the tan vehicle working its way along the edges of the demonstration. The night before, Syrian television had broadcast a less-than-flattering report about an American delegation arriving in the country's fourth-largest city.

"The ambassador of America, in Hama!" one of the protesters shouted.

Within seconds, the car was mobbed by cheering Syrians who pressed against the car until it could barely move. Onlookers threw rose petals and garlands until the driver had to stop and clear the windshield in order to proceed. A chant began from somewhere in the throng and quickly grew into a roar.

"The people want to topple the regime!"

Someone in the crowd captured the moment on a cell-phone video. Grown men leapt for joy, and others waved tree branches or tried to touch the car. Ford, wearing sunglasses, sat behind the driver, eyes straight ahead. He had intended only to bear witness, but now his visit itself had become an event. He directed his driver to leave the city as quickly as possible, but within hours the video shot by cell phone had flashed around the world—including in the Syrian capital, where an enraged Assad railed against Ford's interference in an internal matter.

"The presence of the U.S. ambassador in Hama without previous permission is obvious proof of the implication of the United States in the ongoing events, and of their attempts to increase tensions," the regime said in a statement issued through the Foreign Ministry.

The fuming from the capital was all but eclipsed by the jubilation in Hama, a city that was, at least for that brief moment, Syria's first and only free province. A local organizing committee appointed a pair of civilian guards on motorcycles to serve as an official escort, parting the crowds so Ford's SUV could safely navigate its way back to the Damascus highway. But in the center of town, the celebrating continued late into the evening without a pause, and the tanks in the suburbs stayed behind their lines. On this day, at least, Assad would hold his fire.

Three days later, Ford and his marines stood watch on the embassy's top floor, waiting to see if the heaving rooftop door would hold. The feared backlash had come, and one of the targets, it now seemed clear, was Ford himself.

The Alawite toughs—the same kind that traveled by bus to beat up protesters in cities around the country—continued in their quest to find things to smash. They ripped down the American flag from its rooftop mast, set fire to it, and raised a Syrian flag in its place. From the French Embassy came alarming reports of shots being fired. The assailants there used a battering ram to break into a garage, then proceeded to demolish the ambassador's car. Three embassy workers were hurt in skirmishes before French guards let loose with a warning volley that scattered the mob.

In Washington, the State Department's Near East Division worked the phone lines, looking for anyone in the Syrian government who might possess an off-switch. Secretary of State Hillary Rodham Clinton, furious, called a news conference to denounce the embassy assault and the Syrian leader presumed to be behind it. This time it was Clinton who veered off the White House script, with harsh words that stopped just short of demanding Assad's ouster.

"President Assad is not indispensable, and we have absolutely nothing invested in him remaining in power," Clinton said, sounding out each syllable with an icy resolve. "From our perspective, he has lost legitimacy." It was the first time any U.S. official had publicly challenged the Syrian leader's right to rule.

For whatever reason, the attacks in Damascus's diplomatic quarter abruptly subsided. The police officers who had stood idle as rioters scaled the U.S. Embassy fence now busied themselves doing their jobs, shooing the assailants out of the embassy compound, though making no arrests. From the improvised defensive post on the embassy's top floor, the sounds of conflict gradually softened until the compound was again quiet.

When it was safe, embassy workers ventured outside to survey the damage. Detritus from the morning's mayhem lay scattered everywhere: shattered glass, graffiti, rocks, and rotten fruit. The attackers had nearly destroyed the main entranceway, and had even managed to rip down the metal letters from the U.S. Embassy sign on the front gate. But the more serious scarring was harder to see. The government of Syria had allowed a mob to besiege the American diplomatic mission. And then, whether through inaction or by design, it had let the intruders rampage through the embassy grounds—a violation, in essence, of sovereign U.S. territory.

But what to do about it? After the usual protests were lodged, the White House still had a significant card to play. President Obama had not yet uttered what his staff would call the "magic" words: "Assad must go." Now the debate flared again over whether and when the United States would declare to the world that Assad's expiration date had passed. The pressure for a vigorous U.S. response came from all quarters: from Congress, from Syrian exiles, from editorial writers, from staunch allies such as France. Nearly everyone saw the Assad government as a weak regime—far weaker, surely, than that of Egypt's Mubarak, who had been dislodged from power in a month. Each day's news brought fresh reports of trouble for Assad, from the defections of senior Syrian army officers to the rapid shrinking of the country's foreign-currency reserves. There was a strong White House belief, as the Syria adviser Frederic Hof would later say, that Assad's "days were numbered, and it was a very low number."

But what if Assad refused to leave? What, if anything, was the United States prepared to do? Hof was among a minority of senior advisers who worried that Assad's exit would not be as quick as conventional wisdom suggested. If the Syrian president found a way to hang on, it would be the Americans who would be seen as weak.

"The president doesn't 'do' advice or opinions; if he says Assad should step aside, it's our job to make sure the guy steps aside," Hof would later explain.

Obama did call for Assad's resignation soon afterward, on August 18, 2011—five weeks after the embassy assault, and five months after Assad's first attacks on civilians—in a statement released in coordination with the leaders of France, Germany, and Britain.

"We have consistently said that President Assad must lead a democratic transition or get out of the way," Obama said. "He has not led. For the sake of the Syrian people, the time has come for President Assad to step aside."

Administration officials later acknowledged that the president's statement may have raised expectations for U.S. actions that were not explicitly promised. As Middle East governments teetered in early 2011, the White House found itself repeatedly thrust into the unaccustomed role of "arbiter for legitimacy for various leaders," said Benjamin Rhodes, a former White House speechwriter who became Obama's deputy national security adviser. In the case of Syria, Obama was personally appalled by Assad's use of snipers and tanks to kill protesters. Rhodes described the president as "very disgusted by the behavior of the Syrian regime over a long period of time." Obama felt compelled to put the United States on record as opposing Assad's behavior, Rhodes explained, though it was clear to the White House that "we frankly do not have the available options, short of overwhelming intervention, to forcibly remove Assad from power."

At the time, little else seemed needed. "Everyone thought nature was going to take care of it," said a senior administration official involved in the policy debates. "Assad would be gone, and very soon."

But Syria's president had no intention of leaving, and he still had cards of his own to play. Though perhaps powerless to stop the uprising, Assad, in the summer of 2011, already had a plan in place to change radically what the fighting was about.

As the standoff in Hama was coming to full boil, Assad introduced a new theme in speeches and public statements denouncing the uprising. No longer were the protesters mere "vandals" and "criminals." Now the Syrian leader spoke of a struggle against "*takfiris*"—radical Islamists.

"This kind of ideology lurks in dark corners in order to emerge when an opportunity presents itself," Assad had said in a televised speech to the nation. "It kills in the name of religion, destroys in the name of reform and spreads chaos in the name of freedom."

The notion that the protesters of Hama and Dara'a were religious extremists was patently absurd. Indeed, the early demonstrations were remarkable displays of unity, drawing Sunnis, Shiites, Christians, Kurds, and even some members of Assad's Alawite sect. Yet Assad would continue to insist that Syria was locked in mortal combat against jihadists who wanted to ignite sectarian warfare and transport the country back to the Middle Ages.

The lack of a visible Islamist presence in the uprising seemed at first to undercut the president's claims. But over the months that followed, two different groups—one inside the regime, one based abroad—would take steps to introduce true *takfiris* to the conflict, turning Syria's domestic crisis into an international disaster.

18

"Where is this Islamic State of Iraq that you're talking about?"

In the fall of 2011, Jordan's King Abdullah II phoned his Syrian neighbor Bashar al-Assad to offer a friendly warning. Though couched in diplomatic niceties, it was a message of fearful urgency, a wake-up call to an old friend whose burning house happened to be attached to his own.

The monarch had tried to convey the message in subtler ways, sending personal envoys to Damascus to meet with the president and his ministers. Now he would appeal to Assad directly. Abdullah, almost alone among the region's leaders, saw Syria sliding into a years-long civil war that would split the country and imperil the entire Middle East. A thoughtful response might yet avert the calamity to come. There were no signs of such thoughtfulness coming from Damascus, yet Abdullah would dutifully offer his best advice.

The two men were not particularly close, though they had gotten along well and had much in common. Both were sons of powerful and iconic rulers, and each had been a surprise choice as his father's successor. The two leaders had studied in Britain, and both had glamorous and thoroughly modern wives with Western educations and careers of their own. Even their children were friendly, having bonded over Super Mario video-game competitions during family visits. Yet the two leaders' responses to the Arab Spring unrest had been worlds apart.

In Jordan, as in most of the region's countries, the revolutions in Tunisia and Egypt propelled large crowds of protesters into the streets of the capital, demanding change. Abdullah was prepared for them. He dismissed the sitting prime minister in favor of a popular and reform-minded former general, Marouf Bakhit, whom he charged with the task of cleaning up corruption and making local government more accountable. Then the king began introducing a series of political reforms to speed up national and local elections and devolve more power to the prime minister and his Cabinet. Jordan's opposition movement quickly lost steam in the face of a monarch who seemed as determined to change the system as they were. Abdullah later explained that he welcomed the Arab Spring, because it gave him an excuse to shake up a tradition-bound political system that protected the country's elite: wealthy oligarchs and rich royals who had no interest in giving up their privileges.

Now the king hoped to talk Assad into considering similar reforms, for his own sake and the region's, according to officials present when Abdullah began the diplomatic outreach to his old neighbor. The phone call between the two leaders began with the usual small talk about family. Then Abdullah proceeded to ask about the uprising and to tick off some of the steps he had taken and what he proposed to do next.

Assad cut the king off.

"You should worry about Jordan and yourself," the Syrian said. The call ended shortly after that.

The brush-off stung. Abdullah had expected more of Bashar al-Assad. Assad's father had been a ruthless man, a striver who had climbed from poverty to power through a mixture of cunning and brute force. But Bashar was not his father. After assuming the presidency, he had impressed Abdullah's aides by bringing in a number of young advisers who were intelligent and worldly, some of them having achieved success in international banking or multinational corporations. The Americans weren't the only ones who believed that Syria's president might still prove to be a true reformer, once he had built a sufficient power base to resist challenges from the generals and spy chiefs who controlled the country's security infrastructure.

"The king extended a hand to Bashar, thinking he could pull him in," one of Abdullah's senior aides recalled. "We thought, 'Here's a guy who could actually transform Syria and move it in a different direction.' When the repression began—and then became increasingly violent—we were shocked."

The implosion of a neighboring country was no idle concern. Jordan shares a 233-mile border with Syria, and there were dozens of unofficial crossing points used by tribes that straddled the dividing line. A prolonged conflict would inevitably affect Jordan, Abdullah's advisers knew. There would be refugees, perhaps, and a host of new criminal enterprises pitching camp in the border towns to smuggle in weapons and contraband. Jordanian businesses could lose access to the main transportation artery connecting them to markets in southern Turkey and the European cities beyond. A more serious destabilization could mean a loss of control over major Syrian weapons systems, from antiaircraft missiles that could shoot down passenger jets to Assad's lethal stockpiles of chemical weapons. Even a few shells of stolen VX or sarin gas could kill hundreds, perhaps thousands, in terrorist attacks.

To most security analysts in the fall of 2011, such an extreme outcome seemed unlikely. The common refrain, repeated by intelligence officials from Jerusalem to Washington during the autumn months, was that Assad's "days are numbered." The regime was now losing entire army battalions to defections, and the country's dwindling supply of dollars—crucial for purchasing everything from ammunition and aircraft parts to the loyalty of pro-regime militias—was nearly tapped out. Assad's military commanders had begun confining some of the army's Sunni brigades to their barracks out of fear that they could not be trusted to fight for their president.

But was Assad truly finished? Abdullah wasn't so sure.

The king and his security advisers parsed each day's intelligence reports in endless strategy sessions. Often these were held late at night in the hilltop palace, with the monarch in jeans or sweat clothes, poring over briefing books and quizzing his aides over tiny glasses of Turkish coffee and tea. All signs pointed to a momentum shift in favor of the opposition, yet Abdullah, studying the furious maneuverings of another Arab leader whose hilltop command center was just a hundred miles from his own, could see glimmers of a plan falling into place.

"This is going to take much longer than anyone thinks," Abdullah told his aides.

As the Jordanians saw it, the regime and the opposition each commanded about a third of Syria's population. Between the two was a fearful middle, an anxious mix of ethnic and religious minorities as well as merchants and professionals who were waiting to see which side would prevail. If Assad could play to their fears—if he could successfully paint the rebels as terrorists and religious zealots bent on ethnic and sectarian cleansing—he could turn the fence straddlers into passive allies. More than half the country would support the regime, and Assad could likely count on controlling Syria's most critical real estate: Damascus and Aleppo, the country's largest cities and commercial centers, as well as the crucial seaports along the coast. He could thus afford to cede a few inconsequential desert towns to the rebels, for now.

Assad's bank accounts were running low, it was true, but, again, his predicament was not as dire as it appeared—not as long as he could rely on powerful friends abroad. Iran could be counted on to bankroll its Syrian ally indefinitely, in order to preserve its supply route to Iranian-backed Hezbollah militias along Lebanon's border with Israel. And Russia's Vladimir Putin would be only too happy to sell weapons and parts to his longtime Syrian trading partners, who also happened to be hosts to Russia's only naval base in the Middle East.

As Abdullah surveyed the crisis that fall, it seemed clear that Assad had every intention of clinging to power. And despite predictions to the contrary, he appeared to have enough firepower, money, and troops to keep up the fight for a very long time. Multiple proposals for settling the conflict had been floated, including offers for a comfortable exile abroad that would assure the safety of Assad and his family and spare the country from a destructive civil war. But Bashar al-Assad was not interested.

"This," the king told his advisers, "is going to get quite bloody."

There was yet another ominous development that fall, a slight shift on the rebels' side that barely attracted attention outside the community of intelligence analysts focused on Syria's uprising. It was widely known that Assad had declared a general amnesty in the early months of the uprising, leading to the release of inmates from ordinary prisons, though not the protesters locked in the secret police's special detention centers. Now Syrians were learning just how cynical Assad's goodwill gesture had been. Among the inmates discharged over the spring and summer were a number of radical Islamists who belonged to known terrorist organizations. Some were jihadists who had been picked up while attempting to cross into Iraq to join the insurgency there. Others were suspected al-Qaeda members who had been snatched by the CIA and secretly delivered to Syria under the spy agency's "extraordinary rendition" program. The freed Islamists were too few in number to threaten the regime seriously, but their presence inside the country would help supply a veneer of truth for Assad's extremist claims: now there were, in fact, a handful of authentic jihadists in the opposition camp. It was the same tactic used by the Libyan leader Muammar Qaddafi, who emptied his jails in an apparent attempt to sow strife among the regime's opponents.

Jordanian and U.S. intelligence officials studied the reports with a mixture of incredulousness and alarm. Among the released prisoners were several familiar names. Some had been part of the support network for the Jordanian terrorist Abu Musab al-Zarqawi, running weapons and recruits across the border into Iraq. Now they were free to return to old haunts and perhaps old habits.

Still, measured against the region's other crises, it seemed a small thing.

"There are only a handful of true al-Qaeda types," a Middle East intelligence official said of the jihadists who were observed setting up shop inside Syria in late 2011. "We know exactly where they are. And when this is all over, we know how to get them."

At the same moment, other outsiders were watching the events in Syria with wary hopefulness, like a starving coyote eyeing a buffalo. These were men who had once called themselves al-Qaeda in Iraq, and disciples of Zarqawi. Now they spent their days hiding out in the shabby outer suburbs of Mosul and a handful of other towns, communicating only rarely, for fear of detection. They had adopted a new name—the Islamic State of Iraq—and they maintained the pretense that the organization was a real country, with an administration and departments and even a flag. That the state was fictional was clear even to family members. "Where is this Islamic State of Iraq that you're talking about? We're living in a desert!" one of the leader's wives complained, according to testimony in an Iraqi police case. Yet, to the man at the top of the organization, the Islamic State was already real, and it was about to get bigger, God willing.

The leader was new to the job, having been abruptly promoted from the group's number three slot when the previous leaders were killed in a raid by U.S. and Iraqi troops. Unlike previous commanders, he was not a warrior but a scholar, a professor of Islamic law who held a doctoral degree. At just thirty-two, he was somber beyond his years, a man who prized correctness and was fussily attentive to even the most minor rules governing speech and dress. He had grown up as Ibrahim Awad al-Badri, the son of a conservative Muslim preacher from the Iraqi city of Samarra. His self-chosen jihadist name was Abu Bakr al-Baghdadi.

He was physically unremarkable, a man of medium height with thinning hair and a naturally thick beard that, in middle adulthood, had expanded into an unruly bush. But Baghdadi possessed a prophet's fierce conviction in destiny—the world's, as well as his own. As he had watched the Arab Spring uprisings unfold in the early months of 2011, he could see a divine hand shaping events, jostling and tugging at history's great boughs until the ripened fruit fell at Baghdadi's feet. It was sure to happen anyway, but to nudge things along, Baghdadi began offering helpful suggestions that February, through the Islamic State's media arm, to the masses of protesters in Cairo. After finishing off their country's apostate president, Egypt's throngs surely must recognize their obligation to continue the revolution across the Sinai and beyond, the messages suggested.

"Here in your midst has the market of Jihad opened and become easy to reach!" declared one missive posted to Islamist Web sites in February. "No mature, able-bodied person has any excuse to stay behind with those who refrain from making Jihad."

The same posting included a special plea to empty Egypt's prisons, home to many of the country's most committed and experienced Islamists. Nearly all of the Iraqi group's leadership, including Baghdadi, had served time in the Middle East's notorious detention centers. "Freeing the prisoners is one of the foremost of obligations upon you," the message read. "Do not let things settle unless you free every last one of them."

The entreaties were ignored. To the dismay of Islamists around the world, the crowds besieging government ministries in Cairo and Benghazi showed little appetite for replacing a secular tyrant with a religious one. In Cairo's Tahrir Square, the rhyming slogans chanted by demonstrators ranged from demands for better living conditions—"Bread, freedom, social equality"—to expressions of national pride—"Hold your heads high, you're Egyptian!" Even after Osama bin Laden's death in May, there were no calls for jihad, and no unfurling of al-Qaeda banners or portraits of the slain terrorist leader. Opinion polls showed steadily falling approval for Bin Laden's movement throughout the Muslim world starting around 2004, or just around the time Zarqawi began commanding international attention with videotaped beheadings and suicide bombings. Support for attacks on Muslim civilians—the Islamic State of Iraq's calling card—had fallen even more.

Zarqawi's diminished descendants would occasionally dispatch a suicide bomber into the Iraqi capital to kill and maim. In the months after Baghdadi assumed command, the group claimed responsibility for attacks on bank customers, on parishioners at a church service, and on a queue of young men outside an army recruiting office. But with American troops now out of the country, and with Iraqis focused mainly on the novel political theater of dueling partisans in the Iraqi Parliament, the attacks seemed increasingly pointless to everyone but the terrorists themselves.

Baghdadi's lieutenants could still build a lethal car bomb, and they somehow managed to find a steady supply of hapless adolescents willing to steer a suicide vehicle toward its target. But Zarqawi's old organization was as hollow as its leaders' talk about a Pan-Arab Islamic state. The group was nearly broke. It had lost its sanctuary and freedom of movement, so essential for communication, training, and resupply. And it was selling an ideology that the Muslim world seemed no longer to care for. Five years after Zarqawi's death, the Islamic State of Iraq had become the thing that terrorist organizations fear even more than their own annihilation.

It had become irrelevant.

The decline began soon after the death of Zarqawi, though initially it was hard to tell from the body count.

Stripped suddenly of its charismatic leader and chief strategist, al-Qaeda in Iraq still managed at first to maintain and even surpass the scale of butchery achieved under the Jordanian. The twelve months following Zarqawi's death were the deadliest of the war for U.S. troops, with 904 killed. The monthly Iraqi civilian death toll hit an all-time high of 3,266 in July 2006, the month after U.S. bombs demolished Zarqawi's Baqubah hideout.

But the battlefield was changing. Violence-weary Sunni tribes, banding together into militias that called themselves "Sons of Iraq," were beginning to drive foreign jihadists from their villages, sometimes killing them. President George W. Bush's troop surge of 2007 had flooded the country with thousands of fresh combat soldiers. Most important, America's highly successful "fusion cells"—the anti-terrorism teams of U.S. intelligence and special-forces operatives— had taken the pursuit of Islamist militants to a lethal new level. The cities of the Sunni Triangle that had served as a sanctuary and operating base for Zarqawi were rapidly becoming hostile and even dangerous to his followers, day and night.

At the U.S. special-forces base at Balad, the same formula General McChrystal had used to track and kill Zarqawi was yielding fresh successes each day, and often multiple times a day. The effort continued at a steadily rising tempo through 2008, when McChrystal received his fourth general's star and a promotion to Joint Staff Chief. His replacement, Vice Admiral William McRaven, kept the same policies in place until U.S. combat operations in Iraq officially ended in 2010.

The daily search started with an astonishing array of electronic sleuthing tools, capable of sweeping up every mobile-phone call, e-mail, and text message sent by anyone, anywhere in Iraq. When someone dialed a number that matched a phone in Balad's growing terrorist database, technical teams went to work, tracking the caller's location and movements. U.S. drones and airplanes served as mobile cell towers that could tap directly into calls made from suspicious phones. Airborne surveillance cameras gave U.S. spies enhanced capabilities to trail suspicious cars and trucks.

Equally impressive were the teams of SEALs and Delta operators who set out nightly to kick in the doors of terrorists whose hideouts had been discovered in the previous day's surveillance. By the fourth year of the war, the commandos' tactics had been honed to a fine edge, so that small units of a half-dozen men could carry out multiple raids on a single night. "Joseph," a retired operator who participated in scores of such missions, recalled how the intensity of the fight changed in the months after Zarqawi's death, when the Pentagon authorized an all-out effort to destroy what was left of the Jordanian's terrorist network.

"In 2007, we took the gloves off," said Joseph, who agreed to an interview on the condition that his real name not be revealed. "We were going out on missions and targeting al-Qaeda as hard as we could. Kill-capture missions, not capture-kill. We were handing them their ass, killing al-Qaeda every night."

The workday began at sundown, just as the surveillance teams were coming off their shifts. "We'd have dinner for breakfast," Joseph said. "Then we'd get a brief and we'd go out on a mission. We'd hit a target, going in with [silencers] and night vision, and there would be a gunfight, almost every night. We'd do our own interrogations and develop our own lines of intelligence. And, based on what we found, we'd immediately go after the next thing. And we would do it every single day."

The tactics worked on multiple levels. The accelerated tempo of the nightly operations kept the terrorists off balance, unable to coordinate or plan sophisticated attacks. The raids also produced torrents of fresh intelligence, including insights into the recruitment and training of suicide bombers. The ones Joseph interrogated included teens who had been subjected to heavy indoctrination by imams, and others who just seemed mentally unstable or slow-witted and gullible—"just as dumb as the day is long," he remembered.

Most important, the commandos had found a way to get under the terrorists' skin. The insurgents were no longer the deadliest, most unpredictable force in Iraq. Now it was their turn to be afraid, and exposed. The truth, as Joseph and his comrades discovered, was that the Islamic State's fighters were skilled butchers, but lousy soldiers.

"They're only good at terrorizing people who aren't armed," he said. "They think they're good, but when we would wake them up in the middle of the night, they would crap their pants."

The skirmishes inside the darkened houses were silent and short, often three minutes or less. Those who wisely surrendered found themselves surrounded by bearded, heavily muscled Westerners wearing dark clothes, armed with futuristic-looking weapons, and accompanied by ferocious attack dogs. In Iraqi villages, the story spread of "ninjas with lions" who would burst into town and then vanish again. During the interrogations that followed, Joseph would sometimes seek to perpetuate the legend.

"You've dealt with Americans before?" he would ask.

"Yes," the handcuffed detainee would typically reply.

"Did they look like us?"

"No."

"There's a reason for that," he would say. "I'm here for you. I'm the devil."

The results were soon apparent, and not just in the numbers of killed and captured insurgents. In a single year, from 2007 to 2008, the number of GI casualties dropped from 904 to 314, and then dropped by half again the following year. Iraqi civilian deaths from suicide bombs fell from nearly thirty-nine hundred in 2007 to fewer than seventeen hundred in 2008, the start of a steep decline that would continue through the end of the decade.

The combined effort—the surveillance, the troop surge, the Sunni revolt, and most especially the raids—so weakened Zarqawi's organization that Michael V. Hayden, the CIA director, declared the organization in 2008 to be in "near-strategic defeat." The jihadists who had held sway over Iraq for nearly four years were not completely eliminated, but at last the Americans had discovered a formula for keeping them bottled up.

"We didn't become like them," said an officer who supervised fusion cells as the program was starting to click. "We became what they were afraid of: shadows of the night."

Everyone understood that the pressure could not be sustained indefinitely. The direct costs of invading, occupying, rebuilding, and stabilizing Iraq had drained more than a trillion dollars from the U.S. Treasury, with indirect costs adding another trillion to the taxpayers' tab. A large majority of Americans no longer supported the war, and the Iraqis themselves were anxious to see U.S. combat forces leave the country. The U.S. troop withdrawal began in late 2007, and the last convoy of soldiers to exit the country would roll across the Iraq-Kuwait border on December 18, 2011, ending a deployment that cost nearly forty-five hundred American lives and left more than thirty-two thousand wounded. By the most conservative estimates, the Iraqi civilian death toll was twenty times higher.

The departing Americans were leaving to the Iraqis the task of managing their own security. It would have been a difficult challenge even for a country without Iraq's history of explosive tensions along sectarian and ethnic divides. And, indeed, by almost every measure, the early efforts to create a stable Iraqi society fell short. Sunni distrust of Prime Minister Nouri al-Maliki exploded into open revolt in 2007, following the arrests of prominent Sunni politicians and the dismissals of Sunni commanders in the Iraqi army and security agencies. The following year, the Shiite-led government took steps to disband the Sons of Iraq militias that had helped drive out foreign Islamists, saying it would not tolerate the existence of private militias in the country. Shiite militias, meanwhile, were tolerated and—many Sunnis believed—officially encouraged.

U.S. forces offered the government significant help on the way out. In 2008 and 2010, the Americans delivered a pair of powerful blows against the Islamic State of Iraq, both aimed directly at the group's reconstituted leadership. The first, in October 2008, was a commando strike on a terrorist base located inside Syrian territory, a few miles from the Iraqi border. In a covert operation approved by George W. Bush, special-forces teams in helicopters destroyed the base and killed an Iraqi man described by U.S. officials as one of Zarqawi's longtime logistics agents in charge of the network's supply lines for money and recruits. Then, eighteen months later, American and Iraqi forces jointly attacked a desert hideout near the Iraqi city of Tikrit, just as a meeting of the terrorist group's senior leadership was under way. The Iraqi government jubilantly displayed photos of two corpses pulled from the building's rubble, confirming the deaths of Abu Omar al-Baghdadi and Abu Ayyub al-Masri, the top two commanders of the Islamic State of Iraq since Zarqawi's death.

The insurgents later acknowledged the deaths of "two knights [who] have dismounted to join the group of martyrs." The message also promised certain revenge: a "long, gloomy night and dark days colored in blood." Yet the Islamic State's ability to inflict serious harm on Iraq's government—even a weak, divided Iraqi government—was seriously in doubt.

The jihadists' new chief, Abu Bakr al-Baghdadi, was a man of soaring ambitions, but in late 2011, well into his second year as leader, his boasts were as empty as the group's coffers. The Islamic State of Iraq lacked resources, fighters, and sanctuary. And, perhaps most critically, it lacked a cause—a single big idea with which it could rally its depleted forces and draw other Muslims into the fold.

Soon, within the chaos of revolutionary Syria, it would find all four.

19

"This is the state for which Zarqawi paved the way"

In the sixth month of Syria's uprising, Abu Bakr al-Baghdadi was ready to make a move. He tapped one of his most trusted deputies, a native Syrian and a veteran from the Zarqawi days, to lead an expedition into the Syrian heartland. Outside the capital and other regime strongholds, the institutions that maintained security within Syria were failing, one by one. Here was a chance for Zarqawi's followers to leap to another badly weakened host.

The scouting party was tiny. "There were not more than seven or eight of us," the group's leader later recalled. The men slipped across the Iraq-Syria border, traveling along a pair of desert highways that parallel the Tigris and Euphrates rivers, passing through small Syrian towns that had long served as way stations for fighters heading in the opposite direction. There, far from Syria's contested cities, they met with local contacts, including former members of the Zarqawi network in Syria as well as other jihadists who were newly released from Bashar al-Assad's jails, as the participants themselves would later confirm. The country they encountered was much as Iraq had been nine years earlier: a violent, lawless place where men with weapons moved freely. Unlike in Iraq, there was no threat of Americans suddenly swooping in from above.

"Syria would not have been ready for us if not for the Syrian revolution," the mission's leader, Abu Mohammad al-Julani, acknowledged long afterward. "The revolution removed many of the obstacles and paved the way for us to enter this blessed land."

Under a plan approved by the Islamic State's Iraqi leadership, the men would establish a Syrian-run Islamist militia to join the rebels already battling Bashar al-Assad's government. They called themselves Jabhat al-Nusra, or the Support Front for the People of Greater Syria. The name suggested a kind of auxiliary group coming to the aid of Syria's outmatched opposition. In reality, Baghdadi's designs for the group had nothing to do with helping Syrians. The al-Nusra Front would eventually develop an independent streak, breaking with its parent over everything from ideology to tactics and style. But the original idea, Western intelligence agencies later concluded, was to create a Syrian incubator for the caliphate Baghdadi would some day lead.

"It was to be the face of the organization in Syria, laying the groundwork for the group's expansion," said a U.S. official who helped track the organization's rise. "It was never supposed to be a distinct group."

Over the months that followed, communications between the Syrian colony and the battered Iraqi leadership became a window into Baghdadi's personality and growing ambitions. Like his spiritual predecessor, Abu Musab al-Zarqawi, Baghdadi wasn't chiefly concerned with installing an Islamist government in the Syrian or Iraqi capitals. The goal was to impose Islamic rule without borders, and the way to achieve this was to act boldly, trusting that Allah would bend history itself to suit his purposes. Al-Qaeda's more pragmatic thinkers spoke of the caliphate as a distant goal, one that would have to wait until the Middle East's secular regimes could be toppled. But Baghdadi believed the opposite: raise the caliphate's ancient banner, and righteous Muslims would fall into line.

"He was talking about physically restoring the Islamic caliphate in a way that nobody else did," the U.S. official said. "He would establish an extremist vision of Islam and cleanse the land of apostates. And that would pave the way for a final showdown between Muslims and nonbelievers."

In adopting Zarqawi's vision, Baghdadi also enthusiastically embraced the Jordanian's most grisly excesses. In the years following Zarqawi's death, his immediate successors appeared to take seriously al-Qaeda's warning to avoid the kinds of shocking displays that might offend ordinary Muslims. The videotaped beheadings subsided, and there were fewer of the kinds of gratuitous attacks on Shiite women and children that had become a hallmark of al-Qaeda in Iraq. Now Baghdadi would bring them all back, on a scale that evoked the savagery of the Ikhwan hordes that had swept the Arabian Peninsula a century earlier. And, like Zarqawi, he would find a way to force the world to watch.

Had it not been for the U.S. invasion of Iraq, the Islamic State's greatest butcher would likely have lived out his years as a college professor. Until 2003, life was steering him toward a quiet career of teaching Islamic jurisprudence to twenty-year-olds, rather than strapping bombs to their chests.

Islamist biographers later ascribed to Baghdadi great intellectual gifts and a natural bent toward jihad, though none of this is borne out in the extensive profiles pieced together by Western intelligence agencies. Nothing in his formative years suggested that the man born as Ibrahim Awad al-Badri possessed unusual talents or proclivities, except for a fascination with *fiqh*, or the legal interpretation of the thousands of sayings and edicts contained in Islam's holy texts. He was not a violent troublemaker like Zarqawi, or an adventurer like Osama bin Laden, who moved to Pakistan after college to join the cause of Afghanistan's mujahideen. There were no early flashes of charisma or cruelty. Instead, acquaintances remember a shy, nearsighted youth who liked soccer and kept mostly to himself. Indeed, in his first thirty-two years, Baghdadi seems to have drawn little notice even in his own neighborhood. One family friend recalled a young man "so quiet you could barely hear his voice."

"He always had religious or other books attached on the back of his bike," the neighbor, Tariq Hameed, told a *Newsweek* interviewer, recalling the studious teenager who lived nearby in one of Samarra's lower-middle-class neighborhoods. The son of a Sunni imam who preached in the city, Baghdadi wore the traditional prayer cap and white dishdasha of the religiously devout, and he preferred to spend his free time at the mosque rather than keeping company with other young men from the town, Hameed said. "I never saw him in trousers and shirt, like most of the other guys in Samarra," the neighbor said. "He had a light beard, and he never hung out in cafés."

A single fact about his family background would prove crucial later in life: as a member of Iraq's al-Bu Badri tribe, he could claim to be part of the same ancestral line as Muhammad—a requirement, in the opinion of some Islamic scholars, for anyone seeking to become the caliph, or the leader of the Muslim nation. The distinction did not count for much in gritty Samarra, where there are hundreds of al-Badris and dozens of other tribes that can legitimately claim to be part of the Prophet's lineage. Still, Baghdadi's extended household practically smoldered with religious fervor, which may help explain his youthful devotion and his later drift toward fanaticism. Baghdadi's grandfather bore the title "Haji," having journeyed to the holy Kaaba Shrine at Mecca as a religious pilgrim, and there were numerous preachers and religious teachers among his uncles and ten siblings. His father's sermons were noteworthy, according to one of Baghdadi's jihadist biographers, for their emphasis on the "promoting of virtue and preventing of vice."

He came of age during some of the most turbulent years in modern Iraqi history. Born in 1971, he was in his late teens when the Iran-Iraq War ended in a bitter stalemate after eight years of fighting and a combined loss of at least a half-million lives. He was nearly twenty when the Iraqi army suffered its humiliating defeat in the first Gulf War. Somewhere in between, he likely served his mandatory stint in the Iraqi army, though there is no evidence that he saw combat. What is clear is that he moved to Baghdad as a young man to attend college, and earned a bachelor's degree in Islamic law and theology in 1999. His plunge into the arcane world of seventh-century religious codes appears to have brought out his puritanical side; acquaintances remembered how the college-aged Baghdadi would become irritated when men and women were allowed to dance in the same room during wedding celebrations. "It's irreligious!" he would complain. In any case, he liked the subject well enough to continue his studies well into his early thirties. He was thirty-two and on a track to obtain his doctorate, and a future professorship, when the U.S. invasion of Iraq began on March 20, 2003.

The opening bursts of the U.S. "shock and awe" bombing campaign lit up the world of the Islamic law student, who, better than most, understood the Koran's injunction to defend Muslim lands against invaders. He signed up that same year with one of the many small resistance movements that engaged in hit-and-run attacks against U.S. troops, though his actual contributions appear to have been unremarkable.

And then, a few months later, he was caught. Some of the circumstances of his capture have become obscured, but U.S. records confirm that an Ibrahim Awad al-Badri was seized by GIs during a raid on a house in Fallujah in late January 2004. He was then transported to one of Iraq's most feared destinations, the U.S. detention center known as Camp Bucca.

He arrived on February 4. A military photographer snapped the startled visage of a round-faced man approaching the start of middle age, wearing wire-framed glasses and an outsized beard. For the security-conscious Baghdadi, it remains one of only a small handful of photographs known to exist. The next time he posed for a portrait, more than ten years later, he would be a changed man in every respect. His journey from devout youth to bloodthirsty extremist was about to begin.

The prison where Baghdadi landed was a two-square-mile city of barbed wire and tents, erected on a sun-scorched plain a few miles from Iraqi's border with Kuwait. To those helicoptering in at night, as the U.S. sailors who guarded the prison often did, Camp Bucca looked a bit like Las Vegas: an immense city of light in the middle of empty desert. But inside the wire, it was more like the Wild West.

Built initially by the British for military prisoners of war, the camp expanded rapidly under American control to accommodate huge numbers of Iraqis swept up after the start of the insurgency. Though the camp was designed to house twenty thousand men, the population ballooned at times to more than twenty-six thousand, all living in communal tents in a place where summertime temperatures regularly climbed to 140 degrees. The heat, amplified by an oily Persian Gulf humidity, menaced guards and inmates equally. "It actually feels like you're in a microwave," a boatswain's mate on tower duty told a visiting navy journalist.

The camp's commanders made substantial improvements in later years, replacing tents with air-conditioned cinder-block huts and adding classrooms for literacy and vocational training for carpentry and masonry. But in early 2004, it was the Islamists who controlled life inside the tent villages. Inmates were segregated by creed, and the Sunnis, in their sector, lived under strict Sharia law, self-imposed and brutally enforced. Anyone who disobeyed—or who betrayed the others by showing cordiality toward the Americans—could suffer punishment ranging from a beating to having an eye gouged out. In Compound 30, where the most violent Islamists were kept, prisoners vented their hostility by hurling feces or pellets called chai rocks—a residue of sweet tea mixed with sand and dried in the sun—at passing guard patrols.

One of the camp's senior managers acknowledged that the Camp Bucca of Baghdadi's time was both dysfunctional and, from the perspective of commanders looking to quell the Sunni insurgency, counterproductive. By corralling Islamist radicals and ordinary Iraqis in a lawless desert pen, U.S. officials inadvertently created a "jihadi university" that helped inculcate Islamist ideas into a new generation of fighters, the officer said.

"Extremists mingled with moderates in every compound," Lieutenant Commander Vasilios Tasikas, who ran legal operations at the prison, wrote in a 2009 essay in the *Military Review*. "Unfortunately, U.S. forces had adopted a model of detention operations that assumed that those interned were 'all bad guys' to be 'warehoused' for an indeterminate amount of time and released randomly in arbitrary groups. This approach was not only naïve and myopic, it was also dangerous; predictably, it fueled the insurgency inside the wire."

If Bucca was indeed a jihadi university, Baghdadi would ultimately become its greatest alumnus. Though hardly a tough guy, he found a way to survive and even thrive in prison. Baghdadi forged a number of important friendships and alliances, including one with a Zarqawi disciple called Abu Muhammad al-Adnani, who became his chief deputy and spokesman years later. Moreover, the young Islamic scholar found that his academic expertise gave him a certain stature. The camp's mini–Islamist society needed someone who could interpret Sharia rules, and on that score, Baghdadi was exceptionally qualified. He could lead the daily prayers, in which inmates in their identical yellow uniforms lined up by the thousands on their prayer mats to pledge fealty to Allah. He was also experienced at speaking and teaching classical Arabic, the form used in the Koran and in formal ceremonies and speeches. Baghdadi, having lived his entire life among clerics, could even mimic the singsong delivery of the most learned imams of the great mosques of Baghdad and Mosul. As a vessel, his voice was pleasant yet authoritative, and the men liked to listen to it.

They would not have many opportunities. The scholarly qualities that helped Baghdadi earn respect among fellow detainees also allowed him to gain an early release. Camp Bucca regularly discharged its less dangerous prisoners to alleviate severe overcrowding, a source of constant tension and occasional riots among the inmates. In late 2004, a prison panel reviewed the record for Ibrahim Awad al-Badri and decided that the bespectacled academic posed little threat. He was discharged on December 6, 2004, but not before a medical team took a cheek swab to preserve a record of his DNA. If the same man were to turn up anywhere, dead or alive, in connection with a future terrorist act, U.S. officials could be precisely sure of whom they had.

Baghdadi emerged from his ten-month exposure to U.S. forces with an even greater determination to fight them. Years later, his quest to defeat America became a prayerful refrain. "Deal with America and its allies, O Allah," he would say in one of his public prayers. "Harshen your grip on them. . . . Defeat them with the worst of defeats they will ever suffer. Divide their gatherings, split their body, dismember them completely, and make us raid them, and not them raid us."

For a time, Baghdadi would try to avoid further entanglements with Americans. He was married now, to the first of his three wives, and he was father to at least one child, a four-year-old son. He returned to school after prison and resumed his progress toward a doctorate in Islamic law, which he received in 2007. But the degree was not yet his when Baghdadi was drawn back into the insurgency. His old organization had merged with several others in the advisory council or *shura* created by Abu Musab al-Zarqawi in 2006, and Baghdadi was asked to be one of the council's advisers on matters concerning Sharia law.

A profile compiled by Western intelligence officials suggests that Zarqawi, a dabbler in theology who enjoyed debating with religious scholars, probably knew the man who would eventually replace him. But at the time, Baghdadi was still an obscure figure, even among the jihadists. "Zarqawi was closer than a brother to me, but I didn't know Baghdadi. He was insignificant," Ahmed al-Dabash, a contemporary and member of another militant faction, the Islamic Army of Iraq, told London's *Telegraph* newspaper in 2014. "He used to lead prayer in a mosque near my area. No one really noticed him."

Zarqawi's death in June 2006 changed everything. The heirs to the Jordanian's al-Qaeda in Iraq movement had different ideas about how to run an insurgency, and they quickly reorganized themselves under a new name: the Islamic State of Iraq. Among the dominant leaders now were a number of former officers of Saddam Hussein's vanquished army—Sunni colonels and majors who had allied themselves with Zarqawi but were never fully trusted by him. With the Jordanian gone, the former Baathists moved to assert Iraqi control over the group, from its central hierarchy to the provincial towns that were controlled by the Islamists in all but name. Once again, Baghdadi's credentials made him uniquely valuable: Here was a bona fide Sharia expert with a solid Sunni-Iraqi pedigree who could ensure that the group's scattered cells toed the line, ideologically. Baghdadi was quickly appointed chief of Sharia for a small farming town called al-Karma, just outside Fallujah. Soon afterward, he was placed in charge of religious affairs for all of Anbar Province. Then, in early 2010, he was appointed as the top Sharia official for the entire organization.

The promotion effectively made Baghdadi the third-ranking officer of the Islamic State, subordinate only to the senior leader and the minister of war. It's the post he held on April 18, 2010, when U.S.

missiles and Iraqi rockets flattened a safe house outside the city of Tikrit, eliminating the group's number one and number two leaders in a single blow. At least for the moment, Baghdadi, the bookish academic dismissed by peers as "insignificant," stood alone at the head of the Islamic State of Iraq.

A month would pass before Baghdadi's emirship was made official. Despite his senior ranking, his move to the top of the organization was by no means guaranteed. Indeed, many Western and Middle Eastern intelligence officials believed the job would go to a more seasoned figure with extensive experience commanding and leading operations. Yet, although Baghdadi was still a relative outsider, he won the support of the leadership council's mix of former Baathists and Zarqawists.

Among those who approved of the promotion was a ruthless Iraqi army colonel named Samir al-Khlifawi, the leader of the group's military council. A former Baathist who joined the insurgency after the U.S. invasion, Khlifawi urged Baghdadi to accept the top leadership and promised to serve as his top deputy and mentor, according to documents discovered years later, after Khlifawi's death during fighting in Syria. The white-bearded Khlifawi, more commonly known by his jihadist name Haji Bakr, was regarded by intelligence analysts as a savvy strategist who was chiefly responsible for the Islamic State's early military successes.

Despite his lack of military experience, Baghdadi offered certain advantages to the group. One was the Sharia scholar's willingness to provide religious cover for acts of brutality that clerics around the world had condemned as un-Islamic. Everything that made the group so widely reviled—the beheadings, the suicide bombings, the kidnappings, the extortion, the war against Shiites, the spilling of so much innocent Muslim blood—Baghdadi not only endorsed, but declared legally justified under Islamic law.

His other great asset was his suitability for the role of caliph— symbolically important for an organization that wanted its "Islamic State" claims to be taken seriously. Baghdadi, with his genealogical and scholarly pedigrees, could aspire to heights of leadership beyond Zarqawi's grasp.

Over the years that followed, Baghdadi worked deliberately to prepare himself for the mythical role to which he had been divinely appointed, according to a U.S. official familiar with Baghdadi's history. "He cloaked himself with all the right religious credentials, and paid close attention to imagery, to clothing, to the way he moved and talked," the official said. "He would go to great lengths to show that he was in his rightful place."

It was in the service of that goal that Baghdadi dispatched his emissaries across the border in August 2011, seeking a Syrian launchpad for the caliphate that still languished on the ground in his native country. A successful venture, in Baghdadi's view, would help ensure the survival of his organization for years to come. More important, the Islamic State would be taking a first step toward erasing the artificial boundaries imposed by colonial powers to divide Muslims.

"We have crossed the boundaries that despicable hands demarcated between the Islamic states to thwart our movement," Baghdadi would later say of his Syrian experiment. "This is the state for which Sheikh Abu Musab al-Zarqawi paved the way. It will not retreat in any shape or manner from the territory to which it has been extended."

Weeks had passed since Barack Obama and European leaders had delivered their call for Assad's departure, and Assad was not taking heed. The Syrian's response was to toss a few verbal barbs at the "colonialists" and turn up the violence against the protesters and the volunteer brigades that had sprung up to defend them.

At the White House, the splintering of the country was a subject of concern, but not yet alarm. The consensus among the president's national security aides was that Assad would leave—eventually, according to two officials who attended high-level meetings on Syria that fall. By all appearances, the regime was in trouble, losing territory, soldiers, and even generals to a new rebel force called the Free Syrian Army. History itself was arrayed against Assad, and there was little the United States could or should do on its own to speed up the inevitable, the officials said.

"There was a sense that this thing would run its course, and we would do all we could to contain it," said one senior official present at the discussions. "We really didn't think it would drag on."

But it did. As the conflict edged closer to full-scale civil war, the Obama administration grasped for a lever with which to nudge the sides toward a settlement. There was none to be found. When protests erupted in Egypt and Yemen, the United States had been able to call in old chits, IOUs that had piled up over decades of heavy U.S. economic and military support for the countries' governments and security establishments. In Libya, the Obama administration secured critical legal and moral backing in the form of United Nations resolutions authorizing collective military action to protect civilians and support the rebels. But in the case of Syria, there was nothing like this: No military relationships, no economic aid, not even a significant trading partnership. At the United Nations, Syria's longtime Russian ally blocked even the mildest resolutions criticizing Assad for killing his own people. When European countries voted to boycott the relatively meager imports of Syrian oil, Assad's other major ally—Iran—more than offset the losses by supplying Syria with billions of dollars in bank loans and cash.

And so Assad stayed, month after month, erecting fortresslike defenses around the capital while seeking to wear down the rebels through the wholesale demolishing of neighborhoods by tank and artillery fire. Already, more than four thousand Syrians had died, including nearly three hundred children. Thousands more fled their homes, and those who stayed lived in darkened, ruined communities, desperately short of everything except rage and fear.

Publicly, the Americans pushed for concerted action against Assad at the United Nations and the Arab League. Behind the scenes, the White House worked with allies in seeking inducements that might persuade Assad to accept asylum and leave the country voluntarily. Unspoken altogether, except in the secure meeting rooms, was the acknowledgment that the conflict had at least one salutary effect: as long as it lasted, the uprising would serve as a financial and moral drain on the government of Iran, Assad's most important ally.

One thing appeared certain: there was no appetite, even among the president's most hawkish advisers, for another military entanglement in the Middle East. Even a minor engagement, such as air support or the supplying of arms to rebels, was problematic as long as Russia blocked a UN resolution needed to provide legal cover. The practical obstacles were just as formidable. Unlike Libya's rebels, the Syrian opposition lacked a sanctuary from which it could organize and resupply in safety. And though the rebels had small arms, the Assad regime enjoyed a monopoly on the heavy weapons needed to tip the scales in the rebels' favor. The Obama administration could offer humanitarian aid such as medical supplies, and some nonlethal gear, such as computers and cell phones. But those seeking to defend themselves against Assad's forces would simply have to look elsewhere for rifles, armor, and ammunition. And beyond the reluctance to engage in another war in the Middle East, there were those on the U.S. team who felt arming the rebels would be pointless.

"The reality was, the opposition was not adequate to the task," said the senior security official who participated in debates over action against Assad. "You would have been hard-pressed to find anyone in 2011 who thought the moderates could prevail with enough arms. The truth is, they already had weapons. And it was clear to most of us that we should be pushing for a de-escalation, and not ramping things up even more."

One June afternoon in 2011, as Robert Ford was contemplating what the U.S. Embassy could do about surging violence in Hama, a small group of U.S. congressmen and staff members gathered in the Capitol basement for a private briefing about the events in Syria. Leading the discussion were three American citizens with an unusually keen interest in the fight over Syria's future. The youngest, a twenty-seven-year-old Syrian immigrant, was also a veteran Capitol Hill staffer, well known to many in the room. For Mouaz Moustafa, it was a first introduction to a new job that would prove to be exhilarating and heartbreaking, often in the same day: enlisting American support for Syria's embattled opposition.

For more than an hour, Moustafa and his colleagues answered questions from lawmakers who seemed genuinely concerned and eager to help. Moustafa, experienced at gauging the interest of elected officials in hearing rooms, felt encouraged.

"Everything was still early stages, and people in Congress really wanted to know what was going on," he said, recalling the meeting.

"They were asking good questions. We were hoping that they would be outraged."

It was the first of many such visits for Moustafa, who seemed born for the part he was now playing. A Syrian-born resident of Hot Springs, Arkansas, he possessed communications skills in English and Arabic that had impressed his Capitol Hill bosses as well as influential figures within Washington's small community of Middle Eastern political exiles. Now, in 2011, he stepped into the spotlight in an unexpected way, speaking directly to the American government many Syrians saw as their last resort. Working as a lobbyist for Assad's opponents in a Syria he barely knew, Moustafa was among a handful of Washingtonians who would witness the unfolding calamity from both countries.

"It was that slow car crash where you're trying to yell at the people at the wheel," Moustafa said. "You just want to say, 'Correct the course—just barely, just a bit. We don't all have to die.'"

Moustafa was an ardent believer in American-style democracy, though his path to politics was indirect. The son of an airplane mechanic, he immigrated to the United States as an eleven-year-old whose only knowledge of English came from the *Power Rangers* children's TV show. As an olive-skinned foreigner in his mostly white Arkansas grade school, he was teased mercilessly by other boys, until an adolescent growth spurt turned him into a lanky athlete with exceptional soccer skills. He was a star player through high school and college, and then, after graduation, landed unexpectedly in Washington as an intern for Arkansas Democratic representative Vic Snyder, a member of the House Armed Services Committee. He so impressed his boss that his summer gig turned into a staff position, first with Snyder and then with Arkansas's second-term U.S. senator, Democrat Blanche Lincoln. After Lincoln's defeat in 2010, he worked briefly as a TV journalist before being discovered by a group of Libyan opposition officials who were seeking a lobbyist fluent in both Arabic and the language of official Washington. This was his job in April 2011, when Syrian exiles prevailed on him to work for them instead.

Soon Moustafa was briefing Congress and the White House as director of the Syrian Emergency Task Force, a nonprofit that sought to provide real-time information about conditions inside Syria, as well as the thinking and plans of the anti-Assad opposition. So armed, U.S. policymakers could provide the kinds of assistance that would best help Syria's rebels.

Or they could choose not to.

"The point was to convince people of something that already seemed logical," Moustafa said. Americans are naturally sympathetic toward those who seek to liberate their country from dictatorship, and here U.S. democratic principles "had aligned with U.S. national interests, in terms of what we need to do in Syria," he said. "And we just thought the policy would shift in that direction."

Moustafa made regular trips to the White House to meet with senior members of the president's Syria team, sometimes at his initiation but often at theirs. He sat through long West Wing briefing sessions with Samantha Power, Obama's adviser on human rights who would later become ambassador to the United Nations, as well as Denis McDonough, the president's tough-talking deputy national security adviser, and senior officials from the State Department's Syria desk. All spoke sympathetically about the plight of Syria's embattled opposition. But any talk about possible remedies came with a long list of caveats, legal provisos, and qualifiers.

"There was a lot of 'This is on the table' and 'That is on the table,' but then none of it really was," Moustafa said. "As time went on, that became clearer. The sense was: 'Look, the president came into office saying we were going to get out of these wars.'"

Back in his own office, Moustafa would hold long chats over Skype with Syrian protest leaders, some of whom he later met in person after he began shuttling between Washington and the region. Some refused to be downcast, believing it was inevitable that the Americans would come to their aid. After all, Obama had declared that Assad must go. "The rhetoric from the administration and the rest of the international community was that Assad was over—he has to step down. So their thinking was: 'Let's come out in droves,'" he said. "And they came out. I thought to myself, 'They're getting shot at now, they're going to stop.' But then they'd be back the next week, and the next. And they kept coming out."

Among the defiant ones was Noura al-Ameer, a young Sunni

woman from the Syrian city of Homs whom Moustafa met online and eventually befriended. When the first protests erupted, al-Ameer was twenty-three, a petite brunette and college student who liked political debates and brightly colored head scarves. In the early days, she gushed about the extraordinary unity she observed in Hama's streets, as Syrians from every ethnic group and social class joined in the demonstrations. For a time, nearly every rally featured a pair of protesters carrying a Christian cross and a Koran to symbolize the harmony between faiths.

"There were merchants and workers, doctors and engineers, students and journalists," she remembered later. "All the different sects were there, and all the social classes from across society."

The sense of unity somehow made protesters feel less afraid, she said. Sunni shopkeepers and Alawite law students locked arms, even when riot police began ripping into the crowd with batons and tear gas. The first time it happened, al-Ameer assumed she was going to die. But it didn't seem to matter.

"Even if the regime killed us, we would die happy," she said. "After all the repression we had lived through, it felt wonderful. And it was novel for us. It was almost a fantasy to think we would die for a cause we all believed in."

Al-Ameer did not die, but something else did. Slowly, the symbols of unity disappeared, as stories circulated about sectarian killings and assaults. In her mostly Sunni neighborhood, flyers began appearing in doorways, warning of coming attacks from Alawite death squads. At the same time, al-Ameer's Alawite friends were getting similar warnings about Sunnis. Meanwhile, the regime's notorious goon squads—hired gangs called *shabiha* or "ghosts"—snatched women and children from the streets and then returned them, sometimes dead, other times beaten and tortured, with tales about being brutalized by Alawite thugs. By late 2011, a new chant was added to the repertoire at the daily protests: "Christians to Beirut, Alawites to their coffins."

Then it was al-Ameer's turn to be caught. She was on her way to a visit with her mother when police officers pulled her off a public bus and brought her to one of the intelligence service's special interrogation centers in Damascus. Again she believed she would die. Instead, her captors locked her in a cell and forced her to listen as they beat and tortured one of her friends. When al-Ameer still refused to break, the officers strapped her into a chair and attached electrodes to her temples and chest. The pain shot through her body like liquid fire as her captors laughed to see if she would cry out.

"We're going to exterminate all of you, you Sunnis!" one of the officers said, using epithets that al-Ameer, years later, could not bring herself to repeat.

After she had spent eighty-five days in prison, family members won her release with a bribe paid to one of her jailers. She slipped into Turkey to join the opposition in exile, but by then the mood inside Syria had changed. The unity marches, when the young and old locked arms and carried flowers and olive branches, were gone, replaced by an ugly sectarianism she barely recognized.

"When I was protesting, I was surrounded by all these men and women who were like me, dreaming the Syrian dream," she said. "Today if I go there I won't find them. The regime has stolen them from us."

20

"The mood music started to change"

On January 24, 2012, a previously unknown Syrian rebel group posted a short video confirming what Western intelligence agencies already suspected: the al-Qaeda network's first franchise in Syria was officially open for business.

The formal unveiling came with a media rollout that might have befitted a new car model or the latest Apple gadget. For two days, Islamist Web sites ran banner ads promising a "special announcement," against the backdrop of a clock ticking down the hours. When the time arrived, the al-Nusra Front was introduced with a sixteen-minute video that summed up the group's capabilities and special features. The chief salesman spoke enthusiastically, though carefully keeping his face away from the camera.

"We hereby bring the Islamic nation the glad tidings of a long-awaited event," said Abu Mohammad al-Julani, the man dispatched into Syria five months earlier by the Islamic State's central branch in Iraq. A call for help had been heard, Julani said, and "what else could we do but answer the call?"

By the time the video aired, Julani's band had been offering its brand of assistance for at least three months. A few weeks earlier, a pair of perfectly synchronized car bombs had exploded outside one of the Assad regime's security offices in Damascus, killing forty-four people and serving notice that a new type of combatant had entered the fray. The al-Nusra Front later claimed responsibility; terrorism experts had already concluded that the culprit was likely al-Qaeda or someone trained in the group's methods.

The original parties to the conflict denounced the introduction of suicide bombers into the fighting. "We said from the beginning, this is terrorism," said a Syrian Foreign Ministry spokesman, Fayssal Mekdad. The main rebel opposition force disavowed the use of weapons that killed indiscriminately. The Free Syrian Army "does not use car bombs—it never did before and it never will," declared its spokesman, Ammar al-Wawi. Yet, from that day forward, car bombs were a regular addition to Syria's catalogue of horrors, along with truck bombs, suicide vests, and improvised explosive devices.

Julani, in his occasional video messages, would maintain that his al-Nusra Front was targeting only the regime's forces and not civilians, even those from Assad's Alawite sect. And he insisted that his methods would work, whereas the many others being tried—from nonviolent resistance to hit-and-run guerrilla warfare to a useless reliance on Western aid and Western-brokered peace accords—would not.

"Al-Nusra Front has taken upon itself to be the Muslim nation's weapon in this land," he said. This would be a harsh campaign, but also a holy one, he said, requiring all devout Syrians to "rally around the banner of 'There-is-no-god-but-Allah,'" the black standard borne by the Prophet Muhammad's ancient army and appropriated in modern times by jihadists.

Far from Syria, other Muslim audiences—including those that Julani likely envisioned in recording the video—were more receptive. In the Sunni Arab countries of the Persian Gulf and North Africa, many thousands of religious Muslims began mobilizing in the early months of 2012 to support the jihadists who were at last inflicting real blows on the Syrian tyrant. Young men from Saudi Arabia, Libya, and Tunisia who had watched Assad's massacres of fellow Muslims, shown nightly on Arabic-language cable news channels, began trekking to southern Turkey to join al-Nusra and other Islamist militias that were running recruitment networks in the border towns. In far greater numbers, sympathetic Arabs began donating cash, gold jewelry, and supplies to the Syrian Islamists' cause. Arab governments secretly sent aid as well, usually the lethal kind.

In Kuwait, one of the biggest providers of private funding, a preacher named Hajjaj al-Ajmi, launched a Twitter campaign to persuade his 250,000 followers to donate money to special bank accounts set up to help the rebels. "Give your money to the ones who will spend it on jihad, not aid," al-Ajmi exhorted donors in a video pitch posted to YouTube in 2012. Other supporters held Twitter "auctions" to sell off cars, boats, vacation properties—anything that could be exchanged for cash to help the Syrian rebels. A few wealthy donors—sometimes called "angel investors" by those who benefitted—arranged visits to the battlefield to hand-deliver suitcases full of cash, and were sometimes rewarded by having a rebel brigade rename itself in the patron's honor.

"It's anyone's game," a Middle Eastern diplomat acknowledged at the time, after conceding that his own countrymen were among the benefactors for extremist fighters. "You see different players looking to create their own militias. It is beyond control."

Some countries made an earnest, if belated, attempt to stem the flow of private aid headed for jihadist groups. Saudi Arabia and the United Arab Emirates ultimately tightened restrictions and increased scrutiny of bank transfers to cut down on illicit giving. But others showed little inclination to close the taps. In Qatar and Kuwait— both wealthy Gulf kingdoms and allies of the United States—the Islamists' backers included government ministers who believed the jihadists offered the best chance for defeating the Assad government. Officially, both governments denounced extremism, even as individual ministers privately defended rebel groups that Western governments labeled as terrorists—including the al-Nusra Front, according to U.S. and Middle Eastern officials who participated in such discussions.

"In their view, it's Assad that's the problem, and groups like al-Nusra are the answer," said a senior Middle Eastern intelligence official who worked closely with both countries in coordinating policy on Syria. "That's why they're OK with money and weapons going to al-Nusra. They're the best fighters and they're also Sunni, so, if they win, the new government will be more like them."

—

Qatar, watching the conflict from eleven hundred miles away, could afford to take chances. For Jordan's King Abdullah II, the men with the black flags and Gulf-financed guns and explosives were already uncomfortably close, so much so that Jordanian border guards could sometimes watch the fighting from the observation towers on the Jordan-Syria frontier.

In the summer of 2012, the Islamists drew closer still. Jordan's intelligence service began picking up reports of fighters slipping into the country with weapons, apparently with the intention of spreading the revolution to the Hashemite kingdom. The Mukhabarat's teams watched for weeks as the infiltration teams set up safe houses and began stockpiling supplies for what appeared to be an ambitious plan to strike targets all across Amman.

When the plotters were nearly ready, the Mukhabarat pounced. Eleven suspects were rounded up in a series of raids that seized machine guns, mortars, car bombs, and explosives that had been smuggled into Jordan for the attack. From notes and interrogations, the agency pieced together the outlines of a plan to launch near-simultaneous attacks on multiple civilian and government targets in the capital, from the U.S. Embassy to an upscale shopping mall in the center of town. Had the plan succeeded, dozens, perhaps even hundreds, could have been killed.

The Mukhabarat's men had scarcely finished their work when trouble erupted on the country's border. A passing patrol had surprised a different group of armed Islamists as they were attempting to cross into Syria, setting off a fierce gun battle that left four of the militants dead. Also killed was a Jordanian soldier, the country's first casualty in Syria's year-old civil war.

The king was furious. For months, he had been warning everyone—the Americans, the Europeans, Arab allies, even Assad himself—of the consequences if a full-blown civil war were to erupt in Syria. Inevitably, the sparks from a sectarian or ethnic conflict would drift beyond Syria's borders. It had happened in Iraq, and now it was happening again.

"This is not abstract; this is real. It's next door," the king told senior aides. "And if it continues, it will be knocking at our door."

Through late 2011 and 2012, the monarch worked furiously to build firebreaks to prevent the conflict from widening. Already, Syrian refugees were streaming across the border by the thousands—a single camp, Zaatari, held 30,000 people in mid-2012 and would swell to 156,000 a year later, becoming Jordan's fourth-largest metropolis—so Abdullah boosted his security forces and built intake centers at the border crossings to ensure an orderly and carefully monitored flow into the new tent cities along the frontier. He convened meetings with American, British, and Arab military officials to work up detailed contingency plans for dealing with potential crises ranging from a chemical-weapons attack inside Syria to incursions by Assad's military jets into neighbors' air space. He worked with U.S. and British generals to create special-forces teams that could quickly secure Assad's depots of poison gas in the event of a sudden collapse of central power.

The Western governments were willing to participate in planning exercises, but slow to commit resources. Humanitarian aid trickled in, forcing Abdullah to scramble to find resources to feed and clothe the hordes of refugees on his border. Awkward negotiations began for a clandestine training site in Jordan for secularist rebels, the core of a future "Southern Front" that could advance toward Damascus while Assad's army was mired in fighting in the north and east of the country. Abdullah agreed, despite his fears about getting caught in the crossfire between rival Syrian armies. The training began in 2013, in tandem with a similar, CIA-supported program in southern Turkey. But after authorizing the program, the White House imposed strict limits on both the scale of the training operation and the kinds of weapons and ammunition the fighters would receive. CIA-backed fighters were paid $100 to $150 a month, less than half the salary offered by the Islamists. Ammunition rations were so meager that one commander complained that his soldiers were receiving on average about sixteen bullets per month. Many of the new soldiers wandered off to join other units, taking their weapons with them. "We thought going with the Americans was going with the big guns," one of the CIA-supplied commanders said. "It was a losing bet."

But the most difficult conversations involved other Arab leaders. Jordan, utterly lacking in the oil and gas reserves that fattened its neighbors' coffers, frequently turned to the wealthy Gulf states for aid during times of economic crisis. But now there would be a price: some of the Gulf sheikhs expected Jordan to serve as a conduit for money and weapons headed to the Islamist militias they supported in Syria.

Abdullah was incredulous. Why, he would ask, would anyone supply arms to jihadists whose central aim is to create a seventh-century theocracy in the heart of the Middle East?

"Where are these revolutions going to stop?" he asked one day during a private chat with one of his Gulf counterparts.

"I hope these revolutions continue in the Middle East," said the other sovereign, a man who has publicly acknowledged sharing many of the Islamists' religious views. "I've paid for the support of these groups, and they owe allegiance to me."

"That's not how it works," Abdullah snapped. "You have moved yourself down on the menu. But eventually they're going to come after you."

The flow of money and weapons into Syria continued unabated. In private talks with his aides, Abdullah could see the possible pathways that history might take. One possibility—that Assad, backed by Iran and Russia, would emerge victorious through brute force—now seemed unlikely. An alternate path would see the "loonies"—radical Islamists—seize control in Damascus, though that also seemed remote. A third possibility, if the region were exceedingly lucky, would be a negotiated settlement in which Assad would be forced to surrender power to a Syrian unity government, one that would oversee elections while leaving essential institutions in place to ensure order and safety for Syria's citizens.

There was, however, yet a fourth possible outcome: prolonged violence with no clear resolution. In this scenario, the country known as Syria would disintegrate in a maelstrom that slowly consumed other countries in its wake, destabilizing the region for decades to come. Abdullah, in his discussions with aides, imagined a fractured Syria divided into zones controlled by Sunnis, Alawites, and Kurds, each supported and supplied by foreign partisans. Indeed, the contours of a future divided Syria were becoming clearer, with the regime clinging to defensive positions around the capital and coastal cities and leaving the parched, landlocked interior to the Islamists. "We saw a stalemate coming," one of the king's aides said.

The reality was, the extremists were growing stronger, and so was the pressure from Jordan's allies to back them—passively, if not actively. But Abdullah refused. Alone in his office, he would click through the day's catalogue of videotaped atrocities: captured soldiers executed at close range, priests and imams butchered like sheep, pale young bodies pulled from the rubble of bombed-out apartment buildings. Sometimes he would send the links to his senior advisers. Nothing like this could ever be allowed to happen in Jordan, he told them.

"I have my red lines," he said, as one aide later recalled. "I will not allow support for the radicals, because it will come back to bite us. It will come back to bite my citizens."

In May 2012, Robert Ford was summoned to the State Department Building's seventh floor for a rare private meeting with the woman who had been his boss of record for the past three years. Ford had met Hillary Clinton several times before, but it was unusual for a midlevel diplomat to take the elevator alone to the elegant "Mahogany Row" suite that serves as the personal office of the U.S. secretary of state.

Ford was now an ambassador without an embassy. Officially, he remained the chief U.S. diplomat to Syria, but he had been recalled to Washington the previous October because of concerns about his safety. The rooftop scare in July had been frightening enough, but other incidents in the weeks that followed made clear that Syria's guarantee of protection for foreign diplomats no longer applied to him.

The most terrifying scrape came on a day when Ford paid a call on the leader of one of Syria's few officially recognized opposition parties in Damascus. When the U.S. diplomat arrived at the man's office, a crowd of about seventy-five Assad sympathizers was waiting for him on the walkway outside. Ford and his aides ran through a hail of eggs and tomatoes and managed to slip inside the entrance, just seconds ahead of the mob. The Americans pushed a desk in front of the door to brace it, and Ford turned to his hosts with a sardonic smile. "We're from the American embassy," he said. When the meeting ended, there was a second mad dash to the embassy's cars, which by then had been trashed so thoroughly they could never be repaired. As he ran for his car, Ford convinced himself that he would not survive the day with all his bones and teeth intact. "I didn't think they were going to kill me," he recalled later, "but I thought for sure they were going to beat me up." Somehow all got away unharmed, but Ford's next major outing was to the airport for a flight home. He would not return, and the embassy itself was shuttered three months later.

Clinton knew all about Ford's ordeals, so during their meeting on that May afternoon, the two officials proceeded to talk about the larger power struggles under way in Syria: the Iranians and their growing support for Assad, the latest battlefield trends, the multitude of rebel factions and their allegiances. Ford was going over some of the particulars when Clinton stopped him.

"You know where this is going? This could be a regional disaster," she said. She ticked down a list of possible consequences: spillover violence infecting Lebanon, Jordan, and Iraq; refugee outflows in gigantic numbers; a sectarian war that "stretches from Lebanon all the way to Iraq."

Ford hardly disagreed, though he tried to sound hopeful. Maybe such a crisis could still be avoided, he offered, if the new peace initiative recently launched by the UN's special envoy to Syria, Kofi Annan, gained traction.

"If we can get through the negotiations to get a transitional government stood up—if we can reinforce the opposition enough so they get through a negotiation—maybe we can avoid that," Ford said.

The secretary of state was quiet, pensive. Of the possible scenarios for Syria, they both knew, the least likely was one in which Assad willingly negotiated an end to his own presidency.

"She just didn't think it would ever work with Assad," Ford said afterward.

Ford would play a key role in the UN-brokered negotiations that summer, and for nearly two years after that. Of the myriad obstacles to a solution, one indeed remained constant throughout: Syria's steadfast refusal to consider any settlement in which Assad would lose the presidency.

Yet, already, a new problem was beginning to crowd out the many others facing the White House's Syria team. The tiny bands of jihadists spotted earlier by intelligence agencies had grown into a small army. At National Security Council meetings, the maps displaying the shifting lines now showed pockets of territory under the control of jihadists, including the al-Nusra Front, a group with a clear al-Qaeda pedigree.

Intelligence briefings were soon expanded to include updates on the scores of Islamist groups that were now part of the ever-shifting rebel network. Some groups were thoroughly homegrown and worked cooperatively with the Free Syrian Army's secular command. Others, like the al-Nusra Front, did not. More disturbingly, young Muslim men from around the world were beginning to stream across the Syria-Turkey border to join the fight, evoking the great migrations of volunteer fighters into Afghanistan and Iraq in decades past. To encourage them, al-Nusra's leaders set up Twitter and Facebook accounts offering everything from theological pep talks to practical advice on what to wear and bring.

A few of the arriving foreigners were well known to the spy agencies, having arrived directly from other battlegrounds or having extensive records from incarceration in U.S. detention centers.

"At some briefings," the senior security adviser recalled, "we'd hear, 'Wait till you see who just showed up [in Syria].' And then, the next time, it was 'So—you think that *last* group was bad . . . ?'"

Still other new arrivals were worrisome precisely because they had no record of previous militancy or crime. From Western Europe came hundreds, then thousands of young men, most of them Muslims, and all of them bearing passports allowing them to travel freely throughout the European Union and North America. Suddenly the talk in the West Wing wasn't just about the risk of a destabilizing civil war in the Middle East. It was about a destabilizing civil war with a potential for dispersing thousands of radicalized youths across the continents, more embers carried on the wind. This was enough to keep even the more seasoned national security hands awake at night, the senior adviser said.

"We weren't convinced that al-Nusra was coming for us next week, but we were worried about all these trained jihadis coming back to Europe and having a passport," the senior adviser said. "This is when the mood music in the Situation Room started to change."

From the CIA to the Pentagon, the concerns were given voice in official reports. The State Department's Syria team, which included Ford and other refugees from the now closed U.S. Embassy in Damascus, put together a document for Undersecretary of State William J. Burns that sought to put the latest events and trends in context. The classified report was never made public, but the point, as Ford recalled afterward, was that Syria had drifted into a kind of lawlessness that dangerous groups were beginning to exploit.

"The regime was losing control of eastern Syria—the border points—and some of the border points along the Turkish border, too," Ford later said, summarizing the report's essence. "These are large spaces that extremists will be looking to control, just as they did in Afghanistan and Somalia. And it's important to build a moderate Syrian opposition that can confront those people, as well as Assad."

In the State Department's analysis, the "extremists" consisted mainly of the al-Nusra Front, which was looking increasingly dangerous as the year 2012 neared its end. Not only was the group indisputably linked to al-Qaeda terrorists, but it also was emerging among the rebels as one of their most effective military organizations, as well as a preferred destination for many of the incoming foreign fighters. Even al-Nusra's relatively moderate—by al-Qaeda's standards—behavior was cause for alarm. Though its leaders insisted on imposing strict Sharia law in villages they "liberated," they largely avoided violence against Muslim civilians. Some al-Nusra units actually made a show of picking up trash and delivering food and water to battered neighborhoods, acts that won them respect and even admiration.

What would happen, analysts wondered, if this new brand of "jihadist lite" truly caught hold? What if Syria—a neighbor to Israel, and a true linchpin of the Middle East—were to become the first of the Arab Spring dominoes to fall to a government that was al-Qaeda in all but name?

Since the beginning of the uprising, the White House's entire national security team had been unanimous in opposing direct U.S. interference in Syria's internal conflicts. By the late summer of 2012, the prevailing view had shifted in one significant respect: Key members of President Obama's inner circle now regarded the notion of arming Syria's moderate rebels as undesirable yet necessary—the least objectionable out of a list of exceedingly bad options.

Among the cabinet members urging a more aggressive response was Obama's popular and widely respected secretary of defense. Leon E. Panetta, a former CIA director, brought rare experience to the debate: He helped lead the fight against ISIS's predecessors in Iraq, and he had helped coordinate aid to the Arab insurgency in Libya. At seventy-four, Panetta, the gregarious son of Italian immigrants and former chief of staff for the Clinton White House, was no one's definition of a hawk. But at Langley and the Pentagon he had frequently approved the use of lethal tactics—from the CIA's stealthy drones to missile strikes and commando raids—to kill suspected terrorists in their hideouts overseas. Just a year earlier, Panetta had helped direct the successful mission to kill the world's most famous terrorist, Osama bin Laden.

Now he watched with growing unease as terrorists moved into new sanctuaries created by the chaos that followed the Arab Spring uprisings. With Syria, his initial concern had been regional stability: Sectarian fighting in Syria could spread beyond the country's borders to Turkey, Lebanon, and beyond. But the arrival of hardened jihadists in Syria made the conflict infinitely more dangerous, he believed.

"The intelligence, frankly, was very worrisome," Panetta later recalled. "We were seeing a lot of extremist elements going in, and they were organizing and becoming pretty effective. The last thing we wanted was for them to gain a foothold and use Syria as a base of operations."

At the time, the White House stuck to its policy of providing non-lethal support to the opposition while using diplomatic pressure to bring about Assad's resignation and a new interim government. But the results had been frustrating at best. Kofi Annan, the former UN secretary-general in charge of peace negotiations, resigned in disgust over the summer after repeated setbacks, including Russia's insistent blocking of any measure before the world body that might pressure Assad into stepping down. On the ground, the fighting intensified, and yet neither side could gain a decisive advantage. The Syrian president replenished his weary forces with Hezbollah fighters from Lebanon and used his air force to bomb and strafe rebel positions. Turkey and the Persian Gulf countries sent fresh torrents of cash and weapons to back a rebel force increasingly dominated by Islamists. For the Americans, as Hillary Clinton would later acknowledge, "every option appears worse than the next."

Clinton began privately pushing for what she would call a "carefully vetted and trained force of moderate rebels who could be trusted" with American weapons. As she described the events in her book *Hard Choices,* she invited then CIA director David Petraeus to her house for lunch in July 2012 to brainstorm about ways to recruit and build such a force. If America "was willing finally to get in the game, we could be much more effective in isolating the extremists and empowering the moderates inside Syria," she wrote.

By late summer, following extensive meetings with NATO counterparts and rebel leaders, Clinton was "reasonably confident" that an effective strategy could be put in place, she said. Petraeus's CIA put together a plan for building, training, and arming a moderate rebel army that could eventually overthrow the regime and establish authority in provinces now effectively controlled by Islamists. The plan was presented to President Obama at a White House meeting in late August, and Panetta was among the core group of senior advisers to argue for its acceptance.

"We're outside the game," Panetta would argue. "We don't have any credibility with [Syrian moderates]. We're giving them nonlethal assistance and they're dying."

Panetta was not naïve about the risks. Even the most carefully vetted rebel group might decide to switch sides, or commit a massacre using American-supplied guns. Arms given to friendly fighters could easily end up in the wrong hands.

"There's always a risk," he said. Yet, he told the president, echoing the views of Clinton and Petraeus, "I think we could do this." The alternative—allowing the conflict to run its course—also carried risks, opening the door to even more chaos and an expanded breeding ground for extremists, he argued.

Obama listened thoughtfully and then proceeded to pick at the holes in the CIA's plan, according to officials present at the meeting. There had been many instances in U.S. history where a well-intentioned decision to arm a guerrilla movement had horribly backfired, the president noted, according to Clinton's account. Why would this time be different?

Benjamin Rhodes attributed the president's reluctance to commit to military intervention to his fear that it could mire the country in another Middle East war.

"He was willing to consider options, but the question always was: 'What happens next? What happens the day after you take out a series of runways in Syria?'" Rhodes remembered. "He did not see where a more interventionist military option led us, other than being deeper and deeper in a conflict that is extraordinary complex and shows no signs of having a military solution."

Rhodes also suggested that disagreement between the president and his advisers over Syria was less dramatic than contemporaneous news accounts portrayed it to be.

"I think, candidly, that a lot of people have used this debate to position themselves for posterity as being for doing something in Syria when in fact it wouldn't have made much difference," Rhodes said. The plan presented to Obama that fall "didn't feel fully baked," he said, and the president was unconvinced that arming rebel militias—assuming trustworthy allies could be found—would tip the balance.

"This is a very hard problem, rooted in a decade of war in Iraq and decades of sectarian tensions in that part of the world," Rhodes said. "Sometimes we would like to think we have more agency than we do."

In the end, Obama, who had been elected on a promise to end America's involvement in Middle East wars, rejected the CIA plan. The situation could change in the future, the president allowed, particularly if Assad crossed the administration's "red line" of using or transferring his stocks of chemical weapons. But for the moment, there would be no shipments of U.S. military hardware to Syria's rebels.

The debate would erupt again, but an opportunity had passed. Clinton, disappointed, plunged back into the task of seeking the elusive diplomatic accord that would end the conflict. She also secured an agreement for increasing humanitarian aid—more blankets, food, computers, phones—for Syria's opposition.

"But all of these steps were Band-Aids," she wrote. "The conflict would rage on."

Panetta resigned as defense secretary five months after the August meeting. Looking back more than two years later, he regarded the administration's decision as a costly failure.

"We learned a lot about how to confront al-Qaeda and its affiliates as a result of operations in Pakistan and Afghanistan," he said. "We know how to do this. But we have to be willing to do it."

21

"There was no more hope after that"

The black flags came from the east, as the Hadith's prophecies foretold, carried by men with long hair and beards and surnames taken from their hometowns. They came not on horseback but in small pickup trucks, sometimes dozens at a time, kicking up dust as they headed west across the Iraqi desert. A year after the start of the Islamic State's Syrian venture, Abu Bakr al-Baghdadi was finally moving to assert control over a project that, in his mind, was hopelessly adrift. Now Baghdadi would show his wayward Syrian apostles and the rest of the world how a caliphate was meant to be run.

To ensure unhindered access to the Syrian border and beyond, Baghdadi placed one of his most colorful lieutenants in charge of securing the main Iraqi highway, from western Anbar Province to the Syrian frontier. His pick for the job, the Islamic State's flamboyant Anbar commander Shaker Wahib al-Dulaimi, had already gained local notoriety as Abu Wahib, one of the terrorist group's rising stars, and a man utterly obsessed with his own public image. The twenty-seven-year-old former computer programmer deliberately styled himself after his hero, Abu Musab al-Zarqawi, for whom he briefly served before being arrested and thrown in the Camp Bucca prison in 2006. Now he sought to replicate his mentor's look, from the shaggy black hair, cap, and beard to his penchant for posing unmasked for cameras while affecting the look of a jihadi superhero.

Some of his video outtakes are unintentionally hilarious, as Abu Wahib tries karate moves or attempts to leap through the air while firing his gun. Others are simply cold-blooded.

In the spring of 2013, Abu Wahib's men set up a video camera as their leader stood with his rifle in the middle of a desert highway to flag down a convoy of tractor-trailers heading from Syria into Iraq. After the trucks pulled over, Abu Wahib rounded up three of the drivers and asked each for an ID card to see if he was a Shiite. The video recorder captured the entire exchange.

The men, all Syrians who appear to range from their late twenties to early forties, clearly understand the consequences of a wrong answer, for all three adamantly denied having anything to do with the Shiite faith or the Syrian regime.

"You're Shiites, right?" Abu Wahib asked.

"We're Sunni, from Homs," said the youngest one, a tall, good-looking youth wearing white jeans and a short-sleeved dress shirt.

"Are you sure?"

"We just want to live," said the older one. "We're here to earn a living."

Abu Wahib toyed with them. "What proves to me that you're Sunni?" he asked. "How many kneelings do you make at dawn prayer?"

The men were nervous. "Four," answered one. "Three," said another. "Five," said the third.

Abu Wahib scoffed. "From your talk, you're a polytheist"—a Shiite—he declared. He made the men kneel in the sandy median between the lanes. Then, firing his rifle in short bursts from the hip, he shot each in the back. As they attempted to crawl away, he fired a shot at close range into each man's head.

"So here is the international highway in the hands of the Islamic State!" one of Abu Wahib's masked accomplices yelled. The fighters set fire to the trucks, leaving the drivers' bodies facedown as rivulets of blood seeped into the orange dust. The videotape ended with a recording of Zarqawi's voice.

"Lo and behold, the spark has been ignited in Iraq," the dead leader was heard to say, "and its fires shall only get bigger until it burns the Armies of the Cross in Dabiq."

These were the men with whom Baghdadi now sought to build his Islamic caliphate. The first batch he had sent into Syria had disappointed him. They were too mild, certainly in comparison with their Iraqi counterparts. They were also too Syria-focused and, very possibly, too popular for Baghdadi's liking. Now Baghdadi was ready to start again, with men like Abu Wahib in the vanguard, and with Baghdadi himself setting the tone.

On April 9, 2013, Baghdadi posted a twenty-one-minute audio message on Islamist Web sites, announcing a major corporate restructuring. Officially banished, Baghdadi said, was the group known as the al-Nusra Front. In its place was a newly merged organization that Baghdadi called the Islamic State of Iraq and al-Sham. The latter word, roughly synonymous with the English term "Levant," referred to the lands of the eastern Mediterranean, from southern Turkey through present-day Syria, Lebanon, Jordan, and Israel. English-speakers would know the new organization as ISIL, or ISIS.

In explaining the change, Baghdadi recounted a history of the group's previous incarnations, starting with the early days under Zarqawi, the founder and esteemed "mujahid sheikh." He told a story of how Zarqawi, when he first swore allegiance to Osama bin Laden, explained privately to his followers that he did so for strategic reasons, and not out of some genuine devotion or need.

"I swear by Allah, I didn't need from him money or weapons or men, but I saw in him a symbol," Baghdadi quoted Zarqawi as saying. Now, in a similar vein, it had become strategically important for the Syrian offshoot organization to unite symbolically with its parent, he said.

"Al-Nusra Front was only an expansion of the Islamic State of Iraq, and part of it," Baghdadi said. "So we declare, keeping our trust in Allah, the abolishing of the name of the Islamic State of Iraq and the abolishing of the name of al-Nusra Front, and joining them under one name—the Islamic State in Iraq and al-Sham—and also uniting the banner, which is the banner of the Islamic State."

The message cut a fresh trough of despair across Western capitals. Analysts had long assumed that the al-Nusra Front was an Islamic

State offshoot, though one that had at least temporarily decided to soften its image. Now Baghdadi was asserting publicly that the two organizations were one and the same. Moreover, the more fearsome Iraqi side was taking charge.

But the most emphatic response came from a surprising source: Baghdadi's presumed partner in the merger. No one had bothered to secure the consent of the al-Nusra Front, which, as it turned out, had no intention of fading away. The al-Nusra leader, Abu Mohammad al-Julani, fired back two days later with an audiotaped message repudiating everything Baghdadi had said. "Al-Nusra Front's banner will remain, nothing will be changed in it," said Baghdadi's old comrade and former friend.

Julani then appealed to the world's preeminent jihadist, al-Qaeda's leader, Ayman al-Zawahiri, to settle the dispute. The longtime deputy of Osama bin Laden had famously quarreled with Zarqawi over beheadings and other shock-theater tactics, and the old Egyptian had been equally unhappy with Zarqawi's successors. On June 9, 2013, Zawahiri published an open letter, ordering a halt to the merger and scolding Baghdadi for attempting such a thing without consulting with him first. In an astonishing rebuke, he decreed that Baghdadi would be on probation for a year as leader of the Islamic State of Iraq. After twelve months, Zawahiri would decide to either allow him to stay on the job or "appoint a new emir," the letter said.

Finally, to ensure that no fighting erupted between the groups, Zawahiri said he was sending a personal emissary, an al-Qaeda elder statesman named Abu Khalid al-Suri, into Syria to mediate any future disputes. "Muslim blood is off-limits for other Muslims," Zawahiri declared.

"I call upon all my Muslim brothers and the Mujahedin to stop arguing over this dispute and to stop sedition among the Mujahedin," he wrote, "and to seek harmony and unity, along with winning hearts and uniting ranks among Muslims."

It was a remarkable, and strikingly public, feud between branches of the al-Qaeda network, one that not only contained echoes of the dispute between Zarqawi and Bin Laden but also evoked the earlier rift between Zarqawi and his one-time mentor, Abu Muhammad al-Maqdisi. The squabbling continued to play out for months, with

Islamist scholars and pundits around the world taking sides in Internet forums and chat rooms, arguing over which leader best represented the movement's future.

Baghdadi dealt with al-Qaeda's advice just as Zarqawi did: he ignored it. He issued one additional statement, claiming that he was merely following orders from a higher authority. "I prefer the command of Allah over the command that contravenes it," he said. And then he proceeded to launch his unified Islamic State of Iraq and al-Sham as though the al-Nusra Front did not exist.

Throughout 2013, bands of ISIS fighters would fan out across nearly every part of Syria, from the lawless eastern desert to the populated corridors along the Turkish and Jordanian borders and to the very suburbs of Damascus. But before the assault began in earnest, Baghdadi had a few matters of business to attend to inside Iraq.

He first commenced an organizational overhaul, appointing regional governors, Sharia advisers, and military commanders to oversee operations locally throughout Iraq and Syria. The Islamic State would function like a real government, with flow charts for acquiring approvals and special departments in charge of social media, logistics, finances, training, recruitment, and even the management of candidates for suicide missions, who were kept apart from the regular fighters to ensure proper indoctrination.

Next, Baghdadi would crank up the violence inside Iraq, unleashing waves of bombings that set a new mark for the gratuitous slaughter of ordinary civilians. The body count in Iraq's morgues soon soared to levels not seen since the Zarqawi era, as ISIS dispatched suicide bombers into sports arenas and community soccer games as well as mosques, cafés, and markets. Even Iraqis inured to bloodshed expressed shock when an ISIS recruit drove an explosives-laden truck into an elementary-school playground in Nineveh Province in October 2013, killing thirteen children who were outside for recess.

The final step was an operation Baghdadi called "Destroying the Gates." It started with a trial run in 2012, when his fighters crashed into a small prison near the Iraqi city of Tikrit and freed a hundred prisoners, half of them former terrorists who had been on death row. Then, on July 21, 2013, ISIS struck two of the country's largest prisons in simultaneous nighttime raids that involved multiple suicide bombers and scores of mortar rounds. The biggest of the two raids, on Iraq's notorious Abu Ghraib prison, freed more than five hundred inmates, many of them veterans of Zarqawi's terrorist network.

Now Baghdadi had the core elements he needed for his reinvigorated ISIS army. Already, some of his fighters were moving to take control of small villages and towns in northern and eastern Syria, and now they would be joined by battle-hardened, ideologically disciplined fighters straight from Iraq's worst prisons. Some of the towns they entered were already under the control of other rebel militias, including the al-Nusra Front. When it encountered such forces, ISIS would offer a choice: join, flee, or fight. If the local force resisted, the Iraqis would not hesitate to kill them.

The rift with the al-Nusra Front slowly widened into a chasm. Zawahiri's personal peacemaker, Abu Khalid al-Suri, remained in Syria for a time, still hoping to find a way to end the dispute. In early 2014, he was bunking at the headquarters of an Islamist militia in the northern city of Aleppo when five men charged into the building with guns blazing. One of the assailants squeezed the trigger of his suicide vest, killing al-Suri and six others.

No one took credit for the mission, but al-Qaeda refused to have anything to do with ISIS after that. It urged its followers for the first time not only to stay away, but to oppose Islamic State's endeavors actively. By then it hardly mattered. Baghdadi now controlled the best-armed, most experienced fighters in the Syrian opposition. And they were about to become stronger still.

Syria's eastern provincial capital, Raqqa, is a shabby river town with a long history of being overrun by foreign invaders. The Greeks were first, followed by Romans, Persians, Mongols, and Ottomans, among others. Then it was the jihadists' turn. From midspring to the early summer of 2013, a succession of ISIS convoys rolled into the city in their white pickups, gradually kicking out the last of the Free Syrian Army defenders and setting up the terrorist group's official Syrian headquarters. Raqqa's 220,000 citizens would become the first urban population to experience life in a city fully under the control of the Islamic State.

The newcomers moved quickly, once the city was secure, to establish the new order. A huge ISIS banner was draped around the clock tower in al-Jalaa Square—renamed Freedom Square—and the city's new rulers began promulgating lists of behaviors that would no longer be tolerated.

Secretly snapping photos of ISIS's edicts was a brave young man who called himself Abu Ibrahim. Together with a pair of accomplices, he faithfully documented Raqqa's transformation over the next eighteen months, in photographs and video recordings he would take surreptitiously and post to the Web so all the world could see.

Abu Ibrahim vividly remembered ISIS's triumphant entry into the city. The prelude was a week of heavy street fighting that left scores of bodies lying in the streets and most of the city's civilians trapped in their houses, afraid to venture out for fear of being hit by sniper fire. Stores and bakeries closed, and many families ran out of food. "If you had bread, it was like having a million dollars," he recalled. "These were the hardest days." The fighting gradually waned, as militiamen opposed to ISIS either fled or switched sides. Then, all at once, columns of foreign fighters—mostly Iraqis, Abu Ibrahim later learned—appeared in the streets. ISIS's men raised their black flags over the main government buildings and claimed Raqqa as the new capital of the Islamic State.

"They walked around with their weapons, saying everything was going to be good now," he said. "They even began removing the bodies that had been lying around in the streets."

Many in Raqqa initially did not know what to make of the newcomers, Abu Ibrahim said. Some were relieved at least to see the fighting come to an end. Shops reopened and the city began to feel safe again.

But then the executions started.

The first one witnessed by Abu Ibrahaim involved a young man that ISIS commanders described as a criminal, though the man's offense was never made clear. The condemned man was forced to stand in Raqqa's main plaza, where his sentence was publicly read. Then he was shot in the head as a small crowd looked on. Next, ISIS soldiers tied the corpse's arms to a plank, crucifixion style, and left it to rot in the square for three days.

A second crucifixion followed a few days later. Then came a group execution, in which ISIS soldiers killed seven men and teens in the same square. Some appeared to be stragglers from defeated rival militias, though several were smooth-faced boys. This time the soldiers cut the heads from the corpses and displayed them on fence posts outside a city park.

"People were frightened, which is what they wanted," Abu Ibrahim said. "They wanted everyone to be terrified of them."

Having thus announced themselves to the city, Raqqa's new overseers began moving to eliminate obvious challenges to their authority. The city's three churches were padlocked, and crosses and other Christian symbols were hacked down or covered up. A Shiite mosque with an elegant turquoise dome was blown to pieces. Cigarettes and alcohol—symbols of Western corruption—were dumped into piles and burned. Then ISIS moved to create symbols of its own, starting with a converted police station that was painted black, from top to bottom, and repurposed as an administration building and Sharia court that would decide matters of crime and punishment. Suddenly Raqqa citizens were subject to a bewildering array of new regulations, enforced by the ISIS-appointed Hisbah, or religious police, who were free to interpret the laws as they saw fit.

The city's new rules began with mandatory religious observances— all shopkeepers were required to close for daily prayers, for instance— and expanded to include personal dress and behavior. ISIS banned not only smoking and drinking but also Western music and displays of Western clothing in shop windows. Women could leave their houses only if fully covered, and even then, any outing risked a humiliating inspection by police to ensure that the woman's *abaya* was sufficiently opaque and loose fitting, to avoid revealing any hint of the wearer's physical form.

Punishment for violating ISIS's rules could range from a public scolding or fine to floggings and worse. One unmarried couple was beaten for sitting together on a park bench. Another man was publicly flogged because he married a divorced woman before the mandatory three-month waiting period had ended. Any infraction carried an implicit threat of summary execution, which at times seemed to be carried out almost on a whim, Abu Ibrahim said.

"Sometimes a week or two will go by with no executions, and then suddenly there will be five at once," he said. "For ordinary people, there are fines and fees for everything: for running a business, for parking your car, for picking up your trash. They take your money and they use it to pay the salaries of the foreign fighters. And people are afraid to do anything because of the risk of execution."

But most troubling to Abu Ibrahim was how Raqqa's occupiers treated the city's children. Schools were kept shuttered for months after ISIS seized power, and when they finally reopened, everything had changed. The old textbooks and curricula—the "books of the infidels," ISIS called them—had been tossed out, replaced by religious training. Meanwhile, the city's hundreds of orphaned children and teens were moved to military camps to learn to shoot rifles and drive suicide trucks. Abu Ibrahim would sometimes see the young ISIS recruits in military convoys, carrying guns and wearing oversized uniforms.

"Some are boys younger than sixteen," he said. "When the schools were closed there was nothing for them to do. They see these tough guys with their Kalashnikovs and it affects them. They want to be part of it."

Indeed, ISIS would frequently boast about its youth camps, offering virtual tours on social media of facilities with names such as "al-Zarqawi Camp." Photographs and videos posted to Twitter showed prepubescent boys in military garb, firing weapons and practicing maneuvers. Other images depicted young trainees being directed to execute prisoners with gunshots to the head.

To Abu Ibrahim, the camps were ISIS's attempt at ensuring the movement's survival and hedging against the possibility of future military setbacks. The organization was investing in the creation of cadres of fanatical young followers willing to kill others or sacrifice their own lives if ordered to do so. "They are being brainwashed," Abu Ibrahim said of the ISIS youths, "to create an army of loyal followers for the future."

Meanwhile, ISIS was doing fine with the army it already had. A few months after announcing its entry into Syria, the Islamic State's ranks had swollen to nearly ten thousand fighters, including the bulk of the foreign volunteers streaming into Syria from fifty countries around the world. Rival rebel groups, from the al-Nusra Front to the secular Free Syrian Army, complained that ISIS was winning the competition for recruits—not just because it could afford to pay bigger salaries, but also because it claimed to be fighting for something bigger than Syria.

The group's Twitter and Facebook pages featured daily testimonials from volunteers from Europe, North Africa, and the Middle East touting the many rewards of jihad, both heavenly and temporal. An August 2013 Twitter posting by a Syrian jihadist who called himself Nasruddin al-Shami said he felt he had joined a "global gathering" when he signed up for ISIS. "I chose to be a soldier under this banner, because I found it to be Arab and non-Arab," he wrote. "I found people from the Peninsula, the Islamic Maghreb, the Egyptians, and the Iraqis. I met people from the Levant and Turkey. I met French, British, and Pakistanis. The list is long. They were all beloved brothers whose concern is to support the religion."

A British ISIS recruit told a British broadcaster, "It's actually quite fun.

"What's that [video] game called—'Call of Duty'?—It's like that," he said, "but really, you know, 3-D. You can see everything's happening in front of you. It's real. You know what I mean?"

In Raqqa's downtown markets, bearded, rifle-toting foreigners seemed at times to outnumber locals as the ISIS occupation took on a look of permanence. The group's coffers were fattening quickly, between the fees and bribes assessed to businesses and the sale of more than forty thousand barrels of crude oil per day from oil wells captured by ISIS in its march across the Syrian desert. The jihadists who had been so anxious to capture Raqqa a few months earlier seemed in no hurry now to push on to further conquests, Abu Ibrahim noted. The Islamic State's men would turn aggressive whenever there were punishments to mete out, but between executions and floggings, Abu Ibrahim would see them relaxing in restaurants, gawking at Western Web sites in Internet cafés, or buying knockoff Viagra from the drugstores.

For the occupiers, the Islamic State had finally arrived, at least in miniature. The men with the guns seemed happy with the state of affairs, because they were running the place. For everyone else in Raqqa, Abu Ibrahim wrote, all that was left was the "culture of backwardness and terror, after extinguishing the light of the mind."

In April 2013, as Baghdadi was preparing to announce his restructuring, Mouaz Moustafa slipped into the country, as he had done many times, through a hole in the chain-link border fence of Hatay Province in southern Turkey. He moved easily—this corner of far-northern Syria had been liberated from Assad for nearly a year—and made his way by foot to Khirbet al-Joz, a farming village that had become a kind of in-country base for his Syrian Emergency Task Force. The former congressional aide and his team had made a project of restoring basic services in the town, still scarred by months of fighting and looting. After helping reestablish the police department, he had returned to meet with locals interested in setting up a magistrate's office to settle minor disputes. He never dreamed who else would show up.

At the meeting was a well-dressed lawyer who introduced himself as Muhammad. The man explained that he was representing a client with an interest in the administration of justice in post-Assad Syria. Pressed, he identified the group that had hired him.

"I'm here to represent the Islamic State," he said.

Everyone in the room was floored, from the American visitors to the Christian and Muslim clerics who had unofficially presided over the town since the government forces pulled out.

"It was shocking," Moustafa said. "He was clean-shaven, maybe fifty, wearing a suit. We stopped in our tracks, because we didn't even know how to carry on."

ISIS's man at the meeting had little else to say, and appeared to be mostly listening and taking notes. At one point he interjected that his client tended to prefer Sharia law over secular legal codes.

"We didn't get into a discussion," Moustafa said, "because we didn't want him there."

The man eventually left, but his presence cast a pall. Here was evidence not only of ISIS's presence in Syria, but also of the group's intention to insinuate itself into governance at a microscopic level.

For Moustafa, now two years into his job and more deeply engaged in Syria's struggle than he could ever have imagined, it was another ominous turn. By early 2013, Moustafa had all but despaired of the possibility of a major U.S. intervention in the conflict. Now he spent most of his time looking for practical ways to improve the lives of Syrians in areas of the country outside Assad's control. But for every forward step, there were steps back: infighting among rebel groups; widespread corruption, sometimes fueled by suitcases of cash from Arab governments; a growing sectarian divide that hampered cooperation and sometimes led to reprisal killings. Soon the ISIS problem—the presence of heavily armed extremists at war with everyone else, their replacement of existing courts and police departments with their own system of justice—would eclipse all others, further complicating the efforts by moderate rebels to win Western support for the opposition.

Moustafa's perspective on Syria's unraveling now came at close range. He traveled to Syria constantly, often venturing within a few miles of the ever-changing front lines. He spoke and met regularly with rebel commanders, part of a growing personal network that also included journalists, international relief workers, foreign diplomats, and wealthy donors. After the U.S. Embassy in Damascus closed, Moustafa's reports from Syria became a useful window into parts of the country the Americans could no longer monitor directly. When allegations surfaced that spring about a small-scale use of chemical weapons by the Assad regime, Moustafa was asked if members of his network could help obtain blood and tissue samples for testing. They could, and did.

In May 2013, Moustafa stood next to Senator John McCain when the Arizona Republican made a surprise visit to Syria to meet rebel commanders there. McCain was escorted through a rebel-controlled border crossing and then to a small building that served as a command center for the Free Syrian Army. There, he sat grim-faced as a dozen rebel commanders took turns complaining about Washington's refusal to supply them with weapons, particularly antiaircraft missiles needed to stop Assad's bombing of civilian enclaves. In lieu of the guns and bombs they needed, the militias were receiving surplus army rations—the ubiquitous MREs, or meals ready to eat, in their bland plastic packaging.

"Am I supposed to throw pizzas at those airplanes?" one of the officers asked. Later, McCain would learn that all but two of the twelve officers he met had died in combat.

"We need to have a game-changing action," McCain told a TV interviewer after returning home. "No American boots on the ground, [but] establish a safe zone, and protect it and supply weapons to the right people in Syria who are fighting for obviously the things we believe in."

But at the White House, the president stood firm, insisting that shoveling more weapons into Syria would only make matters worse. "I don't think anybody in the region . . . would think that U.S. unilateral actions, in and of themselves, would bring about a better outcome," Obama told a news conference. The only trigger for a U.S. military response, he said, would be if Assad used chemical weapons, "something that the civilized world has recognized should be out of bounds."

There would be no help from Washington, Moustafa told his exasperated friends. The conflict, now in its second year, would continue as before, with the armies deadlocked while the suffering of civilians grew steadily worse. The biggest change was that risk of violent death now came from multiple sides at once. Two Syrians employed in the relief effort were captured by Assad's forces and later killed. Then two other workers, both of them young men whom Moustafa knew well, disappeared after being stopped at an ISIS checkpoint. Task-force members later learned that the militants had found the workers' laptops, confirming their employment with a Western relief organization. The two were executed, their bodies dumped into a pit.

In late summer, the Assad regime's chemical-weapons attack on civilians in Ghouta, a Damascus suburb, briefly raised expectations of a Western military response. After U.S. intelligence agencies released evidence showing that Assad's army had fired canisters of sarin gas into residential neighborhoods on August 21, Obama signaled his intention to punish Assad for crossing America's one clear "red line." Yet, despite widespread outrage over the deaths, the White House could not muster the political support for a military strike. Congress blocked a vote on a resolution authorizing air strikes against Assad, and the Parliament in Britain—a country presumed to be a key ally in any military campaign—rejected a similar proposal by Prime Minister David Cameron's Tory government. President Obama managed to secure a deal, with Russia's help, to remove all chemical weapons from Syrian territory, and the prospect of military intervention was again pushed aside.

Among Syria's opposition leaders, the collapse, in their view, of Western resolve after the Ghouta attack was a tougher psychological blow than the chemical attacks themselves, Moustafa said. Some rebel groups that had previously aligned themselves with the moderate Free Syrian Army simply gave up and joined the Islamists, who at least paid better salaries.

"People had been ecstatic when they believed the U.S. was finally going to act," Moustafa said. "It was one of those moments when everyone remembers exactly where they were. The regime was scared. We were hearing reports of people fleeing Damascus. Even the idea of bombs falling didn't cause concern. It was, like, 'Thank God. Even if we die in the bombings, at least now things will change.'

"And then, when nothing happened—that was the end," he said. "There was no more hope after that."

Washington's disarray over the chemical strikes looked even worse from the inside. Syria's "wicked problem," as Secretary of State Hillary Clinton famously called it, had split the National Security Council and was now creating casualties among the president's senior advisers.

Frederic C. Hof, the senior diplomat who helped coordinate the administration's response to Syria, resigned in frustration in late 2012. Now Robert S. Ford, the exiled ambassador to Damascus, was beginning to consider quitting.

Ford had been waging a fruitless battle inside the administration, pushing for concrete measures to strengthen the moderate opposition as a counterweight to the Islamists, who were controlling about a quarter of Syria's territory, including border crossings into Iraq and Turkey. He had supported air strikes after Assad's chemical attack on Ghouta in August 2013, and when those failed to materialize, he pushed for direct support to well-known and carefully vetted moderate militias.

"Increase the assistance. Do more," he urged. Despite White House promises, after the chemical attack, to speed up CIA training for rebels in Jordan and southern Turkey, the effort was too small and too slow to make a difference. "We really aren't doing anything," he said.

Making matters worse, Ford was being regularly summoned to Capitol Hill to defend the administration's policies in congressional hearings. Sensing a political opportunity, Republicans hurled insults at Ford in televised hearings, seeking to make the diplomat a symbol for White House ineptitude in managing the crisis. At one hearing, McCain questioned Ford's grasp of the Syrian crisis and suggested that the diplomat was willing to accept Assad's continued butchery of his own people.

"It seems like that is a satisfactory outcome to you," McCain said.

Ford kept calm, but inside he was furious.

"Do I need this?" he thought.

The reality, as Ford understood it, was that Congress was just as divided over what to do as the administration. Hawks such as McCain wanted to arm the rebels, but other Republicans favored military support only for groups that were fighting ISIS. Still other lawmakers—Republicans and Democrats—were leery of any U.S. involvement, reflecting an opinion held by large majorities of the American electorate.

Ford was ready to quit by the fall of 2013, though he was persuaded by State Department colleagues to stay on for another six months. When he finally turned in his resignation letter in early 2014, no one tried to stop him. By then, his efforts within the administration seemed to him increasingly futile, and the highly partisan, highly personalized attacks from Congress had drained his resolve to continue trying.

"I don't mind fighting, but when my integrity is being challenged by people who don't even know what's going on—it's ridiculous," he said.

Ford's resignation was officially announced on February 28, 2014. Days later, McCain asked the ambassador to stop by his office so he could personally thank him for his service.

Ford considered the request for a moment, then politely relayed his reply: "No."

22

"This is a tribal revolution"

In the decade since the group's founding, Abu Musab al-Zarqawi's jihadist followers had been called terrorists, insurgents, and Islamist militants. Now they were a full-fledged army. In the late spring of 2014, the troops of the Islamic State surged across western Iraq and into the consciousness of millions of people around the world. Moving with remarkable speed, ISIS vanquished four Iraqi army divisions, overran at least a half-dozen military installations, including western Iraq's largest, and seized control of nearly a third of Iraq's territory.

Analysts and pundits described the ISIS blitz as sudden and surprising, a fierce desert storm that appeared out of thin air. But it was hardly that. The ISIS conquest of June 2014 was a carefully planned, well-telegraphed act, aided substantially by Iraqis who had no part in ISIS and no interest in living under Sharia law. In the end, the movement's greatest military success was less a statement of ISIS's prowess than a reflection of the same deep divides that had roiled Iraq since the U.S. invasion in 2003.

At the root of the spring's dramatic events was a conflict between Iraq's Shiite government and one Sunni tribe, the Dulaims. It happened to be the familial clan of Zaydan al-Jabiri, the Ramadi sheikh and rancher who had been caught up in the fight against Zarqawi nearly a decade earlier. Zaydan had first watched his fellow tribesmen take up arms against the Americans in 2004, amid soaring anger over the occupation. He had then been a key participant in the anti-Zarqawi backlash known as the Anbar Awakening, when tribal militias helped drive insurgents out of their villages. Now the currents had shifted again, and Zaydan would watch with approval as his entire tribe rose up against an Iraqi government that many Dulaims saw as a greater threat than Zarqawi had ever been.

Zaydan was now fifty, thicker around the middle, but with the same mane of black hair, a successful businessman who wore a tailored suit as comfortably as the dishdasha and keffiyeh he wore to more traditional engagements. He had three wives, and a brick house that could have been plucked out of a tony subdivision in suburban San Diego. But beginning around 2010, Zaydan had come to view Iraq's government as at war with Sunnis like himself. The country's minority Sunnis had ruled Iraq up until the U.S. invasion, when power was handed to Shiites. Now, with American troops out of the way, the score settling had begun in earnest, or so it seemed to the Dulaims. It was objectively true that Sunnis had lost positions of power in the government and armed services, and there were numerous documented cases in which Shiite conscripts had brutalized Sunnis in their homes in the guise of rooting out terrorism. In Zaydan's mind, it was all part of an Iranian-inspired plan to ensure that Iraq never again posed a threat to Tehran's interests in the region.

"The ones who are leading now were thieves, bandits, and sectarian religious parties," Zaydan said, referring to the cohort in power since Prime Minister Nouri al-Maliki's narrow election in 2010. "Even with all the bad things the Americans did in Anbar, they didn't kill people in mosques, and they respected our religion. Those who are with the Iranians do not. They want to get rid of everything called 'Sunni.' I'm not saying the Americans were great, but they were better than these."

Then, beginning in late 2012, Sunni relations with the central government turned sharply worse. On December 21, government security forces raided the home of Rafi al-Issawi, a popular Sunni politician and a former Iraqi finance minister who had been outspoken in his criticism of the Maliki government. Thousands of Dulaims took to the streets in Fallujah, some of them carrying banners that read "Resistance Is Still in Our Veins." The rally eventually grew into a weekly pan-Sunni protest that spread to multiple cities and continued for month after month.

After more than a year of such protests, Maliki had finally had enough. On December 30, 2013, he sent security forces into Ramadi to shut down the demonstrations and break up a tent city that had sprouted in one of the city's plazas. Clashes broke out, and on New Year's Day 2014, protesters set fire to four Ramadi police stations. On January 2, rioting spread to neighboring Fallujah. On January 3, a convoy of armed ISIS militants rolled into town. The jihadists joined tribal militias in street battles with outmatched police and troops, inflicting more than one hundred casualties. Finally, on January 4, the remnants of Fallujah's government evacuated the town, and Islamic fighters raised the black flag of ISIS over the city's administration building.

The Dulaimi-ISIS alliance quickly drew support from other Sunni tribes as well as from a shadowy organization of former Baathists known as the Naqshbandi Order. The Sunni pact waged seesaw battles with army troops for several weeks for control of Ramadi and five other cities, but an uneasy truce settled over Fallujah, with ISIS firmly in charge of the center of town. It was the first time the terrorist group could officially claim an Iraqi city as its own.

ISIS seized the moment to fire off a stream of propaganda images on Twitter, showing its victorious troops parading around the center of the same city from which U.S. marines had ousted Zarqawi's men a decade earlier. Among the fighters posing for photographs was Abu Wahib al-Dulaimi, the flamboyant, publicity-obsessed ISIS commander for Anbar Province who had shot the three Syrian truck drivers on an Anbar highway the previous spring. In one frame, he grimaces, rifle in hand, next to a burning police car, wearing a black overcoat and boots like a Western gunslinger. In another, he walks through one of the captured police stations carrying a stack of files, like some kind of doomsday office clerk. Iraqis who saw the images might have noticed the familiar last name: Abu Wahib's surname identifies him as a member of the Dulaim tribe, making him a kinsman to the men who had organized the Fallujah protests. Enemies before, they were now officially on the same side.

At the White House, President Obama's security advisers viewed the same images with dismay. Administration officials quickly announced plans to speed up the delivery of promised military aid to the Maliki government, including new Hellfire missiles. Security for Iraqis was Maliki's problem now—he had insisted on it—but a terrorist takeover of an Iraqi city could not be allowed to stand.

To Zaydan, however, as for many other Sunnis, the revolt was purely an internal affair, one the Americans and the Baghdad government had completely misread, again.

"This is a tribal revolution," Ali Hatim al-Suleiman, the leader of the Dulaim tribe, told the London-based Arabic-language newspaper *Asharq Al-Awsat.*

"Iraqi spring," explained Tariq al-Hashimi, the Sunni politician and friend of the U.S. ambassador to Syria, Robert Ford, speaking from exile in Turkey after Maliki tried to arrest him.

The Sunnis candidly acknowledged that the tribes had handed ISIS the keys to Anbar Province, but only as a temporary measure. ISIS was merely providing the additional firepower needed to help Sunnis assert long-sought independence from Iraq's abusive central government, they said. Besides, these jihadists were Sunni patriots, not the death-obsessed criminals who had run the organization during Zarqawi's time.

"They changed," Zaydan said of the group. "Their leadership became Iraqi, and their program changed completely. The government claims that Baghdadi is a terrorist, but he's not a terrorist. He's defending fifteen million Sunnis. He's leading the battle against the Persians."

It was true that Zarqawi also had gotten a pass when he burst into Anbar Province with his small band of Sunni militants after the U.S. invasion. Zarqawi also had been a man of the tribe, but a different tribe. Baghdadi, by contrast, was a true Iraqi, raised in Samarra, Zaydan noted. He could be controlled.

"He will not dare talk about Sharia here, because he knows the tribes will not tolerate it," Zaydan said. "These people learned their lesson. They won't try the same things they did last time."

In fact, ISIS already was moving to settle scores in Anbar neighborhoods that had welcomed the group's arrival. Abdalrazzaq al-

Suleiman, a Sunni tribal sheikh and one of Zaydan's Ramadi neighbors, happened to be away on business when a truck filled with black-clad fighters drove up to his farm. The jihadists shot several of Suleiman's bodyguards, destroyed his cars, and then leveled his house with explosive charges. Suleiman's offense: Eight years earlier he had been a leader of the Anbar Awakening movement that cooperated with U.S. troops in driving Zarqawi's followers out of the province.

"They stole everything that was in my house before they blew it up," said Suleiman, who moved to Jordan for safety. "It was my duty and honor to work with the Americans as a tribal leader fighting terrorism. But now it feels like we've been abandoned. We were left in the middle of the road."

On February 11, 2014, two of America's top intelligence officials walked into a Senate hearing room to deliver what is traditionally one of the dreariest presentations of the congressional year: the catalogue of global woes known as the "Annual Threat Assessment." This one would be exceptionally grim. The director of national intelligence, James Clapper, and the chief of the Defense Intelligence Agency, General Michael Flynn, outlined emerging perils from a multitude of sources, including cyber-terrorism, a newly aggressive Russia, North Korean nuclear ambitions, global pandemics, and a potential calamitous unraveling of government authority throughout the Middle East and North Africa. Then, when the topic turned to Syria and ISIS, Flynn made a startling prediction.

"ISIL probably will attempt to take territory in Iraq and Syria to exhibit its strength in 2014," Flynn said, using the federal government's preferred acronym for the terrorist group in his testimony. Black flags were already flying over Fallujah, he said, and the takeover of that city would likely be repeated elsewhere, demonstrating the Islamists' growing strength and "ability to concurrently maintain multiple safe havens."

Flynn used the careful language appropriate to a congressional hearing, but his private assessment of the situation was even more dire. He had gone up against the same terrorist organization a decade earlier, and he understood ISIS's capabilities better than most.

A former chief of intelligence for General Stanley McChrystal, Flynn had helped lead the hunt for Zarqawi in Iraq. He recognized in ISIS the same familiar ideology and tactics. After the prison breaks the previous year, he even recognized many of the names.

"These are children of Zarqawi," Flynn said. "We were able to capture many of the mid-to-high level commanders in the eighteen months after Zarqawi's death. The majority were Iraqis, many of them former military guys who were put in the prison system. They're all out now."

But ISIS also was clearly learning and adapting, gaining new capabilities under Baghdadi's oversight, Flynn explained. Baghdadi was a more careful planner, and he was willing to be both patient and strategic in building alliances and support networks. In short, ISIS's recent gains in Iraq had been no accident.

"They got better because they saw how they were defeated," Flynn said. "Zarqawi was trying to create a civil war immediately to turn the situation in Iraq to his advantage. But the one big mistake he made was that he did not gain enough favor with the tribes in Anbar Province. He stole authority from them and then really abused it, because he was a vicious guy. This new crowd realizes that and they're operating differently."

Slowly, Baghdadi had repaired relations with the Sunni tribes, Flynn said, echoing the assessment made by Zaydan and other tribesmen. The ISIS leader exploited Syria's uprising to rebuild his finances while bringing in fresh recruits and a renewed sense of purpose. And he also had built an organizational structure made up of subject experts in fields as diverse as housing and transportation and strategic messaging.

"This current crowd, they are thinking long term," Flynn said. "They see this as a generational effort."

They were also on the move. Intelligence agencies were spotting unmistakable signs of mobilization for an ISIS offensive. But in which direction? Toward Baghdad, or Damascus?

U.S. intelligence agencies, watching the preparations under way by satellites and other remote systems, became convinced that ISIS was planning a push into the Iraqi heartland, and intended eventually to attack Baghdad itself. CIA analysts dutifully filed their reports, which made their way to the director's office and then to the White House. Any ISIS force that crossed the border, the reports warned, would face a weakened Iraqi army that had fought poorly against insurgents in Fallujah and elsewhere. Just how weakened was hard to tell; after the last U.S. troops left the country, the Maliki government sharply curtailed cooperation with U.S. intelligence agencies.

Yet no one imagined the Iraqi meltdown that would occur in the following weeks, acknowledged a senior intelligence official who watched the events unfold. "Though U.S. intelligence analysts provided ample warning about the ISF's [Iraqi Security Force's] troubles," the official said, "it was difficult for anybody to foresee the rapid ISF collapse."

ISIS's grand offensive began with an attack on its leader's hometown. Just after midnight on June 5, 2014, raiding parties blew up a police station south of the city of Samarra, home to generations of Baghdadi's al-Badri clan. Then, a few hours later, about 150 fighters roared into town on pickup trucks mounted with antiaircraft guns. The jihadists captured Samarra's main municipal building and the city's university, and then began to engage police who moved into defensive positions around the al-Askari Mosque, the ancient edifice whose iconic gold dome had been blown up by Zarqawi eight years earlier. The Iraqi army dispatched reinforcements from Baghdad, and the invaders soon pulled back, but already the fighting had spread to a half-dozen other towns along the highway that ran from Fallujah to the Syrian border.

Meanwhile, the main ISIS column, about fifteen hundred men, moved into position on the outskirts of Mosul. Protecting the ancient city and its 1.8 million people was an Iraqi force that on paper numbered twenty-five thousand. Its real strength was closer to ten thousand, the operational commander of Mosul's Nineveh Province later acknowledged; the rest had dropped out through desertions or were simply no-show jobs on the police department's payrolls, Lieutenant General Mahdi al-Gharawi told Reuters in the battle's aftermath. The city's remaining defenders were ill-supplied, since much of the defenders' armor and heavy weapons had been ordered to the south, to help retake Ramadi and other Anbar Province towns during the January fighting.

"In my entire battalion we have one machine gun," a Mosul battalion commander, Colonel Dhiyab Ahmed al-Assi al-Obeidi, told the news service. By contrast, when ISIS began pouring into his district before dawn on June 6, "in each pickup they had one," he said.

A first column of invaders raced into the city's northernmost Tammoz neighborhood in Humvees and pickup trucks, pouring machine-gun fire into the Iraqi army's defensive front line. On cue, ISIS cells based inside the city also opened up with grenades and sniper fire. The defenders fell back; within hours, columns of ISIS trucks had advanced to within a few blocks of the Mosul Hotel, where Gharawi had set up his command center.

At 4:30 p.m. came the decisive blow. A large water truck packed with explosives barreled into the hotel, exploding in flames and killing or injuring many of the Iraqi force's senior officers.

"The sound shook the whole of Mosul," said Obeidi, whose leg was torn open by the blast.

The rest of the army's defenses collapsed soon after that. By evening, police and army troops were discarding their uniforms and fleeing the battlefield in civilian clothes. Those who were caught were lined up in groups and shot.

By noon on June 10, just four days after the start of the offensive, the jihadists controlled Mosul's airport and most of the town's central district. They emptied the cash reserves from downtown banks and stripped an Iraqi military base of millions of dollars' worth of U.S.-made weapons and equipment. Then they seized control of Mosul's main prison, releasing the Sunni inmates and summarily executing the others—about 670 Shiites, Kurds, and Christians. By the end of the day, Mosul, Iraq's second-largest city, was fully under ISIS's control.

Iraq's army eventually regrouped and launched a counteroffensive that stopped ISIS from advancing into Baghdad, even as ISIS continued to gain ground in other parts of the country. By late June, the terrorist group's total land holdings, from western Syria to central Iraq, was greater than the areas of Israel and Lebanon combined.

The man who presided over this expanse now controlled more than just real estate. He owned oil wells, refineries, hospitals, universities, army bases, factories, and banks. Baghdadi's holdings in cash and financial instruments alone approached half a billion dollars, analysts would later confirm.

There was as yet no real government in place. But in a very real sense, the Islamists now had their state.

On July 4, 2014—a Friday, the Muslim day of prayer—Baghdadi appeared with bodyguards in the prayer hall of Mosul's Great Mosque of al-Nuri, famous for its "hunchback" minaret, which bows inward by several feet from the perpendicular. Local legend holds that the tower's crooked shape was caused by the Prophet Muhammad himself, who passed overhead as he was ascending into heaven.

Those who attended services that day might have perceived a similar warping of the temporal order when the Islamic State's chief officer walked to the front of the mosque to declare the restoration of the caliphate. ISIS had made a similar declaration a few days before, but now Baghdadi was making it official, from the minbar of one of Mosul's most sacred sites.

The former Zarqawi disciple had clearly given much thought to his first public appearance, for he infused each moment with symbolic gestures sure to be recognized by the devout. Baghdadi wore a black robe and turban, evoking the dress of Allah's last prophet on the day of his final sermon. He climbed the steps of the minbar slowly, pausing at each one to emulate another of Muhammad's habits. At the top, as he waited to begin his sermon, he pulled from his pocket a miswak, a carved wooden stick used for oral hygiene, and began cleaning his teeth. Again the act deliberately invited comparison to Muhammad, who, according to an ancient Hadith saying, advised followers to "make a regular practice of miswak, for verily it is the purification for the mouth and a means of the pleasure of the Lord."

He finally faced the audience to deliver a formal declaration of victory. The caliphate, sought by the movement's leaders since Zarqawi's time, was at last real.

"As for your mujahedin brothers, Allah has bestowed upon them the grace of victory and conquest, and enabled them, after many years of jihad, patience, and fighting the enemies of Allah, and granted them success and empowered them to achieve their goal," he said. "Therefore, they hastened to declare the caliphate and place an imam, and this is a duty upon the Muslims—a duty that has been lost for centuries and absent from the reality of the world."

In the sermon, and in a separate audio address, Baghdadi claimed to be less than eager to accept what he called "this heavy responsibility."

"I was placed as your caretaker, and I am not better than you," he said.

Yet he decreed that faithful Muslims throughout the world were to obey him in all matters, as the head of the Islamic State and the guarantor of a new order that would soon become accepted reality for non-Muslims, whether they wished it or not.

"Know that today you are the defenders of the religion and the guards of the land of Islam," he said. "You will face tribulation and epic battles. Verily, the best place for your blood to be spilled is on the path to liberate the Muslim prisoners imprisoned behind the walls of the idols.

"So prepare your arms, and supply yourselves with piety. Persevere in reciting the Koran with comprehension of its meanings and practice of its teachings," Baghdadi said. "This is my advice to you. If you hold to it, you will conquer Rome and own the world."

His sermon finished, Baghdadi, the self-ordained caliph, descended the minbar's steps in the same cautious fashion. He stopped briefly to pray, then marched out of the mosque with his bodyguards, preparing to fight, and then, Allah willing, to rule.

On the June day when Mosul fell, Abu Haytham sat in his office, fielding calls from harried deputies struggling to keep abreast of the events. In the corner, a small television with the sound muted replayed images of victorious ISIS fighters in an endless loop. Some waved and grinned from the backs of pickup trucks; others walked through Mosul's main thoroughfares, past shuttered storefronts and burning police vehicles. Black banners fluttered from car antennas and makeshift flagpoles.

No one had foreseen such a rapid collapse of Iraq's army, even here, at a spy agency that prided itself on avoiding surprises. As he stole glances at the silent screen, Abu Haytham's eyes were bloodshot, and his big hands vigorously worked a set of prayer beads. This had been a stunningly quick turn of events. Yet the trajectory had been apparent for some time.

"Unfortunately, from the beginning, there has been this potential," he said wearily.

He was a brigadier now, a senior officer in the counterterrorism division, where he had spent nearly three decades. Always a serious man, Abu Haytham had grown more somber with age, reflecting the heavier burdens he shouldered. His tidy office was free of adornment except for an ornate copy of the Koran and a photograph of a much younger version of himself, flashing a rare grin and shaking hands with the country's king. An extra suit hung by the door for the days when the workload prevented him from making it home at all.

There were many such days now. The Mukhabarat had been on high alert since the beginning of the Syrian uprising, when the security service had played cat-and-mouse with arms smugglers and jihadi recruits trying to slip across the border. Now the jihadis themselves controlled the border posts on the other side. Jordan remained mostly quiet, for the moment, but there were worrying signs. In the southern town of Ma'an, an Islamist hotbed not far from the abandoned al-Jafr Prison, vandals sometimes spray-painted ISIS slogans on buildings or left black flags planted in the town square. There were no such displays in Amman, where the unraveling of the neighboring states was viewed with increasing dread.

Some Iraqis, particularly the descendants of the East Bank tribes, such as Zaydan al-Jabiri, had been willing to cut a deal with ISIS in order to free themselves from repressive Shiite rule. But the Islamists who seized control of Fallujah and Mosul turned out to be every bit as brutal as their Raqqa counterparts. Captured Iraqi soldiers were paraded before cameras and then gunned down in open pits. Suspected apostates were murdered in the streets, and priceless

Babylonian artifacts—a source of cultural pride for generations of Iraqis—were smashed into powder. Such acts were welcomed by small numbers of religious conservatives whose views aligned with those of the Islamists. But among the Iraqis who had welcomed the Islamist guns, few were interested in Islamist rule. Now it was too late to rescind the invitation.

Abu Haytham, himself a son of the tribe, understood the resentments of Iraq's Sunnis. And he was struck by how effectively ISIS exploited them.

"There's a snowball effect here," he said. "It begins with so many people being dissatisfied because they're not represented within their government."

Daesh, or ISIS, "knew exactly how to make use of these feelings, to benefit itself," he said. "It has been going on now for twelve years, since the very beginning of the Iraq conflict, in 2003."

And not just in Iraq. Already, self-proclaimed ISIS "wilayats," or provinces, had announced themselves in countries beyond the group's birthplace. Soon there would be new chapters in Saudi Arabia, Libya, Algeria, Nigeria, Yemen, Afghanistan, and Pakistan. In each case, the Islamists promised freedom from tyrannical regimes and the creation of a just society, ordered according to godly principles. What they delivered instead was an armed dictatorship defined by corruption, cruelty, and death.

There was nothing the Mukhabarat could do now to reverse that history, or alter the many mistakes and missteps that had led to this day. All that remained for the Jordanians was to strengthen their own defenses against a virulent strain that jumped the country's borders years ago.

"Look how fruitful they have been," Abu Haythan said, gesturing at the images on the screen. "We worked so hard to stop them. They sometimes get sick, but they never die."

EPILOGUE

The spark that set Arab passions ablaze was lit not in Iraq, as Abu Musab al-Zarqawi had supposed, but in a rubble-strewn lot in eastern Syria. It happened on the cool, hazy morning of January 3, 2015, behind a bombed-out building in Raqqa, where the Islamic State's media unit had set up video cameras and a small metal cage. At least two dozen extras in identical masks and uniforms took their places, some forming a gauntlet and others pretending to guard. Finally, the video's featured player was led in. Muath al-Kasasbeh, twenty-six, the Jordanian fighter pilot, now in a loose orange tunic and pants, his hands unshackled, walked unescorted through the mist-shrouded set as though wandering through his own dream.

The first image of al-Kasasbeh since his capture on December 24 depicted a young man whose face was swollen and bruised, evidence of a beating that had taken place sometime after he was seized. Before being led onto the film set, he was made to sit before a camera to tell his own story, or the parts of it that ISIS had wanted him to tell.

"I am First Lieutenant Muath Safi Yusef al-Kasasbeh, Jordanian, from Karak," he began, "an officer in the Royal Jordanian Air Force."

Al-Kasasbeh's recorded account of his December 24 mission mostly followed the actual events. An F-16 pilot with nearly three years of experience, the Jordanian had been assigned to hit ISIS targets inside a grid of coordinates that included the city of Raqqa. His plane was part of an armada of Arab and Western aircraft that had been bombing ISIS since September 2014, when President Barack Obama launched an expanded air campaign in an attempt to drive the terrorist group from its safe havens in Iraq and Syria. Obama had ordered U.S. warplanes and drones into Iraq a few weeks earlier to halt an ISIS advance that threatened Iraq's Mosul Dam and the Kurdish capital, Erbil. Then he announced a broader coalition that included aircraft from Jordan and five other Arab states, including Saudi Arabia, the United Arab Emirates, and Qatar. "This counter-terrorism campaign will be waged through a steady, relentless effort to take out [ISIS] wherever they exist," Obama said in a televised speech.

Al-Kasasbeh's December 24 flight had been just another routine bombing run in the service of this collective mission. The pilot was closing in on his target, and had just nosed his fighter downward, when his wingman spotted flames coming from the rear of his aircraft. At almost the same instant, his cockpit display warned of engine failure, and the jet began to yaw off course. He yanked on the ejection handle and was blasted from the cockpit as the F-16 plummeted toward the Euphrates River.

"I bailed out, and fell in the river," he said in the videotaped interview.

There was no time for his fellow soldiers to attempt a rescue. Al-Kasasbeh was still struggling to free himself from the ejection seat when he was seized by a burly man with a black beard and knit cap. "I am now a prisoner of the mujahideen," he said.

ISIS wasted little time in exploiting its good fortune. Within nine days of the crash—and around the time the haggling over a possible prisoner exchange was getting under way—the group's media unit had roughed out a plan for the execution video they would make. They found a suitable location on the edge of Raqqa, a few hundred feet from the river, and they managed to secure a cage, a cube of thin metal bars with an open floor the size of a large blanket. The crew set up multiple cameras on tripods and parked a backhoe nearby with a load of sand and rock. By the morning of January 3, everything was ready.

The video was to be a professional production, far superior to the jerky, homemade offerings from Abu Musab al-Zarqawi years earlier. The final version includes a long, slickly produced preamble with computer-generated graphics and a series of clips showing Jordan's King Abdullah II giving speeches and shaking hands with Obama. A graphic animation depicts an F-16 jet breaking into pieces, which then magically reassemble themselves into the Arabic script for the video's title, helpfully translated into awkward English: *Healing the Believer's Chests*.

The core of the propaganda film is a montage of video images of the captured pilot juxtaposed with bodies of children and other presumed bombing victims. A camera follows al-Kasasbeh as he walks slowly along a row of masked ISIS fighters, his breath visible in the January air. Then, suddenly, he is inside the cage, his head bowed as though in prayer. The pilot's orange tunic, dry in earlier scenes, is now soaked with fuel.

A masked soldier—a subtitle identifies him as the leader of an ISIS unit that had been bombed in one of the coalition's air strikes—lights a long torch and touches it to a trail of powder leading through the metal bars. In seconds, al-Kasasbeh is engulfed in flames. He jumps and flails, but there is no escape. At last he clasps both arms around his face and sinks to his knees, all but obscured by the fire. Moments later, his darkened form topples over, just before the backhoe crushes the cage and pilot inside with a load of broken concrete and dirt.

As a final flourish, the camera zooms in on a blackened hand visible amid the rubble. Then, in the closing frames, where the film credits normally run, the video shows photographs and names of other Jordanian pilots and announces a bounty in gold coins for anyone who finds and kills one of them.

"So—good tidings," the narrator says, "to whoever supports his religion and achieves a kill that will liberate him from hellfire."

The grisly work was over by midmorning, except for the weeks of studio editing needed to prepare the video for public release. Later that day, and on nearly every day that followed, ISIS continued to dangle the possibility of al-Kasasbeh's release, if only the Jordanians were willing to cut a deal.

It was not the first time ISIS had attempted to shock the world with its savagery. Four months before al-Kasasbeh's capture, the video-taped beheading of kidnapped photojournalist James Foley outraged Western governments and drove American support for a military response against the group. Foley's murder was quickly followed by the killings of a *Time* magazine reporter, Steven Sotloff; a former U.S. Army Ranger, Peter Kassig; and the British aid workers David Haines and Alan Henning. Dozens of others would share their fate, including captured Syrian and Lebanese soldiers, Kurdish women, Iraqi videographers, and Japanese nationals. Libyan jihadists who claimed allegiance to ISIS recorded the executions of Christians in groups of twenty or more at a time.

Yet it was the death of the young pilot that sparked a change among ordinary Arabs. From Jordan's cosmopolitan capital to the conservative Wahabi villages of Saudi Arabia came howls of con-demnation and rage. The beheading of prisoners, brutal though it was, was specifically countenanced by the Koran and regularly prac-ticed by the Saudi government as an official means of execution. But with the burning of a human being—and, in this case, a practicing Sunni Muslim—the Islamic State had broken an ancient taboo.

"Only God punishes by fire," Salman al-Odah, the venerated Saudi scholar and curator of the popular Web site Islam Today, said in a Twitter posting. "Burning is an abominable crime rejected by Islamic law regardless of its causes."

Abdul Aziz al-Shaykh, the Saudi grand mufti, the country's top cleric and a jurist empowered to settle matters of law by religious fatwa, said simply that ISIS was not Muslim: "They are enemies of Islam."

But the most striking repudiation of ISIS came from a man whose teachings were long considered to be part of the radical fringe. Abu Muhammad al-Maqdisi, the jihadist scholar who had been Zarqawi's personal mentor when the two were in prison, had grown increas-ingly critical of Zarqawi's offspring as they marauded across Syria and western Iraq. Maqdisi, still regarded by Islamists as one of the movement's founders and pioneering theorists, had broken with Zarqawi over the killing of Shiite innocents. Now he had begun lodging similar protests with Abu Bakr al-Baghdadi over his butchering of aid workers such as Britain's Alan Henning, killed while in Syria on a mission to ease suffering.

"Henning worked with a charitable organization led by Muslims," Maqdisi noted in an open letter posted on his Web site. "Is it reasonable that his reward is to be kidnapped and slaughtered?"

Maqdisi had lived in Jordan continuously since he and Zarqawi parted ways after the prison amnesty in 1999. Though he had spent much of that time in the Mukhabarat's detention center, he had continued to express his views on the issues of the day in open letters and Web postings. Some Islamists would question whether Maqdisi's opinions were truly his own, or part of a script forced on him by the Mukhabarat. But on at least one point, Maqdisi was fully consistent, both in his writings and in private conversations with journalists and friends: the killing of ordinary Muslims, whether religious pilgrims or Sunni pilots captured in battle, was contrary to Islam.

Indeed, after al-Kasasbeh was captured, Maqdisi offered his services as an intermediary, seeking to facilitate the exchange of the pilot for Sajida al-Rishawi, the failed suicide bomber and death-row prisoner. At one point in early 2015, he exchanged messages with a man believed to be Abu Muhammad al-Adnani, Baghdadi's personal spokesman.

"I am concentrating now on trying to reach a deal that is of legitimate interest to you," Maqdisi said to Adnani in one of the exchanges, later circulated on social-media accounts. If ISIS released the pilot, Maqdisi said to Adnani, they could save the life of a "jihadi sister" and prevent further damage to the group's reputation among Arabs.

ISIS's response was to release the video of the pilot's execution, carried out a full month earlier. Maqdisi was furious.

"They lied to me, and swore solemn oaths," he told the Jordanian broadcaster Roya TV. "Then it became clear to me that they had already killed the pilot."

The break was now complete. Maqdisi, in the interview, proceeded with a sweeping condemnation of the movement he had helped to create. Alluding to his former pupil, Zarqawi, he denounced the errant strain that "began this tradition of slaughter."

"They do not understand conquests and victories except with slaughtering and killing," he said. "They slaughter many of their opponents and they display it in front of television screens, until the people are shocked and say, 'Is this what Islam is?' And we are forced to defend Islam and make clear that this is not from Islam."

Maqdisi was at home in Amman when he uttered the words; Jordan's government had released him from jail months earlier as part of an undeclared truce between the monarchy and the cleric who had once advocated the regime's overthrow. On February 4, 2015, the same day on which Rishawi was executed at Swaqa Prison, Jordan's state prosecutor formally dropped all pending charges against Maqdisi. For the first time since his arrest with Zarqawi more than two decades earlier, Maqdisi's slate with the monarchy was clean.

Prominent Muslim clerics and scholars had condemned previous acts of terrorism, including the September 11, 2001, attacks on New York and Washington. But the criticisms this time came with an explicit acknowledgment, at the highest levels of the Arab world's political and religious institutions, that such statements were no longer enough.

On January 1, 2015, a week after the Jordanian pilot's capture, Egyptian president Abdel Fattah al-Sisi stood before a gathering of Sunni Islam's top religious authorities to call for an Islamic reformation—a "revolution" that would reclaim the ancient religion from fundamentalists and radicals who had perverted its central message. The violence committed by groups such as ISIS and al-Qaeda were but symptoms of a larger crisis that Muslims themselves must address, he said.

"We must take a long, hard look at the situation we are in," al-Sisi told the gathering at Cairo's al-Azhar University, the intellectual center of Sunni Islam for more than a thousand years and the institution that sets the standard for mainstream Muslims on questions of theology and religious practice. "It is inconceivable that the ideology we sanctify could make our entire nation a source of concern, danger, killing and destruction all over the world."

The problem, al-Sisi said, was not with Islam's core beliefs but with the "ideology—the body of ideas and texts that we have sanctified over the course of centuries, to the point that challenging them has become very difficult."

The president drew applause from the room when he turned to address the university's spiritual leader directly—al-Azhar's grand imam, Ahmed el-Tayeb—calling on him to "revolutionize our religion."

"You bear responsibility before Allah," al-Sisi said. "The world in its entirety awaits your words. Because the Islamic nation is being torn apart, destroyed, and is heading to perdition. We ourselves are bringing it to perdition."

Weeks later, after ISIS released the video of the pilot's execution, the grand imam delivered one of the harshest condemnations by a prominent cleric. ISIS was not merely un-Islamic, he said; they were "Satanic." Al-Azhar would later carry out its own crackdown on extremist clerics, removing imams who condoned violence.

Yet it was clear that the banishing of a few imams would not diminish the Islamic State's allure. Among ISIS's thousands of volunteers are young men whose motivation derives less from theology than from a desire to fight authoritarian Arab regimes such as al-Sisi's. Rami Khouri, a Lebanon-based journalist and researcher who has chronicled the rise and fall of Islamist movements over four decades, noted that Zarqawi's intense hatreds were shaped more by prison than by any sermon or religious treatise.

"The radicalization of many of the actors who created al-Qaeda and then ISIS happened in Arab jails," Khouri said. "The combination of American jets and Arab jails was the critical fulcrum around which al-Qaeda and ISIS could germinate."

The king had left Washington vowing that he was "going to war," and he did just that. Even before the royal plane landed in Amman, waves of coalition fighter jets crossed into Syria in what officials would later describe as the largest assault on ISIS positions since the campaign began. The planes struck training camps, barracks, and weapons depots, killing more than fifty militants, an after-action assessment confirmed.

After touching down in Jordan, King Abdullah headed straight into a meeting of his national security staff to plan the next phase. TV cameras were allowed into the room to film the monarch, in a traditional checkered keffiyeh in addition to his tailored suit, vowing to exact revenge for the pilot's death.

"We are waging this war to protect our faith, values and humanitarian principles," he said. As for ISIS—"these criminals," he called them—"they will be hit hard at the very center of their strongholds."

Outside, he was greeted by an extraordinary sight: thousands of Jordanians lining the streets to cheer the king's motorcade. These were young crowds, very different from the bands of middle-aged and older males who usually turn out for pro-government rallies, and many of them lingered on the streets late in the evening, lighting candles and carrying hand-lettered signs. Amman's mosques and Christian churches convened prayer services in the pilot's memory.

More planes left their bases that day, and Jordanians cheered them as well. As a small country that now faced a terrorist army on two of its borders, Jordan had often downplayed its role in the anti-ISIS coalition, hoping to avoid inciting an attack on the kingdom itself. Now formerly restricted military bases allowed photographers to film airmen painting messages on the munitions they were about to drop. "Islam has nothing to do with ISIS," read one note, scrawled on the side of one of the bombs the air force would use in the attack. The Defense Ministry itself, nearly always silent about military missions, publicly announced the new bombing campaign with a statement that bristled with defiance. With only a few planes, and despite a heavy reliance on outsiders for everything from ordnance to fuel, the entire country was banding together, "sacrificing everything to defend the true values of Islam," the Jordanian Armed Forces said.

"This is the beginning," the statement read. "You will know who the Jordanians are!"

The second bombing wave was under way as Abdullah left Amman for the southern town of Karak, home to the al-Kasasbeh clan for generations. Another large crowd assembled to greet the motorcade as it climbed the steep road leading to the nearby village of Ay, where the king would join family members in mourning the pilot's death.

Outside the family's house, Abdullah embraced the pilot's elderly father, and the two turned to walk together. They clasped hands, moving at the head of a long entourage, both wearing the distinctive red-and-white keffiyehs that, to Jordanians, symbolize both the ninety-three-year-old monarchy and tribal traditions far older than the country called Jordan, older even than Islam itself.

As they walked, four Jordanian fighter jets appeared on the horizon, returning from a bombing run north of the border. They streaked past the pilot's house in formation, then turned westward in a wide arc, past the town of Karak, with its crumbling Crusader castle, and over the ancient highway once used by Ikhwan horsemen riding in from the east to murder and pillage. The jets scraped the edges of Zarqa, the industrial town where a troubled youth named Ahmad had grown into a dangerous radical who called himself Zarqawi. Then they landed at the newly bustling Mwaffaq Air Base, where jets from a half-dozen countries, most of them Muslim, were being armed and fueled for strikes against the Islamic State.

The next morning, with fresh bombs attached to their wings, they would head north to attack again.

AFTERWORD

The skinny Belgian kid with the toothy grin was a mere schoolboy when Abu Musab al-Zarqawi began his attacks on Iraqi embassies and mosques in 2003. But had the two met as adults, they might have marveled at the similarities between them, the famous terrorist and the acolyte who would one day bring one of Europe's great cities to its knees.

Both Zarqawi and the young Belgian, Abdelhamid Abaaoud, came from families that were solidly middle-class and only moderately religious. Both attended good schools but dropped out as teenagers to begin a steep slide into delinquency and petty crime. Both were transformed by time in prison, and both traveled abroad to seek redemption and purpose on a foreign battlefield. Zarqawi was twenty-three when he signed up with the mujahideen in Afghanistan. Abaaoud was slightly older, at twenty-six, when he arrived in Syria to join the successors to Zarqawi's old organization, now known as the Islamic State.

Both would aspire to bring the war's horrors back to their native lands. Abaaoud would succeed, spectacularly, as the leader of the November 13, 2015, terrorist attacks on Paris, ISIS's first mass-casualty assault on a Western capital. The Belgian and eight accomplices set off bombs and sprayed bullets across a wide swath of the city's northern and eastern districts, a four-hour killing spree that left 130 people dead and wounded nearly 400 others.

Counterterrorism officials had long clung to the hope that such an event would never occur—that ISIS would remain fixated on the purely local mission of building and defending its caliphate. But here was evidence of a dangerous third phase of the group's violent expansion: After establishing a sanctuary in Syria and completing its conquest of western Iraq, the terrorists were surging into new battlefields far from the Middle East. The foot soldiers for the new campaign were not Middle Easterners or Africans, but young Europeans and North Americans with Western passports and native fluency in French, Flemish, German, and English. They had begun streaming into Syria in 2012, and some, like Abaaoud, had spent years in ISIS's battlefield training academy, learning how to think, pray, and fight as Islamist warriors.

Now, three years later, ISIS's new generation was ready. And the advance troops—a ferocious first wave, sure to be followed by others—would be led by a suburban youth with a cockeyed grin whose most notable previous achievement was burglarizing a neighbor's garage.

The intense courtship that arose between ISIS and Abaaoud was hardly a random occurrence. True, on paper, he offered little: another small-time hoodlum with no military experience or appreciable skills. At the time of his arrival in Syria, the terrorist group was already flush with success, both on the battlefield and in the larger contest for fighters and resources. Hundreds of volunteers were arriving monthly from the Arabian Peninsula, the Caucasus, and North Africa. Yet as early as 2012, the group's leaders were looking ahead to bigger fights and grander prizes. American journalist Peter Theo Curtis, who was taken hostage by the al-Nusra Front when the terrorist organization was officially still a branch of the Islamic State, recalled how his captors spoke of a vision for seeding Europe and North America with sleeper cells that could be called upon to carry out attacks far into the future. Zarqawi's followers wanted cadres of Westerners just like Abaaoud, and they set out purposefully to recruit them.

Jihadists leaders were "inviting Westerners to the jihad in Syria," Curtis wrote, "not so much because they needed more foot soldiers— they didn't—but because they want to teach the Westerners to take the struggle into every neighborhood and subway station back home." Abaaoud was to be an early test of ISIS's strategy. But before he could be deployed, he had to be discovered, vetted, and persuaded. All known evidence suggests that Abaaoud was an exceptionally eager convert.

The oldest of six children born to Moroccan immigrants, Abaaoud grew up in the working-class Molenbeek district of Brussels, where most of his neighbors and schoolmates were of North African or Turkish descent. He dropped out of a prestigious Catholic high school after racking up demerits for bad grades and rowdy behavior. By his midteens he had fallen in with local gangs. At nineteen he had his first criminal conviction, for concealing stolen goods. By his midtwenties the list had grown to assault, burglary, and resisting arrest. Once, while fleeing police, he jumped into a freezing river and had to be treated for hypothermia. He served time in jail, got out, then was arrested again.

Abaaoud's last stint behind bars exposed him to the prison's small circle of Islamists. Most were young men of North African descent, like himself, serving time for gang violence and relatively minor offenses. Like Zarqawi and his disciples years earlier, they were street toughs who adopted a harsh religious code as a way of gaining admittance to an even tougher gang: the jihadists. Along with counterparts in Germany, England, and France, they were part of a generation of disaffected Muslim youth who had become "radical before they were religious," according to Belgian counterterrorism official Alain Grignard, who studied the phenomenon.

"Previously we were mostly dealing with 'radical Islamists'— individuals radicalized toward violence by an extremist interpretation of Islam—but now we're increasingly dealing with what are best described as 'Islamized radicals,'" Grignard said. "Their revolt from society manifested itself through petty crime and delinquency. Many are essentially part of street gangs. What the Islamic State brought in its wake was a new strain of Islam which legitimized their radical approach."

The leader of the cell was a Moroccan-born veteran of the Afghan civil war whom the other Belgian jihadists called "Papa Noel." The forty-two-year-old controlled the group's purse and doled out remittances of $5,000 each to anyone interested in traveling to Syria to join Islamist militias battling the government of President Bashar al-Assad. Eventually at least twenty members signed up, including Abaaoud, who departed for Syria in March 2013 for what would be the first of two combat tours. By early 2014, Abaaoud had a scraggly beard and a nom de guerre—Abu Umar al-Baljiki—and he was posting messages on social media identifying himself as a fighter for the Islamic State.

"It's not fun seeing blood spilled," he says in a March 2014 video uploaded to his Facebook page, "but it gives me pleasure from time to time to see blood of disbelievers run, because we grew up watching the blood of Muslims being spilled" on television.

Soon any hesitancy about spilling blood disappeared. His next video posting showed a laughing Abaaoud dragging the corpses of dead Free Syrian Army soldiers from the back of a pickup truck. "Before, we towed jet skis, motorcycles, and trailers filled with gifts for our vacations in Morocco; now, thank God, we are following His path while towing disbelievers who are fighting us," he says. The slain fighters ostensibly were on the same side, but ISIS viewed all non-Islamist troops as apostates, even those who were aiding the fight against the hated Assad. Indeed, ISIS at times appeared far more focused on destroying rival rebel groups that on battling Assad's soldiers.

By late 2014, Abaaoud was deemed ready for a more important role. In October, a jihadist Web site posted Abaaoud's name on a roster of ISIS fighters killed in battle. Belgian police later concluded that the martyrdom claim was a trick: a "dead" militant would surely disappear from government watch lists, making it easier for Abaaoud to travel in and out of Europe with fake credentials without being detected. By all appearances, it worked: in January 2015, he slipped across Turkey and into Greece to help coordinate a plot by other European comrades to launch a terrorist attack on Abaaoud's native Belgium. The attempt, which involved explosives, assault weapons, and a plan to behead a police officer, was foiled just hours before it was set to begin.

Abaaoud hinted in later Web postings that he had traveled beyond Greece, venturing perhaps as far as Belgium itself to assist with preparations before fleeing back to Syria in February. At no point was he stopped or questioned. "My name and picture were all over the news," he bragged in an interview with ISIS's English-language magazine *Dabiq*, "yet I was able to stay in their homeland, plan operations against them, and leave safely."

Thus emboldened, he would return to Europe once more, this time as leader of an ambitious, multipronged assault on the French capital. Now he would oversee the attack as a field commander, coordinating the teams of suicide bombers and sidewalk assassins, with his childhood friend, an unemployed Belgian mechanic and convicted felon named Salah Abdeslam, serving as his driver and logistics man. After the shootings ended, Abaaoud walked brazenly through at least two of the crime scenes, strolling past covered bodies, harried police officers, and the knots of paramedics working on survivors. With all but two of his nine comrades now dead, he would take cover in a squatter's camp beneath a highway overpass, finally venturing out two days later to ask for help from a female cousin and a family friend who didn't yet know of Abaaoud's role in the mayhem.

He was so proud he could barely contain himself, the friend recalled in an interview.

"The terraces? That was me," he told the woman with a grin, referring to the outdoor cafés that had been raked by gunfire.

Abaaoud mostly seemed his old self, the friend recalled. But when the conversation turned serious, Abaaoud allowed that there had been problems with the operation. Some of the attacks had not gone precisely according to plan, and Abaaoud's mission now was to ensure that the next phase of the attack, just four days away, was free of gaffes. A popular shopping mall in suburban Paris had been picked as a target, along with a nearby police station and a day-care center, he said. This time, Abaaoud made clear, he would do the killing himself.

The friend was troubled by Abaaoud's callousness at the loss of innocent life, and she told him so.

"This is not Islam," she said.

The young man shrugged. "Collateral damage," he said. "That was nothing. After the holidays, you will see."

In the days that followed, as French officials scoured the Paris suburbs in an urgent search for Abaaoud and his surviving accomplices, a number of uncomfortable truths began to emerge.

France had suffered its worst terrorist attack in modern times, and no one had seen it coming. Despite a heightened state of alert following the *Charlie Hebdo* shootings in Paris ten months earlier—and despite increased vigilance by security services regarded as among the best in Europe—French officials had been taken utterly by surprise. Abaaoud and the other plot leaders had managed to travel across Europe without being detected. They had assembled at least seven suicide vests containing an explosive known as triacetone triperoxide, or TATP, likely cooked up in a basement or garage using easily obtainable ingredients. They had been organized, trained, and directed by ISIS commanders a half a world away, yet none of their communications had been intercepted.

More troubling were the identities and backgrounds of the plotters themselves. Of the nine attackers, seven were Belgian or French citizens. At least six had traveled to Syria for jihad and another had trained with Islamists in Yemen. Together they had carried out a sophisticated attack that required extensive coordination, bomb-making capabilities, and at least rudimentary military skills, as well as an icy ruthlessness that allowed them to methodically execute dozens of civilians—mostly young men and women, not much different in age from themselves—at close range.

Experts who studied the profiles of the nine assailants would acknowledge the genius in ISIS's recruitment strategy. The formula that served so well during Zarqawi's time—transforming violent young men into hyper-violent young jihadists—was working brilliantly among ISIS's new European recruits. Youths raised in gang-infested immigrant neighborhoods instinctively understood the connection between respect and fear, said Grignard, the Belgian counterterrorism official. ISIS operated by the same gangster code, while offering its young recruits something most never possessed at home.

"They feel like somebody when they're over in Syria," Grignard said. "If someone crosses you there, you put a bullet in his head. The Islamic State has legitimized their violent street credo."

Not all of ISIS's Western recruits would be inclined to follow Abaaoud's path. Some eventually become disillusioned with ISIS and try to desert or flee, risking imprisonment or death if they are caught. Others quietly return to homes and families to resume their former lives. But within the pool of European and North American ISIS veterans—a group estimated in early 2016 to be about 4,500—a fraction, perhaps several hundred, will be willing to serve as ISIS's invisible army in the West, ready to answer future calls to arms. Given the sheer numbers, some of these hidden cells are likely already in place, said Bruce Hoffman, an adviser on counterterrorism to the George W. Bush administration.

"When you have such a vast universe of recruits, some will have characteristics that will make them more adept at penetrating Western society," Hoffman said. "And if you've bloodied them in combat—if they've had real combat experience fighting Hezbollah in Syria—carrying out an attack in downtown Paris is like a knife slicing through warm butter."

According to Hoffman and other counterterrorism experts, clandestine cells made up of young Westerners could provide ISIS with a means of retaliating for military setbacks in Iraq and Syria. Moreover, they could allow the group to remain dangerous even if ISIS is driven entirely from its Middle Eastern sanctuary. Either way, young veterans such as Abaaoud remain an invaluable weapon for a terrorist organization that possesses increasingly global ambitions and speaks openly of its intention to force Muslims in all lands to choose sides. In a 2015 *Dabiq* article that appeared a few months before the Paris attacks, ISIS warned that it would soon begin targeting Western countries with the aim of deliberately provoking a backlash against Muslims living there. "Muslims in the West," the article said, "will quickly find themselves between one of two choices: they either apostatize and adopt the [infidel] religion . . . or they [emigrate] to the Islamic State and thereby escape persecution."

Abaaoud made his choice, and he prodded other European Muslims to do the same. On November 17, the young Belgian holed up with several accomplices in a small apartment in the suburb of Saint-Denis to finalize preparations for the planned second round of attacks in Paris. Just as Zarqawi had done before the Amman bombings ten years earlier, he enlisted the help of a woman: Hasna Ait Boulahcen, his twenty-six-year-old cousin. Like the female bomber Sajida al-Rishawi before her, Boulahcen had been tormented by conflicting views, and she had recently rejected her non-Islamist friends and tossed away her Western clothes for the black robe and veil. Though she had not known about the Paris attacks, she had told friends that she wanted to emigrate to Syria, perhaps to become a suicide bomber.

Police discovered the hideout and surrounded the apartment building with an assault force of more than one hundred heavily armed soldiers and police. A fierce gun battle ensued, interrupted by a brief pause in which the woman's terrified voice could be heard.

"Can I leave?" Boulahcen called to the armed men outside. "I want to leave!"

Before anyone could reply, one of Abaaoud's accomplices detonated a suicide belt inside the house, killing himself and the cousin. Abaaoud would die as well, his body so badly mangled by bullets and shrapnel that it would take forensic examiners two days to positively identify his remains.

The first wave of ISIS's Western offensive had ended, with nine of the known attackers dead. Police would eventually discover an abandoned getaway car—the one driven by Abdeslam, Abaaoud's childhood friend—in a suburb east of Paris. It would take police another four months to find the driver, barricaded inside a Brussels apartment a few miles from where the two men had grown up.

The identities of other accomplices, a group that at minimum included weapons suppliers and the team that manufactured the seven identical suicide bombs, remained unknown.

ACKNOWLEDGMENTS

The idea for this book about the origins of ISIS began taking shape before there was a terrorist organization called by that name. It arose in part from a long interest in Abu Musab al-Zarqawi, whose personal story became more intriguing to me as I gathered material for my earlier book, *The Triple Agent*. Later, while covering the Arab Spring uprisings of 2011 for *The Washington Post*, I watched with growing interest as Zarqawi's terrorist movement—presumed by many experts to be finished—began to assert itself in Syria's civil war. No one foresaw how the remnants of the old al-Qaeda in Iraq would become a powerful army with territorial claims covering hundreds of square miles. But as far back as early 2012, a few American and Middle Eastern officials were seeing the contours of a global terrorist threat in the making, and some candidly shared their views in private conversations. It is with these individuals—several of whom cannot be named as sources in these pages—that my debt of gratitude begins. This book could not have been written without the assistance of this small group of friends from the intelligence, executive, and diplomatic spheres who, over two years of reporting, generously and patiently shared their knowledge, insights, suggestions, and expertise.

I also am particularly indebted to former U.S. Representative Jane Harman and the Woodrow Wilson International Center for

Scholars for providing critical support for this undertaking. My Wilson Center fellowship afforded me the freedom to report and write without distraction, in the company of gifted writers and inspiring thinkers from around the world. In addition to Representative Harman, I am particularly grateful to Haleh Esfandiari, Robert Litwak, Aaron David Miller, David and Marina Ottaway, former fellow Robin Wright, Andrew Selee, Arlyn Charles, and an extraordinarily resourceful research staff. I also am thankful for the able assistance of intern Craig Browne, an accomplished and energetic Middle East scholar whose knowledge, hard work, and language skills proved to be immensely valuable.

Among the more than two hundred sources interviewed for this book, several were exceptionally generous with their time and knowledge. I am particularly grateful to Nada Bakos, who took time from writing her own memoir to share her recollections, as well as Robert Richer, Michael Hayden, Robert S. Ford, Mouaz Moustafa, Gen. Stanley McChrystal, Lt. Gen. Michael T. Flynn, Leon E. Panetta, Jeremy Bash, Michael Morell, Lawrence Wilkerson, Bruce Riedel, William McCants, Juan Zarate, Bruce Hoffman, Hasan Abu Hanieh, Joas Wagemaker, Marwan Muasher, Kael Weston, John McLaughlin, Sam Faddis, Frederic C. Hof, Zaydan al-Jabiri, Hudhaifa Azzam, James Jeffrey, Abdalrazzaq al-Suleiman, Jonathan Greenhill, Samih Battikhi, Andrew Tabler, Jeffrey White, Abu Mutaz, and Abdullah Abu Roman. Among the many who cannot be identified by name are numerous current and former officials of the Jordanian government and intelligence services, as well as current and former U.S. officials who offered assistance with the understanding that their names and agency affiliations would not be revealed. Critical help in supplying jihadist video and audio material, along with English translations, came from Steven Stalinsky of the Middle East Media Research Institute, and Rita Katz, co-founder of the SITE Intelligence Group. I am indebted to Jean-Charles Brisard for sharing his archives from his excellent 2005 book, *Zarqawi: The New Face of al-Qaeda.*

I could not have attempted this book without the generous support of my employer, *The Washington Post,* and so many *Post* colleagues and friends. I am especially indebted to Marty Baron, Cameron Barr, Kevin Merida, and Peter Finn for their kindness in allowing me to pursue this project. I also am particularly grateful to Jason Ukman, Julie Tate, Souad Mekhennet, Taylor Luck, David Hoffman, Mary Beth Sheridan, William Booth, Doug Frantz, David Ignatius, Kathryn Weymouth, Donald Graham, Greg Miller, Ellen Nakashima, Adam Goldman, Anne Gearan, Karen DeYoung, Craig Whitlock, Greg Jaffe, Liz Sly, Doug Jehl, Karin Brulliard, Jeff Leen, Scott Wilson, Carol Morello, Anne Kornblut, Walter Pincus, Rajiv Chandrasekaran, Laurie McGinley, Kathryn Tolbert, Juliet Eilperin, Chris Mooney, Darryl Fears, and Steven Mufson.

A very special thanks goes to Ranya Kadri, one of Jordan's journalistic treasures and an amazingly resourceful colleague, translator, fixer, and occasional cook and hotelier during my Middle East travels.

I am ever grateful to my literary agent, Gail Ross, for her suggestions, faith, and canny advice, and to the entire staff of the Ross-Yoon Literary Agency for logistical support. I'm indebted as well to the Knopf Doubleday Publishing Group, including Daniel Meyer, Nora Reichard, Michael Goldsmith, Bill Thomas, and Amelia Zalcman. And I'm profoundly thankful for the assistance of my remarkably talented editor, Kris Puopolo, who saw potential in my vague idea for a book about a rising terrorist movement most Americans in early 2013 had barely heard of. Any successes in these pages are a tribute to her strong ideas, peerless editing skills, and seemingly boundless patience.

I was helped immensely throughout this effort by the support and encouragement of a number of friends and family members, especially Paul Scicchitano, James Rosen, Connie Kondravy, Shyam Madiraju, Gene and Denise Jordan, Will Jordan, Ed and Gena Fisher, B. H. Warrick, and my parents, Rev. Eugene and Barbara Warrick. Finally and most importantly, I would like to express my love and gratitude to my children, Victoria and Andrew, for tolerating the many absences, deferred vacations, and my general distractedness, and to my wife, Maryanne, a full partner in this enterprise who cheerfully served as an unpaid researcher, editor, and sounding board as well as an indispensable source of strength and steadiness throughout a challenging two years.

It's good to be home.

NOTES

Prologue

1 "When will I be going home": Researcher interview with Hussein al-Masri, government-appointed lawyer for Rishawi.

1 If she cried or prayed: Author interview with a Jordanian official knowledgeable about Rishawi's prison time and the final days leading up to her execution.

3 from the pilot's own cell phone: Author interview with a senior Jordanian official directly knowledgeable about the prisoner exchange negotiations.

4 He could remember every detail: Author interview with a senior intelligence captain involved in the investigation. A second Jordanian official confirmed key details of the account.

8 "The black flags will come from the East": The prophecy comes from the collection of ancient texts known as the Hadith, specifically from "Kitab al-Fitan," or "Trials and Fierce Battles," associated with Nu'aym Ibn Hamaad in Islam's second generation. For a discussion of the passage in English, see http://www.islamweb.net/emainpage/index.php?page=showfatwa&Option=FatwaId&Id=101399.

9 "The spark has been lit": "Al-Zarqawi's Message to the Fighters of Jihad in Iraq on September 11, 2004," Middle East Media Research Institute, Sept. 15, 2004, http://www.memri.org/report/en/print1219.htm.

9 hardened into resentment: Author interviews with two senior Middle Eastern officials familiar with the king's views.

10 "Can we do anything more for you?": Author interviews with Sen. John

McCain and a senior Middle Eastern official knowledgeable about the exchange.

Chapter 1

15 "There's a terrible loneliness": Quoted in Steven Caton, *Lawrence of Arabia: A Film's Anthropology* (Berkeley: University of California Press, 1999).

15 "a warning of what hell is like": Cole Coonce, *Infinity over Zero: Meditations on Maximum Velocity* (Famoso, Calif.: KeroseneBomb Publishing, 2002).

16 documented by United Nations investigators: See Manfred Nowak, "Report of the Special Rapporteur on Torture," UN General Assembly Human Rights Council, 2007.

16 pressed into service as the doctor: Author interview with the physician Sabha, who narrated his encounter with Zarqawi and the other inmates in al-Jafr.

20 "His radical conclusion": Author interview with Hasan Abu Hanieh.

21 "He is very tough": Author interview with Jordanian journalist Abdullah Abu Roman, who spent time in prison with both men.

22 chiseled through weight lifting: Jean-Charles Brisard, *The New Face of Al-Qaeda* (New York: Other Press, 2005), p. 49.

22 "We have come to die!": Joas Wagemakers, "A Terrorist Organization That Never Was: The Jordanian 'Bay'at al-Imam' Group," *Middle East Journal,* Jan. 2014.

23 *al-takfiris*—"the excommunicators": For more about the *takfiri* ideology, see https://www.ctc.usma.edu/v2/wp-content/uploads/2010/06/Vol1Iss7 -Art61.pdf.

23 "God willing, King Hussein will pardon you": Abu Qadama Salih al-Hami, "Knights of the Unfulfilled Duty: Zarqawi and the Afghan Jihad" (n.p., 2007).

24 "Oh, sister, how much you have suffered": Will McCants, "Letter from Balqa Jail," *Jihadica: Documenting the Global Jihad,* June 22, 2008, http:// www.jihadica.com/letter-from-balqa-jail.

26 "He was not a fighter who lived between the bullets": Wagemakers, "Terrorist Organization That Never Was."

28 called themselves Ikhwan: For a detailed accounting of the Ikhwan movement and its relations with the House of Saud, see Robert Lacey, *The Kingdom: Arabia and the House of Sa'ud* (New York: Avon, 1983).

Chapter 2

30 "I want to see you": Abdullah, King of Jordan, *Our Last Best Chance: The Pursuit of Peace in a Time of Peril* (New York: Viking, 2011).

32   "A cold sensation": Ibid.

32   "We would soon be thrust into the spotlight": Ibid.

33   They stood for hours: Ahmad Khatib, "Jordanians Line Amman's Streets to Bid Farewell," *Jordan Times,* Feb. 9, 1999.

35   "This is God's judgment": Francesca Ciriaci, "Abdullah Proclaimed King," *Jordan Times,* Feb. 8, 1999.

35   "Out of habit, I looked around": Abdullah, *Our Last Best Chance.*

36   Hussein survived at least eighteen assassination attempts: Avi Shlaim, *Lion of Jordan: The Life of King Hussein in War and Peace* (New York: Alfred A. Knopf, 2008).

36   "I didn't know helicopters could": "King Hussein of Jordan," *ABC News Nightline,* originally broadcast Feb. 7, 1999.

37   "I have no idea how": Abdullah, *Our Last Best Chance.*

37   "I'm no angel": Ibid.

39   "the backbone of the country": "Muslim Brotherhood Meets King," *Jordan Times,* March 19, 1999.

39   "Your Majesty, we are with you": Ibid.

43   "Jordan is on the threshold": Tareq Ayyoub, "The Amnesty Law: Complicated and Incomplete," *Jordan Times,* March 29, 1999.

43   Many months would pass: Abdullah, *Our Last Best Chance.*

43   "Why didn't someone check?": Author interview with an official present at the time.

44   "Our friend has come back": Author interview with Dr. Sabha.

Chapter 3

46   "I didn't do anything!": Author interview with two senior officials present at the events.

48   "Gun!" one of the officers shouted: Ibid.

49   "He just spouted ideology": Author interview with Samih Battikhi.

50   troubled since childhood: For more on Zarqawi's family and childhood, see Jean-Charles Brisard, *Zarqawi: The New Face of Al-Qaeda* (New York: Other Press, 2005).

50   Zarqawi's great love remained his mother: Ibid.

51   "He wasn't that smart": Betsy Pisik, "Mother Denies Suspect Is a Terrorist," *Washington Times,* Feb. 24, 2003.

51   "We all knew who he was": Author interview with Hudhaifa Azzam.

52   "Zarqawi was crying": Abu Qadama Salih al-Hami, "Knights of the Unfulfilled Duty: Zarqawi and the Afghan Jihad."

53   "God granted the Muslim mujahidin": Quoted in Fu'ad Husayn, *Al-Zarqawi: The Second Generation of al-Qaeda* (n.p., 2006).

54 He read books about early Islamic heroes: Ibid.
55 "We printed out some of my books": Quoted in ibid.
55 "He wanted everything to be done quickly": Quoted in ibid.
56 "Your penalties only strengthen our faith": Jean-Charles Brisard, *The New Face of Al-Qaeda* (New York: Other Press, 2005).
58 A third officer who took a particular interest: Author interview with Abu Mutaa.

Chapter 4

62 "The time for training is over": Ali H. Soufan, *The Black Banners: The Inside Story of 9/11 and the War Against Al-Qaeda* (New York: W. W. Norton, 2011).
63 "Rob, I have to tell you something": Author interview with Robert Richer.
65 "Despite everything that happened": Author interview with senior Jordanian official.
66 "In a nutshell, Abu Musab:" Quoted in Fu'ad Husayn, *Al-Zarqawi: The Second Generation of al-Qaeda* (n.p., 2006).
71 "Iraq will be the forthcoming battle": Ibid.

Chapter 5

73 "I am where I want to be": Marcella Bombardieri and Jana Benscoter, "Slain Envoy Had Boston Ties on Aid Mission; Foley Was 'Doing What I Want to Do,'" *Boston Globe*, Oct. 29, 2002.
73 Foley crumbled to the pavement: Author interview with two senior Jordanian officials directly involved in the events.
76 "I kept wondering, 'What can I do?'": Author interview with Nada Bakos.
78 "appear based on hearsay": CIA, "CTC Iraqi Support for Terrorism," unpublished report, CTC 2003-1000/HS, Jan. 29, 2003.
79 "simply one of the best": Author interview with a former senior U.S. intelligence official.
80 "I asked tough questions": Richard B. Cheney, *In My Time: A Personal and Political Memoir* (New York: Threshold Editions, 2011).

Chapter 6

86 Charles "Sam" Faddis knew: Author interview with Charles Faddis.
87 "They used to force women": "Under the Microscope," Al-Jazeera TV, Doha, July 1, 2004.
88 "Look, if we can produce solid intelligence": Author interview with Charles

Faddis and descriptions in his book: Mike Tucker and Charles Faddis, *Operation Hotel California: The Clandestine War Inside Iraq* (Guilford, Conn.: Lyons Press, 2009).

90 "It's big enough to be an invasion": Stanley A. McChrystal, *My Share of the Task: A Memoir* (New York: Portfolio/Penguin, 2013).

91 "He was able to forge ties": George Tenet, *At the Center of the Storm: My Years at the CIA* (New York: HarperCollins Publishers, 2007).

91 White House officials were reluctant: Peter Baker, *Days of Fire: Bush and Cheney in the White House* (New York: Doubleday, 2013).

92 "We are considering it": Riad Kahwaji, "Jordan and U.S. Discuss Possible Patriot Deployments," *Marine Corps Times,* Feb. 10, 2003.

93 "fixated on Iraq": Abdullah, King of Jordan, *Our Last Best Chance: The Pursuit of Peace in a Time of Peril* (New York: Viking, 2011).

94 "But I was certain of one thing": Ibid.

Chapter 7

95 "Iraq today harbors a deadly terrorist network": For Colin Powell's Feb. 5, 2003, speech to the United Nations Security Council, see http://www.washingtonpost.com/wp-srv/nation/transcripts/powelltext_020503.html.

95 She continued watching: Author interview with Nada Bakos.

97 "This is bullshit!": Author interview with Samih Battikhi.

97 "We were sick about it": Author interview with Abu Mutaz.

97 "With that speech": Author interview with Hasan Abu Hanieh.

Chapter 8

101 She tried the question: Author interview with Nada Bakos; a second U.S. official familiar with the events confirmed her account.

103 "We had invaded": Author interview with Nada Bakos.

106 sent the van's front section spiraling: Rajiv Chandrasekaran, "Car Bomb Kills 11 in Baghdad," *Washington Post Foreign Service,* Aug. 8, 2003.

107 "We may see more of this": Michael R. Gordon, "Terror Group Seen As Back Inside Iraq," *New York Times,* Aug. 10, 2003.

108 "We've made good progress": E. A. Torriero, "Embassy Attack May Have Tie to Al Qaeda," *Chicago Tribune,* Aug. 9, 2003.

108 "Remnants of the regime": Jim Henderson, "Democracy Is Not Easy, Condoleezza Rice Tells Journalists in Dallas," *Houston Chronicle,* Aug. 8, 2003.

109 "The presence of coalition forces": D'Arcy Doran, "UN Employees' Fears Grew As Security Deteriorated in Baghdad," Associated Press, Aug. 28, 2003.

110 "The explosion went off": Gil Loescher interview with Jeremy Paxman, *BBC News,* broadcast Dec. 18, 2003. For entire interview, go to http://news.bbc.co.uk/2/hi/programmes/newsnight/3330885.stm.

110 "They want to fight us there": George W. Bush press conference, Aug. 23, 2003, Crawford, Texas. Excerpts available at http://www.usembassy-israel.org.il/publish/press/2003/august/082304.html.

111 "Allah was merciful today": Author interview with a senior U.S. official familiar with the investigation.

111 "We should join efforts": "Ayatollah Hakim's Last Sermon," *BBC News* online, Aug. 30, 2003, http://news.bbc.co.uk/2/hi/middle_east/3193341.stm.

112 "Baghdad is bustling with commerce": Tom Infield, "U.S. General: Hezbollah Linked to Iraq Bombings," *Philadelphia Inquirer,* Sept. 6, 2003.

113 "brilliant strategy": Author interview with Bruce Riedel.

Chapter 9

115 "It's factual": Author interview with Robert Richer.

117 "Right before the invasion": Author interview with a former senior U.S. official present during the events.

120 "The ease with which the insurgents": Quoted in James Risen, *State of War: The Secret History of the CIA and the Bush Administration* (New York: Free Press, 2006).

120 "So you guys think": Author interviews with two officials present.

123 no evidence of bullet damage: "Violent Response: The U.S. Army in Al-Falluja," Human Rights Watch, 2003, http://www.hrw.org/reports/2003/iraqfalluja.

123 "We went to them": Author interview with Zaydan al-Jabiri.

Chapter 10

126 "Even if our bodies": "Zarqawi Letter" to Osama bin Laden, U.S. Department of State, Feb. 2004, http://2001-2009.state.gov/p/nea/rls/31694.htm.

129 "I was likely standing less than a block": Stanley A. McChrystal, *My Share of the Task: A Memoir* (New York: Portfolio/Penguin, 2013).

130 "It was pure, unadulterated hatred": Author interview with Stanley A. McChrystal.

131 "before Iraq became truly hellish": McChrystal, *My Share of the Task.*

132 "I would anticipate": "Major Combat Operations Over in Iraq," *PBS NewsHour,* April 14, 2003, http://www.pbs.org/newshour/updates/military-jan-june03-battles_04-14.

133 "What is that?": Author interview with McChrystal.
134 "We fundamentally do not understand": McChrystal, *My Share of the Task.*
137 "The level of organization": Quoted in Brian Knowlton, "U.S. Blames Iraq Attacks on Jordanian-Born Sunni Militant," *New York Times,* March 3, 2004.
137 "Why," she shrieked: Vivienne Walt, "Over 150 Killed in Iraq Blasts," *Boston Globe,* March 3, 2004.

Chapter 11

138 The man he selected for the mission: Author interview with two senior Jordanian officials present during the events.
141 "They're using middlemen": Author interview with Abu Mutaz.
144 "By the time we found them": Ibid.
146 "The men in the Caprice": "Al Qaeda Plans Terrorist Attack in Chemical Weapons Against Jordan," *Petra News Agency,* April 27, 2004. (Full text of confession, unsigned.)
147 "unforeseen negative consequences": Abdullah, King of Jordan, *Our Last Best Chance: The Pursuit of Peace in a Time of Peril* (New York: Viking, 2011).
150 "Yes, there was a plot": Jamie Holguinap, "Terrorist: Wish We Had That Bomb," Associated Press, April 16, 2004.

Chapter 12

151 "Nation of Islam, great news!": Nicholas Berg beheading. video transcript archived by University of Georgia Islamic Studies Department, http://islam.uga.edu/zarqawi.html.
152 "I am reasonably confident": Nicholas Berg letter, *Tom's Photography,* Jan. 4, 2004, http://www.nickberg.org/berg/Email_from_Berg/Entries/2004/1/4_Bergs_Email_from_Iraq.html.
153 "He went where no one else did": Michael Powell and Michelle Garcia, "In a Pennsylvania Town, Friends Recall the Pranks and the Promise," *Washington Post,* May 14, 2004.
155 "No one could figure out": Author interview with Nada Bakos.
158 "Their intention is to shake our will": "President Bush Condemns Brutal Execution of Nicholas Berg," May 12, 2004, http://georgewbushwhitehouse.archives.gov/news/releases/2004/05/text/20040512-2.html.
158 "If you had your thumb": David E. Sanger and Richard W. Stevenson, "Bush Supporters Are Split on How to Pursue Iraq Plan," *New York Times,* May 13, 2004.
160 "Zarqawi jumped the shark": Author interview with Nada Bakos.

Chapter 13

161 "Not a good sign": Author interview with Robert S. Ford.

164 "He spent his entire career": Author interview with Ronald Neumann.

165 "Insurgents and foreign fighters": "USEB 154: 1st Marine Expeditionary Force Discusses Situation in Al Anbar Province," Public Library of US Diplomacy, July 23, 2004, https://www.wikileaks.org/plusd/cables /04BAGHDAD235_a.html.

168 "He surrounds himself with the scum": Author interview with Zaydan al-Jabiri.

168 "swore he'd never personally beheaded": Hannah Allum, "Fallujah's Real Boss: Omar the Electrician," Knight Ridder Newspapers, June 25, 2004.

169 "This is a call for help from the depths": "Al-Zarqawi's Message to the Fighters of Jihad in Iraq on September 11, 2004," Middle East Media Research Institute, Sept. 15, 2004, http://www.memri.org/report/en/print1219.htm.

170 the most "deadly weapons we have": Muhammad Abu Rumman and Hassan Abu Hanieh, *The "Islamic Solution" in Jordan: Islamists, the State, and the Ventures of Democracy and Security* (Amman, Jordan: Friedrich-Ebert-Stiftung Jordan & Iraq, 2013).

171 "I hear and monitor the chaos": Abu Muhammad al-Maqdisi, "Support and Advice, Hopes and Pains," open letter, July 2004, translation provided by MEMRI, http://www.memri.org/report/en/print1473.htm.

173 "We denounce and condemn extremism": For the entire "Amman Message" statement, see "The Official Website of the Amman Message," www.ammanmessage.com.

174 "The ability of a few extremists": Abdullah, King of Jordan, *Our Last Best Chance: The Pursuit of Peace in a Time of Peril* (New York: Viking, 2011).

174 "It should be known": Bin Laden's Dec. 15, 2004, statement quoted in "Bin Laden's Tape: Key Excerpts," *BBC News,* Dec. 27, 2004.

174 "great joy to the people of Islam": Jeffrey Pool, "Zarqawi's Pledge of Allegiance to Al-Qaeda: From Mu'Asker Al-Battar, Issue 21," *Terrorism Monitor,* vol. 2, no. 24 (Dec. 15, 2004), http://www.jamestown.org/single/?tx _ttnews[tt_news]=27305#.VUdYf5N0v64.

Chapter 14

176 "An apostasy against Allah": Jeffrey Pool, "Zarqawi's Pledge of Allegiance to Al-Qaeda: From Mu'Asker Al-Battar, Issue 21," *Terrorism Monitor,* vol. 2, no. 24 (Dec. 15, 2004), http://www.jamestown.org/single/?tx_ttnews[tt _news]=27305#.VUdYf5N0v64.

177 "Local government is in a state of crisis": State Department, "Governor in Trouble-Ridden Anbar Province Held Hostage," cable, Aug. 3, 2004,

retrieved from https://cablegatesearch.wikileaks.org/search.php?q=governor +in+trouble-ridden+anbar&qo=0&qc=0&qto=2010-02-28.

177   "We're not going to put candidates": Author interview with Robert S. Ford.

180   "We are satisfied": "Iraqi Vice-President on Tackling 'Security Chaos,' Coalition Pullout, Government," Al-Jazeera TV, April 29, 2006.

181   the drone picked up the deputy's car: Author interview with a former senior U.S. official familiar with the events.

181   "Just wreck!": Author interview with Nada Bakos.

182   "There was a PowerPoint briefing": Author interview with a former senior U.S. official familiar with the events.

185   "The mujahed movement must avoid": Letter from Ayman al-Zawahiri to Abu Musab al-Zarqawi, translation provided by Combating Terrorism Center at West Point, https://www.ctc.usma.edu/v2/wp-content/uploads /2013/10/Zawahiris-Letter-to-Zarqawi-Translation.pdf.

186   "He does not and should not": Zarqawi, "Zarqawi Clarifies Issues Raised by Sheikh Maqdisi," open letter, July 21, 2005, retrieved from http://thesis .haverford.edu/dspace/bitstream/handle/10066/4760/ZAR20050712 .pdf?sequence=3.

186   "The al-Qaeda Organization": "Al-Zarqawi Declares War on Iraqi Shia," Al-Jazeera, Sept. 14, 2005, http://www.aljazeera.com/archive/2005/09 /200849143727698709.html.

188   It took place on the morning of June 29, 2005: Author interviews with two senior U.S. officials present at the event.

189   "Are you going to get him?": Stanley A. McChrystal, *My Share of the Task: A Memoir* (New York: Portfolio/Penguin, 2013).

190   "By design, often the first time": Author interview with Stanley A. McChrystal.

190   "If we could apply relentless body blows": McChrystal, *My Share of the Task*.

192   "That was a screw-up": Author interview with a senior U.S. official present during the event.

Chapter 15

193   "He put one on me, and wore the other": "Full Text of Iraqi Woman's Confession," Associated Press, Nov. 13, 2005, http://www.nbcnews.com /id/10027725/#.VUdcKZN0v64.

193   listened quietly: Author interview with senior Jordanian official.

198   "Everyone got the call": Author interview with Jordanian intelligence officer.

199   "This was a criminal cruel act": Malmoud al-Abed and Mohammad Ghazal, "Thousands Rally in Unity Against Terror," *Jordan Times,* Nov. 12, 2005.

199 "We're going on the offensive": Abdullah, King of Jordan, *Our Last Best Chance: The Pursuit of Peace in a Time of Peril* (New York: Viking, 2011).

200 "This is our 9/11": Author interview with Robert Richer.

200 "People who would have never worked": Author interview with a senior Jordanian official familiar with the investigation.

200 "Our brothers knew their targets": "Al-Zarqawi Purportedly Says Wedding Wasn't Targeted," Associated Press, Nov. 18, 2005.

201 "Let us not merely be people of killing": Letter from Atiyah Abd al-Rahman to Abu Musab al-Zaraqawi, late 2005, translation provided by the Combating Terrorism Center at West Point, https://www.ctc.usma.edu/v2/wp -content/uploads/2013/10/Atiyahs-Letter-to-Zarqawi-Translation.pdf.

202 "In Iraq, time is now beginning": "Text of a Document Found in Zarqawi's Safe House," Associated Press, June 6, 2006.

203 "In public and private": State Department, "Sectarian Nerves on Edge After Samarra Shrine Explosion," cable, Feb. 23, 2006, retrieved from https:// www.wikileaks.org/plusd/cables/06STATE29555_a.html.

203 "lit the match": Peter Baker, *Days of Fire: Bush and Cheney in the White House* (New York: Doubleday, 2013).

204 Every scene conveyed: Video excerpts can be seen at https://www.youtube .com/watch?v=uB0apnoVf8Y.

205 "my treasured nation": Rusty Shackleford, Ph.D., "Zarqawi Video (with Subtitles) [Updated: Transcripts]," *e Jawa Report,* April 26, 2006, http:// mypetjawa.mu.nu/archives/173861.php.

205 "there were some mistakes made": Edward Wong and John F. Burns, "Iraqi Rift Grows After Discovery of Prison," *New York Times,* Nov. 17, 2005.

Chapter 16

207 "He seemed almost relieved": Author interview with a senior Jordanian official familiar with the events.

212 "We were just trying": Author interview with senior U.S. official present at the meeting.

213 "We're trying to hold on to you": Stanley A. McChrystal, *My Share of the Task: A Memoir* (New York: Portfolio/Penguin, 2013).

216 "We watched a guy dressed in all black come out": Author interview with Stanley A. McChrystal.

217 An autopsy found no evidence: Final Autopsy Report, Abu Musab al-Zarqawi, Armed Forces Institute of Pathology, June 8, 2006.

219 "Why didn't we think of that": Author interview with Rep. Steny Hoyer; see also Peter Baker, *Days of Fire: Bush and Cheney in the White House* (New York: Doubleday, 2013).

219 "I was happy": Author interview with Nada Bakos.

220   "I long had this mental image": Author interview with Abu Haytham.

220   "Your end is close": Author interview with Zaydan al-Jabiri.

Chapter 17

223   small army of men: Author interview with two U.S. officials familiar with the events.

224   "If they get through that door": Ibid.

225   disliked the sight of blood: Joan Juliet Buck, "Asma al-Assad: A Rose in the Desert," *Vogue*, Feb. 25, 2011.

226   "My judgment is that Syria will move": "John Kerry Praises Syria in 2011 Speech," Carnegie Endowment for International Peace speech, March 2011. For entire speech, see https://www.youtube.com/watch?v=GHMiLIZ_iwQ.

227   "The last country in the world": Author interview with Robert S. Ford.

229   twenty-seven interrogation centers: "Torture Archipelago: Arbitrary Arrests, Torture, and Enforced Disappearances in Syria's Underground Prisons Since March 2011," Human Rights Watch, July 3, 2012, retrieved from http://www.hrw.org/reports/2012/07/03/torture-archipelago-0.

229   "The country's problems were being exacerbated": Author interview with Frederic C. Hof.

234   "The presence of the U.S. ambassador": "Syria Says US 'Interfering' As Ambassador Visits Hama," *BBC News,* July 8, 2011.

235   "President Assad is not indispensable": "Clinton Says Syria's Assad 'Not Indispensable'," *Voice of America,* July 10, 2011, http://www.voanews.com/content/clinton-says-syrias-assad-not-indispensable—125382213/142106.html.

237   "He has not led": Macon Philips, "President Obama: 'The Future of Syria Must Be Determined by Its People, but President Bashar al-Assad Is Standing in Their Way,'" *White House Blog,* Aug. 18, 2011, https://www.whitehouse.gov/blog/2011/08/18/president-obama-future-syria-must-be-determined-its-people-president-bashar-al-assad.

237   "very disgusted by the behavior": Author interview with Benjamin Rhodes.

237   "This kind of ideology lurks in dark corners": "Syria Speech by Bashar al-Assad," June 20, 2011, http://www.al-bab.com/arab/docs/syria/bashar_assad_speech_110620.htm.

Chapter 18

239   Now he would appeal to Assad directly: Author interview with two senior officials familiar with the events.

243   "There are only a handful of true al-Qaeda types": Author interview with a senior official familiar with the events.

244 "Where is this Islamic state": Cole Bunzel, "From Paper State to Caliphate: The Ideology of the Islamic State," Brookings Institute, *Brookings Project on U.S. Relations with the Islamic World,* March 2015.

244 "Here in your midst": Wikimedia Foundation, Foreign Affairs Committee, *The ISIS Threat: The Rise of the Islamic State and Their Dangerous Potential* (Google eBook, Sept. 25, 2014).

246–47 astonishing array of electronic sleuthing tools: Author interviews with three U.S. officials who participated in these events at the time.

248 "near-strategic defeat": Joby Warrick, "U.S. Cites Big Gains Against Al-Qaeda," *Washington Post,* May 30, 2008.

249 "We didn't become like them": Author interview with a senior U.S. official who helped oversee the operations.

250 "long, gloomy night and dark days": Steven Lee Myers, "New Qaeda 'War Minister' Warns of 'Days Colored in Blood,'" *New York Times,* May 14, 2010.

Chapter 19

251 "There were not more than seven or eight of us": "Al-Jazeera Interview with Abu Mohamed Golani, the Head of al-Nusra in Syria," Dec. 18, 2013, retrieved from https://www.youtube.com/watch?v=X8uTGdun5Fg.

252 "It was to be the face of the organization": Author interview with a senior U.S. official familiar with intelligence profiles on Baghdadi.

253 "He always had religious": Janine di Giovanni, "Who Is ISIS Leader Abu Bakr al-Baghdadi?," *Newsweek,* Dec. 8, 2014.

254 "promoting of virtue and preventing of vice": Pieter van Nostaeyen, "The Biography of Sheikh Abu Bakr Al-Baghdadi, Amir of the Islamic State in Iraq and Al-Sham," *World Press,* July 2013, https://pietervanostaeyen.wordpress.com/2013/07/15/abu-bakr-al-baghdadi-a-short-biography-of-the-isis-sheikh.

256 "It actually feels like you're in a microwave": Lt. Commander Vasilios Tasikas, "The Battlefield Inside the Wire," *Military Review,* Sept.–Oct. 2009.

256 "Extremists mingled with moderates": Ibid.

257 "Deal with America and its allies": Paul Vale, "Islamic State's Al-Baghdadi Says Group Will Fight to 'Last Soldier,'" Associated Press, Nov. 13, 2014.

258 "Zarqawi was closer than a brother": Ruth Sherlock, "How a Talented Footballer Became World's Most Wanted Man," *Telegraph* [London], Nov. 11, 2014.

259 Khlifawi urged Baghdadi to accept: Matthew Barber, "New ISIS Leaks Reveal Particulars of al-Qaeda Strategy," from "Syria Comment" blog of the University of Oklahoma's Center for Middle East Studies, Jan. 12, 2014.

260 "He cloaked himself": Author interview with senior U.S. official.

260 "We have crossed the boundaries": "The Islamic State in Iraq and Syria Shall Remain," audio message posted June 6, 2013; translation provided by the Middle East Media Research Institute.

260 "There was a sense that this thing": Author interview with a senior U.S. official present during the debates.

263 "It was that slow car crash": Author interview with Mouaz Moustafa.

265 "All the different sects were there": Author interview with Noura al-Ameer.

Chapter 20

267 "We hereby bring the Islamic nation": Video posting, "New Jihad Group in Syria Announces Its Establishment," Middle East Media Research Institute, Jan. 24, 2012.

268 "We said from the beginning, this is terrorism": Quoted in Alexandra Zavis and Katie Paul, "Syria Capital Hit by Massive Bombings," *Los Angeles Times,* Dec. 24, 2011.

269 "Give your money to the ones who will spend it on jihad": David D. Kirkpatrick, "Qatar's Support of Islamists Alienates Allies Near and Far," *New York Times,* Sept. 7, 2014.

269 "It's anyone's game": Author interview with a senior Middle Eastern diplomat.

269 "In their view, it's Assad": Author interview with a senior Middle Eastern intelligence official.

271 "This is not abstract": Author's confidential interview with a senior aide to King Abdullah II.

271 "We thought going with the Americans": Adam Entous, "Covert CIA Mission to Arm Syrian Rebels Goes Awry," *Wall Street Journal,* Jan. 26, 2015.

272 "Where are these revolutions going to stop?": Author interview with senior official familiar with the exchange.

273 "I have my red lines": Ibid.

274 "I didn't think they were going to kill me": Author interview with Robert S. Ford.

276 "The regime was losing control": Ibid.

277 "The intelligence, frankly, was very worrisome": Author interview with Leon E. Panetta. See also Leon E. Panetta, *Worthy Fights: A Memoir of Leadership in War and Peace* (New York: Penguin Press, 2014).

278 "every option appears worse than the next": Hillary Rodham Clinton, *Hard Choices* (New York: Simon & Schuster, 2014).

279 "We're outside the game": Author interview with Panetta.

279 "He was willing to consider options": Author interview with Benjamin Rhodes.

279 "I think, candidly, that a lot of people": Ibid.

280 "But all of these steps were Band-Aids": Clinton, *Hard Choices.*

280 "We know how to do this": Author interview with Panetta.

Chapter 21

282 "You're Shiites, right?": "Who Is the ISIL Iraqi Terrorist Who Executed the Three Syrian Truckers in Syrian–Iraqi border in 2013?," Liveleak.com, retrieved March 2015. More at http://www.liveleak.com/view?i=8d1_1398 584978#mjwHKBEOjIWYc8Ou.99.

283 He told a story: Abu Bakr al-Baghdadi, "Give Good News to the Believers: The Declaration of the Islamic State in Iraq and Al-Sham," audio speech, *World Press,* April 2013, retrieved from https://azelin.files.wordpress.com /2013/04/shaykh-abc5ab-bakr-al-e1b8a5ussaync4ab-al-qurayshc4ab-al -baghdc481dc4ab-e2809cannouncement-of-the-islamic-state-of-iraq-and -al-shc481m22-en.pdf.

284 "Al-Nusra Front's banner will remain": "Jabhat Al-Nusra Leader Abu Muhammad al-Joulani Pledges Allegiance to Al-Zawahiri," audio message, posted April 10, 2013; translation provided by the Middle East Media Research Institute.

284 "Muslim blood is off-limits": "Al-Qaeda Chief Ayman al-Zawahiri's Letter to the Leaders of the Two Jihadi Groups," April 2014, retrieved from https://archive.org/stream/710588-translation-of-ayman-al-zawahiris -letter/710588-translation-of-ayman-al-zawahiris-letter_djvu.txt.

285 "I prefer the command of Allah": Baghdadi statement as translated by Middle East Media Research Institute, *Jihad and Terrorism Threat Monitor* (blog), June 16, 2013.

286 freed more than five hundred inmates: Mushreq Abbas, "Al-Qaeda Militants Raid Iraq's Abu Ghraib, Taji Prisons," *Al Monitor,* July 2013.

287 "These were the hardest days": Author interview with Abu Ibrahim al-Raqqawi. For his blog, see Abu Ibrahim al-Raqqawi, "Raqqa Is Being Slaughtered Silently," http://www.raqqa-sl.com/en; retrieved April 2015.

289 "Some are boys younger than sixteen": Author interview with al-Raqqawi.

290 "What's that [video] game called": "British Jihadi Compares Syria War to Call of Duty," *BBC News,* June 13, 2014.

291 "I'm here to represent the Islamic State": Author interview with Mouaz Moustafa.

293 "Am I supposed to throw pizzas": Author interview with congressional official present at the meeting.

293 "We need to have a game-changing action": Chris Wallace, "Sen. McCain Talks US Action in Syria," *Fox News,* May 5, 2013.

293 "something that the civilized world has recognized": President Barack Obama news conference, May 16, 2013, White House; retrieved from https://www.whitehouse.gov/the-press-office/2013/05/16/joint-press -conference-president-obama-and-prime-minister-erdogan-turkey.

295 "Increase the assistance": Author interview with Robert S. Ford.

295 McCain questioned Ford's grasp: *Syria Hearing Before the Committee on Foreign Relations, U.S. Senate* (Washington, D.C.: Government Printing Office, Oct. 31, 2013).

Chapter 22

297 "The ones who are leading now were thieves": Author interview with Zaydan al-Jabiri.

299 "This is a tribal revolution": Hamza Mustafa, "There Is a 'Tribal Revolution' in Iraq: Anbar Tribal Chief," *Asharq Al-Awsat,* June 17, 2014.

300 "They stole everything": Author interview with Abdalrazzaq al-Suleiman.

300 "ISIL probably will attempt to take territory": Transcript, Lt. Gen. Michael T. Flynn, director, DIA, Statement Before Senate Armed Services Committee, Feb. 11, 2014.

301 "These are children of Zarqawi": Author interview with Michael Flynn.

303 "In my entire battalion": Ned Parker, Isabel Coles, and Raheem Salman, "Special Report: How Mosul Fell," Reuters, Oct. 14, 2014.

305 "As for your mujahedin brothers": "English Subtitles of Full Sermon by ISIS's Abu Bakr Al Baghdadi, Caliph of the 'Islamic State,'" transcript, YouTube.com, July 2014, retrieved from https://www.youtube.com/watch ?v=PxJSm7XwxqA.

306 "Unfortunately, from the beginning": Author interview with a senior Jordanian official.

307 "There's a snowball effect": Ibid.

Epilogue

308 "I am First Lieutenant Muath Safi Yusef al-Kasasbeh": "ISIS Burns Hostage Alive: Raw Video," *Fox News,* Feb. 3, 2015.

309 "This counterterrorism campaign": President Barack Obama, "Statement by the President on ISIL," retrieved from https://www.whitehouse.gov /the-press-office/2014/09/10/statement-president-isil-1.

311 "Only God punishes by fire": Woodrow Wilson Center for International

Scholars, "Muslims Condemn ISIS Killing of Jordanian Pilot," *The Islamists Are Coming* (blog), Feb. 5, 2015.

312 "Henning worked with a charitable organization": "Jihadi Ideologue Calls for Freeing British Hostage," Associated Press, Sept. 20, 2014.

312 "I am concentrating now on trying": "Daesh Releases New Audio Recording of Pilot Negotiation Attempts," *Al-Bawaba News,* Feb. 18, 2015.

312 "They lied to me": Maqdisi interview with Jordan's Roya TV, Feb. 6, 2015, translation provided by Middle East Media Research Institute at http:// www.memri.org/clip_transcript/en/4767.htm.

314 "The radicalization of many of the actors": Rami Khouri, "ISIS Is About the Arab Past, Not the Future," lecture, May 11, 2015, at Woodrow Wilson Center for International Scholars.

315 "We are waging this war": Suleiman al-Khalidi, "Jordanian King Vows 'Relentless' War on Islamic State's Own Ground," Reuters, Feb. 4, 2015.

315 "Islam has nothing to do with ISIS": Ranya Kadri and Anne Barnard, "Jordan, Unabashed, Announces Latest Bombing Raid on ISIS Targets," *New York Times,* Feb. 5, 2015.

315 "This is the beginning": William Booth and Taylor Luck, "Jordan Rages Against Islamic State As Military Vows to Expand Airstrikes," *Washington Post,* Feb. 6, 2015.

Afterword

318 Jihadist leaders were "inviting Westerners": Peter Theo Curtis [Theo Padnos pseud.], "My Captivity," *The New York Times Magazine,* Oct. 29, 2014.

319 he jumped into a freezing river: Christophe Lamfalussy, "De la petite délinquance qui ne révélait en rien de qui allait arriver," *La Dernière Heure,* Nov. 20, 2015.

319 "radical before they were religious": Paul Cruickshank, "A View from the CT Foxhole: An Interview with Alain Grignard, Brussels Federal Police," *CTC Sentinel,* Aug. 21, 2015.

320 "It's not fun seeing blood spilled": Quoted in Guy van Vlierden, "Profile: Paris Attack Ringleader Abdelhamid Abaaoud," *CTC Sentinel,* Dec. 15, 2015.

320 "Before, we towed jet skis": Ibid.

321 "My name and picture": "Interview with Abu 'Umar al-Baljiki," *Dabiq,* Feb. 12, 2015.

321 "The terraces? That was me": RMC interview quoted in "Attentats du 13 novembre: Sonia, celle qui a permis de neutraliser Abaaoud," rmc.bfmtv .com/emission/document-rmc-attentats-du-13-novembre-sonia-celle-qui-a -permis-de-neutraliser-abaaoud-948754.html, Feb. 4, 2016.

323   "They feel like somebody": Cruickshank, "A View from the CT Foxhole."

323   "When you have such a vast universe": Author interview with Bruce Hoffman.

323   "Muslims in the West": "Extinction of the Gray Zone," *Dabiq*, Feb. 18, 2015.

323   "Can I leave?": Jean-Michel Decugis, "La famille d'Hasna Aït Boulahcen porte plainte contre X," Itele.fr, Jan. 20, 2016.

INDEX

ISIS influenced by, 244–46, 251, 252–53,
258, 259, 260, 281–82, 283, 289,
296, 304, 308, 310, 312–13, 314,
316
Islamic fundamentalism of, 28–29, 42–45,
51, 53–56, 59–62, 66, 126–28,
159–60, 169–74, 183–87, 200
Israel opposed by, 48, 70, 150, 200–201
as jihadist, 7–9, 25, 27–28, 46–47, 50–54,
62–71, 75–76, 97–98, 112–13, 116,
126–28, 159–60, 169–74, 185–90,
204–5
Jordanian operations of, 2–4, 67, 72–74,
82–85
Koran studied by, 68, 156, 169–74,
183–84
leadership of, 18, 24–25, 44–45, 67–71,
126–28, 134–36, 159, 170–74,
182–92
Maqdisi's relationship with, 17, 18–21,
25–26, 43–44, 54–56, 59, 66, 171–72,
186, 284, 311–13
McChrystal's operations against, 188–92,
209–20, 246, 301
media coverage of, 149–50, 169, 185, 200
Millennium Plot (1999) and planning of,
62–64, 65, 77, 188
Mukhabarat surveillance of, 4–9, 46–50,
55–65, 81–85, 101–3, 138–50,
193–200, 206–9, 212–13, 220, 270,
305–7, 312
Muslim deaths caused by, 170–74,
184–87
nom de guerre of, 20, 53–54
personality of, 23–25, 44–45, 50–54,
58–61, 67–68, 70–71, 150, 169,
183–84, 189–90, 211
personal security of, 190, 194
photographs of, 95, 97, 182, 204

physical appearance of, 17–18, 25, 95, 97,
151, 204–5, 211, 281–82
recruitment by, 169–70, 189–90, 191,
204–5, 211
religious justifications asserted by, 159–60,
170, 171–74
reputation of, 22, 67–71, 95–98, 150,
157–58, 168–69, 174–75, 184–87,
204–5, 316
Rishawi as agent of, 1–11
safe houses used by, 130–32, 139, 145,
167, 190, 209–20, 246
Sargat training camp of, 69–71, 74, 86–92,
98, 113
second marriage of, 68
sectarian conflict promoted by, 165–66,
202–7, 209
September 11 attacks and, 68–69
as "sheikh of the slaughterers," 159, 160,
169, 185, 204
Shiite opposition to, 171–74, 178, 184–87,
188, 198, 202–5, 213, 214
Sunni support for, 127, 134–37, 171–74,
177–79, 193–205, 207, 220
terrorist operations of, 62–65
third marriage of, 190
U.S. hunt for, 8, 128–32, 188–92, 209–20,
246, 301
U.S. interests opposed by, 70, 126–28,
151–60, 198, 199, 200–201
violence used by, 22–26, 70–71,
135–37, 171–74, 184–87, 189–90,
198–209
Zawahiri's letter to, 184–87
Zarqawism, 171–72
Zawahiri, Ayman al-, 184–87, 204, 284–85,
286
Zeid (son of Sharif Ali), 40
Zengi, Nur ad-Din, 54